Global Cooperation Among G20 Countries

Michael Callaghan • Chetan Ghate
Stephen Pickford • Francis Xavier Rathinam
Editors

Global Cooperation Among G20 Countries

Responding to the Crisis and Restoring Growth

Springer

Editors
Michael Callaghan
G20 Studies Center
Lowy Institute for International Policy
Sydney
Australia

Chetan Ghate
Economics and Planning Unit
Indian Statistical Institute-Delhi
New Delhi
India

Stephen Pickford
Chatham House
London
United Kingdom

Francis Xavier Rathinam
South Asia Research Hub
Department for International Development (DFID)
New Delhi
India

ISBN 978-81-322-1658-2 ISBN 978-81-322-1659-9 (eBook)
DOI 10.1007/978-81-322-1659-9
Springer New Delhi Dordrecht Heidelberg London New York

Library of Congress Control Number: 2013955068

Printed on acid-free paper

Springer is part of Springer Science+Business Media (www.springer.com)

Contents

Part VI Austerity and Growth

Contributors

Shankar Acharya Honorary Professor, Indian Council for Research on International Economic Relation (ICRIER), and former Chief Economic Adviser to the Government of India

Abheek Barua Chief Economist, HDFC Bank, India

Michael Callaghan Director, G20 Studies Centre, Lowy Institute for International Policy, Sydney, Australia

Heribert Dieter Senior Associate, German Institute for International and Security Affairs (SWP), Berlin, Germany

Visiting Professor, Zeppelin University, Friedrichshafen, Germany

Holger Fabig Head of Division, G7/G8, G 20, World Economy, Currency Issues, Ministry of Finance, Berlin, Germany

Ewa Orzechowska-Fischer Analyst, International Finance and Development Division, Department of Treasury, Canberra, Australia

Chetan Ghate Indian Statistical Institute-Delhi, New Delhi, India

Atish R. Ghosh Chief, Systemic Issues and Assistant Director, Research Department, International Monetary Fund, Washington DC, USA

Subir Gokarn Director of Research, Brookings India, New Delhi, India

Former Deputy Governor, Reserve Bank of India, New Delhi, India

Abhijit Sen Gupta Senior Economics Officer, India Resident Mission, Asian Development Bank, New Delhi, India

Pierre Jacquet President, Global Development Network, Washington DC, USA

David Kim Senior Lecturer, School of Economics, University of Sydney, Australia

Takuji Kinkyo Professor of Economics, Kobe University, Kobe, Japan

Yannick Kirchhof Economist, Ministry of Finance, Berlin, Germany

Denis Medvedev Senior Country Economist, Economic Policy and Poverty unit, The World Bank, New Delhi, India

Jae-Ha Park Deputy Dean, Asian Development Bank Institute, Tokyo, Japan

Stephen Pickford Senior Research Fellow, International Economics, Chatham House, London, UK

Jyoti Rahman Manager, International Finance and Development Division, Department of Treasury, Canberra, Australia

Francis Rathinam Department for International Development (DFID), New Delhi, India

Smriti Seth Research Analyst, Economic Policy and Poverty unit, The World Bank, New Delhi, India

Rajeswari Sengupta Assistant Professor of Economics, The Institute for Financial Management and Research (IFMR), Chennai, India

Alok Sheel Secretary, Economic Advisory Council to Prime Minister of India, New Delhi, India

Jong Kook Shin Lecturer, Queen's University Management School, Queen's University, Belfast, Northern Ireland, UK

Gurbachan Singh Independent Researcher, and Visiting Faculty, Economics and Planning Unit, Indian Statistical Institute-Delhi, New Delhi, India

Anand Sinha Deputy Governor, Reserve Bank of India, Mumbai, India

Paul Bernd Spahn Professor Emeritus, Goethe University, Frankfurt am Main, Germany

Emil Stavrev Deputy Division Chief, Multilateral Surveillance Division

Research Department, International Monetary Fund, Washington DC, USA

Chetan Subramanian Associate Professor, Department of Economics, Indian Institute of Management Bangalore, Bengaluru, India

Redom Syed Analyst, International Finance and Development Division, Department of Treasury, Canberra, Australia

Inka Zippe Intern, Ministry of Finance, Berlin, Germany

About the Editors

Michael Callaghan is Director of the G20 Studies Centre at the Lowy Institute for International Policy. Mike has extensive experience on international economic issues, both in the Australian Treasury and the International Monetary Fund (IMF). From 2008 until 2012 he was Executive Director (International) in the Treasury and was Australia's G20 Finance Deputy. Mike also served as the Prime Minister's Special Envoy, International Economy. From 2005 until 2007 he was Executive Director, Revenue Group in the Treasury. Prior to this position he spent four years at the IMF in Washington DC as an Executive Director. Between 1999 and 2000, Mike served as Chief of Staff to the Australian Treasurer, the Hon Peter Costello. Mike has held various senior positions in the Australian Treasury. In 2009 he was awarded the Public Service Medal and in 2013 was made a Member of the Order of Australia.

Chetan Ghate is Associate Professor in the Economics and Planning Unit of the Indian Statistical Institute – Delhi. He is currently a member of the Technical Advisory Committee for Monetary Policy at the Reserve Bank of India. He received his Ph.D. in Economics and M.S. in Applied Mathematics from Claremont Graduate University (USA); Masters in Economics from the Delhi School of Economics (India); and B.A. Economics from Colorado College (USA). He has held faculty positions at the Colorado College, the German Institute of Economic Research, University of Sydney, and Claremont Graduate University. His areas of interest lie in macroeconomic theory and policy. He has published in several leading journals in his field. He recently edited "The Oxford Handbook of the Indian Economy" (OUP) which was selected as one of CHOICE's "Outstanding Academic Titles for 2012". In May 2011, he was a recipient of a Rockefeller Foundation residency in Bellagio, Italy. From 2012-2013 he was the Reserve Bank of India Chair Professor in Macroeconomics at ICRIER (New Delhi).

Stephen Pickford is Senior Research Fellow at Chatham House in London, UK. He has worked on international economic issues for much of his career, and retired from HM Treasury (UK) in 2010, where he was the Managing Director (International and Finance) and the UK's G7 and G20 Finance Deputy. Prior to this he held posts dealing with both European and international finance issues at HM Treasury, and from 1998 to 2001 he was the UK's Executive Director on the boards of the IMF and World Bank. Previous positions included leading the team responsible for Bank of England independence in 1997, and between 1989 and 1993 he worked on macroeconomic policy and forecasting at the New Zealand Treasury. He was educated at the University of Cambridge, England and the University of British Columbia, Canada.

Dr. Rathinam is a research advisor with the Department for International Development (DFID). His recent research work explores the legal, regulatory and political economy aspects of current financial and banking sector reforms in India. Formerly he was a senior fellow at ICRIER. He has a Ph.D. in Economics from Hyderabad Central University and was a visiting fellow at the Institute for Law and Economics, University of Hamburg, Germany. Dr. Rathinam has published in Emerging Markets Review, Macroeconomics and Finance in Emerging Market Economies, Environment and Development Economics, among others.

Abbreviations and Acronyms

CQS	Calculated quota share
EMDC	Emerging market and developing countries
EU	European Union
FCL	Flexible credit line
G20	Group of twenty
G7	Group of seven
GDP	Gross domestic product
GFC	Global financial crisis
IEO	Independent Evaluation Office
IMF	International Monetary Fund
IMS	International monetary system
NAB	New Arrangements to Borrow
PCL	Precautionary credit line
PPP	Purchasing power parity
RFA	Regional financing arrangements
US	United States
WTO	World Trade Organisation

Global Cooperation Among G20 Countries: Responding to the Crisis and Restoring Growth

Michael Callaghan, Chetan Ghate, Stephen Pickford and Francis Rathinam

1 Introductory Chapter

Since the unfolding of the 2008 global financial crisis, the G20 has played a major role in coordinating macroeconomic policies of major economies and reviving the world economy.[1] As the world's primary forum for international economic cooperation, its objectives have been to ensure more sustainable and balanced growth, achieve economic and financial stability and reform the prevailing international financial architecture. In the wake of the crisis, there was a sense of urgency and strong agreement to enact extraordinary policy measures to fend off the collapse of the real sector because of the "collapse of confidence" in the financial sector. The G20 performed spectacularly in this regard: global gross domestic product (GDP) contracted less than expected in 2009 and rebounded faster than expected in 2010.[2]

[1] The global financial crisis of 2008 required a more legitimate and representative forum than the G8 if it was to effect global macroeconomic and financial policy coordination to ward off imminent depression. It was in this context the G20 Leaders Summit was born.

[2] World Economic Outlook (April 09) predicted that world output would contract by 1.4 % in 2009 and grow about 2.5 % in 2010. However, the actual outcome was −0.5 % in 2009 and a 5 % growth in 2010 (Ahluwalia 2011).

M. Callaghan (✉)
Lowy Institute for International Policy, Sydney, Australia
e-mail: mcallaghan@lowyinstitute.org

C. Ghate
Indian Statistical Institute, New Delhi, India
e-mail: cghate@isid.ac.in

S. Pickford
Chatham House, London, UK
e-mail: stephenjpickford@gmail.com

F. Rathinam
Department for International Development (DFID), New Delhi, India,
e-mail: rfrancisxavier@gmail.com

M. Callaghan et al. (eds.), *Global Cooperation Among G20 Countries*,
DOI 10.1007/978-81-322-1659-9_1, © Springer India 2014

These coordinated actions were widely credited for forestalling a second Great Depression, with the G20 declaring victory at their third summit at Pittsburgh in September 2009 ("It worked").

Since 2009, Indian Council for Research on International Economic Relations (ICRIER), along with its partners, has been organizing a high-level annual conference that brings together academics and key policymakers from G20 member countries and International Financial Institutions (IFIs) to deliberate on a range of issues related to the G20. The previous three ICRIER conferences in this series, held prior to the Toronto, Seoul and Cannes G20 summits, had deliberated on the then G20 agenda. Succinct summaries of these conferences have been published and widely circulated among IFIs, think tanks and government officials in both India and abroad. The proceedings served as inputs to policymakers participating in the summits. ICRIER hosted its fourth G20 conference on October 7–9, 2012, at New Delhi in partnership with the Asian Development Bank Institute (ADBI), Department of Economic Affairs (DEA, MoF), International Monetary Fund (IMF) and Konrad-Adenauer-Stiftung (KAS).

Discussions in the fourth conference focussed on six key areas of concern facing the G20:

1. The eurozone crisis: short-run challenges and options
2. Rebalancing the global economy
3. Financial sector regulation
4. A new framework for reforming the international monetary system
5. Capital control policy and emerging market economies
6. Austerity and growth

The overarching theme of the conference was the scope for cooperation and coordination amongst the G20 across several key policy areas.[3] Several issues relating to cooperation and coordination in macroeconomic policy were discussed: the relative efficacy of rules versus discretion-based coordination[4]; how to achieve cooperation across a diverse set of countries especially when cooperation also requires loss of national interest; has the G20 process run its course; how can the process be made

[3] There is a large theoretical literature on the international coordination of macroeconomic policy. See Pilbeam (2006) for a textbook treatment. The principal argument in favour of international coordination is that governments will be tempted to pursue suboptimal policies without it. In short, there will be a failure to internalize the externalities, with the uncoordinated approach leading to Pareto inefficient outcomes. Bird (2012) however argue that policy coordination does not necessarily imply Pareto efficient gains as individual countries may perceive that they would lose from coordinating macroeconomic policy when they subvert domestic policy preferences for policy outcomes that are seen as jointly superior. Further, the bargaining position of individual countries is unlikely to be equal in securing a coordinated outcome.

[4] International policy coordination can take two broad forms: discretion-based cooperation or rule-based coordination. While many examples of policy coordination favour rule-based coordination, discretion-based cooperation is typically superior given extreme unanticipated events for which the existing set of rules cannot cope (Bird 2012). From this standpoint, the London summit of the G20 in April 2009 was an attempt to organize discretion-based coordination.

more inclusive; can the G20 regain its stature as a problem-solving group; how can the G20 strengthen its key function of providing crisis management mechanisms; and given that the basic rationale for the creation of the G20 leaders' process was to manage shocks transmitted by and through the group, how can it best do this.

In addition, broader issues surrounding the role of the G20 in macroeconomic policymaking were also discussed. For instance, many participants felt that the G20 was an informal and political body that brought together the biggest economies in the world as a problem-solving group that looked to the future. To be effective, it should remain a leader's forum. Some participants felt that there were two sub-groups in the G20—the BRICS and the G7/G8. These groups brought a flavour of the past North/South divide, which may limit the sense of a common purpose among G20 members. For legitimacy, various participants felt the need for G20 countries to work more closely with non-G20 countries. Legitimacy would also involve a stronger and more independent accountability process, with regional arrangements linked to the G20. Other points mentioned included a lack of resource commitments by G20 members, that initiatives by the chair were over-emphasized and the credibility of the G20 was hampered by delay in implementing commitments.

Finally, participants felt that there is further scope for cooperation in other areas such as the consultation process and addressing the pace of IMF reforms. Predetermined policy options undertaken by the G20 through a consultation process did help in feeding back into national policymaking processes.[5] This suggests that the role of the G20 as a coordination mechanism will be crucial. Further, the process of reforming international financial institutions has been slower than what the dynamic emerging economies would like. Reforming the composition of the IMF Executive Board to better reflect the changing economic power of member countries would help enhance the IMF's credibility in surveillance and policy advocacy.

1.1 Format of the Volume

Invited contributions from participants in the conference have been divided into six sections which directly mirror the conference agenda. Each section contains one lead chapter by a conference participant which provides an extensive review of the issues of concern for that section. These lead chapters are supplemented by shorter notes by other participants in that session of the conference.

The volume opens with an introductory chapter by the editors outlining the scope of the material covered and synthesizing the rich and broad discussion during the conference. The keynote address delivered by Subir Gokarn (Former Deputy Governor, Reserve Bank of India) constitutes a special opening chapter to the volume.

[5] For example, the Chinese 12th 5-year plan document pretty much reflected what the global community wanted of it.

1.2 Overview of Keynote Address

In his keynote address, *Subir Gokarn* argues that a number of stress points have emerged in the global economy. Given these, he poses the question whether the G20 can regain its stature as a "problem-solving" group, or whether it is just a "wartime" grouping that only works when a crisis is at hand.

The author observes that the emphasis of the G20 has shifted from immediate crisis management to addressing some of the structural factors that were widely seen to have played a role in causing and spreading the financial crisis. This has made the G20 a testing ground for providing a viable solution to macroeconomic policy coordination amongst heterogeneous economies. But the ease with which consensus across the group was found in "wartime" is not being replicated in "peacetime." Given the relatively large number of issues over which coordination is required, the number of possible coalitions and the membership of each country in multiple coalitions raise concerns about the sheer complexity of the coordination process.

2 The Eurozone Crisis: Short-Run Challenges and Options

The Euro crisis has loomed as a major threat to global recovery since 2011. A number of uncertainties, including concerns over whether Greece might have to exit the euro (see Buiter and Rahbari 2012), the crisis in the euro periphery and the fear of a prolonged recession in the euro area, made markets nervous.[6] One reason for market anxiety—and recurring shocks—is the abysmal crisis management by European policymakers. Solvency problems in the periphery countries were initially treated as a liquidity problem, and the proposed support was inadequate, misguided and arrived late.[7] Another problem in Europe was that no orderly mechanism existed for allowing struggling banks to fail (as there was in the USA)[8]. Participants in the conference felt that several risks remain elevated and crucial questions unanswered, such as:

- Why are financial markets still nervous about prospects in the eurozone?
- What reforms are needed to prevent the implosion of the European currency union?
- What is the efficacy of unlimited liquidity as a response to a banking capitalization crisis?

[6] Since 2012 however, coordinated implementation of bank liquidity support, including in particular the Outright Monetary Transactions operation by the European Central bank, along with capital regulation in the euro area and well-guided national policies, has helped calm financial markets.

[7] First the crisis in Greece was denied, then diagnosed and treated for a liquidity problem while it was a solvency problem. Further, ECB worsened market sentiments as it demanded preferred creditor's status after buying Greek bonds on the secondary markets.

[8] For example, the Federal Deposit Insurance Corporation has closed 448 banks since 2008.

- To the extent that debt mutualization is necessary in the euro area, how it could be managed, especially in terms of moral hazard, and how quickly could it be implemented.[9]
- How Grexit or, more broadly, the collapse of the European currency union would play out?
- What are the ways to achieve better fiscal coordination and risk sharing among euro area countries in the medium to long run?
- How would fervent fiscal conservatism in Europe affect European growth prospects and the government finances of member countries, and what would be the impact on the rest of the world (especially EMEs)?
- How can national economies support growth in the short term while maintaining long-term commitments to achieving sustainable fiscal positions?

In the lead chapter entitled "Overcoming the Euro Area Crisis: Reforms and Results," *Holger Fabig, Yannick Kirchhof and Inka Zippe* argue that considerable policy initiatives have been implemented including establishment of the European Stability Mechanism (ESM), a sterilized open-ended bond purchase programme by the European Central Bank (ECB), fiscal consolidation programmes in member countries and the possibility of the direct purchase of sovereign debt by the ESM. Effective fiscal consolidation[10], an early warning system to manage potentially harmful internal macroeconomic imbalances, and the Europe 2020 strategy[11] for strong and sustainable growth have resulted in a marked decline in current account deficits, increased exports and improvement in the competitiveness of the periphery, while wages have increased in France and Germany. An intergovernmental treaty (the Fiscal compact) has been introduced as a new, stricter version of the Stability and Growth Pact. By signing the treaty, 25 countries have committed themselves to introducing uniform, long-term budgetary rules into their national legal systems, preferably at constitutional level. The *European Semester* has also been adopted by the European Council and launched in 2011, with a central task to coordinate economic policies and structural reforms. This improves the integration and implementation of fiscal and economic reforms in the eurozone. The authors also note progress regarding budget balances in the euro area. In particular, structural budget deficits fell on average in the euro area from 6.3 % in 2009 to 3.3 % in 2012. Another key reform step has been the deepening of European banking sector integration. In this

[9] Some argue that debt mutualization should be partial, i.e. the EU should put in place a mechanism for internal transfer where less creditworthy nations should compensate the more creditworthy ones and for monitoring fiscal progress of member countries, and also ensure that the national governments remain responsible to reduce deficits.

[10] Nominal budget deficits declined from 6.4 % in 2009 to 3.2 % in 2012 for EU as a whole, while structural deficits corrected for the business cycle declined from 4.6 % to 2.1 %.

[11] Europe 2020 is a strategy adopted by the European Union to address the shortcomings in the growth models of European countries targeting specifically education, research and innovation, social inclusion and poverty reduction, and climate/energy for achieving smarter, more sustainable and more inclusive growth.

context the discussion of a European Banking Union with bank supervision function has been pushed forward. In sum, the authors argue that Europe has responded effectively and collectively.

Abheek Barua takes a contrasting position and argues that the recent crisis in Cyprus highlights the absence of an established and replicable model for crisis resolution in the euro region. The possibility of a deposit tax not only enhances the risk of bank runs across the region but also could generate sudden stops in liquidity as lending banks became apprehensive that there may be a quick erosion in the liability base of debtor banks.

What is the future for Europe and the euro? Does Europe need more or less integration? There are two views here. First, some participants felt that extensive integration—uniform economic policy and equal social security for all—would do justice neither to the European history nor to the preferences of the people. Economic centralization has a failed history: indeed, super-national banking supervision such as Basel I and II did not help prevent banking crises. The alternate view is that a common framework for supervision, regulation and resolution is necessary as Europe enjoys a common currency and capital market, and has extensive cross-border financial flows within the region. This division of views is taken up in two separate notes by *Heribert Dieter* and *Pierre Jacques*. *Dieter* argues that if governments and institutions like the ECB keep coming to the rescue of the financial sector, the players will become less prudent in the future. Rescue operations will lead to moral hazard. He also argues that Europe can strengthen the ownership of economic and fiscal policies by providing incentives for sustainable economic development. A key provision here is to eliminate the contradictions and inconsistencies of the Maastricht Treaty. *Jacques* argues that there is a clear lack of long-term and shared vision about European integration. Dealing with this requires strong political mobilization. This is the deepest challenge facing Europe currently.

In sum, while Europe's short- and long-run reform initiatives to tackle the euro crisis—fiscal consolidation and steps to improve competitiveness—have been promising, a dominant view was that Europe needs stronger coordination. This implies managed integration to ensure internal burden sharing, restore competitiveness and enhance potential growth.[12]

[12] The session also discussed what would be the likely implication of euro crisis on the Exempted Micro Enterprises (EMEs) and India. Is the slide in growth correlated with intensification of the eurozone crisis? EMEs—like India—would be affected by the crisis through three channels: (1) the confidence channel transmitted through financial markets, (2) regulation-triggered deleveraging of European banks may hurt the quantum of funds available to EMEs and (3) the trade channel. The implications for India would be severe as the EU is India's largest trading partner and half of external commercial borrowings in India are from European banks.

3 Rebalancing the Global Economy

Global macroeconomic rebalancing received considerable attention in the conference. While several issues remain contentious, a general consensus has emerged that reprioritizing domestic policies and reducing domestic distortions are key to rebalancing in an interconnected world. The focus of the debate was on understanding the extent of global macroeconomic rebalancing already achieved, and the need to develop a forward-looking perspective for understanding the changing nature of imbalances. Participants recognized that global imbalances are also dynamic: while the main source of global deficits remains largely the same, the source of global surpluses is now the oil-exporting countries (petrodollars) as opposed to manufacturing-intensive exporting economies (trade surpluses). The changing nature of imbalances—trade surpluses vs. petrodollars—has important implications for reserves and capital flows, and for policy responses.

Did the imbalances in 2008 cause the crisis? While some would argue that it is not external imbalances but financial regulatory failure that caused the crisis, a prevailing view (held, for instance, by Mervyn King and Ben Bernanke) appears to be that global imbalances fuelled the crisis through creating asset bubbles. However there have always been global imbalances: in the 1990s, the widening US deficit was matched by increasing surpluses in Japan and East Asia; in the early 2000s the rise in the US deficit reflected falling US domestic savings rather than strong domestic investment, while during 2004–2008 the US deficit remained large but was matched by a sharp increase in surpluses in China. What is different is the magnitude of the imbalances in the immediate lead-up to the crisis.

In the lead chapter, *Michael Callaghan* argues that the issue of global imbalances should not be presented in terms of a concern over global imbalances per se, but that removing distortions that result in 'bad' imbalances is beneficial to all. He emphasizes that external imbalances are a symptom of structural factors and policy distortions. Hence, not all imbalances are necessarily 'bad'. Imbalances may, for example, be a result of inter-temporal optimization by the private sector. For example, a country with an ageing population relative to its trading partners may choose to save and run current account surpluses in anticipation of dis-savings in the future when the workforce shrinks. Likewise, a country with more investment opportunities relative to its domestic savings will draw on foreign savings. Alternatively, policy distortions that can result in 'bad' imbalances include an export-led strategy through a manipulated exchange rate or structural shortcomings, such as the absence of an adequate social security net that results in excessive private savings. He also points out that the IMF has had little success in persuading countries to reduce their 'bad' imbalances, and there were few clear warnings from the IMF in advance of the crisis. The IMF focussed almost exclusively on the threat of an exchange rate crisis resulting from a pullout from dollar assets, leading to a disorderly decline in the dollar and a spike in interest rates. It did not look at how these imbalances were linked to the systematic risks building up in financial systems.

These arguments suggest the need to examine differences in stages of development, demographic patterns, market failures and other structural shortcomings and how these work through saving and investment patterns and the financial system leading to persistent external imbalances. Hence, imbalances are only symptoms that should be used as a diagnostic tool to identify the underlying causes of the imbalances. The research challenge is in disentangling the causes of imbalances between structural factors and policy distortions.[13] One body of literature[14] suggests that domestic policy distortions played a major role in driving global imbalances in the run-up to the crisis.

What has the G20 done to rebalance global demand and what needs to be done in the future? First, the G20 spent a lot of time identifying quantifiable targets for measuring 'excessive' imbalances. However, it failed to identify the driving force behind the imbalances. And the domestic situations in G20 countries and the sources of imbalances differ widely. As such, policies should be tailored to individual country circumstances, especially the underlying distortions, to anchor the G20 objective of strong sustainable and balanced growth. For example, fiscal consolidation, appropriately timed in advanced economies to reduce the persistent deficits and create fiscal policy space, should be complemented by revival of internal demand in surplus countries to support domestic and global growth.

However, this is easier said than done. A number of concerns remain in rebalancing global demand. First, convincing policymakers to achieve a global public good such as reducing imbalances, especially when a growth model is working fairly well—as in China—would be a difficult task. Here, the G20 may play a decisive role through its peer review process identifying domestic policies for countries that are good for sustaining domestic growth and also for resolving global imbalances. Building on these ideas, *Emil Stavrev* notes that the IMF sustainability report identified seven systemic members as having "moderate" or "large" imbalances that warranted more in-depth analysis. Sustainability assessments indicate that external imbalances have been driven primarily by saving imbalances: i.e. saving in major advanced economies has been too low, and too high in key emerging surplus economies. He argues therefore that policymakers need to continue their efforts to further promote such dual rebalancing which involves a "hand-off"—or trans-

[13] A closer look at the external imbalances in the run-up to the crisis shows that sources vary widely across seven systemic economies (the countries that account for 5% or more of G20 GDP are China, France, Germany, India, Japan, UK and USA). A variety of structural factors reflecting country circumstances have driven savings and investment behaviour: low private and public savings, imbalances between tax revenues and spending commitments and resistance to raising taxes in the USA; low savings in the UK; high savings and over-investment partly reflecting the distortions in the financial sector in Germany; scores of factors including high savings, structural imbalances between tax revenues and spending, declining productivity and a shrinking labour force in Japan; despite high private savings, low public savings and tax revenues, and high spending commitments in India; and exceptionally high private savings and investment, partly inadequate social safety nets, restrictive financial conditions, under-valued exchange rates, subsidized factors of production, limited dividends and lack of competition in product markets in China.

[14] For example, see Blanchard and Milesi-Ferretti (2009).

fer—from public to private demand-led growth in major advanced economies. Dual rebalancing also requires a shift from growth led by domestic demand in major advanced deficit economies towards external demand and vice versa in major emerging surplus economies.

What about emerging markets? In his note, *Takuji Kinkyo* argues that in response to the Asian financial crisis of 1997–1998, crisis-hit Asian countries abandoned *de facto* dollar pegs and officially claimed to adopt floating exchange rate regimes. However, as widely recognized in the literature, there is a discrepancy between *de jure* and *de facto* exchange rate regimes. Kinkyo shows that while China's current account surplus has declined sharply from the peak level before the global financial crisis of 2008–2009, there is evidence that the renminbi still remains substantially undervalued. In particular, he argues that the renminbi is not appreciating fast enough to match the pace of changes in underlying fundamentals, notably the rise in productivity and the accumulation of net foreign assets. The renminbi could, however, become substantially undervalued once global demand begins to grow faster.[15]

In their note, *Jong Kook Shin* and *Chetan Subramanian* argue that global imbalances are not a new phenomenon and have been around for the past three decades. What is important is that the magnitude of the imbalances in the 1980s was relatively modest in comparison to the imbalances immediately prior to the crisis. In addition, the external deficits of the USA and other advanced countries in the 1980s were largely funded by other advanced countries, such as Japan and Germany. In contrast, more recently the imbalances of the advanced countries have been funded by emerging markets.

The authors argue that this pattern highlights one of the important causes for the global financial crisis, namely the demand for risk-free assets which partly reflects poor levels of financial development in the EMEs. The authors argue that this explains the *Lucas Paradox,* where capital flows from the EMEs to developed countries (Lucas 1990).

[15] Another factor is petro-dollars. To quote the Economist, "[t]he biggest counterpart to America's current account deficit is the combined surplus of oil exporting economies which have enjoyed huge windfalls from high oil prices. This year the IMF expects them to run a record surplus of US$ 750 billion, three fifths of which will come from the Middle East. This amount will dwarf China's expected surplus of US$ 180 Billion. Since 2000, the cumulative surpluses of oil exporters amounted to over US$ 4 Trillion, twice as much as that of China" (The Economist 2012). Little attention has been paid to this, as petro-dollars do not show up in international reserves but go into sovereign wealth funds. This does not help the recovery of global demand. This could be corrected partly by exchange rate movements and partly by spending, especially on domestic consumption.

4 Financial Sector Regulation

Participants in the conference recognized that the financial sector has been a big source of shocks to the global economy.[16] Financial sector regulation has also been at the heart of G20 initiatives from the first Leaders' Summit: the G20 succeeded in agreeing on Basel III capital, leverage and liquidity standards, expanding the regulatory perimeter to include systemically important financial institutions (SIFIs), macro-prudential tools and regulation of the shadow banking system.

These reforms have triggered a debate on several questions: were the reforms still too little or did they overreach and excessively impede financial markets? Is the focus on achieving financial stability at any cost? While it is now widely recognized that pre-crisis financial regulation was too lax, is financial regulation after the crisis leading to credit rationing? How can economies reform the financial sector without stifling it? How do countries coordinate financial regulation across jurisdictions; and is it reasonable to have coordination when economies are at different stages of economic and financial development? An area that is of particular interest to India is whether raising fresh capital to comply with the new Basel III norms for Indian banks will be a challenge amidst a slowing economy.[17]

The crisis has also challenged the intellectual foundations—efficient markets, self-regulation, market discipline and financial innovation—that prevailed prior to the crisis. Light touch regulation and supervision were thought to be adequate as markets were efficient in accurately measuring risks and allocating them optimally, and financial innovations were considered to have improved risk management. But the crisis changed these perceptions. One lesson from the crisis is that financial stability is not independent of macroeconomic stability, or the latter independent of the former. Participants in the conference felt that the crisis highlighted many gaps in the regulatory and supervisory framework, including:

- Failure of regulatory policies, particularly capital adequacy and liquidity standards and disclosure requirements to assess risks
- Pro-cyclicality of capital standards

[16] In a May 3, 2013 entry to the IMF direct (blog), David Romer of Berkeley points out that financial shocks are not rare, and should be thought as being closer to commonplace rather than being considered as exceptional events. He suggests that in the past 30 years in the USA, there have been six occasions in which financial developments have posed important macroeconomic risks: the Latin American debt crisis, the 1987 stock market crash, the savings and loans crisis of the late 1980s and early 1990s, the Russian debt crisis of 1998, the dot-com bubble bust of the late 1990s and early 2000s and the housing crisis and financial meltdown of the GFC starting in 2008. See http://blog-imfdirect.imf.org/2013/05/03/preventing-the-next-catastrophe-where-do-we-stand/.

[17] One of the fears of current reform initiatives is that it may lead to credit rationing. Domestically, the most affected segment would be small- and medium-sized enterprises, while globally it would be EMEs, especially trade credits to EME firms. Similarly, countries where a home-grown banking system is absent would get affected most as globally active backs deleverage. This would call for targeted reforms—special provisioning—rather than general relaxation regulatory standards. Second, much of the G20 debate on financial regulations reflects problems of the USA and Europe and is not necessarily relevant for EMEs.

- Too-big-to-fail problems and associated excessive risk-taking behaviour by financial institutions
- The absence of macro-prudential tools
- The position of shadow banking outside the regulatory perimeters
- Failure to appreciate potential risks associated with innovation, compensation structures and associated misguided incentives, the systemic importance of non-banks and the importance of the relationship between banks and non-banks
- Too much reliance on credit rating agencies
- Corporate governance failures

In the lead chapter to this section, *Stephen Pickford* takes stock of many of the above issues and argues that an important aspect to consider is the extent and form of financial sector reforms already undertaken, and the variable impact such reforms may have on economic activity in countries that are at different stages of economic and financial sector development. He argues that in political economy terms it was necessary for governments to tighten regulation in order to address the regulatory shortcomings exposed by the crisis, which required exceptional levels of support and financial resources provided to banks and other financial institutions. Further, malpractice and misbehaviour in private financial institutions has added political pressure for tighter regulation, compounding the pressure already resulting from the high cost of public support for banks during the crisis. Overall, he considers that while the jury is still out on the cost and benefits on a variety of regulatory reforms, there are good political economy reasons for completing the current regulatory programme. This is based on the view that while reforms to address the shortcomings that led to the last crisis may not prevent future crises, at the very least they should prevent a repeat of the last one.

In his note *Jae Ha Park* argues that Asian financial systems have been relatively unaffected by the global financial crisis (GFC) and the ongoing eurozone crisis, reflecting sound balance sheets, prudent risk management and modest exposure to toxic assets. He notes that this strength of the Asian financial system is due to its sizeable non-banking financial firms. In addition, large foreign exchange reserves have provided a cushion against volatile capital flows in most cases. He notes, however, that requirements under Basel III may impose an excessive burden on some emerging Asian economies. Basel III and related supervisory and regulatory measures, which were designed from the perspective of the experience of developed economies during the GFC, may not necessarily be applicable to Asian emerging market economies.[18]

[18] Many participants felt that regulatory concerns of EMEs are different given their developmental needs. The regulatory philosophy in most of the EMEs, especially in Asia (and India), is different—regulators pay close attention and capital and liquidity standards are high. Asian regulators also have used macro-prudential policies—administrative guidance to limit bank-credit growth, real estate loan caps, etc.—which provided a cushion against the crisis. Hence, reforms proposed to address weaknesses in advanced country financial markets may not be applied to EMEs. Though capital and liquidity standards of Basel III are easily achievable for Asian countries, strengthening regulatory capacity and data requirements for implementing Basel III may impose an excess burden. However, it should be noted that international standards such as Basel rules are meant

In his note, *Berndt Spahn* looks at more recent proposals for reorganizing banking supervision in Europe and the euro area in particular. He argues that while the entire gamut of financial sector reforms—ranging from reforms that enhance the quality and quantity of capital, liquidity and leverage ratios, regulating OTC derivatives, identifying systemically important financial institutions and better macro-prudential regulations—will impose new costs and lead to a restructuring of activities, they will not jeopardize the functioning of the financial industry.

Anand Sinha argues in his note that the recognition of the role of systemic risk and the importance of financial stability are the major lessons from the crisis. While there are arguments for both supporting and opposing the new regulations, each has its own merits. The answer therefore lies in striking the right balance to ensure that the new regulations achieve their objective of strengthening the resilience of the financial system while at the same time not adversely impacting on economic growth and the efficiency gains from financial innovation.

In the discussion, many participants felt that while forward-looking provisioning and cross-border resolution mechanisms are being introduced, considerable efforts are still required to identify models or metrics to measure systemic risk and its interaction with the financial system and real economy to effectively use macro-prudential policies for smoothing credit cycles and achieve financial stability. Financial sector reforms have triggered debates over the impact on bank lending and economic growth. It was acknowledged that high capital, liquidity and leverage standards, and restrictions on certain activities for banks have arguably reduced lending to the private sector and stifled innovation, which depresses growth. Sceptics of financial sector reform typically question the ability of regulators to manage the more intrusive regimes. They also show, using historical data, that simple and market-based rules substantially outperform complex rules such as the risk-based Basel approach. On the other hand, the proponents of financial sector reforms argue that the damage unleashed by the crisis is massive, and hence the expected benefits of financial stability outweigh the costs of regulation. Further, given that financial markets failed to assess risk and there was fraud and manipulation, policymakers and the public at large lost trust in the self-regulation of financial markets. The discussion demonstrated that the debate is still inconclusive.

The participants in this session highlighted the need for cooperation in the implementation of standards and the importance of consistent implementation across regions so as to mitigate regulatory arbitrage. These standards are global and non-binding. The G20, however, has entrusted the Financial Stability Board (FSB) with developing a coordination framework for monitoring implementation at national level.

---

for internationally active banks. Countries have a large leeway to implement them as they deem fit—for example, India has proposed to apply it fully, while Japan and the USA have opted it for only the internationally active banks. Finally, an important issue that arises here is the concern over the rapid growth of bank credit. This may be a misleading indicator of "stress" since in EMEs, bank credit is partly driven by more financial inclusion. Universally stringent capital standards (such as Basel III) may disproportionately affect EMEs as globally active banks would reduce their exposure to EMEs to meet new stringent capital standards. Further, if the new standards are implemented in EMEs, this would make development financing and financial inclusion difficult.

Indeed, financial reforms received top billing in the first three summits and have continued to be an important issue in the later summits. The successful implementation of financial reforms would highlight the success of the G20 as a global coordination mechanism. Many considered that rolling back the agenda was not an option.

To summarize, participants felt that several messages can be drawn for the G20's financial regulatory reforms. In the pre-GFC period, financial regulation was not equipped to identify risk concentration and permitted flawed incentives. Macro-policies also failed to take into account the build-up of systematic risk. Hence, it is crucial to fully complete and implement the existing commitments to tighter regulations. However, it is important to take into account the situation of emerging markets, including those in Asia. If there are sector-specific problems, especially pertaining to credit and/or EMEs, then sector-specific and EME-specific solutions must be framed. There may also be a need to consolidate the agenda and focus on implementing existing reform initiatives. This would give regulators and supervisors some time to reflect on what form of regulation and supervision works best in practice. Other broad questions that emerged included what is the optimal FSB–G20 relationship, and how should we assess progress, particularly the trade-off between the safety of the financial system and economic growth.

5 A new framework for reforming the International Monetary System

The G20 agenda for reforming the international monetary system (IMS) includes managing global reserve currencies, managing excessive capital flows and volatility, and providing a global financial safety net. Participants felt that the G20 has made little progress on developing a comprehensive multilateral framework for reforming the IMS. Some relevant questions raised in this session were:

- Is the IMS fundamentally flawed?
- Has the evolution of the IMS kept up with changes in the global economy?
- Will fundamental changes in the global economy make the IMS more multipolar?
- Has the G20 provided a concrete proposal for reforming the IMS?
- What role can global financial safety nets play in mitigating balance of payment crises and reducing IMS-induced global imbalances?
- What is the role of macro-prudential policies in mitigating the deleterious effects of volatile capital flows?

The IMS has evolved from the gold standard to the Bretton Woods arrangements of fixed and adjustable exchange rates (since 1971 when the gold standard was abandoned), and finally to the current system of broadly floating exchange rates. A key feature of the current IMS is that it requires a liquid international asset of stable value (i.e. a reserve asset, which since the demise of the gold standard has been the US dollar). There are, however, several symptoms of instability in the current IMS.

This is evidenced by (1) routinely recurring crises in the post-Bretton Woods period marked by persistent current account imbalances, (2) volatility in capital flows and currency values and (3) a sizeable build-up in international reserves in key emerging economies, which approached $6 billion or over 25 % of global GDP on average in 2008 (Ghosh et.al. 2012).

The root causes of this instability can be traced largely to the following:

- Inadequate global adjustment mechanisms. There are no mechanisms for burden sharing across countries and, as such, the system is prone to inconsistencies and externalities.
- The lack of a global oversight framework for cross-border capital flows. The higher volume of cross-border capital flows creates complex interdependencies, and a universal framework that addresses cross-border capital flows is lacking.
- No systemic liquidity provision mechanism. The size of the collective safety net is inadequate and there is no systematic mechanism to provide liquidity at the global level.
- Structural challenges. There are concerns about a dominant national currency-based system which provides "exorbitant privilege" to the reserve currency issuer. Further, this creates a deep dependence for the rest of the world on the reserve issuer's domestic policies. Furthermore, it raises the possibility of an asymmetric adjustment to imbalances.
- There is a need to accommodate the changing core and to generate the necessary supply of safe assets.

In the lead chapter, *Jyoti Rahman, Ewa Orzechowska-Fischer* and *Redom Syed* suggest that while the current IMS needs reforms, a completely new system is not required. They note that in the 2012 Los Cabos summit, the G20 Leaders further supplemented the IMF NAB (New Arrangements to Borrow) and quota resources with bilateral loans worth more than US$ 456 billion. This has bolstered the IMF's lending capacity. In response to the crisis, the Fund also created a flexible credit line (FCL) and a precautionary liquidity line (PLL) aimed at bolstering market confidence and alleviating balance of payment risks for countries with strong economic fundamentals. However, the GFC highlighted significant weaknesses in the IMF's surveillance methods. A review of surveillance led to major improvements in the surveillance framework with a strengthened focus on spillovers as opposed to an earlier emphasis on exchange rate policies as a primary contributor to external imbalances. The authors also note that while the IMF has been undergoing a set of governance reforms aimed at increasing the representation of emerging markets, further reforms are needed to make the IMF governance structure reflective of changing global realities, and that these reforms should lead to a substantial shift in the IMF quota shares towards the dynamic EMDCs and a change in the IMF quota formula.

In similar spirit, *Emil Stavrev* argues that while the current IMS has survived for over 40 years and has under-pinned strong global growth and increasing integration, it has also exhibited many symptoms of instability. His note summarizes the key problems facing the IMS and discusses potential reforms. The avenues for reform can be found first in strengthening policy collaboration in the core and peripheries through the G20 mutual assessment process (MAP). There should also be a strengthening of IMF surveillance and integration of bilateral and multilateral surveillance. This needs to be further complemented by the monitoring and management of global capital flows. Further work is needed to focus on macro-prudential and capital flow management measures. Finally, the creation of a strong global safety net will be necessary to fully mitigate the above-mentioned instabilities. However, to ensure the success of this plan, it will be important to navigate an orderly and gradual transition to the stronger governance system. Participants in the session recognized that there is an asymmetry in the G20s reform agenda, with a focus on reviving global growth, reducing unemployment and dealing with social issues, while longer-term issues—especially the periodic tendency of instability in the IMS—have not been adequately addressed.

Gurbachan Singh, in his note, focuses on credit lines more specifically. He argues that credit lines (CLs) can serve as safeguards against the pure *sudden stop* of capital inflows into otherwise 'solvent' economies. Since a sudden stop implies a liquidity crunch, it may be difficult for public authorities to raise funds internationally *ex-post* once a sudden stop has occurred. In this context, an *ex-ante* CL gives an option to borrow in the event of a sudden stop. Credit lines can be put into two categories: those that need to be backed by some reserves or liquid assets and those that do not need to be backed by reserves. He proposes that the IMF could serve as a mediator between central banks that use swap credit lines for mitigating a currency crisis. This role is different from the current role of the IMF as a provider of liquidity.

Participants also observed that the objective of the Special Drawing Right (SDR) becoming a "principal reserve asset" was unlikely in the foreseeable future. Overall, the current IMS needs a broader dimension including stronger surveillance, particularly over exchange rate policies, benchmarks and members' obligations, along with more work on global liquidity, the role of the SDR and improved governance arrangements. The IMF has taken a number of initiatives to strengthen its surveillance, including the adoption of an Integrated Surveillance Decision (ISD). But while steps have been taken to improve the analysis and coverage of IMF surveillance, the ongoing challenge is for the IMF to have greater traction with its advice in terms of influencing countries' policies. There is also a need for shared understanding of liquidity requirements by the IMF, Bank for International Settlements (BIS) and the Financial Stability Board (FSB). As regards the use of the SDR as a reserve asset, an international unit of account and an incentive to improve the workings of the adjustment process, further consideration should be encouraged. The composition of the SDR basket should be kept under review and modified as required to reflect the relative importance of economies in international trade and financial transactions.

With regard to national monetary policy, one implication of the use of unconventional policies, such as quantitative easing (QE), is that other countries, particularly EMEs, may lose competitiveness through no fault of their own. No central bank is held domestically accountable for the effect it has on other economies. The use of capital controls remains an important issue for the international community.[19]

Finally, the crisis has provided the trigger as well as the opportunity for reforming the IMS. Positive gains from global economic integration post-Bretton Woods are now under threat as there is an increased risk of instability, retreat to protectionism and competitive depreciations, leading countries to strengthen national reserves and regional reserve pools.

6 Capital Control Policy and Emerging Market Economies

Many participants felt that capital flows are mostly beneficial as they finance productive investment, diversify risk and smooth consumption. But sudden and excessive inflows cause various macroeconomic concerns and financial stability risks such as currency appreciation and asset price bubbles. Participants in this session felt that there were three major issues regarding the use of capital controls:

- The choice between capital controls and prudential measures
- Ensuring capital controls do not substitute for appropriate macroeconomic tools
- Ensuring prudential measures are non-discriminatory

New avenues for future research would include developing a framework for applying the above policy measures for different kinds of capital flows (debt, FDI, etc.) which could require different policy measures to be taken up by the recipient and source countries, and whether it is useful to draw upon the policy measures taken by developed nations and apply them to EMEs whose situations and circumstances may be very different from advanced economies.

In the lead chapter, *Abhijit Sengupta* and *Rajeswari Sengupta* discuss some of the challenges that have emanated from India's increased integration with global capital markets. India's experience with capital flows which remain volatile has complicated monetary and exchange rate management. The authors argue that India has adopted a multiple instrument approach that includes active management of capital flows, especially volatile short-term and debt flows; a moderately flexible exchange rate regime with the RBI intervening with sterilization to prevent excessive volatility and active foreign reserve management. The authors calculate the exchange market pressure (EMP) index in India and track its evolution over the last couple of decades. They also evaluate the extent to which the EMP index has been influenced by major macroeconomic factors and conclude that the EMP has exhibited a great deal of fluctuation during the period 1990–2010. This is due to global and domestic events and has primarily been affected by changes in the trade balance, portfolio equity inflows and stock market fluctuations. In sum, India's ex-

[19] See the Landau report on global liquidity prepared by BIS at the behest of G20 (BIS 2011).

perience in negotiating the macroeconomic "trilemma"—monetary independence, exchange rate stability and capital account openness—given its integration with global capital markets during the last two decades, is commendable. India has opted for the middle ground and has balanced all three objectives by buffering the trade-offs through reserve accumulation.

In his note, *Atish R. Ghosh* draws attention to ongoing research with colleagues in the IMF's Research Department on the use of capital controls in the face of inflow surges; the nexus between capital controls and macro-prudential measures; and multilateral aspects of managing the capital account. His note summarizes this work. He argues that the policy toolkit for addressing financial stability risks could possibly include prudential measures and capital controls that may or may not discriminate between residency and currency. These risk-mitigating policies have all been undertaken by most countries at some time. But this raises the question of choosing between prudential measures and capital controls against financial stability risks. Prudential measures that are non-residency based (i.e. applied to the domestic banking system, and based on currency rather than residency) should be used when the flows come through the economy's financial/banking sector. The cases where flows come through the non-banking or non-financial sector should be handled with the use of capital controls. There are also issues of multilateral cooperation which are of concern to the G20, i.e. how policies should take account of multilateral considerations and mechanisms through which spillover impacts are recognized and worked upon. In addition, there is a renewed interest in international policy coordination arising from imbalances between savings (current account surpluses) and borrowing (current account deficits). Other issues include the possible tools for capital account management, the effects of quantitative easing in advanced economies on capital flows to emerging markets and the role of fiscal and monetary policy as a stabilization tool in emerging markets. Capital controls that are good for one country may not be necessarily good for others.

In the last few years, the world economy has experienced dual-track growth, with strong growth in Asia contrasting with below-trend growth in most advanced economies. There is an interesting contrast between the last few years and the pre-1997 period in which *excessive investment* in the Asian economies was funded by short-term debt denominated in foreign currency, resulting in both a maturity and foreign currency mismatch. Now, the Asian region has *excess savings.* In general, Asia has been able to weather the 2008 crisis. FDI inflows have been strong and have continued to be strong during the GFC. This is because most FDI has been attracted by growing production networks in East Asia. Another factor has been domestic demand-driven growth, which is an attractive factor for FDI. Equity flows are also on the rise: many Asian economies have undertaken financial sector reforms which supports equity flows. Motivated by this, *David Kim* asks whether monetary union in Asia (ASEAN 5 plus three) is a possibility. He notes that the region is far more heterogeneous than both the European Union and Mercosur in terms of per capita income, geographical proximity, industrial structure, political proximity and institutional institutions. Another relevant factor is that these countries are at varying stages of economic development as evidenced by the composition of industrial structure within the region. However, the significant growth in intra-industry trade and foreign direct investment in recent decades has stimulated discussion of closer regional economic integration. To address this, *Kim* notes that a key criterion is the synchronization of business cycles (also referred to as the symmetry of shocks) because the cost of losing an independent monetary policy would be small. He concludes that for regional shocks, several countries within East Asia have uniform responses. This points to the potential benefit of a common macroeconomic policy if the regional shocks constitute a significant proportion of all disturbances.

In sum, many of the participants felt that capital controls are an open field, with the orthodoxy being challenged. Several interesting questions and observations relating to capital controls include:

- What drives capital flows (pull factors or push factors)?
- The composition of capital controls matters (equity-type liabilities versus debt-type flows which tend to be highly volatile).
- The focus should be on gross flows. Net flows are more important for macroeconomic management, but gross flows are more important for financial stability.
- What are the factors affecting gross flows (global factors versus contagion and debt flows)?
- Is there a case for capital controls—what is the empirical evidence?
- Do capital controls help navigate through the impossible trinity?
- What is the appropriate dichotomy in the use of instruments for dealing with monetary policy and macro-prudential policies?
- The need for flexibility and pragmatism (rather than textbook orthodoxy).

Participants also felt that the policy toolkit to address macroeconomic challenges could include allowing the external balance to move towards the medium-term multilaterally consistent equilibrium value. The EMEs following a floating exchange rate would allow the nominal rate to appreciate. The "peggers" would not engage in any sterilized intervention. Other options include

- Accumulating reserves for country insurance
- Lowering interest rates and tightening fiscal policy
- Using capital controls/prudential measures.

7 Austerity and Growth.

This section had two objectives: first, to re-visit the austerity versus growth debate in light of the USA, eurozone and emerging market experiences in the post-financial crisis period; and second, since infrastructure spending is typically cut in fiscal austerity programmes, what does austerity imply for long run growth in national economies. The debate on austerity versus growth is deeply divided. An open research question is whether there are conditions under which contractionary fiscal policy can be expansionary. Further, if short-run stabilization is not the exclusive domain of monetary policy, what fiscal tools are required. In the lead chapter, *Alok Sheel* argues that any overall assessment of the G20 must focus on two metrics: its success as a model for global economic governance and the welfare gains from the globally coordinated response orchestrated by G20 central banks and Leaders after the GFC. He notes that—in one instance—the G20 has not delivered on macroeconomic policy coordination because of the introduction of "expansionary fiscal contractions." This leads to a host of related questions: if fiscal multipliers are potentially high, why is the US recovery not more robust? Could this be because of the fiscal mix? He suggests that Ricardian Equivalence may come in the way of translating additional income into expenditure. In a recession induced by a financial crisis, tax cuts may be less effective than direct government expenditure in stimulating the economy.

He argues that one area that needs more attention by the G20 is the lack of public investment in infrastructure in developing countries. Infrastructure investment could help enhance the effectiveness of macroeconomic policies during a downturn through various channels: first, it would stimulate the economy by creating more jobs and induce household spending; second, it would complement monetary policy transmission channels; third, it would address the instability in the global economy by rebalancing global demand as infrastructure investment is import intensive; and fourth, it would help rebalance demand from the public sector to the private sector. Emphasizing infrastructure investment in G20 deliberations would also calm the markets as they would be convinced of at least one source of growth in global demand. He recommends accelerated financing and implementation of public investment projects in developing economies—which would hasten both global and internal rebalancing, with the associated demand for capital goods creating jobs in advanced countries. He also argues that one area where there is scope for cooperation is coordinating fiscal policy. The task of fiscal re-structuring is complicated by the fact that collective austerity leads to a vicious feedback loop. An immediate priority for fiscal policy is therefore the composition of adjustment: particularly whether the adjustments are growth friendly and not overtly harmful in the short run.[20]

In their note, *Denis Medvedev* and *Smriti Seth* argue that there are mixed views on the role of fiscal consolidations in reducing both public debt and simultaneously reducing the output gap. The proponents of fiscal consolidation argue that a credible consolidation plan would imply a reduction in expected future taxes, and hence an increase in expected future income, which would lead to an increase in current consumption. Hence, fiscal consolidations could be expansionary. In addition, spending cuts would work through the labour market channel as well: it would reduce wages, increase profits, which in turn would increase investment and stimulate long-term growth.

[20] In normal times, sovereign borrowing costs are positively associated with public debt. During a crisis period, however, funds tend to move from high-risk assets to risk-free sovereign bonds. Thus, though there is an increase in the fiscal deficits, there will be a fall in the Treasury bond yields in major developed countries. This fiscal space, if utilized, can stimulate growth which will be a key factor for stimulating growth, and hence fiscal consolidation in the medium to long run.

On the other hand, the proponents of fiscal expansion argue that when expansive monetary policy and private investment cannot pick up the slack, the government should step in. The stimulus can pay for itself, as economic activity picks up, as will tax revenue. Further, a contractionary fiscal policy will work for a country through the export channel if the global economy is growing. If there is a synchronized downturn in many countries, as is the case now, austerity would suppress global demand and aggravate the downturn. However, the effectiveness of stimulus in bridging the output gap depends on the stage of the business cycle and the speed of adjustment of the markets. Also, there is a role for complementary policies, especially monetary policies and supply-side policies.

What should governments do? While it is easy to propose cutting unproductive expenditures and increasing productive expenditures, this is difficult to do in practice. It is not easy to distinguish productive expenditure from unproductive. However, going by the literature, spending on health, education and infrastructures is productive, which would in turn increase productivity in the private sector. Further, how such spending is financed, and what margins are distorted, the composition of government spending would have implications for the effectiveness of a stimulus package.

A policy-induced depression in some sectors should be corrected by reducing subsidies and/or increasing tax in the other sectors—for example, a policy-induced repression in the manufacturing sector in India could be corrected through taxing the agricultural sector or at least by reducing subsidies to the agricultural sector that would tilt the terms of trade in favour of manufacturing. Similarly, reducing wasteful agricultural subsidies in the European Union could free valuable fiscal space. However, these are politically contentious.

Shankar Acharya argues that over the past 30 years fiscal austerity has been notable by its absence in India. The combined deficit of central and state governments has typically been in the range of 7–10 % of GDP, except for 5 years, two in the mid-1990s and three in the mid-2000s. However, while the two best periods of economic growth in India, 1992–1997 and 2003–2008, *have* been associated with significant fiscal consolidation, periods of high fiscal deficits *have not* engendered high growth. Further, the persistence of the high fiscal deficits beyond 2008/2009, while contributing to India's economic resilience in 2008–2010, also helped fuel the high inflation of the post-crisis years, reduced domestic savings and helped induce the worrisome widening of external deficits. The need for successful fiscal consolidation in India therefore remains strong. He also suggests that because India's fiscal policies in the last 25 years cautions against accepting a uniform policy paradigm for all nations at all times on issues of fiscal policy, the ongoing industrial nation debate on austerity versus stimulus may have little practical relevance for India's current fiscal priorities.

Acknowledgement We are deeply grateful to Isher Ahluwalia, Parthasarthi Shome, Rajat Kathuria and members of the ICRIER G20 team for their support related to this volume.

References

Ahluwalia MS (2011) The G20: a new experiment in global governance. In Kaldor M and Vizard P (eds) *Arguing about the world: the work and legacy of Meghnad Desai*. Bloomsbury Academic Publishing, London

Bank for International Settlements (2011) Global liquidity: concept, measurement and policy implications. CGFS Papers 45, Committee on the Global Financial System, November

Bird G (2012) Dealing with global economic imbalances: the political economy of policy coordination, global economic review: perspectives on east Asian economies and industries. J Econ Pol Ref 41(4):299–317

Blanchard O, Milesi-Ferretti G (2009) Global imbalances: in Midstream, IMF Staff Position Note, IMF, SPN/09/29

Buiter W, Rahbari E (2012) Rising risks of Greek euro area exit, citi economics, global economics view, 6 February

Ghosh AR, Jonathan DO, Tsangarides C (2012), Shifting motives: explaining the buildup in official reserves in emerging markets since the 1980s, IMF Working Paper No. 12/34, IMF

Lucas R (1990). Why doesn't capital flow from rich to poor countries?, Amer Eco Rev 80(2):92–96

Pilbeam K (2006). International finance, 3rd edn. Palgrave, London

The Economist (2012) Petrodollar profusion: oil exporters are the main drivers of global imbalances, April 28.

The G20 Since 2008: Some Reflections on the Experience and the Road Ahead

Subir Gokarn

1 Introduction: The Emergence of Questions

Four years after the financial crisis of 2008, the global economy is still in a state of fragility. The early signs of recovery, which were seen as a vindication of the coordinated global policy response in late 2008 and early 2009, have not developed into a sustained revival of the growth momentum that the global economy experienced in the years before the crisis. While the global economy grew by about 4.8 % per year during the 5 years, between 2003 and 2007, it slowed to about 2.8 % in the subsequent 4 years[1]. Further, the post-crisis growth pattern was quite skewed, as emerging market economies (EMEs) initially showed relatively greater responsiveness to the policy stimulus. Recently, however, even these economies have slowed, as perhaps might have been expected in a scenario in which the world's major advanced economies simply failed to sustain whatever early momentum they had generated.

Against this broad backdrop, a number of stress points have emerged in the global economy, which can be seen simultaneously as both outcomes and contributors to the macroeconomic situation. From the perspective of the debate and dialogue in the G20 finance track, two issues had a lot of airtime over the past couple of years. In late 2010, in the wake of enhanced liquidity provisions by the US Federal

This article is a revised version of a speech delivered in October 2012, when the author was with the Reserve Bank of India and represented that institution on the G20 Deputies Forum. I am grateful to my former colleagues Bhupal Singh, S. V. S. Dixit and Anupam Prakash for their contributions to the preparation of this speech and an anonymous referee for useful comments. The content has been updated wherever relevant.

[1] Simple averages of annual growth rates computed from the World Economic Outlook of the International Monetary Fund (various issues).

S. Gokarn (✉)
Brookings India, Brookings Institution,
New Delhi, India
e-mail: subir_gokarn@yahoo.com

M. Callaghan et al. (eds.), *Global Cooperation Among G20 Countries*,
DOI 10.1007/978-81-322-1659-9_2, © Springer India 2014

Reserve, concerns were raised by some EMEs about the impact that this measure would have on their currencies. It was felt that the appreciation of these currencies would reduce the competitiveness of EMEs for essentially no fault of their own. Then, from early 2011 onwards, the unfolding of the sovereign debt problems in Europe evoked concerns about the adequacy of the policy response to them.

On several other issues, the initial promise of concerted collective action within the G20 has given way, perhaps expectedly, to a greater articulation of the differences between the members. On the important and long-standing agenda of the framework for strong, sustainable and balanced growth, there has been a degree of convergence of views on the indicators that might be used to gauge potential stress in economies. However, even as this has happened, there are questions about the uniformity of interpretation of individual indicators in clearly different macroeconomic contexts.

On the very ambitious financial regulation agenda, concerns are being expressed about the capacity of different financial systems to absorb the requirements of the new framework, the requirements these will impose on regulatory agencies and the difficulties in bridging wide gaps between national frameworks (which is needed to make progress towards a globally consistent and coordinated regulatory framework). As regards the reform of the international monetary system, aspirations for changes in the quota and governance frameworks in the International Monetary Fund (IMF) are coming up against differences between countries on what specific factors should determine the new quotas.

In terms of both the stress points and the emergence of differences across what might be seen as "permanent" agenda items, an impression might be created that the G20 process has run its course. After all, the very purpose of this grouping, when it was first created in 1997, was to make the debate on global issues more inclusive by bringing in at least the larger EMEs into it, along with the European Union. The value of this grouping was certainly realized in 2008, when G20 Leaders met for the first time in Washington DC as Heads of the States. Even though the crisis originated in the advanced economies, the complex interlinkages that had developed between them and the other economies in the group carried massive spillover risks, which were clearly manifested in global economic outcomes during late 2008 and early 2009. Consequently, there was little hope of a global recovery taking place without the direct involvement of the entire group. Moreover, as I indicated earlier, the initial signs did suggest that the strategy worked.

However, subsequent developments, both in terms of economic events and outcomes and in terms of the nature of the debate within the G20, raise questions about the relevance and utility of the group beyond a forum for sharing and exchanging views on various issues of global significance. Can it regain its stature as a "problem-solving" group, that is able to generate the kind of consensus and follow-up actions that it did during the 2008 crisis; or, is it just a "wartime" grouping that works only when a crisis is at hand, but does not have the framework to be effective in a "peacetime" setting, in which collective solutions to structural problems need to be found?

2 The Rationale for Continuing

In theory, this is a relatively easy question to answer. The basic rationale for a grouping like the G20 is that it encompasses a set of countries which are strongly interlinked, so that shocks that emanate in one or some of them are almost certain to quickly transmit to the others. In a broader variant of the "no taxation without representation" idiom, the principles of public choice would suggest that it would be in the interest of the overall welfare of the group for each one to have a say in the design and management of shock absorption mechanisms.

Viewed from this perspective, the agenda that the group has set for itself is clearly based on the global public goods nature of each of the items. There are, of course, other global public goods that have resulted in parallel collective mechanisms within which their benefits and costs are distributed. A uniform set of rules for international trade reflected in the World Trade Organization and the ongoing debate on the allocation of responsibilities for mitigation of climate change, as reflected in the United Nations (UN) Framework Convention, are the two primary examples. Clearly, in both these institutions, the representation is much larger than 20, because the implications of inclusion or exclusion are relatively significant for smaller countries.

The specific global public goods that are represented in the G20 finance track agenda relate to macroeconomic and financial interlinkages. Of course, the question has often been asked as to why the group is confined to the 20, when several other economies also face the threat of disruption from shocks emerging from this group.

The arguments for a small grouping are based on limits to coordination and collective action, particularly in "wartime" situations in which speed and timing are of the essence. These arguments are valid, but do not necessarily indicate a specific number of members as being optimal. Nevertheless, as the emphasis of the group shifted focus from immediate crisis management to addressing the structural factors that were widely seen to have played a role in the financial crisis precipitating and spreading globally, this agenda has effectively become a testing ground for whether a viable solution to this particular global public good can be found.

3 Challenges and Responses

The two issues that I referred to earlier—the spillover from domestic monetary actions in one economy into the real sectors of other economies and the implications of sovereign debt stresses in one group of countries for financial and macroeconomic stability in the rest of the group—highlight the challenges and limitations to a collective, cross-country approach.

As regards the first, the conventional mandate of monetary policy in any country is very clearly confined to, with varying degrees of emphasis, domestic price stability, domestic output stability, domestic financial stability and stability of the currency. Different countries may choose to assign weights to each of these objectives in their specific policy rules. However, nowhere in this framework does the price, output, financial and currency stability of other countries appear. No central bank is going to be held domestically accountable for the impact that its actions may have on the economic situation of other countries. Yet, diagnoses of the crisis do suggest that a feedback loop between monetary conditions and financial market outcomes in the advanced economies played a role in the international transmission of the crisis. If capital flows relatively smoothly across countries, the monetary policy actions of one, particularly a large, economy is very likely to impact others.

In response to this, rewriting the textbook on monetary policy to take account of spillovers was way beyond reach. What was more practical and within the ambit of the G20 framework was a consideration of appropriate responses by individual countries to this potentially disruptive force. It was in this context that the issue of the appropriateness of capital controls entered the agenda. The basic framework for this discussion was laid out in a paper published by the Research Department of the IMF, which dealt with the pros and cons of specific types of controls in a given global and domestic macroeconomic environment.

Of course, from the EME's perspective, since the second half of 2011, the situation has actually reversed. What was anticipated as a persistent inflow, reversed direction and, instead of pressures to appreciate, many countries saw their currencies depreciate. Global liquidity conditions still favour a recurrence of inflows, but the state of the global economy now makes all these projections rather tenuous. Notably, the G20's Coherent Conclusions for the Management of Capital Flows adopted in November 2011 represent a hard-won consensus on broad principles. Taking into account and building upon the G20's conclusions, with respect to the liberalization and management of capital flows, the IMF brought out the institutional view on capital flow management (CFM, IMF 2012). Perhaps the debate is not yet over and the group needs to revisit the whole issue in a symmetric framework—one that considers both inflow and outflow scenarios. However, from the viewpoint of the agenda for structural change, this is both an important issue and an illustration of how practical considerations have shaped the debate within the group.

The sovereign debt situation in Europe and the risks it poses to global macroeconomic and financial stability has also received much attention in the finance track discussions over the past couple of years. The situation has evolved rapidly over this period, sometimes in a reassuring direction, sometimes not. The role of other countries in contributing resources to support a potential solution is one concrete issue that has emerged against this backdrop, particularly with reference to the enhancement of the IMF's resource base. More generally, one could, of course, take the view that Europe will create a combination of institutions, incentives and resources that will address the problem. Alternatively, one could argue that this convergence to a solution has been speeded up and facilitated by encouragement from the other countries in the group, who are quite conscious of the likely impact of a failure to resolve the issue on their own economies.

4 The Agenda for Structural Change: A Look Forward

As we look beyond these issues to the larger agenda for structural change, the general question that arises is the effectiveness of the processes by which a broad consensus is arrived at, or, conversely, when an issue is deemed too contentious to remain on the agenda. The G20 has followed a Working Group approach, which allows individual members the time and space to articulate their positions on various issues within each group's domain. In turn, this allows subsets of countries, whose positions are relatively closer to each other on specific issues to converge more quickly and articulate mutually acceptable common positions.

Having referred to the "wartime" vs. "peacetime" distinction a little earlier, I want to re-emphasize its importance in understanding the sustainability of a collective process that is addressing structural issues. A basic insight of cooperative game theory, which is a framework through which all these multilateral mechanisms can be usefully viewed, is the ability of individual players to improve their outcomes by forming credible coalitions. Therefore, it is in every country's interest to seek out others whose positions are closest to theirs.

In this context, the basic distinction between "wartime" and "peacetime" conditions is that in the former, a single coalition encompassing all the members of the group is viable, because the threat is universal and the costs of not responding adequately fall on the entire group. By contrast, in "peacetime" situations, in which structural changes are being discussed, a single coalition is quite unlikely. The process is more likely to move forward in a stepwise fashion, as smaller coalitions are formed around proximate positions. Given the relatively large number of issues involved, even in the finance track alone, the number of possible coalitions and the membership of each country in multiple coalitions obviously raise concerns about the sheer complexity of the process. However, it is really the responsibility of the working groups, complemented by events like the one in which this speech is being delivered, to address these complexities and narrow down the distance between positions as much as possible.

5 The Indian Perspective on the Current Finance Track Agenda

The programme for this seminar is built around the finance track agenda, although some of the sessions have been designed to take a somewhat broader view of the issues covered. The seminar is also intended as a forum for participants to present and discuss country perspectives on the agenda items. I would like to begin the process with some brief thoughts on three issues that are a very important part of the finance track agenda in the foreseeable future, with a view on illustrating how global concerns need to be viewed in a domestic context to arrive at meaningful positions.

5.1 *On the Framework for Strong, Sustainable and Balanced Growth*

The progress on this front, coordinated by a working group co-chaired by Canada and India, has been quite significant. Arriving at a compact set of indicators that might provide early warnings of the build-up of stress in either financial markets or the real economy was clearly a very complicated task. The patterns manifested by various indicators during the crisis provided a useful context; but one episode, or even a small number of them, can hardly be expected to yield a robust and comprehensive early warning framework. Apart from this, perhaps the more challenging issue for this agenda has been to deal with multiple interpretations of a particular indicator, given the specific circumstances of countries.

From India's perspective, two indicators have been important. One, India has a relatively large trade deficit, which is of course moderated by a significant surplus on the invisibles account. If the framework were to look at the size of the trade deficit as an indicator of stress, the inference could be quite different than if the focus were on the current account deficit. Two, rapid growth in bank credit is typically viewed as a sign of potential financial instability, but in an economy in which access to the organized financial system is itself increasing on a trend, the need to distinguish between structural and cyclical components of credit growth is important if it is to be used as a stress indicator.

5.2 *On the International Financial Architecture and Global Financial Safety Nets*

The global economy is fundamentally more interconnected than ever before. The recent financial crisis showed that even those countries with sound policies could be affected by global shocks and thereby highlighted the need to strengthen the global financial safety nets. Therefore, after the crisis, the shortage of liquidity occupied the centre stage of discussion. It was generally felt that the existing liquidity-providing mechanisms were ineffective in handling crisis prevention and crisis resolution. In this context, the issues of augmenting international liquidity, enhancing IMF resources and improving the efficiency of IMF instruments of lending were brought to the fore. India's stance was that IMF should remain a quota-based institution. Therefore, the 14th general review of the quota should be ratified by all the member countries at the earliest with the immediate commencement of quota formula review exercise for the 15th general review.

India has suggested a three-pillar mechanism for global financial safety nets. We have been in favour of a diversified global financial safety net consisting of reserves as the first line of defence (Pillar I). Sound economic policies, effective prudential regulation and an appropriate level of reserves are regarded as the primary lines of defence. It is important to remember that self-insurance gives automaticity, fungibility and usability in crisis prevention and crisis resolution.

Regional financing arrangements and currency swap arrangements also have the potential to meet eventualities, and such initiatives should be promoted (Pillar II). Any safety net should be supported by co-financing arrangements with international financial institutions, which have been very active recently.

As regards enhancement of IMF resources, India has argued that the IMF is a quota-based institution and it should remain one. In this context, we emphasized the importance of early ratification of 2010 quota increases (14th Review) as well as the quota formula and governance reforms. We had committed to contribute US$ 10 billion under NPA which folded into our NAB commitment of US$ 14 billion. In addition, we have now committed US$ 10 billion under the 2012 borrowing arrangement.

In its efforts to address the issue of global imbalances, the IMF was asked to assess the reserve accumulation of large reserve-holding countries. It came out with a reserves adequacy matrix, which is now built into the integrated surveillance decision where external balance assessment is an important element. In this assessment, China, India, Brazil, Russia and Thailand are judged to have excess reserves (IMF 2011). The IMF favours lower maintenance of reserves on the grounds that building of excess reserves in some EMEs is leading to global imbalances.

India's stance on this issue is that reserves should be seen as a part of a diversified global financial safety net approach with reserves and strong fundamentals as the first line of defence. While evaluating the level of reserves and the quantum of self-insurance between countries, a distinction needs to be made between countries whose reserves are a consequence of current account surpluses and countries with current account deficits whose reserves are a result of capital inflows in excess of their economy's absorptive capacity. India falls in the latter category. Our reserves comprise essentially borrowed resources, and we are therefore more vulnerable to sudden stops and reversals as compared with countries with current account surpluses.

Developing a reserve adequacy formula in the face of volatile capital flows and fluctuating commodity prices is a highly debatable issue. Reserves will necessarily remain the primary line of defence against any eventuality in future. It may not be advisable to restrict the level of reserves by instituting subjective formula. Country-specific circumstances need to be given due recognition.

5.3 On Prudential Regulation and the Basel Framework

On the issue of prudential regulation, the G20 commitment is to implement fully and consistently the Basel II risk-based framework as well as the Basel II.5 enhanced requirements on market activities; and securitization by end of 2011 and the Basel III capital and liquidity standards, as per the phase-in arrangements, and review clauses, starting in 2013 and completing full implementation by January 1, 2019.

As far as India is concerned, the Reserve Bank of India announced the draft guidelines for Indian banks under Basel III on December 30, 2011 and the final guidelines on Basel III capital regulations were issued on May 2, 2012. Basel III is being implemented from April 1, 2013[2] in a phased manner. Banks are expected to start disclosing Basel III capital ratios from the quarter ending June 30, 2013. The Basel III capital ratios will be fully implemented as on March 31, 2018. The Indian banks' current capital base and liquidity position are broadly compliant with the Basel III guidelines. Both the capital to risk weighted assets ratio (CRAR) and the core CRAR of Indian banks at 13.8 % and 10.3 % as of end of March 2013, respectively, remained well above the regulatory requirements of 9 % and 6 %, respectively under Basel II. Leverage ratios were around 5 % as against the Basel III requirements of a minimum of 3 %.

Thus, Indian banks start from a position of strength in the process of transition to the Basel III regime, but many challenges lie ahead. For example, raising fresh capital to meet the higher capital requirements under Basel III may pose some challenges especially under an environment characterized by moderating growth and adverse financing conditions. In this context, how the global and domestic economic situations evolve in the coming years will be very important. A quick and sustained turnaround in the global economy will support India's growth momentum by improving both external demand and the overall investment climate. This will, in turn, improve private savings as well as government finances, auguring well for additional capital mobilization for banks in India.

The status report on the implementation of Basel II and Basel III, published by the Basel Committee on Banking Supervision (BCBS) in April (2012), observed that some countries, especially the advanced economies, need to expedite the process of implementation of Basel III in a time-bound manner. In the BCBS assessment of the rules for the European Union and the USA, some gaps have been identified which need to be plugged. We feel that the emerging economies should not be seen as front-runners in the Basel III implementation process.

6 Concluding Thoughts

I have tried to look at the G20 process, using the finance track agenda to illustrate my arguments, through two conceptual lenses: the global public good nature of the agenda items, and the role of coalitions between subsets of countries in order to move the agenda forward. The first perspective underlines the need to continue with the process beyond the immediate compulsions of crisis response, based on the recognition that the agenda for structural change also has significant public good

[2] The start date for implementation was rescheduled to April 1, 2013 from January 1, 2013 to align the implementation date with the financial year (which begins from April 1 each year).

characteristics, which make it necessary for countries to participate in a collective process of coordinated change.

The second focuses on the need to take a realistic view of a process, which has shifted focus from crisis management (wartime) to structural change (peacetime). The ease with which consensus across the group—a single coalition—can be found in wartime is not going to be replicated in peacetime. The way forward, then, is for countries whose positions on individual issues are close to each other to look for convergence and to present a united view to the larger group. This is perhaps a way to either more efficiently reach a broader consensus or decide that this is difficult to achieve on certain issues.

Since, this is a seminar that provides an opportunity for different country perspectives on a series of finance track issues to be articulated; I also tried to present some flavour of the thinking that is going on behind Indian positions on some critical issues, to illustrate the way in which global issues and concerns need to be viewed in a country-specific context in order to arrive at meaningful positions.

References

Basel Committee on Banking Supervision (2012) Progress Report on Basel III Implementation and Procedures for Conducting Country Reviews

IMF (2012) 'The liberalization and Management of Capital Flows—An Institutional View, November 14

IMF (2011) Assessing Reserve Adequacy, February

Ostry J, Ghosh A, Habermeier K, Chamon M, Qureshi M, Reinhardt D (2010) Capital Inflows: The Role of Controls IMF Staff Position Note SPN 10/04

Part I
Eurozone Crisis: Short-Run Challenges and Options

Overcoming the Euro Area Crisis—Reforms and Results

Holger Fabig, Yannick Kirchhof and Inka Zippe

1 Introduction

With the Euro Area sovereign debt crisis starting in May 2010, the institutional arrangements of the Euro Area were tested in the extreme. Private and public debt levels in a number of member states (MS) reached historically high levels. Asymmetric real shocks and the inability to adjust exchange rates in a monetary union have forced unprecedented pressures into the labour market of several MS. Although being far from a uniform process, in some countries public indebtedness has been exacerbated by the financial crisis and recession, and this in turn has contributed to financial instability. In response to this difficult period, as this paper argues, European and national institutions have accepted these challenges and worked collectively towards appropriate policy responses. In particular, the pressing need to undertake fiscal consolidation in many countries and to avoid future fiscal crises in the Euro Area induced a wide array of national and European reform measures.

This paper gives a brief overview of these new policies, new instruments and preliminary results attributable to these measures that have been implemented to solve the financial and sovereign debt crises in the Euro Area. It is shown that comprehensive measures have been taken to respond to the current challenges and that some of these measures are bearing fruits already while others will be visible in the longer term.

Holger Fabig and Yannick Kirchhof are with the Ministry of Finance, Berlin, Germany, where Inka Zippe was an intern in September and October 2012. Views expressed in this paper do not necessarily reflect those of the ministry.

H. Fabig (✉) · Y. Kirchhof
G7/G8, G20, World Economy, Currency Issues, Ministry of Finance, Berlin, Germany
e-mail: Holger.Fabig@bmf.bund.de

I. Zippe
University of Erfurt, Erfurt, Germany

M. Callaghan et al. (eds.), *Global Cooperation Among G20 Countries*,
DOI 10.1007/978-81-322-1659-9_3,

This paper is structured as follows: Each section examines one of the policy reform pillars, comprised of different policy measures that were introduced in response to the Euro Area financial and economic crises. The following section begins with the measures taken to stabilise budgets. Fiscal data are employed as to outline some of the concrete policy achievements that are already observable. Section 3 discusses policy measures that are the building stones towards new economic governance. Some data are provided to show how these measures have already helped stabilise economic imbalances. Section 4 presents the financial assistance mechanisms that were created in the wake of the crisis. Sections 5–7 provide information on additional policy measures taken on financial regulation, the foundations of a banking union and European Central Bank (ECB) crisis management. The diagram below illustrates the architecture of the stabilisation effort.

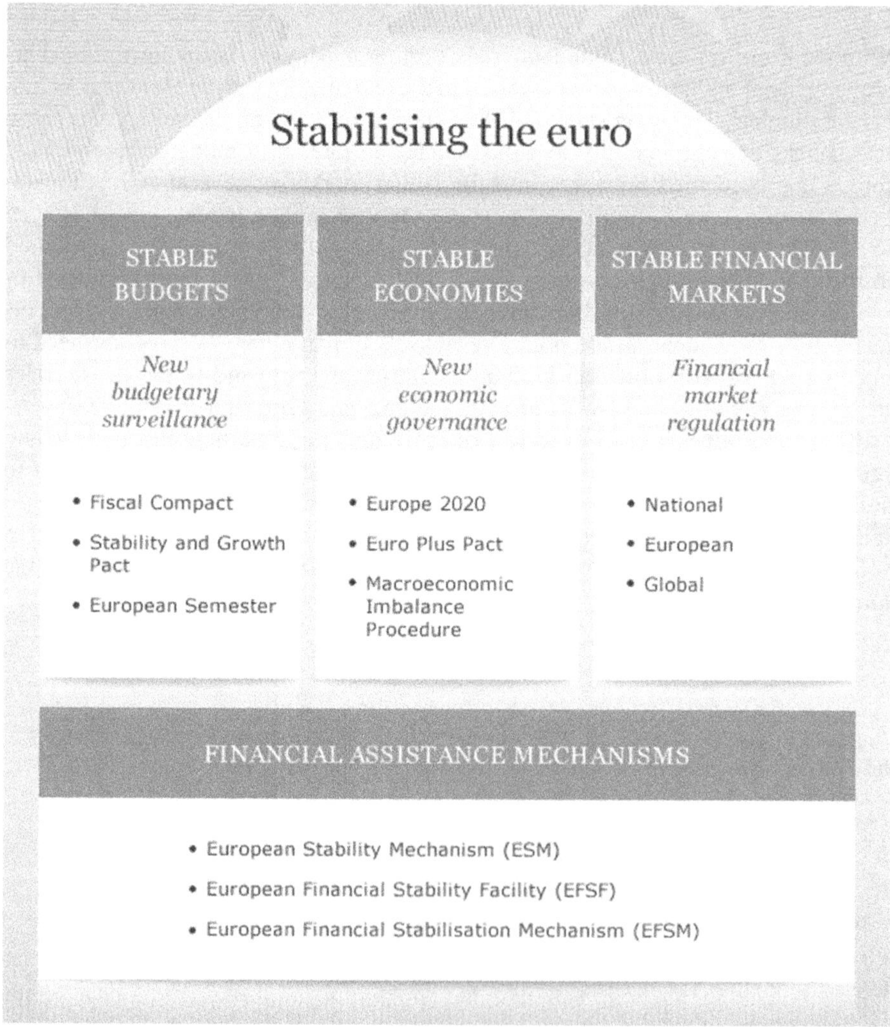

2 Stabilising Budgets

Despite differences in timing and magnitudes of private and public debt developments across Euro Area countries, public and private household indebtedness has generally shown a considerable increase in the most recent past.[1] In response to these developments, concrete Euro Area policies aim at stabilising national budgets in the long term and a new and improved budgetary surveillance process was introduced. The following sub-sections present four key reform measures that were taken—namely the reform of the Stability and Growth Pact (SGP), the Fiscal Compact, the European Semester and the Compact for Growth and Jobs. Recent data are presented to assess the preliminary achievements of these policy actions.

2.1 Reform of the Stability and Growth Pact

The *Stability and Growth Pact* is a rules-based framework for coordinating and monitoring national fiscal policies in the European Union. It was set up in 1997 in order to guarantee solid public finances—an important prerequisite for the correct functioning of the economic and monetary union. The 1992 Maastricht Treaty included convergence criteria for joining the monetary union, which were intended not only to ensure price stability and stable long-term interest and exchange rates but also to set maximum limits on MS' total indebtedness and net borrowing. Government debt was limited to not exceed 60 % of GDP, and deficits to not exceed 3 % of GDP. The SGP further refines these criteria and describes procedures to be followed after violation of these criteria.

By now it is generally accepted that this approach had two main defects: Firstly, it did not adequately allow for cyclical variation in budget positions, and secondly, it did not have an effective mechanism to discipline countries that exceeded the limits. In 2005, therefore, the pact was revised through the introduction of rules requiring structurally balanced budgets, which allowed cyclical effects and one-off items to be stripped out. A structural budget balance target encourages governments to take advantage of cyclical revenue gains during upturns to offset slippage in the overall budget balance during recessions, i.e. to let automatic stabilisers work. The policy intention was to address the first problem. However, the revision still did not offer a solution to the second problem mentioned above, namely it did not provide for effective sanctions when these rules were breached. Ultimately, it was the sovereign debt refinancing problem of some MS of the Euro Area that exposed these weaknesses. In order to rectify these problems, further extensive reforms to the SGP were undertaken. The new rules, which took effect in December 2011, aimed to ensure that greater budgetary discipline was not only demanded but also enforced. To this end, the terms of the pact were substantially modified and made more stringent in several areas. The reformed pact includes a preventive and a corrective arm:

[1] This trend is not confined to the Euro Area.

Preventive Arm

To prevent excessive debt ratios from arising in the first place, MS are expected to substantially reduce their new borrowing. Instead of maintaining a primary focus on limiting deficits to 3 % of GDP, the main emphasis is now on (1) achieving the medium-term goal of a structurally balanced budget and (2) establishing effective sanctions to foster compliance. This is similar to the priorities established under Germany's "debt brake"[2]. MS are required to submit annual Stability or Convergence Programmes[3] outlining the way they intend to achieve or maintain a balanced or close-to-balance budget in the medium term. In the ex post assessment, the Commission determines whether a MS has made sufficient progress towards the medium-term budgetary objective, which must be specified within a defined range of no more than −1 % of GDP. If the Commission finds evidence of significant deviation from the medium-term budgetary objective, this can be followed, in the case of Euro Area MS, by a sanction equal to an interest-bearing deposit of 0.2 % of GDP.

Corrective Arm

For the first time, a numerical benchmark has been stipulated for the reduction of excessive debt: Countries whose debt ratio exceeds 60 % of GDP are required to reduce the difference between their debt ratio and the 60 % target by 1/20 each year, even if their deficit is below 3 % of GDP. Otherwise, they face the sanction of an excessive deficit procedure[4].

---

[2] Since 2011, the German Federal Government has been required to reduce its structural net borrowing step by step through the so-called "debt brake," as enshrined in Germany's constitution. From 2016 onwards, the Federation's net borrowing, adjusted for cyclical fluctuations, will not be permitted to exceed 0.35 % of Germany's gross domestic product. A transitional period, lasting until 2020, has been established for the Länder. From then onwards, they will have to have structurally balanced budgets. A control account has been created, which should be balanced in the medium term. The control account will document non-cyclical deviations from the maximum permissible net borrowing that arise in each fiscal year. To accommodate cyclical fluctuations, additional net borrowing may be incurred during a downturn while in economic good times the resulting cyclical surplus reduces the maximum permissible net borrowing. In an emergency situation, a majority of the Bundestag can approve additional net borrowing. However, this must be accompanied by a binding amortisation plan which provides for the reduction of net borrowing above the standard threshold within an appropriate time frame. This guarantees that higher net borrowing in response to exceptional circumstances does not endanger long-term fiscal sustainability.

[3] Under the provisions of the Stability and Growth Pact, EU member states must each year draw up Stability Programmes (in the case of Eurozone members) and Convergence Programmes (for non-Eurozone countries aspiring to join the Eurozone). In these programmes, the member states must provide details of their fiscal policy strategy and report on their compliance with the Stability and Growth Pact.

[4] The Excessive Deficit Procedure (EDP) operationalises the procedure that is launched when the budget deficit and public debt exceed the thresholds of 3 % of deficit to GDP and 60 % of debt to GDP, respectively, and ensures that member states adopt appropriate policy responses to correct excessive deficits.

In Euro Area countries, the requirements are even more stringent. The reduction of both deficits and debt ratios is now subject to a graduated and largely automatic sanctions procedure. To this end, a new voting procedure has been introduced. A sanctions resolution recommended by the Commission is deemed to have been adopted if it is not rejected by qualified majority of Euro Area members. MS are required to fulfil minimum standards in order to ensure transparency and comparability. These standards include, for example, multiannual budget planning, numerical fiscal rules and more transparency on spending. Moreover, fraudulent statistics on deficits and debts will be subject to strict sanctions in the future. Falsified statistics will be punished by a fine amounting to 0.2 % of GDP.

2.2 *Fiscal Compact*

The *Treaty on Stability, Coordination and Governance in the Economic and Monetary Union* (generally referred to as the *Fiscal Compact)* was signed in March 2012 by all MS of the EU, except for the UK and the Czech Republic. By signing the treaty, these 25 countries have committed themselves to introducing long-term budgetary rules into their national legal systems, preferably at constitutional level. The intergovernmental treaty was introduced as a new, stricter version of the SGP. The key rationale of the treaty was the need of new treaty-based provisions to achieve the reduction of acute excesses of government debt as quickly as possible. The long-term prevention of excessive government debt was acknowledged as an important precondition for the functioning of an economic and monetary union.

Consequently, the treaty does not only inlcude new budgetary rules, but also a strengthening of the deficit procedure and enhanced policy coordination and control. The Fiscal Compact required MS to embed the newly established fiscal principles in their national legislation. By July 2013, ratification of the Fiscal Compact was notified by 21 MS of which 13 belong to the Eurozone. The fiscal governance reforms of the treaty are based on empirical evidence[5] that high public debt levels pose a threat to fiscal sustainability and growth. Therefore fiscal balances should be

[5] A lot of empirical work has dealt with the negative relationship between debt and growth. An often-cited study in this context was published by Reinhart and Rogoff in 2010. Reinhart and Rogoff (2010) found a nonlinear debt–growth relationship, suggesting that GDP growth drops more severely once government debt-to-GDP ratios exceed 90 % (an IMF paper by Kumar and Woo (2010) had similar findings). The existence of a sharp turning point was explained by market perceptions of risk. Most recently, the Reinhart and Rogoff (2010) finding of a debt threshold has been called into question by Herndon et al. (2013) on grounds of identified coding errors and deficiencies in their original data set. In contrast to the finding of a sharp turning point to growth once debt attains a certain level, Herndon et al. (2013) suggest that growth rates merely decline with rising debt, which makes the relationship look rather linear. Beyond the question of linearity, both authors do provide conclusive empirical evidence for a negative association between debt and growth. A look at the literature confirms that firm conclusions on sharp turning points of the growth–debt relationship may be difficult. A more recent IMF publication (IMF World Economic Outlook 2012) found "no particular threshold that consistently precedes sub-par growth performance" but confirms a negative debt–growth relationship.

close to zero "over the cycle". Specifically, the new treaty contains the following changes to existing EU legislation:

1. New budgetary rules: The new treaty contains ambitious targets for national debt brakes. If the debt-to-GDP ratio of an MS is not well below the 60 % threshold, this MS is urged to set a medium-term objective whereby the structural deficit does not exceed 0.5 % of GDP. Thus, the Fiscal Compact goes beyond the existing requirements of the SGP's preventive arm (see above), which caps general government structural deficits at 1 % of GDP. Also, these automatic debt brakes have to be integrated in national law and will be monitored by the Court of Justice of the European Union. Moreover, the granting of financial assistance under the European Stability Mechanism (ESM) is closely tied to the Fiscal Compact. Any country wishing to claim ESM assistance must have ratified the Fiscal Compact and transposed the debt brake provisions into national law. This principle is enshrined in both the ESM Treaty and the Fiscal Compact.
2. Strengthening of the deficit procedure: MS in an excessive deficit procedure are required to put in place a budgetary and economic partnership programme, which is approved and monitored by the Council and the European Commission. If an MS fails to comply with deficit criteria in the future, there will be a semiautomatic opening of an excessive deficit procedure (by reverse qualified majority decision).[6]
3. Tightening of the policy coordination and control: The MS agree to work towards a common economic policy. To improve governance of the Euro Area and to facilitate the discussion and adjustment of all important reform plans of the MS, the Fiscal Compact calls for Euro Summits to be held on a regular basis—at least twice a year.[7]

2.3 *European Semester*

The *European Semester* was adopted by the European Council in June 2010 and first launched in 2011. This instrument's central task is to achieve common timetables for setting up national budgets, to coordinate economic policies and structural reforms within the framework of the Europe 2020 strategy[8] and thereby to improve the consistency, integration and implementation of necessary financial and economic

[6] This means that semi-automatic decisions under the reverse qualified majority voting procedure—which previously applied only to the imposition of sanctions in accordance with the reforms to the Stability and Growth Pact—have now been extended to the launching of excessive deficit procedures.

[7] The treaty also provides for the organisation of a conference of representatives from the European Parliament and national parliaments to discuss budgetary policies and other issues covered by the fiscal compact.

[8] To be further discussed in Sect. 3.

reforms. Moreover, conclusions from the Macroeconomic Imbalance Procedure (MIP) and the Euro-Plus-Pact[9] will also be taken into account.

The European Semester covers a 6-month cycle which begins in January each year. In addition to policy coordination, MS are given political guidance and recommendations while their national budgets are still under preparation. This gives a stronger *ex ante* dimension to the coordination and surveillance of economic policy in the EU. In this way, the EU can react to developments in the MS, and the MS for their part can include European perspectives and guidance in their policies for the following year.

As part of the European Semester, the European Commission produces an Annual Growth Survey at the beginning of each year. The survey outlines the most important fiscal, economic and employment policy challenges faced by the EU and recommends priority measures to deal effectively with these challenges. Based on this report, the European Council formulates horizontal guidelines at its spring meeting in March. In April, the MS submit their Stability and Convergence Programmes (SCP) and National Reform Programmes (NRP) to the European Commission. Based on the Commission's assessment, the Economic and Financial Affairs Council (ECOFIN) adopts country-specific recommendations for the SCP and NRP. These are finally approved by the European Council at the end of June, which concludes the European Semester's 6-month cycle.

2.4 Compact for Growth and Jobs

Many Euro Area countries (in common with many G20 countries) face an unprecedented need to restore fiscal sustainability through credible consolidation plans. For many of these countries, stabilising debt—let alone putting government finances on sustainable positions—constitutes a major challenge and requires sizeable fiscal consolidation. Notwithstanding the pressing need to consolidate, it should be recognised that "slamming on the brakes too quickly" may have serious implications for economic growth and social equity. This means that the long-term benefits of fiscal consolidation must be balanced against short-term (and perhaps medium-term) adverse impacts. However, there is a severe problem with abstaining from consolidation altogether, given the tendency of sovereign risk to adversely affect borrowing conditions in the broader economy.[10]

In many ways, the Compact for Growth and Jobs constitutes a balancing measure that aims to offset potential short-term side effects of consolidation under the

---

[9] Both to be further discussed in Sect. 3.

[10] There are additional reasons to be ambitious in fiscal consolidation: Looking ahead, the observable trend of population ageing in many Euro Area countries suggests more serious challenges for public finances in the future. Countries will be ill-prepared to cover these costs unless public finances are consolidated before the estimated period when demographic transition will be most burdensome on the budget. It also entails permanent costs, which would need to be addressed through structural reforms, including a review of pension entitlements.

Fiscal Compact. The Compact for Growth and Jobs was adopted in June 2012 by the European Council and makes € 120 billion of funds available for direct investments as follows:

- € 60 billion additional EIB (European Investment Bank) lending through capital increase,
- € 55 billion reallocation of Structural Funds and
- € 4.5 billion in Project Bonds.

Nevertheless, the Compact for Growth and Jobs underlines the fact that MS should remain attentive to balance their fiscal accounts and follow "differentiated growth-friendly fiscal consolidation, respecting the Stability and Growth Pact and taking into account country-specific circumstances; particular attention must be given to investment into future-oriented areas directly related to the economy's growth potential and ensuring the sustainability of pension systems" (European Council 2012, p. 8).

2.5 *Preliminary Achievements: Stabilising Budgets*

Despite lingering uncertainty in financial markets, data confirm that progress regarding budget balances in the Euro Area has been made. Budget deficits as a percentage of GDP decreased significantly in the Euro Area on average. More interestingly, however, structural budget deficits also fell on average from 4.6% in 2009 to 2.4% in 2012. In its April forecast, the IMF anticipates a further decline in the average Euro Area structural budget deficit to 1.3% in 2013. Special emphasis should be given to the reduction in the structural deficit because it demonstrates the effectiveness of the structural measures which the Euro countries have adopted to consolidate budgets. Of the deficit reduction anticipated for the 2009–2012 period, around three quarters of the total are due to a decline in the structural deficit and one quarter is due to cyclical and one-off effects.

The goal of sustainable public finances cannot be achieved without reducing structural deficits. Under the SGP, countries that have not yet reached the medium-term budgetary objective of having budgets close to balance are required to reduce their structural deficits by at least 0.5 percentage points each year. Additional requirements apply to countries under excessive deficit procedures. Departing from structural budget consolidation to pursue fiscal policy that has no effect on the cyclical trend would have enormous consequences for individual countries' success in consolidating their budgets. A comparison of two scenarios demonstrates the implications of this for the 2013 budget deficit. The baseline scenario shows structural budget consolidation with a reduction in the structural deficit in line with the Stability and Growth Pact. An alternative scenario of fiscal policy that delivers a constant structural deficit, i.e. with automatic stabilisers operating fully, would in the case of France see its nominal deficit rise to over 5% of GDP in 2013, compared to 3.5% in the first scenario.

International comparison of deficits
(as % of GDP)

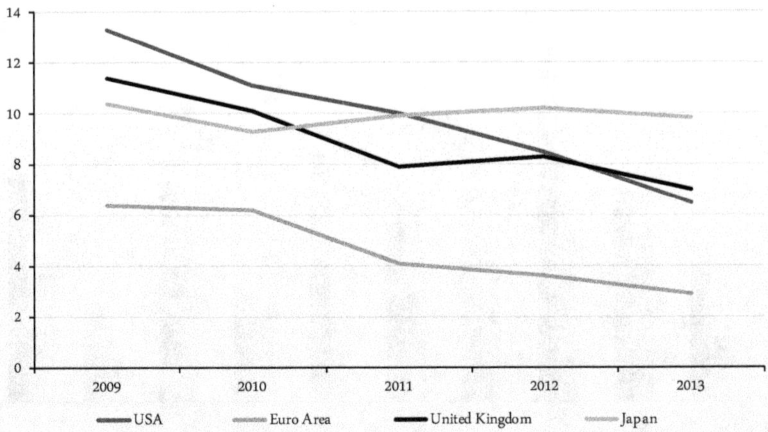

Sources: IWF Fiscal Monitor, April 2013.

Structural deficits
(as % of GDP)

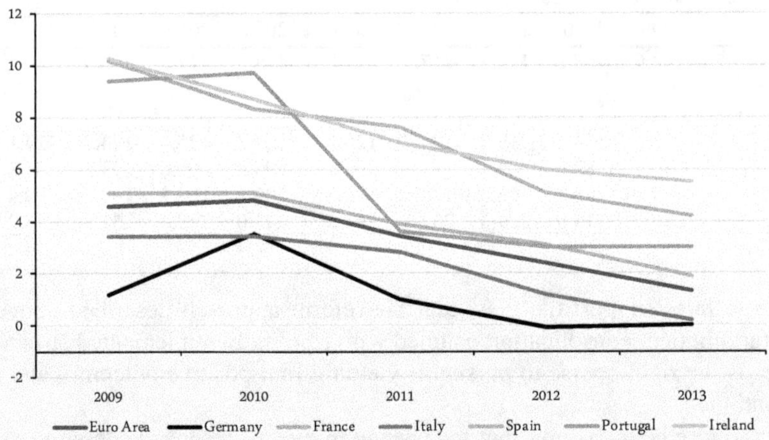

Source: IWF Fiscal Monitor, April 2013

It should also be noted that deficits and overall debt in the Euro Area still appear low by international comparison. In 2012 for example, budget deficits in most parts of the world exceed the 3.3 % of GDP for the Euro Area, with the USA having a deficit of 8.6 %, the UK 8.3 % and Japan 10.1 %. Debt levels also compare favourably with other advanced countries.

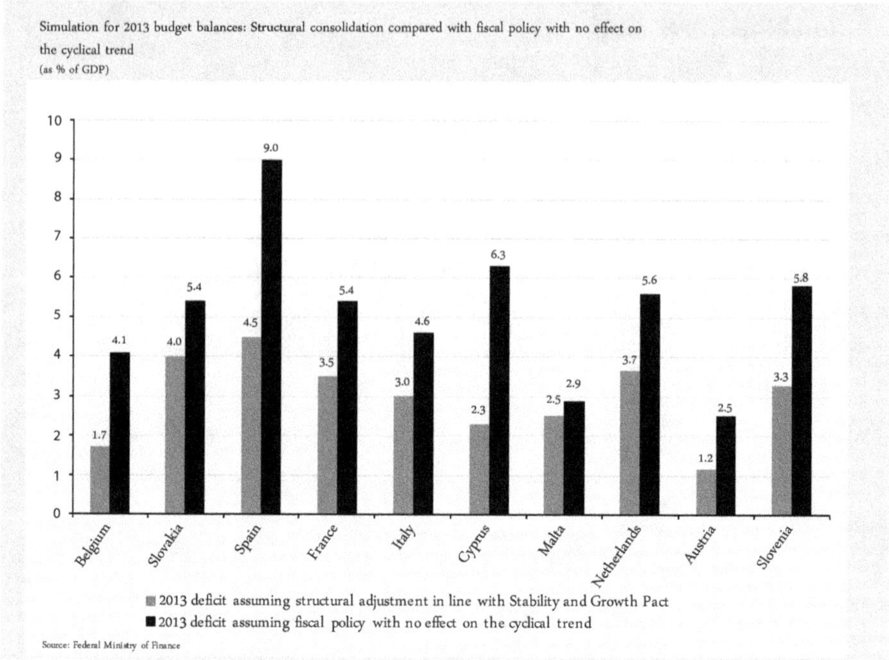

Table 1 Debt levels and dynamics. (Source: IMF Fiscal Monitor April 2013)

General government gross debt (% of GDP)

	2009	2010	2011	2012	2013	2014	2015	2016	2017	2018
G20—advanced economies	102.0	108.8	113.3	117.7	117.9	118.2	117.7	116.9	116.1	115.1
G-7	106.6	114.7	119.9	124.7	125.2	125.8	125.4	124.7	124.1	123.4
Eurozone	80.1	85.6	88.1	93.1	95.1	95.3	94.6	93.5	91.8	89.9
USA	89.1	98.2	102.5	106.5	108.6	109.8	109.5	109.3	109.4	109.7
Japan	210.2	215.0	229.3	237.1	244.5	247.0	249.7	251.5	253.2	254.8

These facts support the view that the reform approach described above, with structural budget consolidation coupled with resolutely implemented structural reforms, is the right course to pursue, is yielding first positive outcomes and should be continued.

The figure below shows that the change in overall responsiveness to *Going for Growth*[11] recommendations across Organisation for Economic Co-operation and Development (OECD) countries from 2009-10 to 2011-12 was particularly high in the European crisis countries. This confirms the notion that especially countries such as Greece, Spain, Ireland and Portugal are committedly following structural reforms. One can be reasonably hopeful that the positive impact of these reforms on growth will materialise once the usual time lags have passed.

[11] Going for Growth is the OECD's flagship report on structural policies, where it identifies and reviews progress on key priorities to achieve strong and sustained growth in each OECD country.

Change in responsiveness to Going for Growth recommendations across OECD countries from 2009-10 to 2011-12

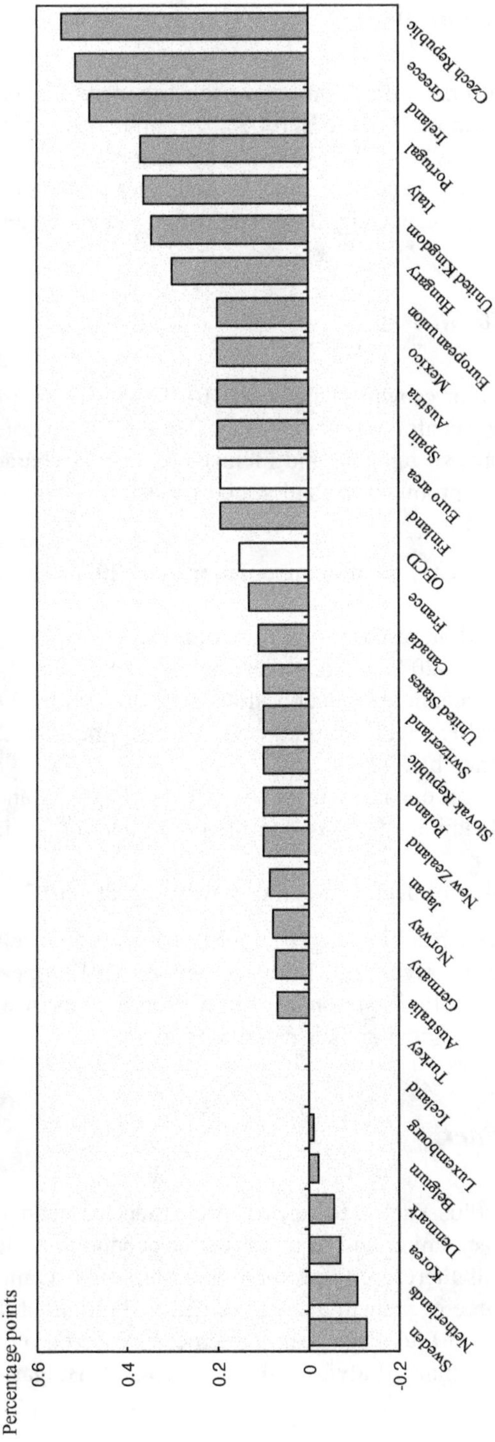

Source: OECD (2013), *Economic Policy Reforms 2013: Going for Growth*

3 Stabilising Economies

The second major reform pillar is the move towards new economic governance. Major steps in this realm include the Europe 2020 Strategy, the Euro Plus Pact and the MIP, which are briefly described below. Although many of the positive results of these policies may only become visible in the longer term, some of the policies are bearing fruits already, especially the correction of macroeconomic imbalances.

3.1 Europe 2020 Strategy

Europe 2020 is a 10-year growth strategy (2010–2020) which replaces the Lisbon strategy. The strategy's central aim is to ensure that the EU emerges stronger from the crisis, with a smart, sustainable and inclusive economy characterised by high levels of employment, productivity and social cohesion. Therefore five headline targets were formulated:

1. Raising the employment rate of the population aged 20–64 from 69 % to at least 75 %,
2. Investing 3 % of GDP in research and development,
3. Achieving the "20–20–20" climate protection and energy targets by achieving at least a 20 % cut in greenhouse gas emissions compared with 1990 levels, raising the share of renewable energy in final energy consumption to 20 % and increasing energy efficiency by 20 %,
4. Reducing school drop-out rates from the current 15–10 % and increasing the share of the population aged 30–34 completing tertiary education from 31 % to at least 40 % and
5. Reducing the number of people at risk of poverty by at least 20 million.

In order to achieve these headline targets, the MS have set themselves concrete national targets in the above five areas. In the context of the European Semester, MS submit annual reports on their National Reform Programmes in which they detail progress made towards achieving their national targets.

3.2 Euro Plus Pact

The aim of the Euro Plus Pact is to further strengthen the economic pillar of the economic and monetary union and to attain better economic policy coordination. Its primary objective is therefore to promote and harmonise competitiveness, and to foster a higher degree of growth and convergence throughout the EU. Adopted in March 2011, the Euro Plus Pact is an agreement of the euro countries and six non-euro countries Denmark, Latvia, Lithuania, Poland, Bulgaria and Romania.

The pact focuses primarily on measures in policy areas that fall under the national competence of the MS themselves, such as:

- fostering competitiveness,
- boosting employment,
- enhancing the sustainability of public finances and
- reinforcing financial stability.

Every year the heads of state or government of participating MS commit themselves to a set of concrete actions in these priority areas, to be realised over the next 12 months. The choice of specific policy actions to achieve the common objectives remains the responsibility of each country. National Reform Programmes as well as Stability and Convergence Programmes must include reporting on the implementation of these measures. These programmes are then assessed by the European Commission, the European Council and the Eurogroup as part of the European Semester. Involving heads of state or government in the Euro Plus Pact ensures a high level of political commitment and visibility. This increases the pressure on MS to actually implement the planned measures on time. Furthermore, the pact demonstrates that MS are ready to intensify the coordination of national policies.

3.3 Macroeconomic Imbalance Procedure

The financial and sovereign debt crises have shown that existing instruments for monitoring fiscal and economic policies were incomplete. This allowed economic tensions and imbalances to arise in certain countries, which ultimately posed risks to the macroeconomic stability of the Euro Area and the EU as a whole. With the adoption of the euro, current account imbalances became entrenched within the Euro Area, as core countries tended to run surpluses and peripheral countries deficits.[12] The worsening of the current account balances of the peripheral countries seems to have occurred *pari passu* with the increasing surpluses of the core countries. These imbalances appear particularly pronounced by historical standards. While the Euro Area as a whole has remained close to external balance, considerable divergence in the current account balances among MS have emerged. The EU's new macroeconomic imbalance procedure was created to deal with this issue using appropriate instruments.

The new procedure aims to identify MS with—or at risk of—macroeconomic imbalances that may consequently threaten the stability of their own economy, the Euro Area and the EU as a whole. Such imbalances may result, for example, from overheating domestic economies, rapidly expanding credit volumes or fast-rising home prices. The procedure focuses in particular on MS with major competitive weaknesses. It contains an early warning system—an indicator-based scoreboard

---

[12] For the purpose of this paper the periphery includes Greece, Portugal, Spain, Ireland and to a lesser extent Italy, while the core comprises Germany, the Netherlands, Austria and France.

that helps identify macroeconomic risks in MS at an early stage. If the indicators trigger an alert for a country, that country is bound to initiate corrective measures. As a last resort, (e.g. in the event of repeated failure to take appropriate countermeasures) MS can even face financial sanctions. Formally, the MIP is embedded within the European Semester.

3.4 Preliminary Achievements: Stabilising Economies

First of all, it should be noted that many of the results of the substantial reforms in economic governance may only become observable in the longer term. Despite this time lag, there is some evidence that the correction of macroeconomic imbalances is making progress already. This may be interpreted as a sign of the first successes arising from the structural reforms implemented to date.

The figure below shows that the precrisis trend of diverging current account balances within the Euro Area has generally reversed since 2008. Current account deficits in particular have fallen in Spain, Greece and Portugal. Recent data by the European Commission show that current account deficits as a percentage of GDP fell from 9.6 to 0.5 % in Spain, from 12.6 to 1.5 % in Portugal and from 14.9 to 4.6 % in Greece between 2008 and 2013.

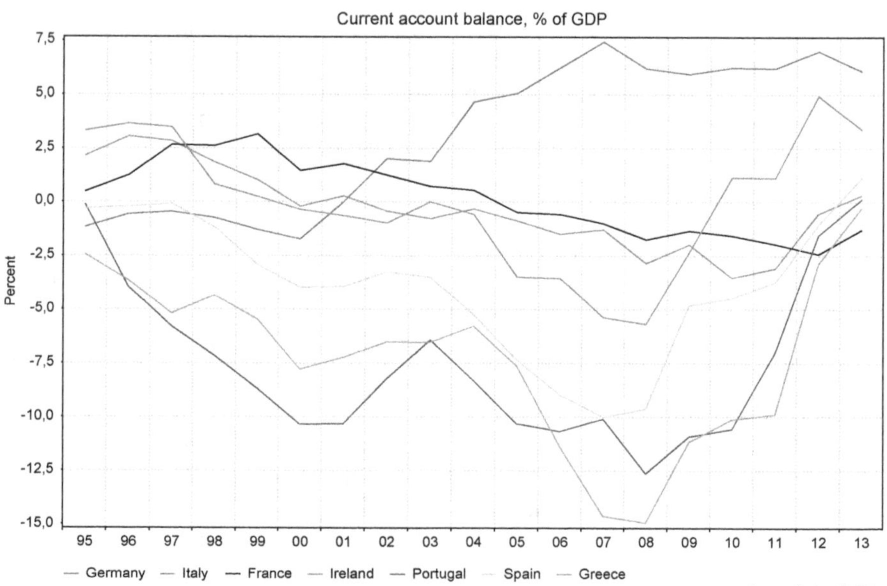

Although an important factor behind this, the decline in current account deficits is not just a result of the fall in domestic demand leading to lower imports. Recent supply-side improvements also contributed to the correction of current account imbalances: Exports have climbed considerably in some deficit countries. In Portugal and Spain for instance, annual export growth between 2010 and 2012 averaged around 7 %. Germany's current account surplus with other Euro Area countries has decreased substantially compared with the precrisis period, with domestic demand being bolstered by growth in employment and income. Although a more nuanced view may point out intercountry difference, the tendency is that current account imbalances decline. In many deficit countries, the excesses in the domestic sectors over the past years (i.e. a strong focus on domestic consumption, frequently in conjunction with a boom in construction) are increasingly being corrected. A reallocation of labour and capital resources from shrinking domestic sectors to growing export-oriented sectors is underway.

Export growth: Average for 2010-2013 (in %)

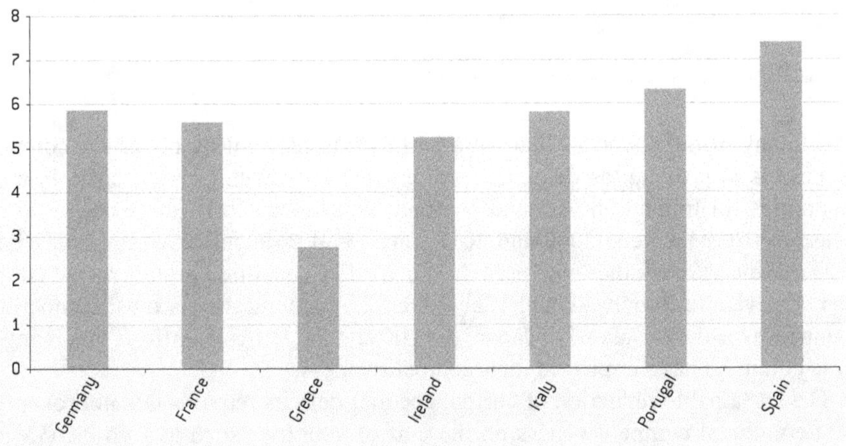

Sources: European Commission; Ameco database; own calculations

A change in relative prices is important to create incentives to achieve this realignment. If the restructuring continues, the economies concerned will experience lasting stabilisation, providing a boost for their labour markets, among other things. Nevertheless, time is required for the shift in the focus of production from domestic consumption to exports, and this is leading to a temporary increase in unemployment. Complementary structural reforms are important so as to open up new job prospects and prevent unemployment from becoming entrenched.

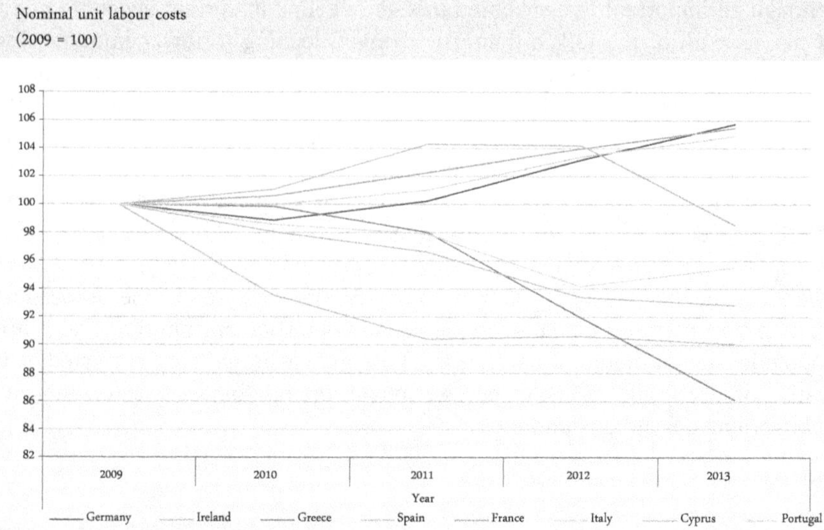

Sources: European Commission, Ameco database; own calculations

In many of the countries that were particularly hard hit by the crisis, competitiveness is improving, as demonstrated, e.g. by falling unit labour costs in these economies. In Ireland and Greece, nominal unit labour costs are expected to decrease by 10 % between 2009 and 2012. Spain and Portugal have seen unit labour costs fall by 6 % over the same period. The World Economic Forum's recent Global Competitiveness Report—which places Germany among the six most competitive countries worldwide, ahead of Japan, the UK and the USA—confirms that many of these countries have improved their competitiveness.

The sustainable reduction of current account deficits requires this improvement in international competitiveness on the part of countries such as Cyprus, Greece, Portugal and Spain to continue. Steps must be taken to ensure that wage developments in these MS continue to grow competitiveness and that rigidities on product markets continue to be dismantled.

4 Financial Assistance Mechanisms

The refinancing crisis in several Euro Area members made it necessary to establish a package of financial assistance mechanisms. Measures such as the European Financial Stability Mechanism (ESFM), the European Financial Stability Facility (EFSF) and ultimately the ESM were set up to support MS in difficulty and thereby preserve financial stability.

4.1 European Financial Stability Mechanism

The EFSM is part of the temporary euro rescue package put together in 2010 (along with the EFSF and contributions from the IMF) and contributes € 60 billion to the rescue package's capital resources. Germany's share of the funding corresponds to its share of the EU budget, which is around 20%. Once the permanent ESM was coming into force, the EFSM was wound down.

4.2 European Financial Stability Facility

The EFSF is another element of the temporary euro rescue package put together in 2010 to respond to the acute sovereign debt crisis. The EFSF is a private-law corporation founded under Luxembourg law. It is authorised to grant emergency loans through mid-2013 to countries in the Euro Area if their problems pose a risk to the stability of the monetary union as a whole. It borrows on capital markets in order to lend, and the Euro Area countries provide pro rata guarantees on those loans up to a total of € 780 billion.

The EFSF has a lending capacity of € 440 billion. In the case of default, the MS are liable to the amount of their capital share. The financial assistance packages are only available to countries that adopt strict austerity and reform programmes to ensure that the causes of the debt crisis are addressed. This will be monitored by the so-called Troika of European Commission (EC), ECB and IMF. The chart below shows the EFSF's deployed funds as of February 28, 2013. In Juli 2013, EFSF and the EFSM were replaced by the permanent ESM (see below).[13]

[13] Not shown in the diagram below, Spain has been provided with sector-specific financial assistance up to € 100 billion in EFSF/ESM credits in order to stabilise its banking sector (this includes a security buffer, as the exact amount of assistance needed is not known yet). The credit will first be channelled to FROB, the government's restructuring fund, which will then distribute assistance to troubled banks. As of September 2013, € 41.4 billion have been effectively used.

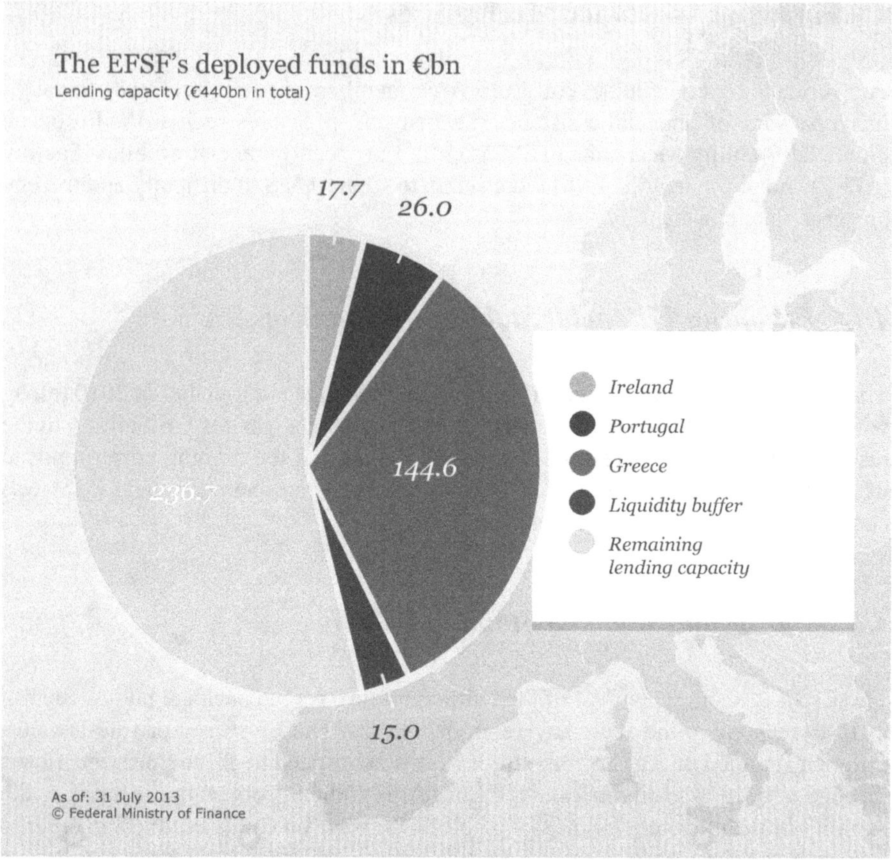

In addition to granting emergency loans, the EFSF (like its successor ESM) is authorised to use the following instruments:

1. Precautionary financial assistance: Like the IMF, the EFSF grants credit lines to MS with sound economic fundamentals that are experiencing short-term financial difficulties. The aim is to safeguard market confidence in otherwise strong economies and to prevent an actual crisis that might then spread to other countries.
2. Financial assistance to recapitalise financial institutions: Where specific problems in an MS's financial sector pose a risk to financial stability, the EFSF can grant loans to MS authorities that may be used to recapitalise financial institutions. European state aid legislation must be complied with. The recipient MS rather than the financial institution is responsible for repaying the loan and complying with the conditions attached.
3. Primary market purchases: The main objective of this instrument is to allow a country to retain access to the primary bond market or to allow it to regain access—for example after completing an adjustment programme. In such cases the EFSF participates by purchasing that country's new issues.

4. Secondary market interventions: Where the ECB has evidence of an extraordinary situation arising on the financial market or threats to financial stability, sovereign bonds can be purchased on the secondary market in exceptional cases. The aim of this measure is to support the functioning of the sovereign bond markets and to guarantee sufficient liquidity on those markets. Work is currently ongoing to implement the two options agreed in October 2011 to optimise the EFSF's lending capacity by partially guaranteeing sovereign bonds and to create Co-Investment Funds allowing a combination of public and private funding.

4.3 European Stability Mechanism

All Euro Area MS have agreed to establish the permanent ESM by international treaty as an international financial institution. Its purpose is to mobilise financial resources and make them available to Euro Area MS that are experiencing financial difficulties. It uses the same instruments as the EFSF (see above). The assistance is provided only under strict economic policy conditionality and only when it is indispensable for safeguarding the stability of the Euro Area as a whole.

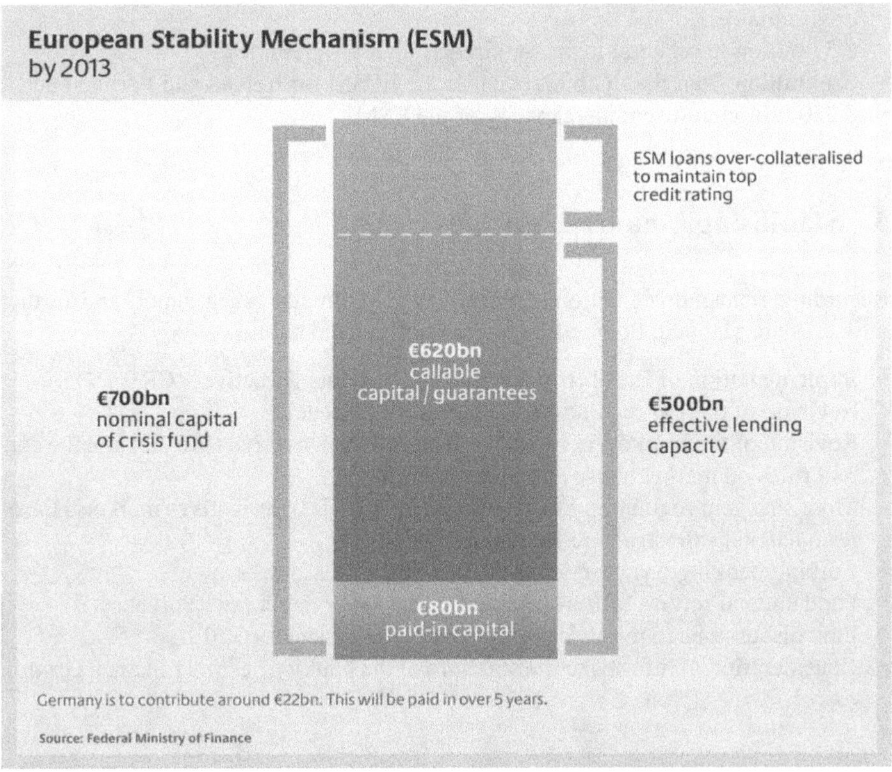

The policy conditions are agreed as part of a macroeconomic adjustment programme that targets the affected country's economic and financial imbalances. In addition, the financial assistance is linked to ratification of the Fiscal Compact and—after the expiry of the relevant implementation period set out in the Fiscal Compact—coupled to implementation of the new debt rule. The Eurozone finance ministers have agreed to allow the ESM to enter into force already in 2012, earlier than initially envisaged. National ratification procedures have been finalized in the MS. The ESM will have a subscribed capital of € 700 billion. This is made up of € 80 billion of paid-in and € 620 billion of callable capital. The capital will be paid in five tranches, with the first two tranches paid during the course of 2012, and the remaining tranches to be paid in 2013 and 2014.

The ESM Board of Governors comprises the Euro Area's finance ministers. Decisions are taken by unanimity, but for issues that require quick decisions, a majority representing 85 % of the capital shares is sufficient. The ESM also has a Board of Directors that is responsible for the day-to-day management of the ESM. In order to facilitate private sector participation, Collective Action Clauses (CAC) will be included (from 2013) in newly issued government bonds of all MS. In a restructuring situation an agreement between the state and its private creditors will thus become easier.

In sum, the European firewall capacity now totals around € 800 billion and consists of:

- € 188 billion pledged EFSF funding for Ireland, Portugal and Greece (second programme),
- € 53 billion in bilateral loans for Greece (first programme),
- € 49 billion from the EU budget under the EFSM for Ireland and Portugal and
- € 500 billion new lending capacity of the ESM.

5 Stabilising Financial Markets

Regarding financial regulation, Europe has also already taken action and further measures are planned. Some of them are briefly listed here:

- Implementation of Basel III (Capital Requirements Directive—CRD IV).
- Revision of the EU regulation on credit rating agencies.
- Revision of the Markets in Financial Instruments Directive (MiFID) and the current rules on market abuse and investment funds.
- More stringent regulation of over-the-counter (OTC) derivatives markets (European Market Infrastructure Regulation—EMIR).
- Curbing banking pay practices that encourage recklessness.
- Fundamental reform of European insurance supervision law (Solvency II).
- First discussions to regulate the shadow banking sector (G20).
- Consideration of reforms to the structure of the banking sector (Liikanen Group).

6 Banking Union

Another key reform step was the deepening of European banking sector integration. In this context the discussion of a European Banking Union with common bank supervision, restructuring and resolution has been pushed forward. The recent crisis demonstrated the speed and extent to which problems in the financial sector of one country may spread to another. This is especially the case in a monetary union: Local financial turmoil may quickly threaten the stability of the entire Euro Area banking system. The rationale for a banking union is thus that such developments and the underlying financial structures need to be managed jointly by EU or Eurozone MS.

This more integrated financial framework is being built upon three components: a Single Supervisory Mechanism (SSM), a Single Resolution Mechanism (SRM) for banks and a system of deposit protection.

Following the political accord of EU ECOFIN ministers in December 2012, negotiations about the new SSM were concluded in 2013. The agreement will become operational in 2014 and will see the ECB (in collaboration with national supervisory bodies) having direct oversight of large Eurozone banks. To avoid conflicts of interest, an important feature of the SSM is the effective separation of monetary policy and banking supervision tasks within the ECB. A second important feature of the SSM is that national authorities of non-Euro Area MS have an option to participate in the SSM. Obviously, the concentration of more powers at the ECB implies a higher level of accountability and transparency. The Council's proposal of December 2012 addresses this issue by creating a Review Panel of SSM decisions from a legal point of view and, in particular, by defining the accountability of the SSM to the European Parliament. Last, but not least, the SSM builds the precondition for a possible direct recapitalisation of banks by the ESM.

A second element of the Banking Union is the establishment of an SRM. The draft Bank Restructuring and Resolution Directive lays out a harmonised toolbox of resolution powers and bail-in instruments. Negotiations are well underway.

The third element of the Banking Union is the establishment of a common system of deposit protection. A system, built on common EU standards, will be important in the future to ensure enhanced depositor confidence in the robustness of European banks. This element can also help reduce the risks of financial fragmentation that results from contagion fears. The corresponding draft Deposit Guarantee Schemes Directive is still under discussion.

7 ECB—Measures

Since the eruption of the sovereign debt crisis in the Euro Area in May 2010, the ECB has been in the spotlight of crisis management and resolution and agreed to a number of non-conventional measures:

1. *Securities Market Programme (SMP):* Since May 2010, the ECB repeatedly purchased government bonds from Eurozone countries on the secondary market. The current outstanding amount is € 190,7 billion as of September 24, 2013. The SMP expired in September 2012.
2. *Outright Monetary Transactions Programme (OMT):* The OMT was introduced in September 2012 and replaced the SMP. Under its provisions, government bond purchases are possible under strict conditions. A necessary condition for Outright Monetary Transactions is strict and effective conditionality attached to an appropriate EFSF or ESM programme. Such programmes can take the form of a full EFSF/ESM macroeconomic adjustment programme or a precautionary programme (Enhanced Conditions Credit Line), provided that they include the possibility of EFSF/ESM primary market purchases. The involvement of the IMF shall also be sought for the design of the country-specific conditionality and the monitoring of such a programme. Transactions will be focused on the shorter part of the yield curve, and in particular on sovereign bonds with a maturity of between 1 and 3 years may be bought without limit on secondary markets, and the ECB has waived its preferred creditor status. All purchases will be published and thus made transparent, although there have been no purchases yet. The excess liquidity generated will be fully sterilised through repo or open market operations.
3. *Longer-Term Refinancing Operations I and II (LTRO):* In 2011, the ECB Council announced two refinancing operations with a maturity of up to 36 months to support the real economy and to improve the liquidity situation in the euro money market.[14]
4. *Covered Bond Purchase Programme (CBPP):* In order to support the covered bond market which had suffered significantly in the crisis, the ECB launched the CBPP. [15]
5. *Emergency Liquidity Assistance (ELA):* ELA is an alternative to conventional refinancing operations of the central banks when regular refinancing is temporarily not possible. Commercial banks can get emergency loans from national central banks under certain conditions and after approval by the ECB's governing board. In the past, the ECB has decided to grant ELA to, inter alia, Ireland, Greece and Cyprus. The outstanding amounts of ELA operations are not explicitly published in the national central bank balance sheets or the aggregated balance sheet of the Eurosystem.

[14] LTRO I and II took place in December 2011 and February 2012, respectively, and accounted for the amount of € 489 billion (net allocation € 200 billion) and € 529 billion (net allocation € 314 billion) respectively. Due to recent early repayments the current volume of longer-term refinancing has been reduced to € 705 billion as of June 28, 2013. Net allocation represents the difference between the LTRO operation and ordinary refinancing operations that expired at the same time and were not replaced by another ordinary refinancing operation in the same amount.

[15] The first CBPP which ran until June 2010 had a nominal amount of € 60 billion. As of September 24, 2013, the outstanding amount was € 43 billion. In November 2011, the ECB launched a second purchase program for covered bonds amounting to € 40 billion maturing in October 2012 (CBPP2). The outstanding amount was € 15,7 billion as of September 24, 2013.

6. *Collateral requirements* for commercial banks have been substantially lowered for a number of ECB operations.

8 Conclusion

Europe has embarked on a remarkable journey of comprehensive reform to tackle the euro crisis. First results on fiscal consolidation and competitiveness have already been achieved. Other benefits of the reform measures will only be realised in the longer term. Despite the challenges the Euro Area has faced, and is facing today, the euro remains a strong reserve currency with low inflation. It is imperative that short-term crisis management measures are supplemented by sustained policy action to achieve sound public finances and higher growth potential in the longer term. Success will certainly not come overnight. What is needed is vigorous, steady policy implementation along agreed timetables.

Acknowledgements We are grateful to our colleagues at the Ministry Reinhard Felke, Robert Völter, and Stefan Freitag for useful comments on an earlier version of this paper.

References

European Council (2012) Council Conclusions of 28/29 June 2012, EUCO 76/12
Herndon T, Ash M, Pollin R (2013) Does high public debt consistently stifle economic growth? A critique of Reinhart and Rogoff. PERI Working Paper 322
Kumar M, Woo J (2010) Public debt and growth. IMF Working Paper
IMF (2013) Fiscal Monitor of April 2013: Fiscal Adjustment in an Uncertain World
IMF World Economic Outlook (2012) The good, the bad, and the ugly: 100 years of dealing with public debt overhangs (Chapter 3). IMF (October 2012)
Reihnhart C, Rogoff K (2010) Growth in a time of debt. Am Econ Rev 100(2):573–578

Predicting the Euro: A Practitioner's Perspective

Abheek Barua

For a financial market practitioner, the task of predicting the Euro seems to present new and daunting challenges every year. For one thing, the turn of events in Cyprus in the second half of March 2013 points to the continued existence of unknown pockets of risk in the region. Although Cyprus was known to have its share of financial troubles emanating largely from its banking system and had been negotiating a bailout with the troika of the European Union (EU), International Monetary Fund (IMF) and the European Central Bank (ECB) since 2012, financial markets woke up to the possibility of a 'shock' to the Euro-zone economy from this tiny Mediterranean island (it accounts for just 0.2 % of gross domestic product (GDP)) barely a month before it hit the headlines. The markets' focus shifted to Slovenia and Malta in the wake of the problem in Cyprus but the probability of a banking/fiscal crisis unexpectedly emerging from some other part of the currency union is certainly not negligible (see Table 1). Thus, as recently as the first quarter of 2013 Europe remains a somewhat uncharted minefield.

The crisis in Cyprus brings another issue to the table—the absence of an established and replicable model for crisis resolution. The impact on the financial system of funding a relatively paltry 17 billion euros could have been a merely localized blip on the Europe-watcher's radar screen were it not for the ad hoc manner in which it was handled (Loynes and Mckeown 2013). The troika[1] agreed to provide 10 billion euros but proposed that the rest be raised through a levy on bank deposits, a large fraction of which was covered by deposit insurance. This was a departure from the usual set of conditions such as tax increases, pension reforms and public sector reform along with 'haircuts' for creditors that were imposed for recipients of assistance in the past like Greece, Ireland or Portugal. Protracted negotiations

[1] The troika is used to refer to the three organizations that have negotiated bailouts within the Euro zone. They are: (a) The European Union, (b) The European Central Bank and (c) The International Monetary Fund. The details of the agreement between the troika and the Cyprus government were revealed in a document that was released by the European Commission.

A. Barua (✉)
HDFC Bank, Mumbai, India
e-mail: Abheek.Barua@hdfcbank.com

M. Callaghan et al. (eds.), *Global Cooperation Among G20 Countries*,
DOI 10.1007/978-81-322-1659-9_4,

Table 1 Overstretched financial systems in smaller nations could pose significant risks going forward. (Source: Eurostat)

Fiscal position and bank assets in 2012 (% GDP)			
	Government debt	Fiscal balance	Bank assets
Cyprus	84	−4.9	716
Estonia	10	−0.5[a]	109
Luxembourg	21	−1.5[a]	2107
Malta	73	−2.6[a]	760
Slovenia	48	−4.2[a]	144
Slovakia	51	−4.8[a]	81

[a] Estimates from European Commission's (EC's) latest economic forecasts

between Cyprus and the EU resulted in an arguably better but almost equally arbitrary resolution. Among other things (one of the largest banks was effectively wound up entailing hefty write-downs for holders of both junior and senior debt), a massive 40% tax was levied on deposits in two major banks above 1,00,000 euros.

There is an argument that since these big-ticket deposits were largely from offshore depositors taking advantage of interest rate arbitrage, low taxes and a lax regulatory mechanism (Know your Client or KYC norms are notoriously liberal in Cyprus), it made it somewhat fair to force them to participate in the bailout. This might be a politically popular view particularly in the 'core' economies of Europe who have been funding the bulk of the bailouts in the region. However, it involves the kind of subjectivity and value judgment that could set a dangerous precedent and is best avoided as a basis for policymaking. The fact is that the response to the crisis underscored the lack of progress in what one could describe as 'system-building'.

It is possible, of course, that the mode of resolution of the Cyprus crisis is likely to emerge as the 'system'. Contrary to what the majority of European policymakers have suggested, Cyprus might not be a 'unique' case and could constitute a template for future bailouts. The willingness of European policymakers (as in Cyprus's case) to risk contagion for a relatively small amount of funds and push the entire region to the brink of crisis might not reflect their incompetence alone. It could be read as a sign that the core economies, particularly Germany, are becoming increasingly reluctant to bear the cost of bailouts. Instead they are likely to improvise solutions (like a levy on deposits or a hefty 'bail-in' surcharge for residents) to bridge fiscal gaps or financial gaps that banks might encounter. The increase in this 'internal' funding of these gaps could either exacerbate recessionary tendencies or, as in the case of Cyprus, lead to a virtual collapse of the financial system. The possibility of a deposit tax also enhances the risk of bank runs across the region at the faintest whiff of a funding problem in the future. This could, in turn, feed sudden stops in liquidity as lending banks become apprehensive of a quick erosion in the liability base of debtor banks.

Were the 'Cyprus model' to indeed emerge as the model for crisis resolution in the future, it is likely to give some of the fiscally stretched peripheral economies a reason to introspect yet again the costs and benefits of participating in the Euro project. The costs of sacrificing monetary and increasingly fiscal control and coping with the economic consequences of what is often (from an individual country's perspective) an overvalued exchange rate could outweigh the benefits of financial assistance that come with increasingly difficult riders (Krugman 2013). Thus, Cyprus has effectively resurrected the risk of exit of one or more of the peripheral economies from the union.

That said, it would be somewhat unfair to entirely overlook the progress that the region has made in terms of new policy mechanisms or the economic fundamentals. On the policy front, the commitment to Outright Market Transactions (OMT) by the ECB in September 2012 has perhaps made the most substantive difference to market sentiment, and has enhanced the ability of fiscally challenged economies to fund their deficits through sovereign bond offerings (European Central Bank 2012). A full-blown OMT would involve an open-ended liquidity backstop offered by the central bank to purchase government bonds of an economy that faces funding strain. This is likely to ensure that the government is able to raise funds at 'reasonable' rates. The OMT is part of a larger package wherein a troubled economy approaches the troika, agrees to conditions that could relate to fiscal consolidation or restructuring of key sectors like banking. While there could be some direct support in the form of a loan from the European Stability Mechanism (ESM) and the IMF, if more finance is needed it will have to be raised from the market with the liquidity support from the central bank.

It might be useful to analyse exactly how the OMT works to alleviate stress. One thing that the financial crisis of 2008 has underscored is the close link between liquidity and solvency. A sudden stop in liquidity flows to a sovereign bond market, driven by the fear of insolvency of a fiscally stressed sovereign (Calvo 1988), could lead to a sharp rise in its bond yields (the effective interest rate at which it borrows). As the interest bill rises, it could drive a rapid deterioration in the fiscal gap and, in a classic example of a self-fulfilling prophecy, actually enhance the risk of insolvency (De Grauwe 2011). The rise in sovereign bond yields also leads to capital erosion of banks and to the extent that these bonds are held by the domestic banking system, it enhances their insolvency risk as well. The OMT creates a buffer against a sudden stop in liquidity and thus simultaneously reduces the risk of insolvency. This sets off a virtuous cycle—the perception of lower insolvency risk gets priced into the sovereign bond curve, lowers cost of funding the fiscal gap and actually improves the solvency of the economy.

Conventionally, the risk of sovereign default is seen as a function in a large part of the debt–GDP ratio (Mody and Sandri 2011). The probability of default is typically seen to rise exponentially above a threshold level for this ratio. The OMT substantially reduces the probability of default for all levels of the debt–GDP ratio. Thus with an unchanged or larger debt burden, the risk of default reduces significantly. A good reflection of this is in the manner in which Credit Default Swaps (CDS) spreads have compressed in most of the fiscally stressed states. For instance, the 5-year Spanish CDS spread averaged around 474 bps in 2012 prior to the ECB's OMT programme but has subsequently averaged around 290 bps after the launch of the OMT programme. Similarly, the Italian 5-year CDS spread averaged around 451 bps prior to OMT but has averaged around 270 bps since its launch.

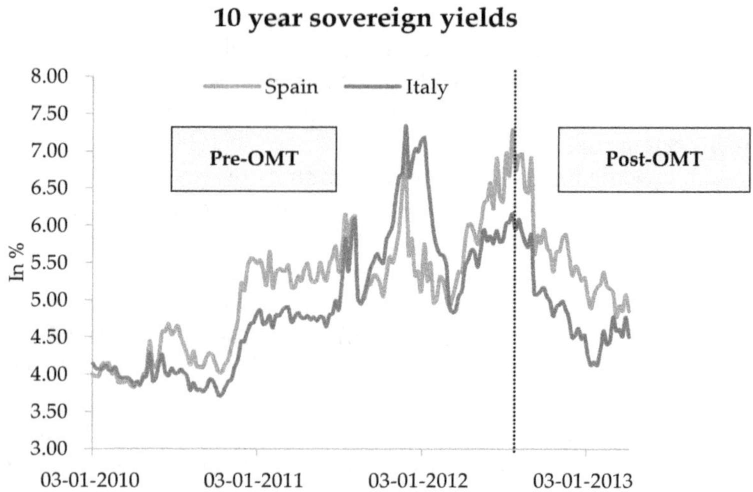

Fig. 1 Peripheral sovereign yields have fallen since the inception of the OMT. (Source: Reuters and HDFC Bank)

The OMT seems to have had an impact on the region and financial markets in two different ways. It has led to a decline in the bond yields of the periphery (see Fig. 1). It also appears to have resulted in a 're-rating' of the Euro manifested in a marked upward shift in its trading range vis-a-vis the US dollar and other free-floating currencies like the Pound sterling and the Japanese yen. It has also reduced the volatility of the single currency quite substantially (see Fig. 2). Thus, the markets have viewed the OMT as a credible policy measure to back the ECB President Mario Draghi's (2012) promise that he would do 'whatever it takes to save the Euro'.

The rerating of the Euro is not due to the OMT alone. There has been some improvement in fundamental economic parameters as well. Current account balances (see Fig. 3) have improved for a number of the peripheral economies. In most cases, this improvement has come partly on the back of an improved export performance and not just a contraction in imports driven by a recession. Part of this improvement in export growth could have come in response to improving labour productivity captured in falling unit labour cost numbers (see Fig. 4; Bootle and Loynes 2013).[2] These are important steps forward in the process of 'internal-rebalancing' that is seen to be imperative for the coexistence of the core and periphery within the common currency arrangement. The financial markets appeared to have recognised this and have again priced this into the valuation of the Euro and sovereign yield spreads.

[2] It is important to note that the unit labour costs are calculated from macroeconomic aggregates and changes in the composition in output as well as a rise in informal employment could be partly responsible for the decline although it is unlikely that they would explain it entirely. Surprisingly, the fall in unit labour costs is not fully reflected in either export or consumer prices.

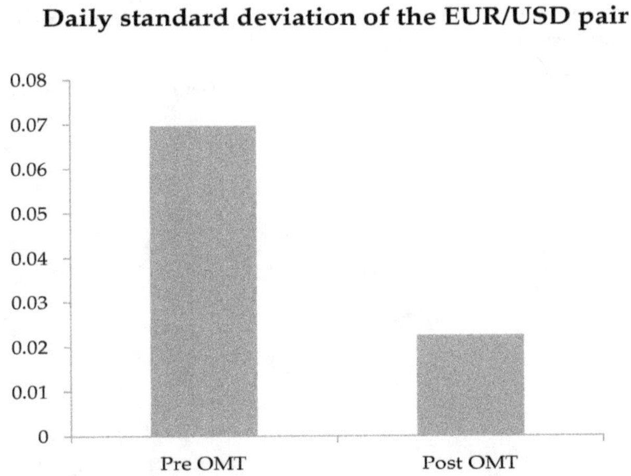

Fig. 2 Volatility in the Euro has diminished since the launch of the OMT. The Pre-OMT period is from January-2011 to August-2012 and the post OMT period is from September 12 to present (which includes the Cyprus bailout period). The calculations are based on a daily data. (Source: Reuters and HDFC Bank)

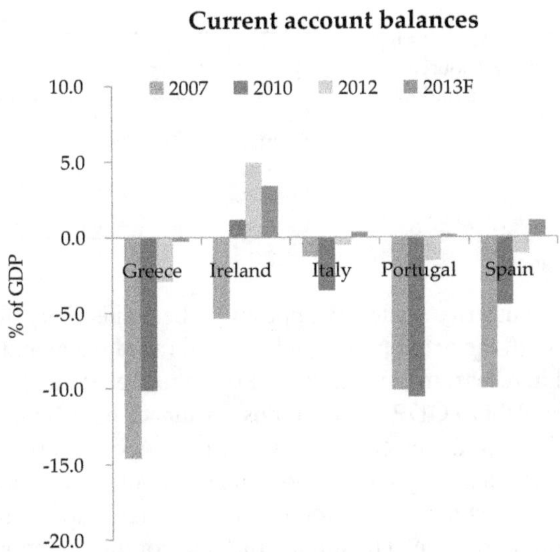

Fig. 3 Peripheral current account balances have improved. (Source: IMF, world economic outlook April 2013)

Thus if the assessment of the financial markets is correct, the probability of survival of the Euro project has certainly increased. This does not rule out periods of turmoil such as the 'Cyprus episode". It also does not rule out the prospect of a small economy exiting the union. However, the likelihood of the entire union falling part (a possibility that the financial markets had considered just a year ago) has virtually disappeared.

Survival is one thing. The other question that market practitioners, with exposures to the Euro, have to grapple with is the speed or the ease with which the region returns to a normal growth path. Unfortunately, the prognosis for the short term (that financial markets tend to focus on) is far from optimistic. For one thing, the clichéd

Fig. 4 Peripheral unit labour costs have fallen. (Source: Eurostat)

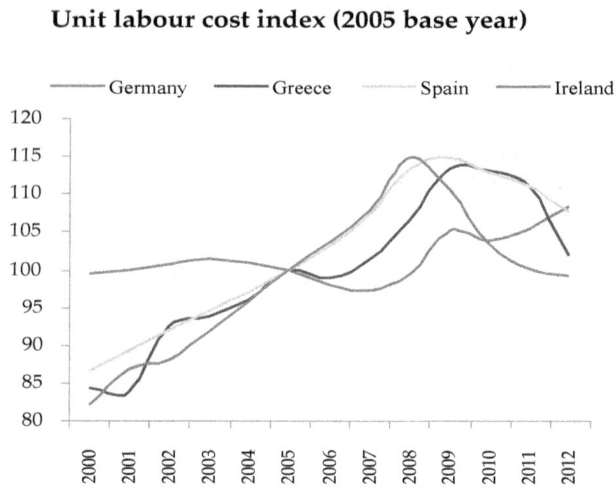

Table 2 Growth rates in the periphery. (Source: IMF, world economic outlook April, 2013)

GDP growth rate (In YoY %)	2011	2012	2013F
Greece	−7.1	−6.4	−4.2
Portugal	−1.6	−3.2	−2.3
Ireland	1.4	0.9	1.1
Spain	0.4	−1.4	−1.6
Italy	0.4	−2.4	−1.5

growth-austerity trade-off appears to be quite sharp for the European periphery. Almost all the economies that have embraced fiscal and institutional reform remain mired in recession (see Table 2). Prolonged recession has not helped the fiscal cause and the debt to GDP ratios in most instances have actually deteriorated (Table 3).

This should not come as a surprise. A conventional Keynesian model (Gros 2011) with a multiplier of more than one coupled with a debt–GDP ratio over 100 % would predict a deterioration in the debt–GDP ratio in the short term in response to fiscal compression. The impact of GDP contraction would tend to outweigh the reduction in debt. However, in the long term, GDP growth would return to a 'normal' path while the debt reduction would be permanent. This would entail a fall in the debt–GDP ratio. Currently the austerity-embracing periphery is displaying all the symptoms of the short-run and austerity appears to be self-defeating. This certainly makes the task of fiscal consolidation more challenging. The financial markets' response to this deterioration in growth and fiscal balances would depend on whether they take a short-term view or are willing to 'price in' the potential long-term gains in fiscal parameters. At this stage, they seem to be losing patience, and a significant section of market participants are now calling for a less-aggressive approach to fiscal correction. This is likely to mean more turbulence in the months to come.

Table 3 Debt–GDP ratios in the Euro-zone periphery. (Source: IMF, world economic outlook April, 2013)

Gross government debt as a % of GDP					
	2007	2010	2011	2012	2013F
Greece	107.3	147.9	170.6	158.5	179.5
Portugal	68.3	93.2	108.0	123.0	122.3
Ireland	25.0	92.2	106.5	117.1	122.0
Spain	36.3	61.3	69.1	84.1	91.8
Italy	103.3	119.3	120.8	127.0	130.6

References

Loynes J, Mckeown J (2013) Cyprus: disaster averted but with lasting effects. European economics update, Capital Economics

Krugman P (2013) Cyprus, Seriously. New York Times

European Central Bank (2012) Technical features of the Outright Monetary Transactions program. 9

Calvo G (1988) Servicing the public debt: the role of expectations. Am Econ Rev 78:647–661

De Grauwe P (2011) Managing a fragile Euro-zone. Center for Economic Studies, IFO. Institute Forum 12(2):40–45

Mody A, Sandri D (2011) The Euro-zone crisis: how banks and sovereigns came to be joined at the hip. IMF working paper, 2–3

Draghi M (2012) Speech by Mario Draghi President, European Central Bank (July 26, 2012) at Global investors conference, London

Bootle R, Loynes J (2013) Have the peripheral economies regained competitiveness. European Economic Focus, Capital Economics

Gros D (2011) Can austerity be self-defeating? The Center for European Policy Studies

Monetary Integration in Europe and the Drawbacks of Centralization

Heribert Dieter

1 Introduction

The continuing financial crises in some member countries of the eurozone have intensified the debate about reforms of monetary integration. The deep and lasting crises in a number of member countries of the European Monetary Union have demonstrated that the original architecture of the Treaty of Maastricht has to be revised. It did not prevent Greece, Ireland, and other economies from implementing unsustainable fiscal policies. However, the two alternatives suggested by the proponents of deeper integration—either deeper integration regarding monetary and fiscal policy, or a return to antagonistic, national policies—are far from being inevitable. By contrast, it is possible to make the monetary union more crisis proof while at the same time giving the European nations a high degree of responsibility for their own economic development. The frequently cited assertion that transferring—i.e., centralizing—hitherto national competencies to the European level would make fiscal policy and financial regulation easier to manage is not convincing. That approach ignores the downside of centralization. Far-reaching centralization may result in new problems and will weaken, not strengthen, the economic dynamism of the European Union (EU).

For 3 years the eurozone has been agonizing over a financial crisis that has its origins in some of the member countries. But the crisis has lingered on and there has been no return to steady growth. Recent turbulence—the elections in Italy in February 2013 and increasing public opposition to further austerity programs in economies affected by crises—is underlining the political problems of European crisis management.

H. Dieter (✉)
German Institute for International and Security Affairs, Berlin, Germany
e-mail: heribert.dieter@swp-berlin.org

Zeppelin University, Friedrichshafen, Germany

M. Callaghan et al. (eds.), *Global Cooperation Among G20 Countries*,
DOI 10.1007/978-81-322-1659-9_5, © Springer India 2014

This situation has led to urgent demands for a quick solution to end the crisis by creating new, deeper forms of cooperation in the eurozone. Proponents of this line of thinking argue that cooperation in Europe can only succeed by immediately creating a fiscal or banking union. However, alternatives do exist. An evolution of the Treaty of Maastricht is possible and would better serve the heterogeneity of the EU than a centralization of economic policies, which would inevitably result in a reduction of sovereignty for the European nation-states.

The lasting corrections are certainly causing great trouble for the affected citizens. But the current adjustments—for instance, the shrinking of the construction sector in Spain and Ireland—have nothing to do with the fiscal compact, and they have very little to do with the eurozone. It is, however, true that the architecture of the eurozone did not provide economies with instruments to cool off the exuberance. Interest rates were too low for booming economies like Ireland and Spain, and in addition an inflow of foreign capital resulted in further overheating of these economies. The development of instruments against unwanted capital inflows should be discussed in the context of the further development of the eurozone.

2 The Financial Sector has Captured the Debate in Europe

Given the rather moderate level of debt in eurozone economies compared with the UK, the USA, or Japan, the lasting panic is somewhat surprising. The financial sector continues to insist that it needs to be rescued and has successfully captured the debate in Europe. European policymakers have either forgotten basic principles of market economies or are too timid in their application.

In essence, a government faced with a financial sector that has gambled too much and is burdened with debt can choose between two structurally different paths. The first is to take responsibility for the activities of private sector companies and bail them out. Capital injections are helping banks that would otherwise collapse. In one way or the other, a government then socializes the losses of private banks. This is the method being applied in Spain, and from today's point of view the rescue operations of the Irish government may have been wrong. The largest Irish bank, Anglo Irish, was provided with fresh liquidity in autumn 2008, but the rescue operation was based on lies of the bank's management, which was revealed in 2013 through the publication of taped conversations between bank managers (Norris 2013). With hindsight, it might have been wiser to let the struggling Irish banks fail and use taxpayer's money only for the protection of depositors, not of bondholders and other investors.

Of course, this would have been an approach entirely appropriate for a market economy. Banks that do not understand their business should be permitted to leave the market and should not be rescued. In a market economy, first of all the shareholders of incompetent banks should lose their capital and the affected banks should—if closing them looks too risky—be nationalized. If the shareholders' capital is not sufficient to cover the losses, bondholders of the affected banks ought to make a contribution to the rescue operation. In most cases, a haircut for share- and bondholders will be sufficient. In exceptional cases—like Cyprus—there ought to be contributions from holders of bank deposits.

This second approach—permitting banks to fail and primarily drawing on share- and bondholders to cover losses—is quite unpopular, both in Spain and the wider eurozone. But why is that the case? Why have many policymakers and many journalists categorically ruled out large-scale bank closures? A political economy analysis suggests that this reflects the increasing political influence of the financial sector on policymakers. Of course, banks always claim that they have to be rescued.

The successful campaign of the financial sector is also reflected in the increased use of the term "systemically relevant." While it is obvious that many banks claim that status for themselves, the fact that the European Central Bank (ECB) is using this term more often underlines the influence of the finance industry. ECB Vice-President Vítor Constâncio suggested in April 2012 that there are 36 systemically relevant banks in the eurozone. Of course, he also argued that mechanisms should be developed to stabilize—that is, to rescue—these banks, should they lose money.

In the USA, shareholders of banks have to take responsibility much faster than in Europe in resolving failing banks. Since 2008, the Federal Deposit Insurance Corporation (FDIC) has closed 445 ailing banks. If a bank gets into trouble, the shareholders lose their investments and the FDIC either closes the bank completely or sells marketable parts of it. The FDIC protects the depositors for up to 250,000 dollars per customer. The closing of banks—including the then sixth largest US bank, Washington Mutual, in 2008—has been a major factor in the disciplining of the US financial sector.

If governments and institutions like the ECB keep coming to the rescue of the financial sector, the players will become less—not more—prudent in the future. Rescue operations lead to moral hazard. The irony is that, in Europe, the financial sector has successfully managed to link its own interests with those that favor European cooperation and integration. Even left-leaning parties are singing the siren song of the rescuers and have failed to acknowledge whose song they are singing. At the end of the day, the question is: Why have some private sector companies been successful in putting their economic interests above those of the taxpayers?

The high level of influence of the financial sector is, of course, not a phenomenon restricted to Europe. In 2009, the former chief economist of the International Monetary Fund (IMF), Simon Johnson, criticized the disproportionate influence of Wall Street on US economic and fiscal policy. Johnson even argued that the USA was exposed to a "quiet coup" and demanded breaking the power of the "financial oligarchy." If that did not happen, Johnson suggested, it would be very difficult for the American economy to return to a sustainable growth path. But the determined actions of the FDIC described above demonstrate that policymakers have been trying to address this issue.

Viewed this way, there is thus not a conflict between nations, but between interest groups within the eurozone. The main beneficiaries of the rescue operations have managed to put their commercial interests above the interests of taxpayers, which is a smart move on their part. Needless to say, a Europe that continues to serve privileged interest groups will not be a successful competitor in the twenty-first century.

Contradictions in the management of the European crisis are being critically observed, particularly in emerging economies. Disbelief in Asia stems primarily from the apparent unwillingness of European policymakers to apply well-established principles of a capitalist economy. How is it possible that Europeans have forgotten how market economies work and which incentives have to be given? Yet many policymakers and academics have been calling for a rapid solution of the crisis. Supranational solutions are considered superior despite evidence that they do not work any better than national solutions.[1]

3 Cornerstones of Maastricht 2.0

The question of course is whether there are any alternatives to the current push for centralization. It is clear, of course, that there are: Europe can evolve without a great leap forward, which is rejected by a sizable number of citizens in the eurozone, where support for integration varies considerably between countries. One should not forget that the Maastricht Treaty offers several advantages, many of which are worth preserving. The common currency reduces transaction costs within the eurozone without forcing the participating countries into a centrally planned fiscal policy straightjacket. This approach acknowledges the diversity of European societies much better than a one-size-fits-all concept.

In contrast to the bipolar view favored by the advocates of centralization, there are more than two alternatives for the future development of the eurozone. Europe can both strengthen the ownership of economic and fiscal policies by individual societies as well as provide incentives for sustainable economic development. The key factor is the elimination of contradictions and inconsistencies of the Maastricht Treaty. The three most important points are as follows:

1. There is a contradiction between the no-bailout clause (Article 125, Treaty on the Functioning of the European Union) and the absence of an exit option. This regulatory gap has been successfully exploited by Greece. To prevent a recurrence, the Treaty of Maastricht should be supplemented by an exclusion clause: Member states that do not fully service their payment obligations should have to leave the monetary union within 6 months after the default.
   This amendment would leave the responsibility for sustainable fiscal policy where it belongs: with individual member countries of the eurozone. The potential loss of economic benefits of membership in the monetary union would offer a sufficient incentive to implement a sustainable fiscal policy.

[1] See, for example, Haldane 2009; Levinson 2010.

2. States should be able to leave the eurozone if they consider the benefits of membership to be lower than the costs. A monetary union does not have to act as a straightjacket for societies and impose certain and everlasting monetary and exchange rate policies on them. Because of the current compulsory membership, the monetary union also ceases to be attractive to both members and nonmembers.
3. Individual countries should be permitted to protect themselves against unwanted capital inflows. The prevailing doctrine—only unrestricted capital flows ensure rising prosperity—has to be called into question after recent experiences. Both the IMF and the G20 have recently acknowledged the need for restrictions on capital flows in certain circumstances. Temporary restrictions on capital inflows may enable individual economies to curb excesses in the markets and to shield an economy from their negative effects.

Today, countries are not allowed to limit capital flows within the European Union. Article 63 of the Treaty on the Functioning of the European Union prohibits any restrictions. Capital flows thus enjoy the same protection as trade in goods and services or the unrestricted movement of labor. But treating capital flows and goods equally is questionable. In the past, capital flowed within the eurozone from countries with current account surpluses—like Germany—to countries with current account deficits, namely today's crisis countries. Economies could not protect themselves against an inflow of hot money. In Spain and Ireland, the inflows fueled unsustainable property booms.

4 Europe 2020—Centralized Planned Economy or Return to National Ownership?

In the financial crisis, Europe has been stumbling toward an economic system that is reminiscent of a planned economy. The mechanisms of the market have the potential to be deactivated permanently while a weakly legitimized institution—the ECB—is being endowed with far-reaching powers. The creeping disempowerment of national governments and parliaments by the ECB is alarming from a (German) constitutional perspective, and it should lead to the further strengthening of Euro-sceptical assessments. The author Hans Magnus Enzensberger has described this process as the disenfranchisement of the European citizen and has insistently warned about this risk.

But there are alternatives for European integration. A revised treaty—Maastricht 2.0—should aim at minimizing the transfers of sovereignty to the supranational level, insist on the compliance of contracts, and strengthen national ownership of economic policies in the member countries of the European Monetary Union.

References

Norris F (2013) In Ireland, dire echoes of a bailout gone awry. The New York Times, 4 July 2013. http://www.nytimes.com/2013/07/05/business/in-ireland-dire-echoes-of-a-bailout-gone-wrong.html?pagewanted=all&_r=0. Accessed 15 July 2013

Haldane A (2009) Rethinking the financial network. Speech by Andrew Haldane to the Financial Student association, Amsterdam, April 2009. http://www.finextra.com/Finextra-downloads/featuredocs/speech386.pdf. Accessed 15 July 2013

Levinson M (2010) Faulty Basel. Why more diplomacy won't keep the financial system safe. Foreign Affairs 89(3):76–88

Reflections on the Euro Crisis

Pierre Jacquet

Once largely eclipsed by, first, the dynamism of the US economy and then the formidable expansion of emerging countries, the Eurozone has ominously come back to the fore of global preoccupations. It seems to matter again, but mainly through the harm that its current predicament can bring to the world economy. The Eurozone seems to cumulate four major crises in a potentially lethal combination: a crisis of current and potential growth, a crisis of government debt, a banking crisis, and a political crisis characterized by a patent lack of trust and shared vision.

In such a context, this short paper argues that the focus that emerged on the urgency of fiscal consolidation misses the point and can have deleterious effects. The paper starts with a short discussion about the fiscal situation before briefly addressing the other dimensions of the crisis and concluding.

1 Confidence vs. Fundamentals

On the face of it, it may seem quite surprising that the Eurozone became trapped in a government debt crisis, starting in a country—Greece—whose gross domestic product (GDP) barely represents 2% of the GDP of the zone, and threatening to engulf other countries. This crisis erupted after a long period of fiscal consolidation, which stopped in the aftermath of the 2007–2008 global financial and economic crisis when most governments within and outside the Eurozone deliberately chose to support economic activity to avoid economic depression. As a result, public debt ratios deteriorated substantially.

This evolution clearly led to concerns about the sustainability of public debt. However, a cursory look at the graphics below suggests that this cannot be the whole story behind the Eurozone crisis. Figure 1 depicts the current (2012) fiscal situation of the countries of Organisation for Economic Co-operation and Develop-

P. Jacquet (✉)
Global Development Network, New Delhi, India
e-mail: pjacquet@gdn.in

M. Callaghan et al. (eds.), *Global Cooperation Among G20 Countries*,
DOI 10.1007/978-81-322-1659-9_6, © Springer India 2014

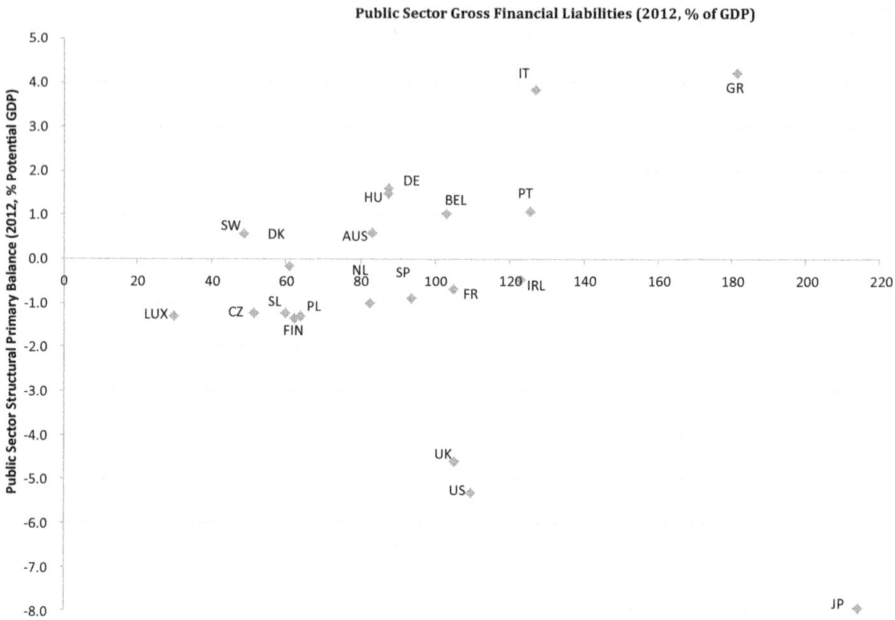

Fig. 1 Fiscal situation in 2012. (Source: OECD Economic Outlook, Volume 2012, Issue 2, November 2012)

ment (OECD), showing the combination of the ratio of public debt to GDP, and the ratio to potential GDP of the "primary structural balance," namely the fiscal balance corrected for the effects of the business cycle and before interest payments on public debt. That balance, thus, is a good proxy for the structural fiscal stance maintained by governments. Figure 1 shows that the debt and deficit situation is not characteristically more severe within the Eurozone than it is for countries outside the zone and outside the European Union. For example, Japan, with a debt ratio well above 200 % of GDP and a structural primary deficit higher than 8 % of potential GDP, seems to be in a more difficult position. The USA and the UK both have public debts higher than 100 % of GDP (and higher than the aggregate Eurozone ratio) and primary structural fiscal deficits of the order of 5 % of potential GDP (against a surplus close to 1 % of potential GDP in 2012 for the Eurozone). As for Eurozone countries, their response to the financial crisis has led to a dramatic worsening of their public debt ratios, but most have small primary structural deficits, and the most indebted countries, including Greece, even have substantial primary surpluses.

The current level of debt ratio and public deficits, however, gives little indication about debt sustainability, which is a forward-looking concept: debt is sustainable when the present value of future income covers the initial debt plus the present value of future liabilities. Any assessment, therefore, has to rely on projections of future income and liabilities, which we know are fragile. Yet, one approach to sustainability is to look at the conditions in which the debt-to-GDP ratio can remain

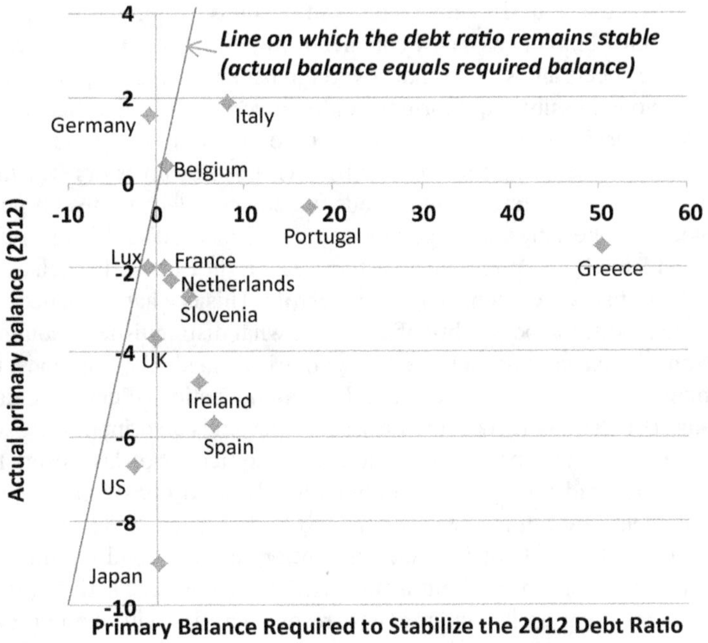

Fig. 2 Simple debt dynamics. (Source: OECD Economic Outlook, Volume 2012, Issue 2, November 2012)

stable. Simple arithmetic about the dynamics of public debt from one year to the next allows us to compare the actual primary balance (fiscal balance before payment of interest on the public debt) with the primary balance that is required to stabilize the debt ratio: the higher the initial debt ratio, and the larger the difference between the interest rate on the public debt and the growth rate of the economy, the larger the primary fiscal surplus needed to stabilize the debt ratio. Figure 2 shows the required and actual primary fiscal balances of various countries in 2012. The degree of unsustainability (defined by the stability of the public debt ratio) can be measured by the distance from the line on which the actual balance equals the required one. Unsurprisingly, Greece comes out as the country with the largest unsustainability problem. Data from 2012 also confirm that Portugal, Spain, Ireland, and, to a lesser extent, Italy also face sustainability problems. However, so do Japan, the USA, and the UK as much as France or The Netherlands, and part of the problems for Eurozone countries also come from a self-fulfilling prophecy: lack of confidence of markets has translated into much higher interest rates on public debt, which considerably affected the debt dynamics from 2009.

If debt sustainability (thus defined) does not really appear as the discriminating factor, what then explains the crisis in the Eurozone and the lasting lack of market confidence with respect to public debt? One of the simplest explanations, also emphasized by Paul Krugman (2011), is that there may be a vicious circle at play, notably due to the lack of decisional and political unity within the zone. In fact, the Greek bankruptcy both opens a new channel of fragility through the deterioration of banks' balance sheets and signals that sovereign bankruptcy is possible. In that context, there are two possible equilibriums: either investors consider that governments are capable of servicing their debt, in which case interest rates will remain low and investors' confidence will be proven justified ex post, or investors fear the risk of default, in which case interest rate spreads widen and interest rates on public debt may explode. In the latter case, governments will face difficulties in refinancing their debt, which will in turn prove investors' fears right ex post. In such an explanation, self-fulfilling expectations play a crucial role. This is what happened in 2012 in the Eurozone. Now, the possibility of default is what distinguishes a country within the Eurozone from a country outside it: in countries outside the Eurozone, there is a clearly identified lender-of-last-resort and the monetization of debt remains an option because countries borrow in their own currency and can print money, so that the option of default is not open. Within the Eurozone, lender-of-last-resort functions and monetization did not appear as options available to borrowing governments, while adjustment through lower spending and higher taxes could prove lethal and unacceptable, so that default remained an option and the "bad equilibrium" prevailed. This led the European Central Bank (ECB) to intervene actively, if arguably belatedly, by stepping up its lender-of-last-resort facilities with the introduction of the Outright Monetary Transactions (OMT) scheme in September 2012, an unlimited bond-buying program designed to restore minimum investors' confidence. The ECB thus demonstrated that—if allowed to do so credibly, which requires minimum support from major governments in the zone—it could effectively address the confidence problem highlighted above.

2 The Euro as an Unfinished Business

Thus, the crisis in the Eurozone is at least as much a crisis of governance as it is an economic crisis with clear fundamentals. As such, it is a tough combination of economic and political woes. European politics, in particular, appears as a major factor in understanding the current problems. As we know, the ECB eventually jumped in decisively to address the liquidity problem brought by the crisis of confidence and to play the lender-of-last-resort for the banking sector. Yet, beyond crisis management, and in order to face up to future challenges, deeper reforms are needed. There is, however, a severe political problem among Eurozone members, namely a lack of trust that prevents serious consideration of the economic situation and of economic policies that would be appropriate.

The economic agenda, however, is inescapable. It has three dimensions, mirroring the three crises analyzed by Shambaugh (2012): economic growth, fiscal profligacy, and the banking crisis.

The growth prospects within the Eurozone are currently alarming (for a discussion, see Darvas et al. 2013). The growth performance was disappointing already

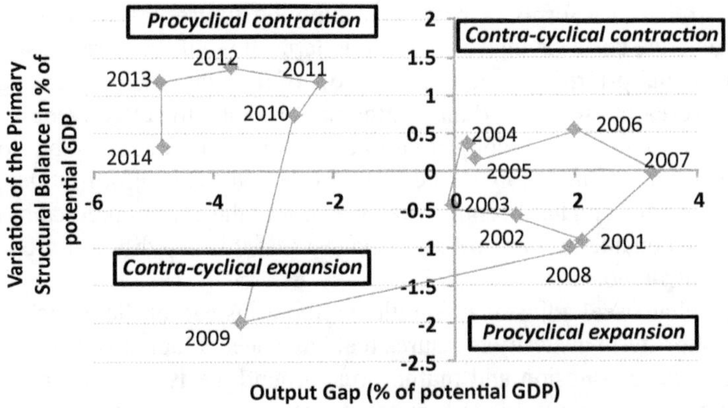

Fig. 3 Orientation of the Eurozone economic policy (2001–2014) (Source: OECD Economic Outlook, Volume 2012, Issue 2, November 2012. Figures for 2012 are estimates. (Figures for 2013 and 2014 are OECD November 2012 projections))

before the crisis, and has deteriorated since then. The concern is twofold: first, in the short term, there is a lethal interplay between politics within the zone, the prolongation of the crisis (notably through the banking sector), and the recognized need for fiscal adjustment. The lack of trust (notably between "virtuous" Northern European countries, including Germany, and the "undisciplined" South) has the result of making fiscal austerity both a principle and a condition for any cooperative approach. As a result, governments embark on fiscal tightening, which deepens the current slowdown and is likely to be self-defeating, since lower economic growth pushes fiscal deficits and debt higher. Figure 3 points to the striking tendency, within the Eurozone in the aggregate, to conduct pro-cyclical policies: instead of dampening the economic cycle, economic policies have accentuated it. Over the 15 years between 2001 and 2014, on the basis of November 2012 OECD data (including estimates for 2012 and projections for 2013 and 2014), economic policies were counter-cyclical only during 2004–2007 and in 2009. We now seem to have entered a long period of pro-cyclical contraction of the economy, which certainly does not help improve growth or fiscal balances and has turned into a vicious circle.

Disappointing potential growth prospects are the second concern. Not only is the economy close to stagnation, but also the estimated rate of potential growth is hardly above 1%. Persistent underemployment also threatens to affect skills and result in yet lower potential growth. This compounds the political problem because European integration and the creation of the Euro have clearly not succeeded in raising potential growth. Moreover, the current focus on short-term fiscal adjustment does little to help reorientate economic policies toward structural reforms. Yet, if politics allowed it, there is a way out of the seeming dilemma, because debt sustainability is a medium-term challenge rather than a short-term urgency. What is needed is not short-term fiscal tightening, but restoring the sustainability of the future path of government spending through credible measures. This, however, points to the need for deep structural reforms of programs implying future policy commitments in order to generate costs savings over the long term. It would require questioning political and social priorities, redefining the role of the State (notably through higher education, research, social, and innovation policies) and the effectiveness of public service delivery, not with an objective to dismantle State functions, but to identify them, streamline them, and make them more effective. This reform of the State has long been overdue and has become a key way out of the current predicament. Political economy considerations, however, suggest that this is a difficult proposition to gain political support for.

This is what fiscal adjustment should be about instead of the panicky and self-defeating short-term austerity measures that have been adopted in practice. Yet, the lack of European cohesion and mutual trust around the issue weakens the ability of governments to persuade markets to accept such a longer-term view of crisis resolution. There are various components that can be usefully discussed toward a meaningful European fiscal union, but the most pressing is restoring dialogue and trust about longer-term prospects and policies. In the absence of such dialogue, the focus is on short-term indicators and this is counterproductive.

Finally, substantial progress has been achieved through various discussions on the European Banking Union, even though the exact contour and membership of this union are yet to be finalized (for a discussion, see notably European Commission 2012; Pisani-Ferry et al. 2012; Elliott 2012). There are three main and related issues to address: a single joint mechanism for effective banking supervision, a joint or harmonized deposit guarantee system, and the adoption of procedures for dealing with troubled banks. The current plan for the Banking Union is to include all Eurozone member countries, and the Union will also be open to non-Eurozone member states willing to join. The ECB is expected to be in charge of a single regulation and supervision for the Banking Union as of March 2014, but the discussion on deposit guarantees and bank crisis management still needs to be finalized.

Looking back at the 3 years that have elapsed since the eruption of this already very long crisis leaves an observer with mixed feelings. Much has been achieved: the ECB has stepped in and taken major decisions to deal with the market liquidity problem, protracted discussions and measures have ultimately succeeded in calming the worst market fears and keeping the Eurozone together. Yet, the crisis is by no means behind us; the lack of trust between member states is obvious; disagreements abound on the lessons to draw from the crisis in terms of EU and Eurozone governance reforms. Moreover, above all, there is a clear lack of long-term and shared vision about European integration. Such vision cannot spontaneously emerge from technical discussions on how best to manage interdependence, especially during crises. It requires a strong political mobilization, which is currently absent. This is the deepest challenge facing Europe's future.

References

Darvas Z, Pisani-Ferry J, Wolff G (2013) Europe's growth problem (and what to do about it). Bruegel Policy Brief 2013/03, Bruegel, Brussels, April 2013

Elliott DJ (2012) Key Issues on European Banking Union. Trade-offs and some recommendations, global economy and development working paper 52. The Brookings Institution, Washington D.C.

European Commission (2012) Proposal for a Council Regulation conferring specific tasks on the European Central Bank concerning policies relating to the prudential supervision of credit institutions. COM (2012) 511 final, European Commission, Brussels, September 12, 2012

Krugman P (2011) Euro crisis is not due to failure of Welfare State. The New York Times, November 11, 2011

Pisani-Ferry J, Sapir A, Véron N, Wolff GB (2012) What kind of European Banking Union? Bruegel Policy Contribution, Issue 2012/12, Bruegel, Brussels, June 2012

Shambaugh JC (2012) The Euro's three crises. Brookings papers on economic activity, Spring 2012, The Brookings Institution, Washington D.C. pp 157–231

Part II
Rebalancing the Global Economy

The G20, IMF and Global Imbalances: The Policymakers' Perspective

Michael Callaghan

1 Introduction

Global imbalances have been a focus of attention by economists for a considerable time.

In the first decade of this century, the USA ran very large current account deficits while China and other countries in East Asia, in particular, ran large surpluses. These were dramatically reversed from 2009 onward in the wake of the global financial and economic crisis, yet they remain a topic of debate, including the role of global imbalances in contributing to the crisis[1].

Concern currently ranges from whether external imbalances will re-emerge with the recovery, and, in turn, that the risks they pose will reassert themselves, to the view that rebalancing global demand, which will lead to a reduction in imbalances, is the key to achieving a sustained pick-up in global growth.

An enormous amount has been written on the topic of global imbalances. The objective of this paper is not to cover this issue in detail, but to advance the proposition that, while examining the causes and consequences of global imbalances is fertile ground for economists and academics, it does not generally capture the attention of the national policymaker. In particular, this is because it is difficult for the policymaker to win the domestic political debate needed to implement policy changes and reforms by saying that the measures will lead to a 'reduction in global imbalances'.

This is not to say that external imbalances are not an area of concern that can materially affect economic performance in individual countries, or that there are no circumstances where measures should be taken to reduce them. However, from a pragmatic public policy sense, perhaps the issue could gain more domestic traction

[1] Blanchard and Milkes-Ferretti (2011).

M. Callaghan (✉)
G20 Studies Centre, Lowy Institute for International Policy, Sydney, Australia
e-mail: mcallaghan@lowyinstitute.org

M. Callaghan et al. (eds.), *Global Cooperation Among G20 Countries*,
DOI 10.1007/978-81-322-1659-9_7, © Springer India 2014

if it is not presented in terms of global imbalances per se, but on why removing distortions that result in 'bad' imbalances is beneficial to all.

In fact, focusing on global imbalances can prove to be a distraction from dealing with the underlying problems. For example, while the G20 was focused on developing indicative guidelines to identify large imbalances, the European debt crisis was unfolding.

In terms of winning the public policy debate in order to get measures accepted, the focus should be presented squarely on what is required to achieve sustained economic and jobs growth, and not in terms of dealing with global imbalances.

But this is easier said than done.

2 Past Global Imbalances

Global imbalances are, of course, not a new phenomenon.

Prior to the First World War, there were massive capital flows from Western Europe to economies with plentiful investment opportunities such as Argentina, Australia and Canada. Prior to 1914, current account surpluses in Britain, France and Germany reached over 9% of gross domestic product (GDP) while the deficits in the recipient countries exceeded 5%.

In terms of more recent experiences, Blanchard and Milesi-Ferretti have compiled a summary that divides the period from 1996 into three sub-periods.[2]

- Between 1996 and 2000, the US current account deficit widened from 1.5% of GDP to 4.3%, reflecting a sharp increase in US investment during a period of strong economic growth. The main surplus counterpart was Japan, where the lasting impact of the crisis of the early 1990s continued to depress investment. In emerging Asia, investment collapsed following the Asian Financial Crisis and most countries in the region moved into large current account surplus.
- During 2001–2004, the USA remained in deficit but the driver was now a fall in domestic saving rather than strong investment, with public saving falling by over 5 percentage points between 2001 and 2004.
- From 2005 to 2008, the US current account deficit remained large, with a number of other countries, including in South and Central Europe, recording sizeable deficits associated with asset booms. The counterparts to the deficits were China, with a fivefold increase in its surplus between 2004 and 2007 and a rapid build-up in international reserves, along with rising surpluses in the oil exporters and in Germany. While investment increased in these regions, the increase in saving was larger. Obstfeld and Rogoff identified three interlocking causes for the

[2] Blanchard and Milesi-Ferretti (2011).

widening in global imbalances during this period: the escalation of global commodity prices; an acceleration of financial innovation in the USA and European banks' demand for US structured products.[3]

Over the period from 1996 to 2008, advanced economies were running large deficits while emerging market economies were running large surpluses. This appeared to be puzzling, with capital 'running uphill' from dynamic emerging markets to mature advanced economies.

The impact of the global financial crisis saw a substantial narrowing of global imbalances in 2009 as growth plummeted, and asset prices and commodity prices fell. Although, as the IMF notes, even as global economic output remains well below potential and financial conditions are still highly uncertain, current account divergences have widened modestly in recent years as commodity price increases have raised surpluses for oil exporters.[4]

3 Should Policymakers Have Worried More About Global Imbalances?

This is an issue for much analysis and debate.

As Blanchard has pointed out on numerous occasions, there are 'good' imbalances and 'bad' imbalances.[5] 'Good' imbalances are when saving goes to where it can be most productively used. Imbalances may reflect differences in saving and investment patterns across countries owing to differences in stage of development, demographic patterns and other fundamental drivers.

- Examples of 'good' imbalances include a country with an ageing population relative to its trading partner chooses to save and run current account surpluses in anticipation of dissaving that will occur when the workforce shrinks. Another example is a country with investment opportunities well in advance of the level of domestic savings finances part of its investment through foreign saving. By way of a country example, Australia has a large current account deficit. However, this is not considered to be a cause of concern because foreign capital is financing domestic investment, particularly in the resource sector, that is likely to yield high rates of return and expand export capacity. Although net foreign liabilities are growing as a share of GDP, the size of the trade balance adjustment needed to ensure long-run sustainability appears achievable.[6] Singapore illustrates the sustainability of long-term current account surpluses. It has sustained a current account surplus to build up substantial diversified foreign investment holdings

[3] Obstfeld and Rogoff (2009).

[4] 2012 Staff Reports for the G20 Mutual Assessment Process (MAP), June 2012 IMF, Washington DC, USA.

[5] Blanchard and Milesi-Ferretti (2011).

[6] Garton et al. (2010).

given that it is a small economy dependent on world trade.[7] Whether this represents a 'good' imbalance may be debatable, for it could be argued that these surpluses are the result of distortions that encourage very high saving rates.

'Bad' imbalances are those that result from domestic problems or distortions.

- Examples of imbalances that can be detrimental include large current account surpluses that reflect structural shortcomings that lead to high national saving, such as a lack of social insurance or poor firm governance that allows them to retain excessive earnings.
- Conversely, detrimental low private saving may be the result of a bubble-driven boom in asset prices that are accommodated by policy shortcomings or distortions. In addition, high current account deficits could be driven by high public sector borrowing.
- Another distortion leading to imbalances may be through the rapid accumulation of reserves by countries either seeking to pursue an export-led growth strategy.

A further concern is that large imbalances may lead to 'disruptive adjustments'. As noted below, this was perhaps the main focus of attention with respect to imbalances prior to the global financial crisis.

Did the existence of large global imbalances in the period prior to 2008 cause the global financial crisis? Views are divided. As Obstfeld and Rogoff have noted:

> …controversy remains about the precise connection between global imbalances and the global financial meltdown. Some commentators argue that external imbalances had little or nothing to do with the crisis, which instead was the result of financial regulatory failures and policy errors, mainly on the part of the US. Others put forward various mechanisms through which global imbalances are claimed to have played a prime role in causing the financial collapse.[8]

The Governor of the Bank of England, Mervyn King, stated: *'global imbalances helped fuel the crisis'*.[9] The chairman of the US Federal Reserve, Ben Bernanke, said: *'In my view…it is impossible to understand this crisis without reference to the global imbalances in trade and capital flows that began in the latter half of the 1990s'.* Stephen Grenville observed that only a modest role should be given to external imbalances in terms of attributing blame for the crisis, but some adjustment in these imbalances is still desirable. This is not because external imbalances in themselves are inherently undesirable, but because some of the specific components of today's current imbalances are unsustainable.[10]

The IMF's recent pilot External Sector Report provides a 'balanced' summary when it notes[11]:

---

[7] Grenville (2009).

[8] Obstfeld and Rogoff (2009).

[9] King (2011).

[10] Ibid.

[11] IMF (2012).

> External imbalances added to global vulnerabilities by exacerbating domestic asset bubbles/busts and the attendant spillovers to the real economy. As with earlier emerging market crises, external imbalances were a symptom rather than the major driver of the global crisis, whose main causes were loose financial supervision and monetary policies which generated unsustainable asset booms in major advanced economies.

The debate over whether large global imbalances contributed to the global crisis illustrates the imprecision that can come from focusing on the existence of imbalances per se and not focusing directly on the cause of the imbalances. As the IMF notes, external imbalances can be a symptom of problems. Nevertheless, it is always better to focus on the causes of the problems rather than the symptoms.

However, imbalances are a symptom of the aggregate of many factors affecting the economy—some good, some bad, and the challenge is to separate out these influences. As with human health, it is often hard to identify underlying problems by just looking at some symptoms. Yet the challenge is to identify and tackle underlying problems causing the imbalances and to do so before they manifest themselves as chronic imbalances and become destabilizing.

In hindsight, the answer to the question, 'should more have been done about external imbalances prior to the crisis', is clearly 'yes'. The distortions that contributed to the rise in excessive external imbalances should have been addressed. However, at the time, the situation may not have been so clear-cut and the concern over the threat posed by large external imbalances may have been misplaced.

4 Why Multilateralism Pre-G20 Failed to Deal With Global Imbalances

In the period leading up to the financial crisis, the main multilateral responsibility for dealing with global imbalances rested with the IMF. But the ultimate responsibility for taking action to correct imbalances rested with the countries making up the membership of the Fund. In general, the Fund had little success in persuading countries to reduce their 'bad' imbalances.

The IMF's Independent Evaluation Office's examination of the performance of the IMF prior to the crisis concluded that, overall, there were few clear warnings from the IMF in advance of the impending crisis.[12] In fairness, the Fund did stress the need to deal with the risk of a disorderly unwinding of global imbalances.[13] It did not look, however, at how these imbalances were linked to the systematic risks building up in financial systems. Instead, it focused almost exclusively on the threat of an exchange rate crisis resulting from a pull-out from dollar assets, leading to a disorderly decline in the dollar and a spike in interest rates.

In the event, although there has been an unwinding of imbalances as a result of the financial crisis, it has not been accompanied by the anticipated US dollar crisis.

[12] IEO (2009).

[13] Ibid.

Rather than a flight from the US dollar, the greenback has become a safe haven against a background of financial instability.

As an example of the IMF's views on imbalances, the April 2005 IMF World Economic Outlook (WEO) focused on 'Globalisation and External Imbalances'. Here, the Fund noted its concern that large external current account imbalances, particularly the large US deficit, may result in large exchange rate adjustments with possibly disruptive effects on global financial markets.[14]

But the Fund also noted in the 2005 WEO that other observers were less concerned, arguing that a benign resolution of global imbalances was more likely given the existence of deep economic and financial markets. Larger external current account deficits and surpluses were presented as the natural outcome of increased scope for cross-border trade in financial assets.

Blanchard states that the potential risks presented by the imbalances were the focus of much discussion, which culminated in the 'multilateral consultations' held by the Fund in 2006–2007.[15] The multilateral consultations involved the USA, the euro area, China, Japan and Saudi Arabia. The objective was to outline the policy measures that should be undertaken by each of the countries in order to reduce global current account imbalances. However, the multilateral consultations could hardly be regarded as a great success in terms of countries adopting mutually consistent policies designed to reduce global imbalances.

Moreover, in a paper by Paul Blustein, which is based on unpublished IMF internal briefings and discussions, he suggests that the whole concept of the mutual consultations was primarily a way of defusing pressure from the USA for the Fund to categorize the Renminbi as 'fundamentally misaligned' and for the Fund to launch special consultations with China over its exchange rate policy.[16] The account provided by Blustein suggests that political 'wheeling-dealing' was the main driving force behind the multilateral consultations. The policy prescriptions were presented by the IMF, but countries were not willing to commit to them. If Blustein is right, the multilateral consultations process was conceived by the IMF, led by the IMF and was never embraced by the countries involved. In contrast, the G20 Mutual Assessment Process (MAP) is a country-led exercise, where the G20 invites technical assistance and advice from the IMF. As such, there should be a better prospect that the policy commitments made as part of the G20 MAP will have greater country ownership than was the case in the multilateral consultations.

5 The G20 Focus on External Imbalances

The quest to reduce global imbalances became a focus of the G20, in particular through the work of the IMF in assisting with the development of the MAP under the Framework for Strong, Sustainable and Balanced Growth. The evolution of the

[14] IMF (2005).

[15] Blanchard and Miles-Ferretti (2011).

[16] Blustein (2012).

G20's work has been summarized by Jean Pisani-Ferry, who has divided the G20's involvement in macroeconomic coordination into three phases:[17]

- The first phase from 2008–2009 was when the G20 focused on, using Pisani-Ferry's words, 'saving the world'. The focus was on coordinating a global stimulus, enhancing the resources of the IMF, and adding to global liquidity through a general SDR allocation.
- Phase two from 2010–2011 was when the G20 turned to what Pisani-Ferry describes as the *'conceptually debatable and politically delicate issue: the so-called global imbalances'*. He states that the intellectual background to the policy agenda was the fear that the recovery would leave pre-existing imbalances largely untouched.
- Phase three from 2011 to 2012 is described as the period of 'assisting Europe'. While the Cannes and Los Cabos summits were meant to be discussing global issues, both were largely hijacked by the euro crisis. In terms of responding to the threat posed by the euro crisis, Pisani-Ferry concludes, somewhat harshly, that the G20 failed to live up to its self-proclaimed title as the 'premier forum for international economic cooperation'.

How successful were the G20's efforts to deal with global imbalances in 2010–2011? The record is chequered, at best. Much of the debate was viewed in bilateral terms, in particular the trade imbalance between the USA and China, with the USA being concerned that China was maintaining an undervalued exchange rate in order to boost its export competitiveness.

As noted previously, there is a view that US pressure for the Renminbi to be labelled 'fundamentally misaligned' led the IMF to develop the multilateral consultations in 2007. In a similar vein, USA's frustration over the imbalance in its trade relationship with China and perceived undervaluation of the Renminbi resulted in the G20 embarking on a path in 2010 to develop 'indicative guidelines' to assess persistently large imbalances.

Immediately prior to the G20 meeting of Finance and Central Bank Governors in Korea in October 2010, the US Secretary to the Treasury, Tim Geithner, essentially proposed a cap be placed on the size of current account deficits and surpluses of G20 countries. Secretary Geithner wrote to his fellow G20 Finance Ministers on 22 October 2010 proposing, ' G20 countries should commit to undertake policies consistent with reducing external imbalances below a specified share of GDP over the next few years'. While the figure was not mentioned in his letter, it was widely understood that the proposed cap was 4% of GDP. This was a controversial proposal, which was opposed by a number of countries, including China and Germany. However, initially it came from Korea; the chair of the G20 in 2010 Changyong Rhee, the Korean G20 Sherpa, described Korea's support for a quantifiable current account target as a pragmatic response to the currency tensions that were mounting prior to the Seoul G20 summit.[18]

---

[17] Pisani-Ferry (2012).

[18] Rhee (2011).

The USA appeared to be looking for a way out of the exchange rate gridlock it had with China—a means to reframe the discussion with China and to foster a broader adjustment process involving both deficit and surplus countries.

An obvious problem with the concept of a quantitative target for the current account balance is that it fails to focus the policy attention on the causes of the imbalance or distinguish between 'good' and 'bad' imbalances. As Rhee noted:

> Critics pointed out that the current account imbalance is a result of international competitiveness, as well as a result of inter-temporal optimization of private sectors that reflect age profiles and savings–investment gaps[19].

With some G20 members strongly resisting the idea of a specific target for current account deficits and surpluses, the negotiated compromise was an agreement by the G20 at the Seoul Summit to:

> ...strengthen multilateral cooperation to promote external sustainability and pursue the full range of policies conducive to reducing excessive imbalances and maintaining current account imbalances at sustainable levels. Persistently large imbalances, assessed against indicative guidelines to be agreed by our Finance ministers and Central Bank governors, warrant an assessment of their nature and root causes of impediments to adjustment as part of the MAP, recognizing the need to take into account national or regional circumstances, including large commodity producers.

After much discussion by officials, a set of indicative guidelines for identifying persistently large imbalances was adopted by G20 Finance and Central Bank Governors at their meeting in April 2011. The process was to a large extent 'reverse engineered' to ensure that the imbalances of major economies were included in the assessment. Seven economies were identified for *sustainability assessments of imbalances:* China, India, Japan, France, Germany, USA and the UK.

These indicative guidelines were used by the IMF to assess the underlying causes of the imbalances and make corresponding recommendations. The overall policy implication coming from the assessments identified by the IMF in the *Sustainability Report* prepared for the Cannes Summit was straightforward:

> Broadly speaking, sustainability assessments indicate that imbalances have been driven primarily by saving imbalances—too low in major advanced economies and too high in key emerging surplus economies.[20]

Policy recommendations were tailored to suit the circumstances of individual countries but essentially involved appropriately timed and paced fiscal consolidation across the major advanced deficit economies and to offset weaker demand in major advanced partner countries, an increase in internal demand in the major surplus economies, in particular China, by reducing the distortions that have kept savings high.

Changyong Rhee concluded that the significant outcome from the Seoul Summit was that it provided political momentum to reduce global imbalances, '*an objective that has been long declared but has lacked follow through*'.[21]

---

[19] Ibid.

[20] IMF (2011).

[21] Rhee (2011).

It is still not possible, however, to say that the long-awaited 'follow through' has been delivered. In the IMF's October 2012 WEO, it notes that, despite recent improvements, global imbalances and associated vulnerabilities are likely to remain well above desirable levels unless governments take additional, decisive action. The IMF's assessment in early 2013 was that 'global imbalances have narrowed considerably, but old challenges remain unaddressed'.[22] The Fund's view is that much of the adjustment in global imbalances in recent years has come from demand compression in crisis-stricken economies, rather than from necessary fiscal and structural adjustments.

Pisani-Ferry's view is that the G20 has failed to deliver in reducing global imbalances and the reasons for this failure include[23]

- There was no consensus among economists on the risks involved in the persistence of global imbalances. Moreover, the pattern of imbalances had changed with the reduction in the Chinese surplus and rise of those of oil-producing countries.
- Previous attempts at global discussions on imbalances, such as the IMF's 2007 multilateral consultations, had failed to deliver any meaningful result.
- It was not clear that the participating countries were ready to change their own policy for a change in a partner's policy. The G20 economies were not prepared to enter into the 'grand bargain' called for by Mervyn King.[24]

Pisani-Ferry also notes that as other problems come along, such as sovereign solvency risks in Europe, a continued focus on global imbalances may be seen as a distraction. To keep focusing on the same issue in international forums may help narrow down differences, but the process takes time. It also takes time to get a large group of countries like the G20 to embrace more cooperative action when some of the participants are not used to speaking openly with others about their policy choices. However, keeping the policymakers focused on one set of issues may be at the expense of other, more pressing issues. The focus of the G20 following the 2010 Seoul Summit on the development of 'indicative guidelines' to assess persistently large imbalances was a distraction within the G20. A great deal of time, effort and political capital was used up in the first few months of the French presidency in 2011 to agree on the indicators to identify which countries to assess for persistently large imbalances, despite the fact that it was already clear which countries had imbalances that needed to be assessed. While the focus of the G20 in the first months of 2011 was on developing 'indicative guidelines', the European debt crisis was building and was portrayed as 'hijacking' the Cannes Summit in November 2011.

---

[22] IMF (2013).

[23] Pisani-Ferry (2012).

[24] King (2011).

6 The IMF's Pilot External Sector Report

While progress within the G20 on reducing external imbalances may not have been a priority at Los Cabos, the IMF has recently initiated a new product focused on external imbalances with its Pilot External Sector Report.[25] The need for such a product was identified in the IMF's 2011 Triennial Surveillance Review, and it is intended to provide a mutually consistent analysis of the external positions of major world economies.

One advantage of the approach taken in the external sector report is that it recognizes that not all imbalances are undesirable and it focuses on current account imbalances that differ from those warranted by fundamentals and desirable policies. The Report examines the drivers of external positions and assesses the extent to which they: (1) abate over the cycle; (2) reflect policy distortions and potential vulnerabilities and (3) are warranted by fundamentals.

The conclusions from the pilot report are not surprising, with the assessment that policy actions are needed across many nations as most of the economies analysed had balances that were to some degree out of line with fundamentals. In terms of policy adjustments, the conclusion was that many advanced economies needed large and evenly paced fiscal consolidations. In many emerging markets, structural reforms were required, including more flexible product and labour markets, changing social protection to reduce precautionary saving, and, in some cases, reduced foreign exchange intervention and capital flow management measures.

7 Will the IMF's Pilot External Assessment Report Result in a Renewed Focus on Reducing Global Imbalances?

As with all IMF surveillances, the effectiveness of the External Assessment reports will depend on how persuasive the analysis is and how it can contribute to domestic policy debates. While the External Assessment Report can be said to be delivering on the IMF's mandate to exercise surveillance over exchange rates by examining broad aspects of members' external positions, it may not receive the necessary traction required to achieve policy action because dealing with global external imbalances is not seen as a policy priority of members.

The focus of countries at the moment is on achieving growth, and, for policy advice to resonate, it should be clearly focused on what steps are necessary to achieve economic growth and reduce unemployment. It is difficult to see a policymaker picking up the language in the Report and arguing that ambitious policy reforms are required in order to 'move current accounts to the levels implied by fundamentals and desirable policies'.

---

[25] IMF (2012).

The other aspect that may reduce the effectiveness of the External Assessment Report is that there is still the element of 'black box' in terms of assessing whether current accounts differ from those warranted by fundamentals and desirable policies.

The comments in the IMF's October 2012 WEO provide the basis of an approach to the issue of dealing with current account imbalances, which may get more resonance with policymakers. The IMF points out those policies that would most effectively lower global imbalances and related vulnerabilities that serve the self-interests of the countries concerned, 'even when considered purely from a domestic viewpoint'. Politicians will always put the prime focus on the 'domestic viewpoint'. There will not be domestic support for policy measures unless it is evident that there are domestic benefits. It is rare to find a domestic constituency prepared to support economic pain at home for the overall health of the global economy, even if the latter ultimately benefits the home country as well. In fact, from the policymaker's perspective, in seeking public support for policy measures, the case is likely to be presented 'purely from a domestic viewpoint'. As summed up by Dadush and Suominen[26]:

> …the reality is that none of the large G20 economies will correct the drivers of the imbalances—China pushing for domestic consumption or the United States defusing its fiscal time bomb—unless domestic politics align and such actions are in these nations' interest. They will not do so just because the G20 decided these might be global desirables.

As such, if the IMF wants to gain greater traction with its policy advice aimed at reducing external imbalances, it would be wise to present this more forcefully in terms of the domestic gains accruing to countries.

8 Conclusion

As noted at the outset, the conclusion from this brief overview is that, while a focus on efforts to reduce global imbalances is fertile ground for economists and academics, it does not capture the attention of the policymaker. The challenge facing the policymaker is to convince an often sceptical public that a proposed course of action is in the best interest of the public. This is unlikely to be the case if the reason for a policy course of action is presented as helping to reduce 'global economic imbalances'. What people are interested in is obtaining and maintaining a job and improving their standard of living.

This is not to say that external imbalances are not an area of concern, or that there are no circumstances where measures should be taken to reduce them. But it is not always clear that imbalances are a problem. Moreover, it is not clear that authorities have the instruments to control external imbalances. For example, the USA may implement a credible medium-term fiscal consolidation plan, yet if its status as a safe

[26] Dadush and Suominen (2011).

haven grows against a background of global instability, capital will continue to flow into the USA and the exchange rate will appreciate. The US deficit would increase. However, this does not diminish the need for the USA to pursue medium-term fiscal consolidation, and this should be the focus of the Fund's policy advice. Moreover, with the ageing of populations in Asia, there are sound reasons to see these countries run large current account surpluses in the medium term.

Furthermore, as Pisani-Ferry has noted, focusing on global imbalances can prove to be a distraction from dealing with underlying problems and more immediate risks.[27] The G20's focus in the first half of 2011 on developing indicative guidelines for assessing persistently large imbalances was a distraction.

In terms of winning the public policy debate in order to get measures accepted, the focus should be squarely presented on what is required to achieve sustained economic and jobs growth, and not in terms of dealing with global imbalances.

References

Blanchard O, Milkes-Ferretti GM (2011 March) (Why) Should current account balances be reduced. IMF Staff Discussion Note

Blustein P (2012 June) A flop and debacle: inside the IMF's global rebalancing acts. CIGI Papers

Dadush U, Suominen K (2011) Is there life for the G20 beyond the global financial crisis? J Glob Dev 2(2)

Deutisch A, Dyer G (2010) Obama calls for G20 to act on imbalances. Financial Times, 9 November 2010

Grenville S (2009 September) External Imbalances and the G20. Lowy Institute for International Policy

Garton P, Sedgwick M, Shirodkar S (2010) Australia's current account deficit in a global imbalances context. Treasury Economic Roundup, (1):29–50

IEO Background Paper. (2009 December) IMF performance in the run-up to the financial and economic crisis: bilateral surveillance in selected IMF member countries

IMF (2005 April) World economic outlook, globalization and external imbalances

IMF (2011) G20 Mutual assessment process: from Pittsburgh to Cannes—IMF Umbrella Report

IMF (2012 July) Pilot external sector report

IMF (2013) Global prospects and policy challenges, meetings of G20 Finance Ministers and Central Bank Governors February 15–16, Washington DC

King M (2011 February) Global Imbalances: the Perspective of the Bank of England. Banque de France Financial Stability Report

National Perspectives on Global Leadership (2012) Soundings Series No 7: Los Cabos, Centre for International Governance and Innovation, Canada

Obstfeld M, Rogoff K (2009 October). Global imbalances and the financial crisis: products of common causes. Federal Reserve Bank of San Francisco Asia Economic policy conference

Pisani-Ferry J (2012 June) Macroeconomic coordination: what has the G20 achieved. Think Tank 20

Rhee C (2011 September) From Seoul to Cannes; What has the G20 Delivered so far. FPQ

Vox (2011) Research. www.voxeu.org/article/g20-and-global imbalances. Accessed 26 June 2011

[27] Ibid.

Global Imbalances: Causes and Policies to Address Them

Emil Stavrev

Global imbalances, which culminated in the wake of the Great Recession, have been one of the most complex macroeconomic issues facing economists and policy makers. They have reflected differences in a number of factors in many countries, including saving, investment, and portfolio decisions. The cross-country differences in saving patterns, investment patterns, and portfolio choices can be "good"—a natural reflection of differences in levels of development, demographic patterns, and other underlying economic fundamentals. However, they can also be "bad", reflecting distortions and risks at the national and international level.

To understand the nature of large imbalances, their root causes, and impediments to adjustment that may undermine growth, IMF undertook an in-depth assessment of global imbalances in the context of the G20 Mutual Assessment Process (MAP).[1] The Sustainability Report identified seven systemic members (China, France, Germany, India, Japan, the UK, and the USA) as having "moderate" or "large" imbalances that warranted more in-depth analysis. Sustainability assessments indicated that global imbalances have been driven primarily by saving imbalances—generally too low in advanced deficit economies and too high in emerging surplus economies—owing to a combination of equilibrium factors (demographic patterns), structural weaknesses, and domestic distortions. The assessments further suggested that corrective steps, including through collaborative action, aimed at addressing structural impediments and underlying distortions, would be needed to better support G20 growth objectives.

[1] The result from the analysis was published in a 2011 Sustainability Report—see for details: https://www.imf.org/external/np/g20/map2011.htm.

E. Stavrev (✉)
Multilateral Surveillance Division, Research Department,
International Monetary Fund, Washington, DC, USA
e-mail: EStavrev@imf.org

M. Callaghan et al. (eds.), *Global Cooperation Among G20 Countries*,
DOI 10.1007/978-81-322-1659-9_8, © Springer India 2014

1 Imbalances—Conceptual Issues

A framework approach of "internal and external balance" provides a sound analytical foundation for analyzing global imbalances. The framework is well suited toward identifying, assessing, and addressing "large and persistent" imbalances in key dimensions that could jeopardize G20 growth objectives. The key elements include notions of *external* and *internal balance*, which are grounded in the concepts of macroeconomic equilibrium over the medium term (see Blanchard and Milesi-Ferretti 2009, 2011 for further discussion).

The framework allows us to study the linkages between internal and external imbalances. The current account reflects the excess or shortfall of national saving over investment, and, thus, connects external and internal imbalances. Moreover, viewing current accounts through the prism of saving–investment balances provides a good sense of various interlinkages and the levers for adjustment. The analysis of internal imbalances focuses primarily on public finances—cyclically adjusted primary balances (CAPBs) and public debt—since large fiscal imbalances are likely to bear upon external imbalances, can stifle growth, and can heighten vulnerability to market financing pressures. The examination of external imbalances focuses primarily on the current account—a core component of the balance of payments, which provides a concise summary of a country's net external position.

Imbalances are not prima facie "bad" and warrant remedial action only to the extent that they are underpinned by distortions.[2] In particular, imbalances may reflect differences in saving and investment patterns and portfolio choices across countries, owing to differences in levels of development, demographic patterns, and other underlying economic fundamentals. Imbalances can be beneficial if they reflect the optimal allocation of capital across time and space. For instance, to meet its life-cycle needs, a country with an aging population relative to its trading partner may choose to save and run current account surpluses in anticipation of the dissaving that will occur when the workforce shrinks. Similarly, a country with attractive investment opportunities may wish to finance part of its investment through foreign saving and thus run a current account deficit. Such imbalances are not a reason for concern.

At the same time, however, imbalances may also reflect policy distortions, market failures, and externalities at the level of individual economies or at a global level. Imbalances can be detrimental if they reflect structural shortcomings, policy distortions, or market failures. For instance, large current account surpluses may reflect high national saving unrelated to the life-cycle needs of a country but instead that related to structural shortcomings, such as a lack of social insurance or poor governance of firms that allows them to retain excessive earnings. Similarly, countries could be running large current account deficits because of low private saving,

[2] For further discussion see: Blanchard and Milesi-Ferretti 2009, "Global Imbalances: In Midstream?," IMF Staff Position Note 09/29 (www.imf.org/external/pubs/ft/spn/2009/spn0929.pdf).

owing to asset-price booms that are being fueled or accommodated by policy distortions in the financial system that impede markets from equilibrating.

Imbalances could also reflect systemic distortions, reflected, for instance, in the rapid accumulation of reserves by some countries to maintain an undervalued exchange rate. Such imbalances are a cause of concern, since they could undermine the strength and the sustainability of growth.

2 Explaining Imbalances

The sources of external imbalances in the run up to the crisis vary significantly across the seven economies, largely reflecting factors that have led domestic saving to differ widely. Current account deficits before the crisis have reflected low public and private saving in key advanced deficit economies, or low public saving, which has been partly offset by high private saving. Surpluses, on the other hand, have reflected high national saving in key emerging surplus economies, owing, in particular, to exceptionally high private saving that exceeds high private investment, or positive private saving–investment balances in key advanced surplus economies, due to high saving and low investment, which has offset high (modest) public dissaving in some cases.

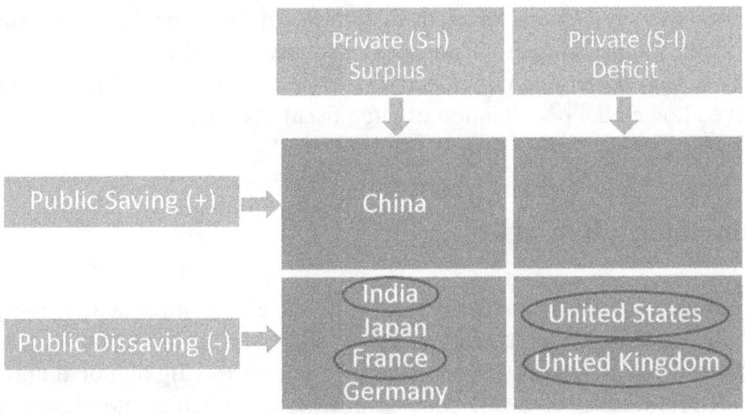

A variety of structural and equilibrium factors have driven public saving behavior. Fiscal deficits have been underpinned by several forces, specifically: (i) persistently low growth, reflecting a decline in productivity, a shrinking labor force, and low investment (Japan); (ii) structural imbalances between tax revenues and spending commitments pre-crisis, including underfunded entitlement obligations (France, the UK, and the USA); (iii) the lack of fiscal rules and strict enforcement mechanisms to impose sufficient budgetary discipline; (iv) political economy considerations exerting strong pressure on spending and resistance to raising taxes (India, Japan, and the USA); and (v) financial repression in some emerging economies.

However, domestic policy distortions (defined broadly as factors that impede a market from equilibrating) have also played an important role in driving imbalances.

Distortions in financial systems in key advanced economies have fueled low private saving and large current account deficits. The distortions, pertaining to regulatory and supervisory frameworks, were partly responsible for a fundamental breakdown in market discipline and mispricing of risk (reflected in credit and housing booms) and contributed to a widening of external imbalances in major advanced deficit economies, notably the USA and UK. Weak private saving–investment imbalances before the crisis have played a role in fueling current account deficits in major advanced economies.

The high national saving in China reflects significant underlying distortions. Policy distortions or gaps—inadequate social-safety nets, restrictive financial conditions, an undervalued exchange rate, subsidized factor costs, limited dividends, and lack of competition in product markets—have underpinned exceptionally high national saving and, in turn, current account surpluses. Large current account and balance of payment surpluses have, in turn, led to massive reserve accumulation in China (and elsewhere), contributing to the low-cost financing of US current account deficits.

Weak investment in advanced surpluses economies also reflects policy distortions (Japan and Germany). Specifically, favorable private saving–investment balances reflect, in part, either distortions that keep private investment growth weak, while corporate savings are large, or distortions in the financial sector may be a drag on domestic investment. Distortions have also played a role in fueling public dissaving in some emerging deficit economies (India), where tight financial restrictions have allowed the perpetuation of large fiscal deficits.

3 Concluding Remarks

Global imbalances have narrowed markedly, as global trade and activity have slowed down. Most of the adjustment took place during the Great Recession of 2008–2009, when global growth was negative. The narrowing of global imbalances mainly reflects weaker domestic demand in external-deficit economies rather than stronger demand from external-surplus economies. However, healthier adjustments have also taken place: fiscal balances in external-deficit economies have improved, while domestic demand in China has been strong and oil exporters have increased their social spending, bringing down their large surpluses.

Additional decisive action by policy makers is needed to durably reduce global imbalances and the associated vulnerabilities. It must be emphasized that the policies that would most effectively lower global imbalances and related vulnerabilities are very much in the national interests of the countries concerned, even when considered purely from a domestic viewpoint. Many external-deficit economies need strong medium-term fiscal adjustment programs. The policy priorities for emerging market economies with external surpluses and undervalued currencies are to cut back official reserve accumulation, adopt more market-determined exchange systems, and implement structural reforms, for example, to broaden the social safety net.

Broadly speaking, sustainability assessments indicate that imbalances have been driven primarily by saving imbalances. Specifically, saving in major advanced economies has been too low, while it has been too high in key emerging surplus economies. This, in turn, implies that policy makers need to continue their efforts to further promote the dual rebalancing acts—a shift from public to private demand led growth in major advanced economies and a shift from growth led by domestic demand in major advanced deficit economies toward external demand and vice versa in major emerging surplus economies.

Accordingly, country-specific policies are needed to address underlying distortions to facilitate the dual rebalancing acts. Such policies will also help anchor the shared G20 growth objectives of strong, sustainable, and balanced growth. In particular, fiscal consolidation that is appropriately timed and paced is needed across major advanced economies to reduce persistent deficits, create policy space, and anchor sustainability. Fiscal consolidation will, however, depress growth in the near term. Hence, closing the output gap will require complementary policies. In addition, growth in these countries will need to be fueled by higher net exports. To offset weaker demand in major advanced countries, internal demand will need to increase elsewhere, notably the surplus countries, to support domestic and global growth. This will require lower national saving in key emerging surplus economies, notably by reducing the distortions that have kept saving exceptionally high. There is also room to bolster domestic demand by reducing private saving–investment balances in advanced surplus economies, notably by lowering corporate saving and boosting investment by reducing distortions.

References

Blanchard O, Milesi-Ferretti G-M (2009) Global imbalances: in midstream? In: O Blanchard, Il SaKong (eds) Reconstructing the world economy. International Monetary Fund, Washington

Blanchard O, Milesi-Ferretti G-M (2011) (Why) should current account balances be reduced? IMF Staff Discussion Note 11/03. International Monetary Fund, Washington

Exchange Rate Flexibility and Economic Rebalancing in China

Takuji Kinkyo

1 The Flexibility of China's Exchange Rate Regime

China has long been accused of keeping the renminbi undervalued so that its export competitiveness can be maintained (IMF 2004; Bergsten et al. 2009). In response to the international pressures to increase flexibility in the exchange rate regime, the Chinese government introduced a new exchange rate regime in July 2005. Under this regime, the renminbi would be managed with reference to a basket of currencies rather than a single currency of the US dollar. However, the renminbi–dollar rate is kept within a narrow band by massive official interventions in foreign exchange markets and its central rate has been allowed to appreciate only gradually.

In response to the Asian financial crisis of 1997–1998, crisis-hit Asian countries abandoned *de facto* dollar pegs and officially claimed to adopt floating exchange rate regimes. However, it is widely recognised that there is a discrepancy between *de jure* and *de facto* exchange rate regimes (Calvo and Reinhart 2002). In fact, there is no consensus on the type of *de facto* exchange rate regimes in post-crisis Asian countries (Reinhart and Rogoff 2004; McKinnon 2005; Cohen 2008; Kawai 2008).

Drawing on methodology originally developed by Frankel and Wei (1994), Kinkyo (2012) empirically examines the behaviour of exchange rates to identify *de facto* exchange rate regimes in East Asia after the crisis of 1997–1998. Engle's (2002) dynamic conditional correlation (DCC) model is used to estimate the time-varying conditional correlation among the exchange rates of four Asian currencies (Thai baht, Korean won, Indonesia rupiah, and Chinese renminbi) and three major

T. Kinkyo (✉)
Graduate School of Economics, Kobe University,
2-1, Rokkodai, Nada-ku, Kobe 657-8501, Japan
e-mail: kinkyo@econ.kobe-u.ac.jp

Policy Research Institute, Ministry of Finance,Tokyo, Japan

M. Callaghan et al. (eds.), *Global Cooperation Among G20 Countries*,
DOI 10.1007/978-81-322-1659-9_9, © Springer India 2014

currencies (US dollar, euro, and Japanese yen)[1]. In doing so, the paper seeks to identify the anchor currency and measure the time-varying degree of exchange rate flexibility in post-crisis Asia.

Figure 1a–d reproduces the results of Kinkyo (2012) using the updated data covering the period from the first week of 1994 to the last week of June 2013. The DCC model is estimated for weekly changes in the currency values, which are measured using the Swiss franc as a numeraire. Prior to 1997, all four Asian currencies exhibit correlations close to 1 against the dollar. The results indicate that the dollar served as a nominal anchor for these currencies and their *de facto* exchange rate regimes were dollar pegs before the Asian financial crisis. Following the collapse of dollar pegs in the wake of the crisis, there was a sharp decline in the correlation between the crisis-hit Asian currencies (baht, won, and rupiah) and the dollar. In sharp contrast, the correlation between the renminbi and the dollar remained as strong as before the crisis, indicating that China's dollar peg survived the crisis.

The correlation between the three crisis-hit currencies and the dollar rose again after 1999. However, the correlation became weaker and much more volatile than before the crisis. The correlations of these Asian currencies with the yen and the euro remained as weak and volatile as before the crisis. These results indicate that the degree of flexibility in the post-crisis exchange rate regimes in Thailand, Korea, and Indonesia has increased substantially. There seems to have been neither a revival of dollar pegs nor a shift towards multiple-currency basket pegs in these countries. Their exchange rate regimes can be best characterised as managed floating rates with a varying degree of flexibility.

A notable exception is China. There seems to have been no fundamental change to the exchange rate regimes in China throughout the sample period. Although the renminbi–dollar correlation declined below 0.9 immediately after the introduction of a new exchange rate regime in 2005, it soon returned to a level above 0.98 and remained at approximately the same level until mid-2013. The strong renminbi–dollar correlation indicates that the renminbi continued to be managed very tightly with reference to the dollar.

2 The Undervaluation of the Renminbi

While the pace of the renminbi's appreciation has been slow, its accumulated appreciation has been substantial since 2005 and China's current account surplus has declined sharply from the peak level before the global financial crisis of 2008–2009. However, there are also some indications that the renminbi still remains undervalued

[1] The DCC model is a class of multivariate generalised autoregressive conditionally heteroscedastic (GARCH) models, which not only allow the conditional variance of a variable to depend on the realised volatilities in previous periods but also allow for volatility spillovers in the sense that volatility shocks to one variable could affect the volatility of other related variables. See Enders (2010, pp. 179–180) for an accessible description of the DCC model.

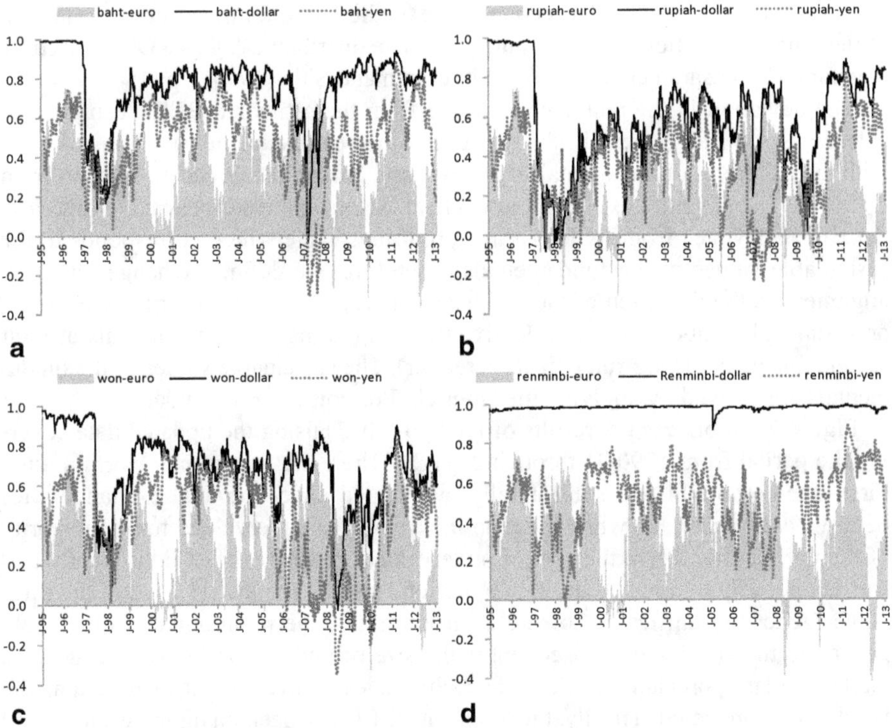

Fig. 1 **a** Conditional correlation (Thai baht). **b** Conditional correlation (Korean won). **c** Conditional correlation (Indonesian rupiah). **d** Conditional correlation (Chinese renminbi)

substantially. For example, China's exports continue to grow faster than the global average and its current account surplus would rise again as a share of world GDP according to the International Monetary Fund (IMF)'s projection.[2] These observations naturally raise the following questions: To what extent has the undervaluation of the renminbi been rectified? Will the reduction of undervaluation be sustained? If not, what are the causes and what should be done?

Kinkyo (2013) addresses these questions by estimating the equilibrium exchange rate of the renminbi using Clark and MacDonald's (1999) behavioural equilibrium exchange rate (BEER) approach. The real exchange rate is explicitly modelled as a function of a set of fundamental variables, namely, the productivity differential, net foreign assets, and terms of trade. The productivity differential will capture the Balassa–Samuelson effect (Balassa 1964; Samuelson 1964)[3]. Estimates of the BEER are derived from the equilibrium relation between the real exchange rate and

[2] China's current account surplus as a share of world GDP is calculated using the data from the IMF's World Economic Outlook Database published in April 2013. The share is projected to rise from 0.30 % in 2012 to 0.66 % in 2017, which is close to the pre-crisis peak of 0.69 % in 2008.

[3] The Balassa–Samuelson effect is a tendency for countries with higher productivity in the traded relative to the non-traded goods sector to have more appreciated real exchange rates.

the fundamental variables. The econometric method used for the test and estimation of the long-run relationship is the autoregressive distributed-lag (ARDL) procedure developed by Pesaran et al. (1996) and Pesaran and Shin (1999).

The deviation in the real exchange rate from the estimated BEER can be considered as a misalignment in the sense that the real exchange rate is not in line with the underlying fundamentals. However, the fundamentals can also depart from their sustainable values as a result of cyclical factors and disturbances. In this case, the BEER deviates from its long-run equilibrium value which corresponds to the sustainable values of the fundamentals. Therefore, we define exchange rate misalignment as the deviation of the real exchange rate from the long-run equilibrium or sustainable value of the BEER given by calibrating the fundamentals at their sustainable values (long-run BEER, hereafter). The sustainable values of the fundamentals are derived by applying the Hodrick–Prescott filter to the data.

Figure 2 reproduces the results of Kinkyo (2013) using the updated data covering the period from 1990Q1 through 2011Q4. There are four points worth noting. Firstly, the renminbi was substantially overvalued under the dual exchange rates before 1994.[4] Secondly, while the renminbi remained undervalued for the majority of the period after 1994, the size of undervaluation was reduced significantly and was temporarily eliminated during the period between the late 1990s and the early 2000s. After the unification of the exchange rates, the renminbi was effectively pegged to the US dollar. Consequently, the size of undervaluation was reduced as the US dollar appreciated against other currencies; conversely, it increased as the US dollar depreciated. Thirdly, the long-run BEER has been on an increasing trend for most of the sample period. The major factors that contributed to the increase in the long-run BEER are the Balassa–Samuelson effect and the accumulation of net foreign assets. There was a reversal in this trend due to the worsening of terms of trade in the early 2000s. However, the long-run BEER returned to an increasing trend after 2005 as the accumulation of net foreign assets accelerated. Finally, the size of undervaluation remained large even after a new exchange rate regime was introduced in July 2005. Despite its continued appreciation under the new regime, the renminbi remained substantially undervalued before the global financial crisis. After the Lehman shock in September 2008, the renminbi's pace of appreciation accelerated following the strengthening of the US dollar. As a result, the misalignment of the renminbi was reduced significantly. However, the reduction in its undervaluation proved to be temporary as the renminbi began to depreciate again following the weakening of the US dollar after 2009. Consequently, the average size of undervaluation reached 10 % in 2011 (see Fig. 3).

These findings suggest that the fundamental cause of the renminbi's persistent undervaluation is the lack of flexibility in China's exchange rate regime. The renminbi is not appreciating fast enough in nominal terms to close the gap arising from the changes in underlying fundamentals, notably the rise in productivity and the accumulation of net foreign assets.

---

[4] Prior to the unification of exchange rates in January 1994, China adopted a dual exchange rate regime.

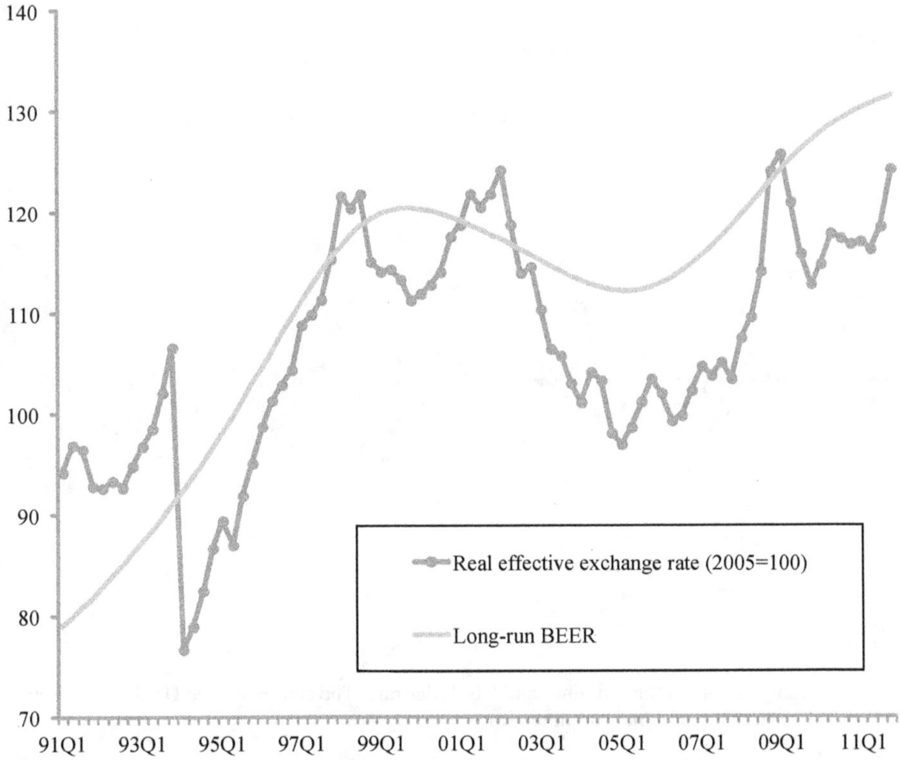

Fig. 2 Long-run BEER of the renminbi

The fundamental solution to the renminbi's chronic problem of undervaluation is to introduce a more flexible exchange rate regime under which the exchange rate is determined more closely by market supply and demand. By doing so, the exchange rate should be allowed to converge to the equilibrium value consistent with underlying fundamentals over the medium term, thereby preventing large and persistent misalignments.

3 Promoting Economic Rebalancing in China

Greater flexibility in the exchange rate regime will help China to promote economic rebalancing through two broad channels. Firstly, by allowing the real exchange rates to appreciate in line with underlying fundamentals, exchange rate flexibility will reduce exports and increase imports, thereby narrowing external imbalances. Real exchange rate appreciation will also promote rebalancing in China's production and investment structures. The undervaluation of the renminbi effectively provides

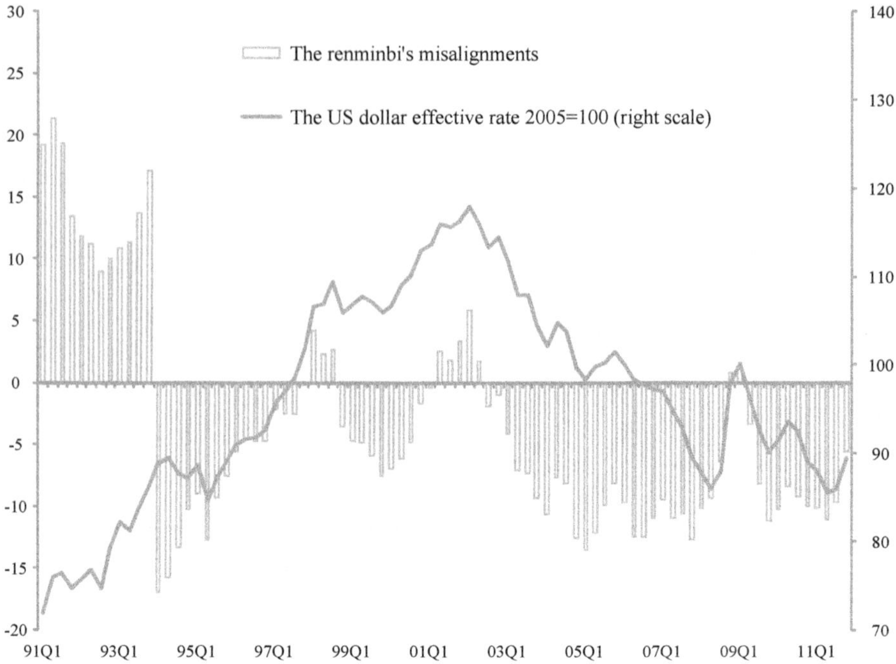

Fig. 3 Misalignments of the renminbi and US dollar rate. The source for the US dollar effective rate is IMF, International Financial Statistics

manufacturing sectors with subsidies by increasing the relative price of tradable goods to non-tradable goods. Eliminating the bias in relative prices will contribute to shifting production and investment towards the service sectors and away from the manufacturing sectors. One of the key driving forces that will facilitate such rebalancing is a sectoral shift in foreign direct investment (FDI). China's growth in the manufacturing sector has been led by FDI, and nearly half of China's exports are accounted for by foreign-owned enterprises. Real exchange rate appreciation will discourage FDI in export-oriented manufacturing sectors while encouraging FDI in the service sectors by rebalancing the relative price between the two sectors.

Another possible channel for rebalancing is interest rate liberalisation that allows bank deposit rate to rise. Currently, bank deposit rates are kept low by the central bank to create profit margins for commercial banks. In return, commercial banks are required to purchase bills issued by the central bank to sterilise massive foreign exchange market interventions. In this regard, exchange rate flexibility is a prerequisite for interest rate liberalisation (Lardy 2012). Interest rate liberalisation will allow deposit rates to rise, which will increase household income and consumption provided that the income effect dominates the substitution effect.[5]

[5] The response of household-saving rates to changes in interest rates will depend on the relative strength of substitution and income effects. Lardy (2012) argues that the primary motivation of

Exchange rate flexibility is also required to enhance monetary policy autonomy. As the proposition of impossible trinity suggests, fixed exchange rates and an autonomous monetary policy cannot co-exist with free capital movement.[6] As China promotes further integration with global capital markets by removing capital controls, exchange rate flexibility will be necessary to create greater room for countercyclical monetary policy that safeguards against capital flow volatility. Greater macroeconomic stability secured by effective monetary policy will stimulate household consumption by decreasing uncertainty and thus reducing precautionary saving.

In summary, greater flexibility in China's exchange rate regime is necessary to eliminate distortions in relative prices and create the preconditions for further economic reforms. In these important ways, exchange rate flexibility will help China promote economic rebalancing and achieve sustainable growth.

References

Balassa B (1964) The purchasing-power parity doctrine: a reappraisal. J Polit Econ 72:584–596

Bergsten CF, Freeman C, Lardy NR, Mitchell DJ (2009) China's rise: challenges and opportunities. Peterson Institute for International Economics and Center for Strategic and International Studies, Washington DC

Calvo GA, Reinhart CM (2002) Fear of floating. Q J Econ 117:379–408

Cohen BJ (2008) After the fall: east Asian exchange rates since the crisis. In: Macintyre A, Pempel TJ, Ravenhill J (eds) Crisis as catalyst: Asia's dynamic political economy. Cornell University Press, London, pp 25–44

Clark P, MacDonald R (1999) Exchange rates and economic fundamentals: a methodological comparison of BEERs and FEERs. In: Stein J, MacDonald R (eds) Equilibrium exchange rates. Kluwer, Boston, pp 285–322

Enders W (2010) Applied econometric time series, 3rd edn. Wiley, New Jersey

Engle RF (2002) Dynamic conditional correlation—a simple class of multivariate GARCH models. J Bus Econ Stat 20:367–381

Frankel J (1999) No single currency regime is right for all countries or at all times. NBER working paper 7338, National Bureau of Economic Research, Massachusetts

Frankel J, Wei S-J (1994) Yen block or dollar block? Exchange rate policies of the east Asian economies. In: Ito T, Krueger AO (eds) Macroeconomic linkages: savings, exchange rates and capital flows. Chicago University Press, Chicago, pp 295–333

IMF (2004) People' Republic of China: 2004 Article IV Consultation IMF Country Report 064/351. IMF, Washington DC

Kawai M (2008) Toward a regional exchange rate regime in east Asia. Pac Econ Rev 13:83–103

Kinkyo T (2012) De facto exchange rate regimes in post-crisis Asia. Econ Bull 32:2155–2165

Kinkyo T (2013) Is the Renminbi appreciating fast enough? In: Kinkyo T, Matsubayashi Y, Hamori S (eds) Global linkages and economic rebalancing in east Asia. World Scientific Publishing, Singapore, pp 193–209

Chinese households to save is to achieve a target level of savings in an environment of underdeveloped social security systems. Under such circumstances, the income effect is likely to dominate the substitution effect; thus, household saving rates will increase in response to an increase in deposit rates.

[6] See Frankel (1999) for the discussion of impossible trinity in the context of the choice of exchange rate regimes.

Lardy NR (2012) Sustaining China's economic growth. Peterson Institute for International Economics, Washington DC

McKinnon RI (2005) Exchange rates under the east Asian Dollar standard: living with conflicted virtue. MIT Press, Massachusetts

Pesaran MH, Shin Y (1999) An autoregressive distributed lag modelling approach to cointegration analysis. In: Strom S (ed) Econometrics and economic theory in 20th century: The Ragnar Frisch Centennial symposium. Cambridge University Press, Cambridge, pp 371–413

Pesaran MH, Shin Y, Smith RJ (1996) Testing for the existence of a long run relationship. DAE Working Paper, No. 9622, University of Cambridge

Reinhart CM, Rogoff KS (2004) The modern history of exchange rate arrangements: a reinterpretation. Q J Econ 119:1–48

Samuelson PA (1964) Theoretical notes on trade problems. Rev Econ Stat 46:145–154

Global Imbalances and Financial Fragility

Jong Kook Shin and Chetan Subramanian

1 Global Imbalances

Global current account imbalances are not a new phenomenon and have been around since the 1980s. However, as pointed out by Serven and Nguyen (2010), two key features distinguish the global imbalances of the 1980s from the ones that we have witnessed in the last two decades: First, the magnitude of the imbalances in the 1980s was relatively modest compared to what we have witnessed more recently. Second, the external deficits of the USA and other advanced countries in the 1980s were largely funded by advanced countries such as Japan and Germany. In contrast, the recent imbalances of the advanced countries have been funded by emerging markets. This means that the most recent phase of global imbalances is characterized by the Lucas Paradox, (Lucas 1990) wherein capital flowed from poorer to richer countries. The pre-crisis debates largely centered on the sustainability of these current account imbalances and the threats they posed to the global economy.

The broad consensus in the pre-crisis period was that global imbalances were not sustainable. This was because they reflected macroeconomic imbalances such as exchange rate misalignment among major countries, the low savings rates, and widened fiscal deficits of current account deficit countries. The correction of these imbalances would necessitate a US current account adjustment, a reversal of capital flows and a major depreciation of the dollar. The general consensus among the proponents of this view was that the magnitude of the exchange rate and trade adjustment required was significant and the global economy would be subject to a hard landing.

C. Subramanian (✉)
Department of Economics and Social Sciences,
Indian Institute of Management Bangalore, Bannergatta Road,
Bengaluru 560076, India
e-mail: chetan.s@iimb.ernet.in

J. K. Shin
Management School Riddel Hall, Queen's University,
185 Stranmilis Road, BT9 5EE, Belfast, Northern Ireland, UK
e-mail: j.shin@qub.ac.uk

M. Callaghan et al. (eds.), *Global Cooperation Among G20 Countries*,
DOI 10.1007/978-81-322-1659-9_10,

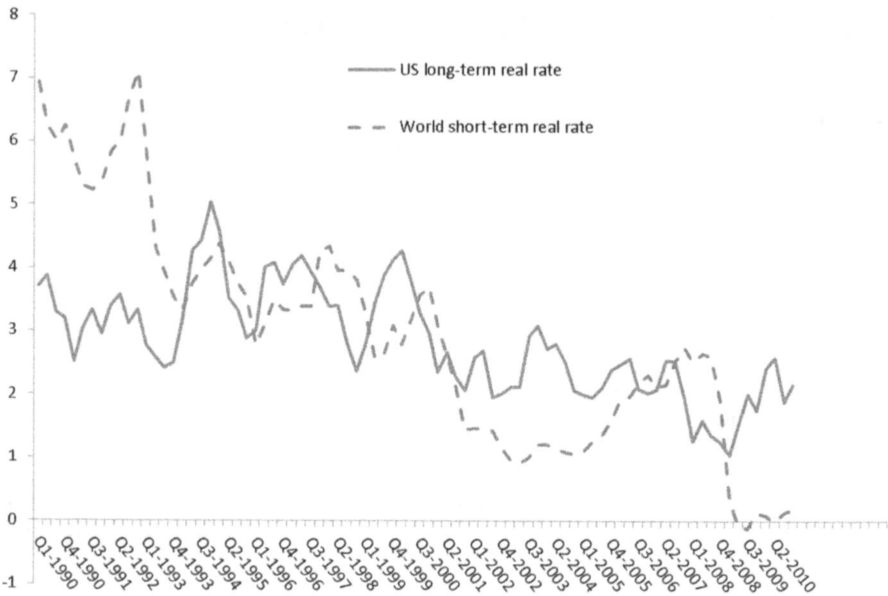

Fig. 1 Real interest rate on public debt: long term (10 years) and short term (3 months). (Source: OECD)

2 Global Imbalances and the Crises

In the wake of the crises, a number of authors have argued that global imbalances were perhaps the single largest contributing factor and therefore its elimination should be made a global priority. However, the link between global imbalances and crises is tenuous at best and must be treated with some degree of caution.

According to a prominent view, the global savings glut arising in emerging markets depressed world interest rates (Fig. 1) and led to the formation of the asset price bubble that triggered the financial market crises. However, critics (Gourinchas 2012) have pointed out that the real interest rate is determined by global savings and investment and not by the pattern of its geographical distribution. In other words, a given world real interest rate is equally consistent with large, small, or no current account imbalances.

Borio and Disyatat (2011), in an interesting paper, point out that the net capital inflows and current account balances tell us little about global financing patterns, an issue which is at the core of understanding the global financial crisis. Current account numbers simply indicate changes in net claims on a country arising from trade in real goods and services and exclude, for example, all the transactions involving only trade in financial assets. It is however the trade in financial assets that makes up a large chunk of cross-border activity. It is their rapid expansion that is potentially more threatening to financial and economic stability. In the run up to the global financial crisis, for example, gross capital flows into and out of the USA expanded roughly three times faster than net claims on the country, thereby indicating that the

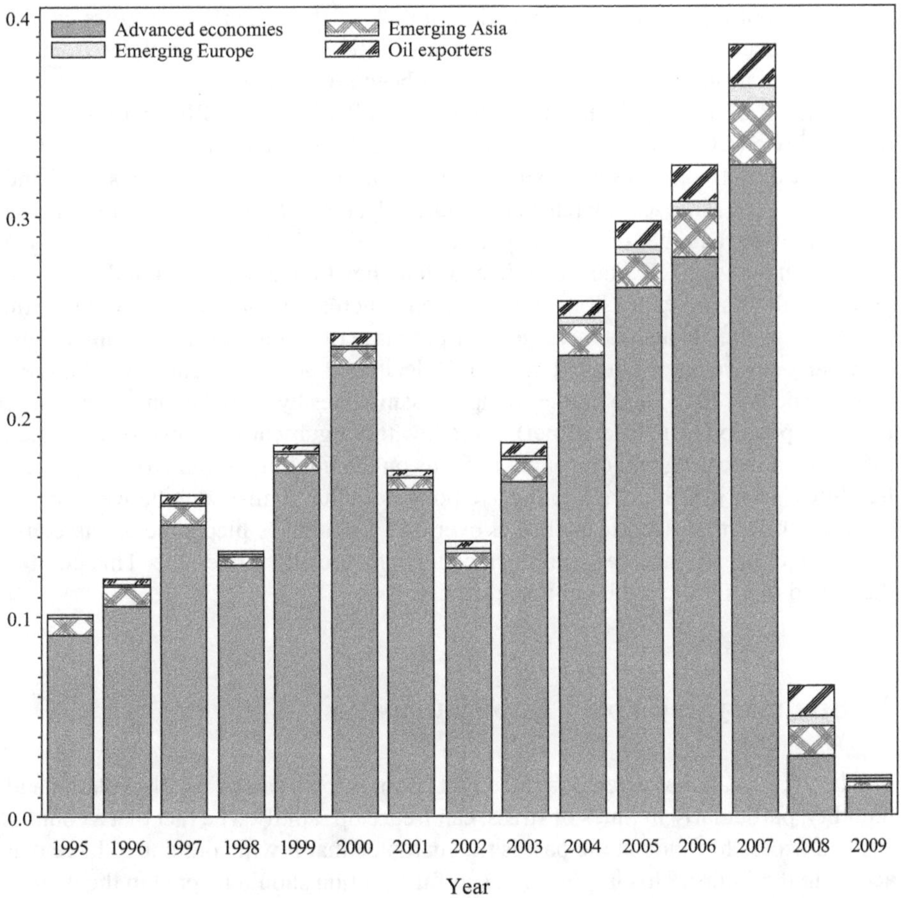

*Gross capital flow = capital outflow by domestic residents + capital inflow by foreigners

*Advanced economies: Australia, Canada, Denmark, the Euro area, Japan, New Zealand, Sweden, the UK and the US. *Oil exporters: Algeria, Angola, Azerbaijan, Ecuador, Equatorial Guinea, Gabon, Iran, Kazakhstan, Kuwait, Libya, Norway, Oman, Russia, Saudi Arabia, Syria, Trinidad and Tobago and Venezuela. *Emerging Asia: China, India, Indonesia, South Korea, Malaysia, the Philippines, Singapore and Thailand. *Emerging Europe: Bulgaria, Czech, Estonia, Hungary, Latvia, Lithuania, Poland, Romania, Slovakia and Slovenia

Fig. 2 Gross capital flows as a percentage of world GDP. (Source: IMF)

current account did not play a dominant role in determining financial flows into the USA.

The weak link between net capital flows and the global financial crises has led a number of authors to look at gross instead of net positions and flows. There is a growing consensus that dangerous levels of gross assets can build up even in the absence of any net international flows and it is these flows which eventually set off the financial turmoil. Gross flows rose from about 10 % of world gross domestic product (GDP) in 1988 to over 30 % in 2007 (Fig. 2). Borio and Disyatat (2011) find that, contrary to popular perception, a bulk of the expansion in gross capital flows had been driven by flows between advanced economies. The flows from, or between, emerging markets have in contrast been relatively modest.

Broner et al. (2011) document both gross capital inflows (CIF) and gross capital outflows (COD) for the period 1970–2009 for 103 countries. Their analysis finds that over the past four decades the volatility of gross capital flows (CIF and COD) has been large and increasing. Importantly, the volatility of net capital flows is much lower than that of gross capital flows. This reflects the increasing positive correlation between CIF and COD. In addition, they find that gross capital flows are procyclical: During expansions, foreign agents increase their purchase of domestic assets and domestic agents increase their purchase of foreign assets. During crises, especially severe ones, both CIF and COD decline, though CIF tends to fall more.

Gourinchas (2012) also argues along the same lines by focusing on gross capital flows or positions (instead of net). He takes the argument on gross flows a step further by advocating that one ought to focus on the liquidity of the gross assets and liabilities—not just the magnitudes. He points out that a mismatch between short-term liabilities that need to be rolled over and a country's pledgable assets could lead to liquidity imbalances, making a country financially vulnerable. This point is illustrated in a simple model in the appendix.

3 Summary and Policy Implications

The last few years have demonstrated that capital flows can be highly volatile and liquidity, particularly in times of stress, can freeze up rapidly. The fact that a country has had access to funds in the past is no guarantee that it will continue to have that access in the future. This implies that careful attention should be paid to the pattern of gross flows as net flows would not reflect these vulnerabilities.

The period since the crises has seen the global economy characterized by a dual pattern of growth. On the one hand, the advanced economies which were worst hit by the crises have had a very sluggish recovery. This is in contrast to the emerging markets which have been quick to rebound and have exhibited robust growth rates. Monetary policy, as a result, has been set to be expansionary in the advanced economies. The differential patterns of growth and the record low interest rates have induced large capital inflows into emerging markets. Taylor (2012) points out that there is growing evidence to suggest that in order to prevent the resultant appreciation of their exchange rates, central banks in emerging markets tend to hold their interest rates lower than what would be appropriate for domestic stability. Such a policy makes these countries financially vulnerable and poses a risk to global stability. Borio and Disyatat (2011) suggest that such spillovers and externalities associated with monetary policy in individual countries call for some form of policy coordination.

Central banks also ought to rethink how they should respond to potential asset price bubbles arising out of capital flows. Conventional wisdom suggests that monetary policy should not target asset prices as there could be unintended consequences for inflation and growth. However, this issue needs to be revisited. The run up to the global financial crisis was characterized by low and stable inflation and robust growth—the so-called "great moderation". Many central banks are therefore focusing on maintaining financial stability in addition to inflation and growth stability. However, there needs to be a clearer understanding on the trade-offs that might arise between these objectives. Another area of focus for researchers and policy makers should be to develop tools to assess whether credit bubbles are developing.

Shortage of liquid assets continues to plague the global economic system. The crisis has exacerbated the problem, if anything. Emerging markets, in their quest for safe assets, continue accumulating large amounts of international reserves thereby posing a threat to financial stability. As Gourinchas (2012) argues, the resolution of this so-called global liquidity imbalances, which was at the heart of the crisis, is far more important than the consolidation of current account imbalances. In this regard, a systematic use of central bank swap lines and multilateral provision of liquidity under International Monetary Fund (IMF) supervision are all steps in the right direction.

It follows from the discussion above that gross capital flows rather than net flows (current account balances) have contributed to the fragility in the global financial system. Given that gross capital flows are critical in determining the health of the financial system, it becomes imperative to study and understand the composition of these flows. One of the root causes of financial crises is that liabilities are often funded by short-term debt instruments. These transactions carry counterparty risk and are therefore a threat to global stability. Rogoff (2011) makes an interesting point that government policy actually incentivizes the appetite for debt. Tax systems in many countries favor debt over equity. Central banks have often bailed out debt far more aggressively than equity. Perhaps reducing the reliance on debt and increasing the share of liabilities funded by equity might make these capital flows less volatile and the financial system more resilient.

4 Conclusion

In this paper we argue that in assessing the financial health of a system one needs to focus on gross rather than net capital flows. The bulk of cross-border flows over the last couple of decades has been characterized by transactions in pure financial assets. These transactions are not captured by net capital flows and current account balances. The current account therefore is a poor indicator of the financial soundness of a system. Given the importance of gross flows, we examined the challenges that increased capital flows present to the financial stability of emerging market economies. We also focus on the implications and policy responses to increased cross-border flows.

Appendix

Model

We present a simple example to illustrate how, despite having a sound net debt position, a crisis could be triggered off by the presence of large gross debt. The model essentially follows Chang and Velasco (2001, *CV*) with minor modifications. We consider a small open economy with ex ante identical agents. There are three time periods in the economy denoted by $t=0,1,2$. There exists a single good which is freely traded and whose price is fixed and is normalized at a dollar. The domestic agents are endowed with e dollars. At $t=0$, goods can be invested in a foreign long-term technology such that each dollar invested yields $R>1$ dollars at the end of period 2. However, if the technology is liquidated in period 1, the return from this investment is $r<1$. On the other hand, there is a world capital market that is liquid and deep. One dollar lent at $t=0$ yields a gross return of 1 dollar at either $t=1$ or $t=2$. Domestic agents can lend as much as they want but can borrow a maximum of $f>0$.

As in *CV*, each domestic agent discovers her type at $t=1$. Specifically, she discovers with probability λ that she is impatient and derives utility only from period 1 consumption, c_1, or with probability 1-λ, that she is patient and derives utility only from period 2 consumption c_2. Type realization is $i.i.d.$ across agents and there is no aggregate uncertainty. The ex ante expected utility of domestic agents is

$$\lambda u(c_1) + (1-\lambda)u(c_2) \tag{1}$$

where $u(c)$ is $\frac{c^{1-\sigma}-1}{1-\sigma}$. In such a setup with no aggregate uncertainty, *Home* agents can benefit from pooling their resources, which rationalizes the existence of a bank. The bank maximizes the utility of the representative depositor conditional on the realization of her type. The problem is solved using the Revelation Principle wherein the social optimum is obtained by maximizing (1) subject to

$$k \le d_0 + e \tag{2}$$

$$\lambda c_1 \le d_1 + rl \tag{3}$$

$$(1-\lambda)c_2 + d_0 + d_1 \le R[k-l] \tag{4}$$

$$d_o \le f \tag{5}$$

$$d_0 + d_1 \le f \tag{6}$$

$$c_1 \le c_2 \tag{7}$$

$$c_1, c_2, k, l \ge 0 \tag{8}$$

where k denotes the amount invested in the long-term overseas project, d_0 and d_1 are the foreign debts at $t=0$, 1, respectively, and l denotes the liquidation amount of the long-term project at $t=1$. Equation (2) restricts the long-term investment to be less than the endowment plus borrowings. Equations (3) and (4) represent the feasibility constraints in periods 1 and 2. Equations (5) and (6) are the external feasibility constraints and (7) is the truth-telling constraint. Following *CV*, at the social optimum, there is no wastage of resources, leading to the following conditions:

$$\tilde{l} = 0 \tag{9}$$

$$\lambda \tilde{c}_1 = \tilde{d}_1 \tag{10}$$

$$(1-\lambda)\tilde{c}_2 + \tilde{d}_0 + \tilde{d}_1 = R\tilde{k} \tag{11}$$

$$\tilde{k} = \tilde{d}_0 + e \tag{12}$$

$$\tilde{d}_0 + \tilde{d}_1 = f \tag{13}$$

where the tilde denotes the social optimal values of the respective variables. Equations (9)–(13) can be reduced to a single equation:

$$(1-\lambda)\tilde{c}_2 + R\lambda\tilde{c}_1 = R\omega \tag{14}$$

where $w \equiv e + f[R-1]/R$ and can be interpreted as the social wealth of the *Home* country. The social optimal is obtained by maximizing (1) subject to (14), which yields

$$\lambda \tilde{c}_1 = \theta\omega \tag{15}$$

$$(1-\lambda)\tilde{c}_2 = (1-\theta)R\omega \tag{16}$$

where $\theta = 1/\left[1 + \frac{(1-\lambda)}{\lambda} R^{\frac{\sigma=1}{\sigma}}\right] \in [0,1]$. Denoting the gross and net foreign debt flows[1] at the end of $t=0$ as d_0 and $n_0 \equiv d_0 - k$, respectively, it follows that

$$\tilde{d}_0 = \tilde{k} - e = (1-\theta)\omega + f/R - e \tag{17}$$

$$\tilde{n}_0 = -e \tag{18}$$

[1] =0.67; in this simple setting, net (gross) capital flows amount to net (gross) debt flows.

Bank Runs: Gross vs. Net Capital Flows

CV show how a decentralized bank deposit system can lead to bank runs. In the section, we explore the link between gross and net capital flows and bank runs. Under the deposit system described by *CV*, each agent surrenders her endowment in period 0 and capacity to borrow from the international capital market to the bank. The bank implements the socially optimal borrowing and investment described in the previous section, i.e., $\tilde{k}$ and $\tilde{d}_0$ in period 0 and $\tilde{d}_1$ in period 1. In exchange, the agent is given the right to withdraw either $\tilde{c}_1$ in period 1 or $\tilde{c}_2$ in period 2 at her discretion. It is further assumed that the bank serves withdrawal requests sequentially. In other words, agents can withdraw $\tilde{c}_1$ in period 1 if the bank is still open upon their arrival. If the withdrawal request exceeds a preset liquidation threshold $\bar{l}$ (which will be discussed shortly), the bank closes and stops its operation. *CV* show that such a demand deposit system gives rise to multiple equilibria. Intuitively, if each agent expects all other agents including the patient ones to withdraw their deposits at $t=1$, it becomes optimal for an individual agent to withdraw her deposit in $t=1$. In other words, it becomes optimal for an agent to withdraw deposits before the bank runs out of liquid assets (i.e., reaches its upper limit of liquidation, $\bar{l}$).

If the domestic banking sector can commit to repayment of all foreign debt[2], the maximum liquidation of a long-run project, $\bar{l}$ must satisfy

$$R(\tilde{k}-\bar{l}) = \tilde{d}_0 + \tilde{d}_1$$

Combined with (13), this condition implies

$$\bar{l} = \tilde{k} - f/R \tag{19}$$

Under this scenario, foreign lenders are always willing to give $\tilde{d}_0$ and $\tilde{d}_1$ to the bank because they know they will be repaid in full regardless of the bank's situation. When there is a bank run in period 1, the bank decides to go bankrupt if the withdrawal request exceeds the maximum liquidity available:

$$z = \tilde{c}_1 - (\tilde{d}_1 + r\bar{l}) > 0 \tag{20}$$

In other words, a bank run-driven financial meltdown happens if a measure of bank illiquidity z is a positive number. We next investigate the role of the net and gross foreign capital flows in such a financial crisis. Using (19), (12), and (18) we can rewrite (20) as:

$$z = \frac{\theta\omega}{\lambda} - f\left(\frac{R-r}{R}\right) + [1-r]\tilde{d}_0 + r\tilde{n}_0 \tag{21}$$

---

[2] =0.67; more realistically, banks may not be able to commit to pay back all their foreign liabilities; however, it can be shown that our key results are unchanged in this setting.

It follows from (21) that the illiquidity measure z varies directly with both $\tilde{d}_0$ and $\tilde{n}_0$. In other words, it is not just the net but also gross foreign capital flows that increase the possibility of a financial crisis.

Result As long as the gross capital flow $\tilde{d}_0$ is high enough a financial crises could occur even with a negative net foreign capital $\tilde{n}_0$.

A financial crisis can occur due to liquidity mismatches and sentiments despite good fundamentals ($R > 1$). Since the long-term investment yields higher return than borrowing costs, it is optimal for *Home* agents to use a leverage. However, as the size of the leverage increases, the risk of a financial crisis also increases. More interestingly, it can occur as long as the size of the gross capital flow $\tilde{d}_0$ is large enough. Put simply, in such a setup a net capital flow need not be a good indicator of financial fragility. The presence of larger gross capital flows can trigger a crisis even if the net capital flows are in balance.

References

Chang R, Velasco A (2001) A model of financial crises in emerging markets. Q J Econ 116(2): 489–517

Broner F, Didier T, Erce A, Schmukler S (2011) Gross capital flows: dynamics and crises, CEPR Discussion Paper No. 8591

Borio C, Disyatat P (2011) Global imbalances and the financial crisis: link or no link? BIS Working Papers 346, Bank for International Settlements

Gourinchas P-O (2012) Global imbalances and global liquidity mimeo. University of California, Berkeley

Lucas RE Jr (1990) Why doesn't capital flow from rich to poor countries? Am Econ Rev 80(2): 92–96

Servén L, Nguyen H (2010) Global imbalances before and after the global crisis. World Bank Policy Research Working Paper 5354

Rogoff K (2011) Global imbalances without tears. http://www.project-syndicate.org/commentary/rogoff78/English March 2011. Project Syndicate

Part III
Financial Sector Regulation

Financial Regulatory Reforms: Not Far Enough, or Too Far?

Stephen Pickford

1 Introduction

The global economic and financial crisis which began in 2007 produced the most significant downturn in the global economy since the Second World War. Its impact is still being felt, with many advanced economies not having regained the output lost during the crisis, and the crisis in the euro area is ongoing. Most emerging markets have also experienced significant slowdowns from their growth rates in the earlier part of the decade (albeit still growing relatively quickly). Moreover, substantial policy responses are still underway.

One of the major causes of the crisis was due to failings in the financial sector, both by private institutions and by public regulators. Private institutions took excessive risks, as evidenced by the sub-prime crisis in the USA. This rapidly spread to other advanced economies (especially in Europe), not only through their exposure to securitised products and their interlinkages with US financial institutions, but also as the crisis exposed weaknesses in their own financial systems and institutions. Wholesale financial markets seized up, major institutions had to be rescued by their governments and the entire global financial system was facing a meltdown.

The policy response to the crisis, led by the G20 from the Washington summit in late 2008 onwards, was intended both to restore confidence and to fix the perceived failings at the heart of the financial crisis. It started a process of root-and-branch reforms to financial regulation that have been the most extensive, complex and globally coordinated ones ever seen.

In embarking on this agenda, there was general acceptance that a number of assumptions that had underpinned the pre-crisis approach to regulation were wrong. The 'light-touch' approach that was seen by most policymakers prior to the crisis as the most appropriate and effective model, was based on a particular view of the world, that transferring risk between institutions through securitisation made the system more resilient as a whole, and that relying on internal risk models was

S. Pickford (✉)
Chatham House, London, UK
e-mail: stephenjpickford@gmail.com

M. Callaghan et al. (eds.), *Global Cooperation Among G20 Countries*,
DOI 10.1007/978-81-322-1659-9_11,

the most efficient form of supervision, which encouraged needed innovation in financial products and markets. The crisis caused a rethink of these assumptions, and the major financial centres embarked (through the G20) on a programme of reforms based on a revised view of the world.

The intention was to make the financial system more resilient, and the reform agenda covered almost all parts of the financial system: institutions, markets and products. Measures already agreed include:

- Enhancing the quantity and quality of bank capital,
- Requiring enhanced liquidity buffers,
- Imposing leverage ratios,
- Making major changes to derivatives markets,
- Imposing restrictions on compensation systems in private institutions, in order to reduce incentives to take excessive risks, and
- Requiring changes to the corporate governance of private institutions.

They have been taken forward largely through an internationally coordinated process, reflecting the global nature of the finance industry and the potential for regulatory arbitrage. Although many reforms have already been agreed in international fora, at least in general terms, there is still a long way to go before they are implemented fully in all jurisdictions.

However, as many parts of the global economy remain in poor health, questions are being asked as to whether the reform agenda is adding to economic problems rather than solving them. This paper examines these arguments, and addresses the question: have the reforms not yet gone far enough, or have they gone too far?

Section 2 looks at the origins of the global economic and financial crisis, especially the role of the financial sector. Section 3 examines the intellectual response to the crisis, and the impact it had on a number of pieces of 'received wisdom', and Section 4 traces the policy responses resulting from this rethinking. The following three sections then look at possible criticisms of the post-crisis agenda of reforms to financial regulation—that it has gone too far and damaged growth; that the internationally coordinated approach was not appropriate for emerging markets, especially in Asia and that the increasing complexity of regulation was not only unnecessary but also counterproductive. The final section draws some tentative conclusions about the regulatory reform agenda going forward.

2 The Origins of the Crisis

The global crisis began in 2007 and deepened in 2008, as Lehman Brothers collapsed, causing financial markets to freeze. At the time, the problems facing the global economy were clear. There was a risk that the global recession could turn into a depression that rivalled the 1930s, and the pressure on policymakers to act was overwhelming.

The crisis began in financial markets, as the problems facing sub-prime loans in the US housing market started to emerge, as did the scale of the wider impact on markets through securitisation and complex derivatives[1]. However, macroeconomic issues were also seen as playing a part. In particular, some observers have viewed the build-up of foreign exchange reserves in major emerging markets (especially China) as having added to the downward pressure on interest rates globally, and encouraging the 'search for yield' that fed increased risk-taking by financial institutions.

In the aftermath of the Lehman's collapse, G20 Leaders met in Washington to provide a response to the crisis. The summit communiqué—the 'Declaration on Financial Markets and the Global Economy' (G20 2008)—attributed the blame for the crisis to a combination of causes, including a lack of international coordination in macroeconomic policies, and inadequate structural reforms, which "contributed to excesses and ultimately resulted in severe market disruption."

However, it also pointed clearly to policy failures and shortcomings in the behaviour of private financial institutions—weak financial regulation and poor supervision allowed a build-up of financial market risks, which investors failed to appreciate. In the words of the Declaration:

> During a period of strong global growth, growing capital flows, and prolonged stability earlier this decade, market participants sought higher yields without an adequate appreciation of the risks and failed to exercise proper due diligence. At the same time, weak underwriting standards, unsound risk management practices, increasingly complex and opaque financial products, and consequent excessive leverage combined to create vulnerabilities in the system. Policy-makers, regulators and supervisors, in some advanced countries, did not adequately appreciate and address the risks building up in financial markets, keep pace with financial innovation, or take into account the systemic ramifications of domestic regulatory actions.

The resulting Action Plan set out a raft of measures to be taken by G20 members to design and implement financial reforms to address these shortcomings. These actions covered: regulatory regimes; prudential oversight; risk management; integrity in financial markets and international cooperation in these areas.

3 Rethinking Approaches to Regulation

Embarking on this agenda, G20 countries were recognising that a number of assumptions that had underpinned the pre-crisis approach to regulation in many countries were wrong. In particular, the intellectual underpinnings of the 'light-touch' approach that was seen by most policymakers prior to the crisis as the appropriate and effective model for regulation and supervision was called into question.

Among the assumptions underpinning the pre-crisis approach to regulation and supervision were that:

[1] See for example, various issues of the IMF's *Global Financial Stability Report* (IMF).

- Macroeconomic stability would guarantee financial stability,
- Distribution of risk around the system would make the system more resilient as a whole,
- Markets were efficient and could transfer risk to the parts of the system that were best able to handle those risks,
- Models based on previous historical experience could accurately measure risk,
- Supervisors could rely on internal risk models of private institutions and
- Light-touch regulation and supervision encouraged innovation, and all financial innovation was useful.

The crisis came after many years of rapid growth, low inflation and rising asset prices. This 'great moderation'[2] fostered the view that lending could safely be expanded because it was underpinned by rising collateral values (in particular real estate values), which in turn led to further asset price increases.

Although it was recognised that there were risks associated with mortgage lending, the process of securitisation created parcels of assets, which were supposed to blend high-risk and low-risk underlying assets in a way that produced acceptable levels of overall risk for end investors. This allowed originating banks to reduce their own exposure to risk. Spreading these risks through the financial system was also believed to make the system more resilient as a whole, because any one institution had limited exposure.

The increasing complexity of these securitised products also presented a challenge to supervisors (as well as to investors holding the products). The solution, building on the move in Basel II to increase reliance on internal models, was for supervisors to rely on banks' own assessments of the riskiness of their assets using models of historical behaviour.

At the same time, financial innovation was seen as leading to greater efficiency, in both the financial sector itself and the wider economy. Spreading of risk allowed banks to economise on capital, which reduced their costs.

The onset of the crisis caused all these assumptions to be called into question.

4 Responses to the Crisis

Given the role of regulatory failure as a contributory factor behind the crisis, reform of financial regulation has been a priority issue for the G20 since it began as a Leader-led process in 2008, and in 2009 it was designated as the "premier forum for our international economic cooperation" (G20 2009).

Financial sector strengthening formed a key part of the G20 discussions at the first G20 summit in Washington in November 2008. A comprehensive action plan

[2] Charles Bean in a speech to the European Economic Association (Bean 2009) describes the pre-crisis period as "characterised by an unusually high degree of macroeconomic stability, with steady growth and low and stable inflation in most of the advanced economies."

was formulated and a number of international institutions, in particular the Financial Stability Forum (FSF), were tasked with taking forward different aspects of the plan. The FSF had been established in 1999 and brought together finance ministries, central banks and regulators of the major financial centres. Following the Washington summit, the FSF was given a broad oversight role for financial sector reform; its membership expanded to include all the G20 countries, renamed the Financial Stability Board (FSB) and provided with greater resources and more responsibilities.

The G20 stressed that, while financial regulation was primarily a national responsibility, there was a clear rationale for coordinated international action—"our financial markets are global in scope, therefore, intensified international cooperation among regulators and strengthening of international standards… and their consistent implementation is necessary to protect against adverse cross-border, regional and global developments affecting international financial stability" (G20 2008). Therefore, the issue of financial stability became a key public policy issue for G20 countries, individually and collectively. However, the pace of implementation of reforms and actions to address and resolve failing financial institutions has varied markedly between countries, with the IMF, for example, criticising the slow pace of efforts in a number of European countries to deal with bad loans on banks' balance sheets (IMF 2011).

In successive summits over the last 5 years, the programme of financial sector reforms led by the G20 (and largely implemented by the FSB) has increasingly expanded its scope and drilled down into greater detail.

Over this period, the agenda has grown substantially in complexity, in five dimensions:

- The range of *institutions* covered by the supervisory net has risen dramatically, from banks and insurance companies initially, to cover hedge funds, other forms of 'shadow banking' and the financial infrastructure institutions (clearing and settlement systems, and credit rating agencies);
- The coverage of *instruments* under detailed regulation has increased, notably for asset-backed securities, and over-the-counter (OTC) derivatives;
- The level of *detail* on capital, liquidity, leverage, accounting standards and conduct of business issues has also expanded dramatically. For example, Basel I ran to 30 pages, Basel II to 347 pages and Basel III to 616 pages;
- The *processes* around supervision have also been strengthened, for example, the setting up of supervisory colleges, and processes for bank resolution, especially for systemically important financial institutions (SIFIs) and
- Measures have been introduced aimed at regulating the *behaviours* of financial institutions, for example, guidelines on compensation and corporate governance.

To illustrate the scope of the reform agenda in its first 2 years, the G20 called for:

- Strengthening of the FSB;
- Changing the approach to risk management in private financial institutions, including through controls on compensation systems;

- Instituting a new bank capital and liquidity framework to constrain leverage and maturity mismatches, capital buffers and leverage ratios;
- Addressing the 'too-big-to-fail' issue through a resolution framework and more intensive supervisory oversight for SIFIs as well as building a robust core financial market infrastructure and
- Instituting mandatory international recovery and resolution planning and risk assessment by international supervisory colleges, in particular for global systemically important financial institutions (G-SIFIs).

In addition, at the Seoul summit in 2010, the G20 mandated a further programme of work covering (G20 2010):

- International peer review of implementation of reforms at the national level;
- Strengthening regulation and supervision of hedge funds, OTC derivatives and credit rating agencies;
- Creating a single set of global accounting standards;
- Further work on macroprudential policy frameworks and
- Strengthening regulation and supervision of the shadow banking system and derivatives markets.

At the Cannes summit in 2011, the G20 committed to the full implementation of this reform agenda and the creation of a global legal entity identifier (FSB 2012a) to identify parties to financial transactions. Los Cabos repeated these commitments and pledged to make national resolution regimes consistent with the Key Attributes developed by the FSB (FSB 2011).

These measures have primarily been taken forward internationally through the FSB and the standard-setting bodies (including the Basel Committee, the IASB and IOSCO)[3], but much of this agenda has to be implemented by the relevant national regulators and supervisors[4]. While the political priority of international coordination on financial regulation has advanced quickly, detailed implementation of regulations at the national level is lagging behind. Nevertheless, compared with the speed of progress on regulatory reform before the crisis, much greater and faster progress has been made than would have been likely with the pre-2008 structures for international cooperation.

[3] The Basel Committee on Banking Supervision (BCBS) is a committee of banking supervisory authorities whose purpose is to encourage convergence towards common banking regulations and standards. The International Accounting Standards Board (IASB) is an accounting standard-setting body tasked with developing a single set of "high quality, understandable, enforceable and globally accepted" international financial reporting standards. The International Organisation of Securities Commissions (IOSCO) is an association of organisations that regulates the world's securities and futures markets.

[4] Implementing regulation and supervision is still essentially a national responsibility, since it derives from national laws backed up by national fiscal authority. This is particularly so when a bank has to be resolved and/or recapitalised, since there is usually a need for public resources (or at least guarantees). Banking union seeks to elevate this to the European level (ESAs, ESRB, single supervisory mechanism, single rule-book, harmonised deposit guarantee schemes, single recovery and resolution framework).

5 Are There Negative Impacts from the Reforms?

In the early phase of the crisis, there was general consent that financial reforms were necessary in order to begin the process of repairing financial markets, resolving failed banks and restoring confidence. In turn, this was seen as necessary in order to allow economies to start growing again.

In political economy terms, it was also necessary for governments in some countries to be seen to tighten regulation, in order to justify the exceptional levels of support and financial resources they had provided to banks and other financial institutions. Given the role that failings, in private institutions, played in the crisis and in the subsequent recession in many (mainly advanced) countries, the degree of public trust in banks had fallen. Furthermore, subsequent scandals involving banks, including the manipulation of London Interbank Offered Rate (LIBOR) interest rates, breaches of anti-money laundering provisions and losses caused by 'rogue traders', have further damaged the public perception of banking. Thus, malpractice and misbehaviour in private financial institutions have added further political support for tighter regulation, adding to the pressure already resulting from the high cost of public support for banks during the crisis.

The crisis has also caused a rethink in the major financial centres about the role of banking, their business models and their approach to risk, given the implicit and explicit guarantees against bank failure provided by governments.

This moral hazard argument has led to the Dodd–Frank legislation[5] in the USA (based on the 'Volcker rule' ban on proprietary trading). In the UK, the independent banking commission[6] chaired by John Vickers proposed ring fencing retail bank operations from investment banking as well as higher capital requirements than proposed by the Basel committee, and the government is preparing legislation to implement this approach. In addition, the EU set up the Liikanen commission[7] to look at ways of separating retail and investment banking operations.

However, questions have begun to be asked as to whether the financial regulation reform agenda (both the G20-led reform process and these additional national reforms) has gone too far. These revolve around two propositions, that:

- Tighter regulation is having a negative impact on economic growth, through higher interest rates, reduced supply of credit and lower lending volumes and
- It is stifling innovation in the financial sector (which drives efficiency in the overall economy).

---

[5] The Dodd–Frank Wall Street Reform and Consumer Protection Act (US Senate 2010) was enacted in 2010.

[6] The Independent Commission on Banking (ICB 2011) was established in 2010 to consider reforms to the UK banking sector to promote financial stability and competition. In its report in 2011 it recommended that banks should 'ring-fence' their retail operations from their investment banking arms.

[7] The European Commission's High-level Expert Group on Bank Structural Reform (EU 2012a), chaired by Erkki Liikanen (governor of the Bank of Finland), reported in October 2012.

Much of the initial questioning came from the financial sector itself, and was regarded as the industry 'talking its own book'. However, as economic growth in many advanced economies has remained sluggish at best, and as corporates (especially small and medium-sized enterprises) have cited lack of access to bank finance as a factor preventing them from expanding their operations, complaints about the impact of tighter regulation have become more widespread. Increases in bank capital requirements have come in for particular criticism as both restricting the supply of lending and increasing loan spreads, as banks have sought to rebuild profitability.

The evidence on the impact of regulation on lending is far from clear. On the volume of lending, the counterargument from the banks is that there is insufficient demand for loans from corporates and households, reflecting uncertainty about the economic outlook. Furthermore, on spreads, it is also unclear whether these are simply reflecting the riskiness of lending in the current economic climate.

Nevertheless, governments in some countries have introduced policies to respond to the perceived restrictions on lending. For example, in the UK, the Bank of England has put in place the Funding for Lending scheme (Bank of England 2012), which provides liquidity to banks at low interest rates, as long as the banks on-lend the funds to borrowers, also at lower rates. It is too early to judge whether the scheme is having the desired effect, but earlier versions suffered from low take-up, suggesting that lack of demand for finance was at least part of the explanation.

The other main line of argument criticising the effects of tighter regulation is that it discourages innovation in the financial sector and, thus, indirectly harms the wider economy. It is particularly hard to judge whether this is happening, and if so, how far it is due to tighter regulation. However, innovation in financial technology, in the form of securitisation, was one of the causes of the crisis. So one could argue that it was an explicit aim of the reforms to slow the pace of at least the most harmful forms of financial innovation. The proposed Financial Transactions Tax (EU 2012b), which is being introduced by a number of European countries, is also intended to discourage 'speculative' forms of financial activity.

While financial innovation has the potential to provide better services and products to companies and households as well as to reduce costs, it is far from clear how much impact these innovations have had in practice on the wider economy.

6 What has been the Impact on Emerging Markets?

The reform agenda was largely designed and driven by advanced economies, which host major financial centres. Until the changes to the composition of the FSB, many emerging markets were not members of the body, which was tasked with taking forward the reform agenda.

Since most of the financial sector problems identified as causes of the crisis originated in advanced economies, this was perhaps not surprising. However, questions have been raised as to whether the agenda is appropriate for emerging markets, especially in Asia.

Asian financial systems were in relatively good shape prior to the crisis and were largely unscathed by the crisis. Their banks typically had relatively sound balance sheets, modest exposure to toxic assets and prudent approaches to risk management. To some extent, this reflected their successful economic performance. For example, a decade ago, Chinese banks were widely thought to have had large numbers of problem loans on their balance sheets, but rapid economic growth through the 2000s and rising asset values meant this problem did not come to a head.

In addition, the regulatory framework in many Asian economies was also more conservative than in most advanced economies, reflecting the experience of the Asian financial crisis in the late 1990s and the policy changes put in place to strengthen financial systems following that episode. However, it also reflected relatively underdeveloped financial systems, dominated by banks and with limited capital markets.

In this sense, the G20-led reform agenda has had less relevance for these emerging economies because their financial systems had not developed the full range of financial products, which proved to be problematic in advanced economies, or the same level of complexity in interlinkages between institutions that led to the systemic crises experienced in many advanced economies.

As the reform agenda was less directly relevant for emerging markets in their current state of financial development, it is possible that implementing regulatory reforms has diverted scarce capacity from other tasks, such as broadening and deepening their financial markets. However, it is also likely that emerging markets have benefitted indirectly from the impact of the reform agenda in making advanced countries address weaknesses and fragilities in their own financial systems, given the interconnected nature of financial markets worldwide.

The FSB, in collaboration with the IMF and World Bank, produced a report in 2012 (FSB 2012b), looking at the extent to which the regulatory reforms may have had unintended consequences for emerging markets and developing economies (EMDEs). This study reported widespread support among EMDEs for the objectives of the agreed reforms and noted that many EMDEs did not expect significant adverse effects from the implementation of the reforms.

However, some issues were raised about the impact of certain reforms, including Basel III, policy measures for G-SIFIs and OTC derivatives reforms. In addition, some EMDEs raised concerns about the impact on them of financial reforms in advanced economies, including higher capital requirements for European banks and the implementation of the Volcker rule in the USA. More generally, spillovers and home bias in the design or implementation of reforms by advanced economies were seen as a problem by some.

Prior to the FSB's expansion to include all G20 members, only a few emerging markets with systemically important financial centres (including Singapore and Hong Kong) were members of the FSF. However, expansion to other emerging markets did give them a stake in the reforms and a greater voice in their design.

7 Is There Over-complexity?

As the financial reform agenda has expanded, it has also become more detailed and complex. In part, this is a reaction against the 'light-touch' philosophy, which was seen as part of the problem.

However, again questions are being raised as to whether regulation is becoming too complex and intrusive. In a speech last year at the Jackson Hole conference (Haldane and Madouros 2012), Andy Haldane[8] raised some of these issues. His arguments were two-fold:

- Firstly, that detailed regulation and supervision require an enormous amount of information, which is costly and could cause supervisors to ignore the bigger picture and general trends.
- Secondly, that complex rules are actually less effective than simple rules when taking decisions under uncertainty.

On Haldane's first point, he argues that the most effective decision-making rule when future states of the world and their probabilities are known is to develop state-contingent rules. However, in the real world of extreme complexity, collecting and processing the information necessary to define these states and probabilities for decision-making are extremely costly.

The costs of regulation have already increased over time. Haldane notes that in 1935, there was one regulator for every three banks in the USA, whereas there are now three regulators for every one US bank. There are different models of supervision; for example, in Spain it is usual for supervisory staff to be bedded out in the banks they are supervising. But whatever the starting point, the regulatory reforms are almost certain to increase the resources devoted to supervision by the authorities and to compliance by the institutions being supervised. Moreover, the level of complexity of regulation and supervision has also increased substantially.

If greater resources devoted to supervision and compliance reduce the risk of financial crises, this could well be judged to have been a price worth paying. However, Haldane also argues that more complex rules make supervisors adopt a more risk-averse, box-ticking approach, which makes it more likely that by concentrating on the detail, they will miss the bigger picture.

He also makes the even more telling point that for decision making under uncertainty, complex rules tend not to be as effective as simple rules, in part because the future is uncertain and the past may not be a good guide to the future. Haldane performs a rerun of history, for a sample of about 100 large and complex global banks and finds that a simple leverage ratio, with assets equally weighted performs better than for Tier 1 regulatory capital ratios with risk-weighted assets, and has a statistically significantly better ability to predict bank failures.

If these results have general applicability, they carry fundamental conclusions for public policy. In particular, they suggest that the thrust of the current regulatory

[8] Executive Director, Financial Stability at the Bank of England.

reform agenda, towards greater complexity and more detailed supervision, requiring greater amounts of detailed information from financial institutions, is heading in the wrong direction. At the very least, this suggests that more evaluation of new regulations in terms of their ability to avoid bank failures and improve financial stability is needed.

8 Concluding Remarks

The extensive agenda of financial reform initiated, following the onset of the crisis was seen as an indispensible response to address one of the major causes of the crisis and to reduce the probability of it happening again.

However, as the reforms are in the process of being implemented and further changes are in train, questions have already been raised as to whether the reform of regulation has gone too far. These questions revolve around three propositions:

- That the reforms are restricting lending, damaging growth and stifling innovation in the financial sector;
- That the agenda is designed to address the problems of advanced economy financial sectors, and has been a distraction for emerging markets from more important priorities and
- That the increasing detail and complexity of regulation and supervision are more costly and less efficient, than simpler forms of regulation.

The jury is still out on these issues. However, they represent a substantial reaction to the early consensus on the way forward to make the financial system more stable and need to be taken seriously. If they are right, they cast doubt on the way forward in regulatory reform.

Given the current state of the debate, four main conclusions could be drawn.

First, there are good political economy reasons for completing the current programme of reforms. It is clear that the pre-crisis system of regulation and supervision had serious shortcomings in some (mainly advanced) countries. These shortcomings (which were one significant reason for the crisis) put financial stability at risk and, as a result, imposed substantial wider economic costs. Fixing these shortcomings probably will not avoid any future crises, but they should at least prevent a repeat of the last one.

Reversing the current reform measures, many of which have been agreed internationally and are in the process of being implemented by national regulators and supervisors, would be difficult to justify, given the weight of evidence of past regulatory shortcomings in many jurisdictions. Although it might find support among financial institutions, many governments would also find a reversal of reforms hard to defend to public opinion, which has become more hostile to financial institutions as a class, given further scandals (such as LIBOR fixing) and the substantial public resources spent on rescuing failed institutions.

Second, the speed and timing of tighter regulation (in particular requiring banks to hold more capital) may have hindered recovery of confidence and economic growth. However, the evidence is not clear-cut. It is difficult to determine whether low levels of lending are due to constrained supply or restrained demand. The complaints tend to be concentrated on specific parts of the market, especially SMEs and some infrastructure spending, which appear to have faced most difficulty in gaining access to finance. Moreover, they are related to the particular circumstances when economies are struggling to recover.

The experience varies from country to country, but where it is seen to be a problem there may be a case for targeted responses, such as guarantee schemes for loans to specific sectors. However, a general rollback of regulatory reforms to respond to sector-specific and time-limited problems would not be appropriate.

Third, some parts of the reform agenda may not be directly relevant to the situation of emerging markets, which tend to have less developed financial systems and are less prone to the problems faced by institutions in advanced economies. However, unlike in the past, emerging markets have been more involved in the reform process. In addition, in a wider sense, they will have benefitted from greater resilience of financial systems in advanced economies.

Fourth, the evidence that increasingly detailed and complex regulation may be facing diminishing (or even negative) returns has to be looked at seriously. But if more rigorous supervision makes the financial system significantly more stable and reduces the probability of failures, the additional costs it imposes on the supervisors and the institutions being supervised are almost certainly worthwhile.

However, if more complexity is actually less effective (as Haldane suggests), then there should be more focus on simple approaches such as the leverage ratio, this suggests the need for a change in direction for regulation and supervision. A sensible way forward may be to take stock of the evidence about the most effective form of regulation and supervision, including experience so far with the more detailed and complex forms of regulation already implemented, before embarking on a new wave of reforms.

Experience shows that the cost of getting financial regulation and supervision wrong can be enormous, in terms of financial failures and wider economic costs. The reform agenda initiated in 2008 was a serious attempt to put right those shortcomings. However, regulation and supervision need to evolve to keep pace with changes in the financial system, and it is now time to look again at what is the most effective way to guard against the risks inherent in the financial system.

References

Bank of England (2012) Funding for lending scheme. http://www.bankofengland.co.uk/markets/Pages/FLS/default.aspx, Accessed 14 Oct 2013

Bean C (2009) The Great Moderation, the Great Panic and the Great Contraction. Schumpeter lecture at the Annual Congress of the European Economic Association, Barcelona, 25 August 2009. http://www.bis.org/review/r090902d.pdf?frames=0, Accessed 14 Oct 2013

EU (2012a) Report of the European Commission's High-level Expert Group on bank structural reform http://ec.europa.eu/internal_market/bank/docs/high-level_expert_group/report_en.pdf, Accessed 14 Oct 2013

EU (2012b) Statement on an EU financial transactions tax. http://europa.eu/rapid/press-release_MEMO-12–762_en.htm?locale=en, Accessed 14 Oct 2013

FSB (2011) Key attributes of effective resolution regimes for financial institutions. http://www.financialstabilityboard.org/publications/r_111104cc.pdf, Accessed 14 Oct 2013

FSB (2012a) A legal entity identifier for financial markets. http://www.financialstabilityboard.org/publications/r_120608.pdf, Accessed 14 Oct 2013

FSB (2012b) Identifying the effects of regulatory reforms on emerging market and developing economies: a review of potential unintended consequences http://www.financialstabilityboard.org/publications/r_120619e.pdf, Accessed 14 Oct 2013

G20 (2008) Declaration of the Summit on Financial Markets and the World Economy. http://www.g20.utoronto.ca/2008/2008declaration1115.html#principles, Accessed 14 Oct 2013

G20 (2009) The Pittsburgh Summit statement. www.g20.utoronto.ca/2009/2009communique0925.html, Accessed 14 Oct 2013

G20 (2010) The Seoul Summit document. http://www.g20.utoronto.ca/2010/g20seoul-doc.html

Haldane A, Madouros V (2012) The dog and the frisbee. http://www.bankofengland.co.uk/publications/Documents/speeches/2012/speech596.pdf, Accessed 14 Oct 2013

ICB (2011) Independent Commission on Banking. http://webarchive.nationalarchives.gov.uk/+/bankingcommission.independent.gov.uk, Accessed 14 Oct 2013

IMF (2011) Global Financial Stability Report http://www.imf.org/external/pubs/ft/gfsr/2011/02/pdf/sum.pdf, Accessed 14 Oct 2013

US Senate (2010) http://www.banking.senate.gov/public/_files/070110_Dodd_Frank_Wall_Street_Reform_comprehensive_summary_Final.pdf, Accessed 14 Oct 2013

Asian Perspectives for Financial Regulatory Reforms after the Asian Financial Crisis

Jae-Ha Park

This paper discusses the causes and lessons learned from the 2008 global financial crisis (GFC); the financial reform process after the GFC, related issues, and debates; and the strengths, weaknesses, and challenges for Asian financial systems and the implications for emerging Asian economies.

1 Causes and Lessons of the GFC

One of the most important causes of the global financial crisis (GFC) was insufficient and inadequate financial regulation and supervision in some major global financial centers. Before the crisis, it was widely accepted that there were sufficient measures, particularly in the USA and Europe, for self-regulation, market discipline, and financial innovation to check shocks and prevent a crisis from developing. However, the GFC revealed a number of flaws in financial regulation and supervision, including: inadequacy of the macroprudential supervision; shadow banking; "too-big-to-fail" problems; insufficient capital and liquidity standards; inadequate transparency on derivative products; and procyclicality. From the experience of the GFC, a number of lessons can be learned. First, market discipline failed to constrain the excessive risk-taking behavior of financial institutions. Second, regulatory policies, including capital, liquidity, and disclosure requirements, failed to mitigate risk management weaknesses, particularly in the USA and Europe. Third, corporate governance failed, including ignorant and negligent boards. Fourth, there was under-appreciation of the importance of the relationships between banks and nonbanks. Fifth, there was overreliance on credit rating agencies. In addition, we have learned about the potential high cost of innovation, compensation structures/asymmetric incentives, and the systemic importance of nonbanks. These lessons highlight for emerging markets, particularly in Asia, the importance of having

J.-H. Park (✉)
Asian Development Bank Institute, Tokyo, Japan
e-mail: jhpark@adbi.org

M. Callaghan et al. (eds.), *Global Cooperation Among G20 Countries*,
DOI 10.1007/978-81-322-1659-9_12, © Springer India 2014

sound financial systems to promote long-term and balanced development, as well as to absorb various types of shocks.

2 Financial Reform Process After GFC

After the GFC, diverse financial reform measures were taken by various organizations and countries to make financial systems more resilient and better able to serve the needs of the real economy. The range of the reform itinerary includes: strengthening prudential regulation, reducing systemic risk, increasing regulatory scope, improving internal risk management and compensation systems, developing global accounting standards, and improving measures to deal with noncooperative jurisdictions such as tax havens, money laundering, and terrorist financing.

Among the various organizations that were the locus of coordination, the Financial Stability Board (FSB) took several measures including: complying with Basel III requirements, raising the capital requirement for banks, getting more over-the-counter (OTC) derivatives centrally cleared on platforms, improving the resolvability of systemically important financial institutions (SIFIs), etc. The FSB's measures are aimed at reducing the moral hazard of SIFIs by reducing the probability and impact of an SIFI failure and also by improving resolution capacity. The Basel Committee on Banking Supervision (BCBS) took various prudential regulation measures to increase quantity and quality of bank capital and mitigate procyclicality by introducing a capital buffer and leverage ratio. They also took measures for risk coverage by imposing more capital requirements on trading and maintaining liquidity by establishing long-term and short-term liquidity standards. Similarly, the International Monetary Fund (IMF) took measures for recoupment of existing losses and financing for future crisis[1].

The European Union (EU), Japan, and the USA agreed to work together on clearing platforms for OTC derivatives (FSB 2013). Switzerland has focused on holding more capital than required and is dealing with resolvability in a unique way—a capital rebate if its banks can demonstrate resolvability. From 2013, Canada, Switzerland, and the USA agreed to implement the leverage ratio, not based on risk-weighted assets that run alongside the Basel risk-weighted approach. The leverage ratio is to be calculated as an average over each month. The numerator of the ratio of the Basel III requirement is Tier 1 capitals. The denominator is to be calculated in accordance with financial accounting principles that apply to the bank but with a consistent application of regulatory netting principles to gross assets. Securitized assets will be treated according to the accounting treatment for such assets

[1] IMF took various burden-sharing measures, including: introduction of International Financial Transaction Tax, Windfall Tax, Capital/Liquidity Insurance Fee, etc.

(Shearman & Sterling LLP 2011). The US Dodd–Frank law of 2010 has also placed some regulations on the financial industry and is geared toward protecting consumers with rules like keeping borrowers away from abusive lending and mortgage practices by banks.

Thus, the G20 has already come to several important agreements to enhance global financial regulatory reforms, but some remain to be finalized yet. The G20 agreements reached so far include: requirements for greater quantity and quality of capital; requirements for liquidity; the maximum leverage ratio for commercial banks; standards for OTC derivatives markets (by 2012); and identification, surveillance, regulation, and resolution of SIFIs, especially global ones (G-SIFIs). Several issues are expected to be finalized soon by the G20 including: strengthened oversight of shadow banking; issues related to compensation and credit rating agencies; development of macroprudential frameworks and tools; convergence to strengthen international accounting standards; and strengthened adherence to international supervisory and regulatory standards. Despite all these various measures, there is much discussion and debate going on in the international financial community about the need for more regulations, as well as about the impact, implementation, prioritization, and necessity of consistent implementation of all measures by all countries.

3 Current Status, Progress, and Future Issues

Although many reform measures have been proposed and discussed, they have yet to be fully implemented almost 4 years after the GFC began. National implementation of Basel III started on 1 January 2013, and as of April 2013 rules are fully in force in 13 countries (Australia; Canada; People's Republic of China (PRC); Hong Kong, China; India; Japan; Mexico; Saudi Arabia; Singapore; South Africa; and Switzerland) (BIS 2013a). However, as the introduction of Basel III has been delayed in the USA and the EU (including UK), doubt remains about its timely introduction in emerging market economies. The BCBS finalized a framework for dealing with domestic systemically important banks (D-SIBs), which was approved in November 2012 (BIS 2013b). D-SIB regulations will be fully implemented by 2016 and various opinions on the selection criteria and surcharge level will be considered by conducting pilot testing of selection and surcharges during 2013–2015. Progress on the implementation of shadow banking regulation includes initial recommendations on supervision being announced at the G20 Finance Ministers Meeting in November 2011; the final policy measures will be made by the G20 leaders' summit in September 2013 (FSB 2012a). Countries agreed to implement recommendations for OTC Derivatives Market Reforms by the end of 2012. At the November 2012, G20 Finance Ministers Meeting, the FSB OTC Derivatives Working Group's (ODWG) fourth progress report on implementation was presented (FSB 2012b). Countries were asked to make changes in their legal and regulatory frameworks and to address cross-border issues, regulatory mismatch, and conflicts by the end of 2012. On progress in improving the FSB governance structure, at the Los Cabos Summit in June 2012, G20 leaders agreed to continue to review the representation in the FSB governance structure (FSB 2012c). However, in the November 2012 G20 Finance Ministers Meeting, the Republic of Korea called for the FSB to review and report about its representation arrangements that differentiate seats according to member countries.

International consistency is a critical factor for efficient implementation of the proposed financial regulation measures. Without international consistency, issues will continue to arise about regulatory arbitrage and business migration from more to less controlled jurisdictions. There are also various arguments and questions on the adequacy and appropriateness of the microprudential and macroprudential regulations for ensuring systemic stability, including: (i) are these measures sufficient for ensuring systemic stability; and (ii) are these too tight and overburdening the development of the financial industry?

Furthermore, there are conflicting views over implemented and proposed financial regulatory reforms. According to some views, financial regulations must be strengthened to prevent a future financial crisis (Caruana 2009; Lagarde 2012). However, others argue that regulations that are too tight and strong could strangle the financial industry and weaken economic growth (Subbarao 2012; Sriram et al. 2012). For example, substantial benefits are expected from the implementation of Basel III strategies, including: greater resilience of banks and other financial institutions during financial turbulence, enhanced transparency, improved economic and financial stability, better international cooperation and thus reduced risk of financial crises. However, the potential costs may be significant as well, including: increased regulatory burdens, higher transactions costs, delay in financial sector development, and growth slowdown.

While there are debates on future financial regulations, the lessons of the GFC should be remembered. In particular, it should not be forgotten that loose and soft-touch regulations have failed, incurring huge costs to the global economy. Therefore, future financial regulations should be tight and strong enough to maintain financial stability. In addition, in considering any regulatory reforms it is necessary to consider the many scandals related to financial transactions in recent years such, as Barclays' attempt to manipulate the London interbank offered rate (LIBOR), J.P. Morgan's huge loss from derivatives, HSBC's money laundering, and Standard Chartered Bank's breaching of US rules. Moreover, any future regulatory reform should not adopt the pre-crisis views of self-regulation, market discipline, financial innovation, etc.

Hence, reform efforts need to continue to strengthen financial regulations so as to limit malpractices and misbehavior in the financial industry. Such measures should also establish mechanisms to limit reckless behavior in the financial industry and ensure a stable and growth-supporting financial system, as it is critical for long-term, sustainable, economic growth. Therefore, considering the importance of a stable financial system, the current reform proposals cannot be considered too stringent and threatening overkill of the financial sector.

4 Asian Perspectives: Strengths, Weaknesses, Challenges, and Implications

Asian financial systems have been relatively unscathed by the GFC and the ongoing eurozone crisis, reflecting sound balance sheets, prudent risk management, and modest exposure to toxic assets. This strength of the Asian financial system is due to its sizable nonbanking financial firms and large foreign exchange reserves that provided a cushion against volatile capital flows in most cases. Asian regulatory frameworks were also more "conservative," with less regulatory capture and less ideology about the virtues of free financial markets. Asian regulators had a number of macroprudential policies to deal with a crisis, such as administrative guidance to limit bank-credit growth and real estate loan caps.

However, despite these strengths, Asian financial systems are still relatively bank-dominant, with smaller bond markets and a modest role for securitization and derivative products. Asia also has a low degree of regional financial integration in portfolio investment and depends on London and New York. Moreover, Asian financial systems have limited regulatory capacity to address procyclicality, exposure to activities of large global financial firms, growing non-bank financial activities, and rising financial complexity over time. They are also vulnerable to volatile capital flows and "double mismatches." The 1997–1998 Asian financial crisis underlined a number of substantial inadequacies in Asian financial markets, including: underdevelopment of domestic bond markets and deficiencies in corporate governance, transparency, and financial regulation.

Although Asian financial systems have been resilient to the GFC and the eurozone crisis, this partly reflects immature financial systems that need to be developed to accommodate sustainable economic growth while promoting financial stability. Much of the G20 debate on financial regulations discussed earlier mainly reflects the viewpoints and problems experienced in Europe and the USA and is not necessarily relevant for emerging Asian economies. Consequently, it is necessary to avoid the "one size fits all" approach; rather, emerging Asia's regulatory capacity can be improved by taking measures relevant to the region. Most Asian banks can meet more stringent capital, liquidity, and leverage requirements under Basel III. However, regulations to address weaknesses in US and European banks should not be directly applied to Asia, as complex derivatives products are less developed in the region and many Asian banks have large retail funding bases.

Asian regulators need to review macroprudential policy best practices. Regulatory capacity also needs to be strengthened. However, data requirements for Basel III implementation may impose an excessive burden on some emerging Asian economies. Basel III and related reforms, supervisory and regulatory measures, were designed from the perspective of the experience of developed economies during the GFC. The application of all these directly in developing Asia's context may not be fully relevant. The need for tighter financial regulation and supervision in Asia must be balanced with the need for financial development, deepening, and integration to support sustainable growth in the region. To enhance financial stability, emerging Asian economies need global and regional cooperation to continue efforts to strengthen adequate financial regulation to limit malpractices in the financial industries.

As Asia has been relatively untouched by the GFC and the eurozone crisis, the region does not need to take aggressive measures that are being carried out by a number of European countries, or emergency responses similar to those taken by Asian countries following the 1997–1998 Asian financial crisis. However, both positive and negative lessons from the economic and financial integration in the EU need to be understood as the integration may provide an important benchmark for similar processes in Asia. The region may not be ready for monetary integration for many years to come, but will increasingly require exchange rate policy coordination. In Asia, intraregional exchange rate volatility hurts intraregional trade. Therefore, greater exchange rate cooperation and coordination among Asian economies deserves closer policy consideration to avoid contagion (Zandonini 2013; Tang 2012). In particular, financial integration processes in emerging and developing Asia may focus more on such measures as: domestic financial market development and liberalization, effective national and regional level regulatory and supervisory frameworks, and capacity building to monitor and manage capital flows.

To further advance regional financial integration, Asia needs to further develop bond markets by strengthening the Asian Bond Market Initiative (ABMI), the Asian Bond Fund (ABF), and the Credit Guarantee and Investment Facility (CGIF). Similarly, the Association of Southeast Asian Nations (ASEAN) capital market integration initiative should help promote the harmonization of market regulations, taxes, exchanges, and liberalization of capital flows. Regional macroeconomic and financial surveillance and safety nets may be developed further by strengthening regional approaches, such as the Chiang Mai Initiative Multilateralization (CMIM), ASEAN+3 Macroeconomic Research Office (AMRO), and by working closely with international organizations like the FSB, the IMF, and the World Bank. Similarly, for regional financial stability, an Asian Financial Stability Dialogue (AFSD) could be introduced. It could be the Asian equivalent of the Financial Stability Forum and promote a regional policy dialogue covering policy development on financial reform and regulation, the establishment of standards for governance and transparency, increasing coordination on conducting early warning system analysis, and improving investor confidence.

It is also important to identify potential major systemic risks to Asian economic and financial stability emanating from the GFC and eurozone crisis, and what steps, including regional cooperation, can be taken to minimize the potential impact of those risks. In particular, to sustain Asia's growth, regulators in the region need to take various measures at the national and regional levels, including: improving investor-friendly financial regulations, ensuring predictable and transparent enforcement of financial regulations, and improving financial infrastructure and corporate governance. All these strategies taken at the national and the regional level may complement the strengthening of Asia's financial system to make it more resilient to any potential crisis risks arising regionally or globally.

References

Bank for International Settlements (BIS) (2013a) Progress report on implementation of the Basel regulatory framework. Basel: Bank for International Settlements. http://www.bis.org/publ/bcbs247.pdf. Accessed 11 Apr 2013

Bank for International Settlements (BIS) (2013b) Report to G20 Finance Ministers and Central Bank Governors on monitoring implementation of Basel III regulatory reform. Basel: Bank for International Settlements. http://www.bis.org/publ/bcbs249.pdf. Accessed 12 Apr 2013

Caruna J (2009) Minimising the impact of future financial crises: six key elements of regulatory reform we have to get right. Banque de France, Financial Stability Review, no. 13, September

Financial Stability Board (FSB) (2012a) Overview of progress in the implementation of the G20 recommendations for strengthening financial stability. Report of the Financial Stability Board to G20 leaders. Basel: Financial Stability Board. http://www.financialstabilityboard.org/publications/r_120619a.pdf. Accessed 12 Apr 2013

Financial Stability Board (FSB) (2012b) OTC Derivatives Market Reforms. Fourth Progress Report on Implementation. Basel: Financial Stability Board. http://www.financialstabilityboard.org/publications/r_121031a.pdf. Accessed 12 Apr 2013

Financial Stability Board (FSB) (2012c) Strengthening oversight and regulation of shadow banking: an integrated overview of policy recommendation. Basel: Financial Stability Board. http://www.financialstabilityboard.org/publications/r_121118.pdf. Accessed 10 Apr 2013

Financial Stability Board (FSB) (2013) OTC Derivatives Market Reforms. Fifth Progress Report on Implementation. Basel: Financial Stability Board. http://www.financialstabilityboard.org/publications/r_130415.pdf. Accessed 13 Apr 2012

Lagarde C (2012) IMF/CFP Policy Roundtable on the future of financial regulation. http://www.imf.org/external/np/speeches/2012/041712.htm. Accessed 10 July 2013

Shearman & Sterling LLP (2011) The New Basel III Framework: implications for banking organizations. http://www.shearman.com/files/Publication/f4e80b99-f0a1-4e3a-90f0-3bf21c7d0ce0/Presentation/PublicationAttachment/8d4e19cc-1ba3–4501-8fe6–63a6633d5b6b/FIA-033011 The_new_Basel_III_framework__Implications_for_banking_organizations.pdf. Accessed 5 July 2013

Sriram MS, Chaturvedi V, Neti A (2012) Too big versus too small to be counted. BIS Paper no. 62, January. http://www.bis.org/publ/bppdf/bispap62.pdf. Accessed 10 July 2013

Subbarao D (2012) Financial regulation for growth, equity and stability in the post-crisis world. BIS Paper no. 62, January. http://www.bis.org/publ/bppdf/bispap62.pdf. Accessed 10 July 2013

Tang HC (2012) Is there a Case for exchange rate policy coordination in Asia? ADB Policy Brief no. 4, December.

Zandonini M (2013) Multiple currencies for a multipolar world: all change…or Not? International Economics IE 2013/01. Chatham House, London.

The Challenge of Financial Stability and Regulation from a European Perspective

Paul Bernd Spahn

1 Background

From the early 1980s, the European banking industry has experienced significant institutional and procedural deregulation as well as cost reductions from progress in information and transaction technologies, and from the evaporation of reserve requirements. As a consequence, the industry started to act globally, developing new and by volume vastly growing instruments for financial investments and taking on board unprecedented (and not always well understood and managed) risks. Given the regulatory ease on the industry in the past, the financial crisis and subsequent actions to re-regulate banking was resented as "overkill" by some, but not going far enough by others. The divisive positions on banking regulations are typically heightened by emotions resulting from apparent dysfunctions of the industry ranging from supposedly excessive bonuses, speculation on banks' own accounts with the risks being shifted to taxpayers, to outright fraud, including the rigging of financial data such as the London interbank offered rate (Libor), an important benchmark for financial dealings. All this has undermined confidence in the European banking industry.

Reforming financial regulation is not easy under these auspices. It has to reconcile short-term emergency responses (to reestablish trust and to avoid a meltdown of the financial system) with structural mechanisms of a longer-term bearing and the need to ease the transition to a new regime in order to avoid shocks to the real economy that would affect the growth of investments, production, consumption, and employment.

While Basel III, the main regulatory codex for banking, was originally conceived in a longer-term framework, it has clearly been sharpened under the pressure of the crisis. Additional emergency measures to reestablish trust, such as stress testing, have put new strain on the industry without producing unambiguous results, although they may have helped to soothe markets. Moreover, the catalog of further

P. B. Spahn (✉)
Goethe University, Frankfurt am Main, Germany
e-mail: pbspahn@mac.com; pbspahn@gmail.com

M. Callaghan et al. (eds.), *Global Cooperation Among G20 Countries*,
DOI 10.1007/978-81-322-1659-9_13, © Springer India 2014

demands for regulation inspired by frantic policy making is long. It includes the request for rules on corporate governance and on controlling bonuses; bans on certain operations in investment banking (such as short selling, or the "Volcker rule" on "proprietary trading," i.e., on making speculative investments on a bank's own account); the supervision of commodity derivatives markets; pleas for structural changes such as the separation of commercial and investment banking; the obligatory use of central counterparties for trade of certain instruments; greater transparency of trading activities in equity markets, including "dark pools" (liquidity that is not available on public platforms); new safeguards for algorithmic and high-frequency trading (HFT) activities that could pose possible systemic risks; or the taxation of financial operations and/or assets. In Europe, the discussion is further obscured by proposals to reorganize the supervision of banking institutions at the supranational level.

2 Assessing the Impact of Banking Regulation

The judgment on whether banks may face new challenges under recent legislation such as Dodd–Frank in the USA or the pending implementation of Basel III in both the USA and Europe is not easy given that much is still in flux and some measures may still be "watered down" during the process. Moreover, not all reform proposals sketched above are contained in these pieces of regulation as yet. This renders it difficult to determine appropriate benchmarks for judgment.

I shall address the subject from a European perspective mainly based on Basel III and other proposals such as those discussed in the context of a new European Markets in Financial Instruments Directive (MiFID). I shall also look into the more recent proposals for reorganizing banking supervision in Europe and the euro area in particular.

The main pillars of Basel III and farther-reaching reform proposals can be characterized as follows:

- *Raising the quality, consistency, and transparency of the capital base*: These measures concentrate on enhancing the quality of capital by harmonizing supplementary components such as reserves, hybrid, and subordinated debt, and by eliminating supplementary components that exceed 100 % of the core capital (Tier III capital). It is hard to argue that these provisions would impair the banking business. On the contrary they render banking more resilient (although they may imply extra costs for some institutions).
- *Enhancing risk coverage*: The provisions emphasize new risks in the capital adequacy ratio, such as off-balance sheet risks, derivative related exposures, resecuritization, or counterparty credit risk, for instance. Ignoring such risks had proved to be destabilizing during the crisis. The supervisory measures proposed are of course imperfect substitutes for an effective risk management at the level of the firm (which proved, alas, to be deficient), but they contribute to

establishing a level playing field and to limiting the danger of a competitive race to the bottom and the playing down of risks. This should be to the benefit of the banking industry in general.

- *Constraining the buildup of leverage and introducing financial safeguards*: These provisions aim at mitigating the risk of a destabilizing deleveraging process that could damage the financial system and affect the real economy; and they are also geared toward enhancing transparency.
  It is arguable what a healthy leverage ratio would be[1], but it is obvious that excessive leverage during the pre-crisis years has exacerbated the crisis, bearing on asset prices, and hence on the banks' capital and profitability, and reducing credit availability. Controlling the process of deleveraging is perhaps the greatest challenge for the financial industry, and it will undoubtedly reduce the role of investment banking and constrain the industry's return on capital, needing assistance by monetary authorities during a transition phase (e.g., quantitative easing). But the overall gains in long-run stability and profitability for the society as a whole are likely to outweigh short-run speculative profits based on excessive leveraging.
- *Providing countercyclical buffers and limiting excess growth of credit*: These measures will certainly interfere with banking operations that benefit from procyclicality. Further, they will bear on profitability through the need to make forward-looking provisions that can be relied upon under stress over the business cycle. It is obvious that such provisioning will constrain the distribution of dividends, share buybacks and generous compensation payments, and they will be resented for these reasons. Yet, they are effective tools to address the relevant market failures, aggravated by herd behavior and collective action, by introducing harmonized minimum standards for all banks, which then puts them on equal footing. However, uniform rules on capital adequacy ratios may have an unwarranted price for those institutions that are less exposed to global risks such as savings banks and credit unions. This is why the recent policy decisions regarding financial safeguards differentiate between different groups of financial institutions in Europe.
- *Addressing systemic risk and interconnectedness*: The crisis has clearly exposed the systemic role of larger institutions whose risk portfolios are highly interconnected and may collapse under a shock, which jeopardizes financial stability in general. Capital adequacy rules for such institutions are to be increased by combinations of capital surcharges, contingent capital, and bail-in debt. Again, this will bear on these banks' profits and, from their perspective, could be resented as "overkill". But the long-run gains, if not for the industry then definitely for taxpayers, will certainly outweigh the costs. It could of course be argued that these costs are borne unilaterally by the systemically relevant institutions, which bears on their competitive position. But the extra costs can be shifted into the price

[1] It should be noted however that the UK bank's leverage, until the 1960s, was about 12% (or below before WW I), excepting the two wars. It reached a triple of that value before the financial crisis (Miles 2010, p. 8).

of their sophisticated financial services for which they do not face competition from ordinary banks. Given a heated discussion on the role of systemically relevant banks, subjecting them to macro-prudential supervision and higher capital adequacy standards is politically preferred to radical proposals such as to break them up into smaller units that would be unable to face the challenges of global banking.

- *Introducing a global liquidity standard*: This is an innovative tool in the inventory of banking supervision whose benefits and costs are difficult to assess. Under normal circumstances, a bank should manage its liquidity in pure self-interest. But the crisis has revealed the inadequate provisioning of liquidity by individual banks despite sound capital adequacy, and moreover the uncertainties and distrust among banks have produced liquidity shocks on interbank markets that had to be cushioned by the central bank intervention. Creating a common framework for minimum liquidity standards is unlikely to hurt the business of banks as it will corroborate the interbank market and hence reduce the costs of providing liquidity under strain—provided there are sufficient high quality liquid assets available for banks to meet the standards. It also sets a level playing field for all, which limits the scope for ruinous competition.
- *Channeling certain over-the-counter (OTC) operations through central counterparties*: It is obvious that OTC transactions blur market transparency while unfairly benefiting from services provided by central counterparties (such as price setting). Channeling particularly risk-sensitive transactions through institutionalized counterparties may indeed be more costly, because formerly hidden settlement risks now enter the price explicitly, but it clearly adds to market transparency and stability. This should benefit all market participants, including banks. Of course the main beneficiaries will be the central counterparties themselves of which banks may be the owners. For the financial industry as a whole, the measures are likely to be profitable as the costs can be shifted, at par among banks, onto the final users of the services.
- *Separating commercial from investment banking and banning certain operations*: This topic is highly contentious and, probably, intrudes too far into the structure of the banking sector and its business. However it makes sense to ring-fence depositors and commercial banking from risky financial investments. This could easily be done *within* a bank (as for different lines of business in insurance). The transfer of resources between business lines within the institution should be unrestricted, but be carried out with risk-adjusted transfer prices. Following this rule should be in the commercial interest of banking institutions themselves. As a side effect the overblown profits of investment banking are likely to be reduced in favor of commercial banking. Whether the banks can organize such dealings without common supervisory standards that prevent competitive conflicts among different business lines is doubtful however. Matching commercial and investment banking in a fair play without producing competitive, and inefficient, crowding out of resources remains an unresolved piece of the puzzle where further thinking on supervisory intervention and standard setting is needed.

- As to the outlawing—or controlling—of certain financial operations, a hands-off approach is likely to be commendable. For instance, if short selling were to be forbidden, an important instrument to counter overheating markets would be eliminated. This can only amplify emerging price bubbles. Innovative products such as derivatives may indeed conceal risks, but they may also be used for hedging risks. The appropriate answer must be proper pricing and a better rating of structured products, in particular where resecuritized, according to evaluation rules that attach *the lowest rating* of components onto the entire package, for instance.[2] The contentious Volcker rule is likely to increase the costs of investment banking, but it needs exemptions and privileges in order to become operational. These create loopholes that will undoubtedly be exploited aggressively by innovative firms, which would entail new inequities and inefficiencies that do not just harm customers, but the industry more generally.
  Another case in point is HFT. Allegedly needed to secure liquidity, this kind of trading has degenerated into a race, at the speed of electrons, for tiny arbitrage gains to be reaped from automated processing. Only the technologically most advanced banks can compete for such gains where the winner takes all. Whether this type of "liquidity" is really needed to allow financial institutions to run smoothly or whether it is just an apology to protect this type of "margin reaping" is debatable. As an aside, the interplay of complex trading algorithms is suspected to provoke artificial and excessive volatility through unruly non-linearities in the software.
  Whether HFT renders the financial industry more efficient and serves to keep the financial costs for the ultimate user in the real economy at bay is highly doubtful. On the contrary: the fact that central counterparties seem to grant direct access on site to these privileged traders' computers, and even to spy into the order book pre-trading, must be considered discriminatory at least; at worst it could be criminal (analogously to insider trading).
  I consider such practices unfair and distorted. They could, perhaps, be best controlled or curtailed by financial transaction taxes whose assessment and collection is embedded in the automaticity of the trading algorithm. Given that transactions costs have fallen dramatically over the years, an additional tax on financial transactions at a tiny rate is unlikely to represent a serious challenge for the financial industry.

Whether the proposed measures in banking regulation are sufficient, or do not go far enough, remains an open question. However, it is definitely counterproductive to

[2] For instance structured CDOs allowed institutional investors (such as insurers) to gain access to assets below investment grade, which—on their own—would not have been eligible for their portfolio. As, over time, the share of riskier subprime home equity loans in CDOs increased (from 5% in 2003 to 6% in 2007), hard-to-sell tranches were repackaged (CDO squared or cubed), or "synthetic" CDOs were created from risky credit-default swap contracts, "both the rating agencies and the investment banks failed to recognize the amount of risk inherent in these products" (Barnett-Hart 2009, p. 15). Despite these developments and the massive growth of the CDO market, ratings remained virtually unaltered.

insist on micromanaging the banking business from outside through overly detailed supervisory regulation; and it would be counterproductive to push the reform agenda through swiftly as a *big bang*. Cautious phasing and consistent regulation across countries is needed. Managing the transition process gradually is critical because the deleveraging of credits needs time and assistance from monetary authorities to prevent a breakdown of the real economy.

True, there are a number of pending problems to be resolved, especially as to balancing commercial and investment banking, the inclusion into financial supervision of bank spin-offs (such as special investment vehicles), quasi-banks, and non-banks (such as hedge funds). In this regard actual supervisory rules and propositions may be regarded as incomplete needing further elaboration. Overall, the record of supervisory reforms in banking appears to be balanced and result oriented.

3 The Reorganization of Banking Supervision in Europe

The crisis has emphasized the need to better control financial conglomerates that operate beyond national borders and employ ever more complex financial products and dealings. Further, the increasing integration of international financial markets poses additional risks should one of the important global players fail. Hence, global banking represents a macro-prudential challenge that can only be addressed conjointly at a supranational level. The reorganization of financial supervision in Europe responds to such challenges.

The previous loose organization of European financial supervision relied entirely on national supervisory bodies with some coordination through three European advisory committees with no legal personality (for banks, the Committee of European Banking Supervisors, CEBS). In 2011, the committees were transformed into full-fledged and independent authorities with legal personality and much broader competences. The European Banking Authority (EBA)[3], successor of CEBS, aims at "preventing regulatory arbitrage, guaranteeing a level playing field, strengthening international supervisory coordination, promoting supervisory convergence and providing advice to the EU institutions in the areas of banking, payments and e-money regulation as well as on issues related to corporate governance, auditing and financial reporting."[4]

EBA still works through national authorities for lack of its own supervisory apparatus, but it has substantial powers in the setting of binding standards and of non-binding guidelines ("legislation"), information gathering, consumer protection, the supervision of rating agencies, and even direct supervisory powers in the case

[3] The other two authorities are EIOPA, the European Insurance and Occupational Pensions Authority, and ESMA, the European Securities and Markets Authority.

[4] See http://www.eba.europa.eu/Aboutus.aspx.

of a breach of Union law, action in emergency situations and the settlement of disagreements.

The three authorities cooperate through joint committees on matters of common interest such as anti-money laundering, financial conglomerates, cross-sectoral risks, consumer protection, and financial innovation.

In addition, a new institution was created to place emphasis on the stability of the financial system as a whole: the European System Risk Board (ESRB). Its purpose is to better protect citizens, to rebuild trust in the financial system, and to provide macro-prudential oversight[5].

The structure of the European financial supervision is depicted in Fig. 1.[6]

The euro crisis has spurred further moves toward centralizing European financial supervision of banks. On September 12, 2012, the European Commission proposed to establish a single supervisory mechanism (SSM) for banks in the euro area. In this mechanism, the ultimate responsibility for specific supervisory tasks related to the financial stability of all euro area banks rests with the European Central Bank (ECB). National supervisors will continue to play an important role in the day-to-day supervision and in preparing and implementing ECB decisions.[7]

The establishment of the SSM is complemented by a single rulebook for banking supervision in the form of capital requirements, harmonized deposit protection schemes, and a single European recovery and resolution framework, which are all considered to be relevant steps toward realizing the "Banking Union" of the euro area. Non-euro European countries may join on a voluntary basis. EBA continues to preserve the integrity of the single market, but it cannot overrule decisions by the ECB, which are binding only for euro countries and voluntary members of the club. This renders the ECB the dominant leader in EBA decision making that is likely to prevail in banking supervision for the European Union (EU) as a whole. Moreover the ECB will be able to carry out early intervention measures when a bank breaches, or risks breaching, regulatory capital requirements by requiring banks to take remedial action. As a new lender of last resort and its involvement in a single bank resolution process will give it unprecedented powers that have already met criticism.

The criticism is based on fears of a conflict of interest that cannot be excluded. As the chief warden of the monetary system, the ECB has to make decisions that could provoke market reactions and be politically challenged: the decision, for instance, to recapitalize a particular bank, or to close and unwind it. Although there would be a strict separation of supervisory and monetary policy functions within the

[5] According to the ESRB Regulation: "The ESRB shall be responsible for the macro-prudential oversight of the financial system within the Union in order to contribute to the prevention or mitigation of systemic risks to financial stability in the Union that arise from developments within the financial system and taking into account macroeconomic developments, so as to avoid periods of widespread financial distress. It shall contribute to the smooth functioning of the internal market and thereby ensure a sustainable contribution of the financial sector to economic growth."

[6] From (Sell 2011).

[7] See http://europa.eu/rapid/pressReleasesAction.do?reference=IP/12/953.

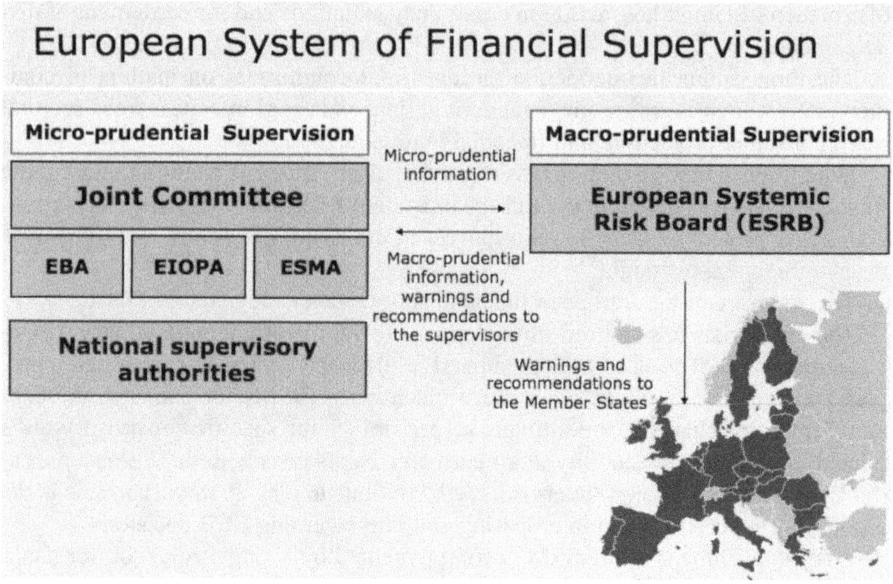

Fig. 1 European system of financial supervision

monetary authority, the ultimate decision is always with the Governing Council, so conflicting interests could indeed emerge. This calls for an independent legitimate arbiter, which could be the European Commission. But it entails strengthening the legitimacy of European institutions more generally, which has been dragging on for so long.

Finally the Commission's timetable is extremely ambitious: The new mechanism was to be put in place in January 2013 for systemically relevant institutions and the coverage would be complete by 2014. This timetable could not be maintained but the move toward a European banking union has gained momentum through a decision, on June 27, 2013, of the Economic and Financial Affairs (ECOFIN) Council on a draft directive[8] establishing a framework for the recovery and resolution of credit institutions and investment firms. The proposed directive is aimed at providing national authorities with common powers and instruments to preempt bank crises and to resolve any financial institution in an orderly manner in the event of failure, while preserving essential bank operations and minimizing taxpayers' exposure to losses.

At whatever speeds the course of creating the Banking Union for the euro area will advance, its high ambitions have found wide political support, and the gist of the proposals is likely to be enacted progressively. This should silence those who believe that financial regulatory reforms in Europe do not go far enough.

[8] No.11148/1/13 REV 1.

4 Conclusions

Financial regulatory reform is a continuing process that has been accelerated by the financial crisis. The response as enshrined in evolving codices such as Basel II and III was to not only reemphasize sound principles of financial management such as capital adequacy or constraints on leverage, but also address new aspects such as countercyclical capital provisions, liquidity buffers, or systemic risk and interconnectedness. None of these provisions will jeopardize the functioning of the financial industry although they will impose new costs and lead to a restructuring of activities.

The reorganization of banking supervision in Europe is still in the making. The persisting challenge is to coordinate financial supervision among a large number of member countries with a financial industry that thrives on cross-border operations and risk transfers. It imposes the need for national authorities to cooperate on matters of common interest such as anti-money laundering, financial conglomerates, cross-sectoral risks, consumer protection, and financial innovation. The proposed framework for a European Banking Union is ambitious in that it aims at centralizing banking supervision under the umbrella of the European Central Bank, which is highly prone to generate political conflicts, not the least between the euro zone and Europe's most important financial centre, London.

References

Barnett-Hart AK (2009) The story of the CDO market meltdown: an empirical analysis. Dissertation, Harvard College, Cambridge Massachusetts

Miles D (2010) Leverage and monetary policy, Monetary Policy Committee, Bank of England. Speech delivered at ESRI/FFS Conference, Dublin, 12 October 2010

Sell M (2011) The new architecture for European financial supervision, Bundesanstalt für Finanzdienstleistungsaufsicht (BAFin), Germany. Speech delivered at ESE Conference, Luxembourg, 28 September 2011

Financial Regulatory Reforms: Striking a Balance

Anand Sinha

Regulatory reforms undertaken in the aftermath of global crisis have generated a serious debate regarding their adequacy, efficacy and also of their need and relevance. Some argue that the reforms are a case of overkill comprising onerous measures such as enhanced capital and liquidity requirements which will adversely affect economic growth and profitability of banks. The structural measures such as prohibition under the Dodd-Frank Act on proprietary trading by US banks, bank holding companies and their affiliates, or moving OTC derivatives to the central counterparties are also criticised to be negatively impacting market liquidity and financial firms' ability and willingness to innovate. The proponents of reforms, however, aver that the reforms are imperative to put the crisis battered financial system back on track, restore systemic stability and facilitate long-term growth. This paper, analyzing both the arguments, suggests that the answer lies in striking the right balance by devising a regulatory framework which ensures stability, encourages innovation and promotes growth.

Regulatory reforms undertaken as a policy response to the global financial crisis have generated as serious a debate as the crisis itself. The crisis is unprecedented in terms of its coverage, impact and longevity. The policy response to the crisis, too, has been quite extensive and as some would say, onerous. Going by Newton's third law of motion (*every action has an equal and opposite reaction*), it is fair to expect that reaction (policy response to the crisis) matches action (the crisis), in magnitude. Many, however, hold the view that this law has been violated inasmuch as the policy reaction is a case of overkill.

The crisis has highlighted many gaps in the conceptual framework. Some of the gaps are: the notion that macroeconomic stability ensures financial stability; light-touch regulation and supervision are adequate because financial markets are sophisticated and efficient which can distribute risks to those who can handle these risks; risk models measure risk accurately and all financial innovations are useful. Serious gaps have also emerged in macroeconomic modelling and, above all, in the understanding, or lack of understanding, of systemic risk and how to deal with

A. Sinha (✉)
Reserve Bank of India, Mumbai, India
e-mail: anandsinha@rbi.org.in

M. Callaghan et al. (eds.), *Global Cooperation Among G20 Countries*,
DOI 10.1007/978-81-322-1659-9_14, © Springer India 2014

it. The crisis has challenged the intellectual foundations of macroeconomic and financial policy making. New theories have been written debunking the old ones and a new regulatory framework is being put in place to make the financial system more resilient. The redesigned regulatory framework encompasses measures, such as enhancing the quality and quantity of capital to be maintained by banks, reducing leverage, enhancing risk coverage, stipulating liquidity ratios and maintenance of countercyclical capital buffers, amongst others. More importantly, the recognition of the role of systemic risk and the importance of financial stability are the major lessons learnt from the crisis.

1 Reforms: Not Far Enough or Overkill? A Continuing Debate

The new regulatory framework, inasmuch as it requires higher quantum of better quality capital and liquidity buffers leading to reduced leverage, has raised intense debate over the impact they could have on economic growth and the profitability of banks. It is argued that increased capital requirements would impinge on the profitability of banks, forcing them to either increase their lending rates to maintain their margins or cut down on lending to preserve their capital base, both of which may have a large negative impact on economic growth. The proposed restrictions on activities permitted to be undertaken by banks and the ring fencing of certain banking activities have also led to concerns in some quarters. The prohibition under the Dodd–Frank Act on proprietary trading by US banks, bank holding companies and their affiliates, despite certain carve outs has, particularly, caused discomfort from the perspective of the negative impact on market liquidity and cross-border implications.

There is also a serious debate on the impact of these regulations on innovation in the financial system. Regulations, such as the proposals to standardise the bespoke financial derivatives and moving their settlements to central counterparties (CCPs), are argued to be impacting firms' ability and willingness to innovate. By stifling the innovating ability of firms, the regulations, it is being argued, would impact the development of the financial system and, eventually, economic growth.

Another interesting debate is about the efficacy of increasingly complex regulations. It is argued that for a set of the world's most complex banks, simple weighted measures appear to have greater pre-crisis predictive power than risk-weighted alternatives (Haldane 2012). Moreover, the pursuit of increased risk sensitivity in formulating regulations has considerably increased the complexity, due to the use of complex models and difficulties in measuring accurately the model input parameters. Therefore, it is concluded that increasing the complexity of regulations is not necessarily the solution to build resilience and avert crisis.

On the other hand, many feel that these regulations are necessary to preserve systemic stability and to ensure long-term growth. The crisis has wreaked havoc on the global economy with significant economic and social costs. To strengthen the financial system and enhance the systemic stability with a view to minimising the incidence of such crises in future, it is argued that stronger regulation is necessary. It is also argued that the benefits of financial stability would outweigh the costs of regulation and, therefore, there is a good reason for revamping the regulatory framework. In response to the criticism of increasing complexity of regulations, it is said that such complexity is a by-product of the desire for risk sensitivity and without proper measurement, risk may build-up undetected (Ingves 2012). Further, because of incentive effects, simple measures are more likely to be arbitraged, with banks undertaking riskier activities while reducing the less risky ones (Byres 2012).

A recent discussion paper put out for comments by Basel Committee for Banking Supervision (BCBS 2013) attributes the increased complexity of the regulatory framework to factors such as continuous innovation within financial markets, alignment with banks' risk management practices, adaptation of rules to accommodate new products etc., and also posits that some complexity within the regulatory framework is inevitable, as banks' business models cannot be simplified beyond a limit. Nevertheless, the BCBS recognises that maintaining a reasonable balance between simplicity and risk sensitivity is critical.

These debates are still inconclusive and the judgment on whether these regulations are a necessity or a case of overkill is broadly dependent on which side of the fence one is on, i.e., whether one is a regulator or associated with a regulated financial sector entity. There are, of course, many others not in either of the two categories, who hold strong views. While even critics broadly agree on the idea that regulations need a revamp, the critical question remains, how much regulation is adequate? At what point do regulations start to have diminishing returns—regulatory costs outweighing benefits? And does financial regulation—which is global in scope—cater to the local needs of specific jurisdictions?

2 Striking the balance

The arguments, both supporting and opposing new regulations, have their own merits. While new regulations do moderate innovation and lead to increased costs, which could impact the economic growth in the short term, the redesigning of regulation to address the gaps that led to the crisis is imperative. The answer, therefore, lies in striking the right balance to ensure that the new regulations achieve their objective of strengthening the resilience of the financial system, while at the same time not adversely impact economic growth and socially useful innovation.

2.1 Impact on Growth

Basel III stipulates the maintenance of equity capital of 7% (including the capital conservation buffer of 2.5%) as against the earlier requirement of 2%. This substantial increase in equity capital requirements, coupled with other changes such as liquidity standards etc., would increase the cost of funding for banks, which could have, eventually, an adverse impact on economic growth. However, these costs need to be seen in perspective. These are the costs that the system would endure in the short term for the long-term benefits arising out of higher stability and reduced frequency of banking crises. It is established that the effects of banking crises are long lasting and the damages they inflict on economies are significant. Therefore, the increased costs arising out of new regulations need to be seen as costs incurred in building stronger systems, which offer payback in terms of reduced incidence of crises.

The Macroeconomic Assessment Group of the Basel Committee had concluded that if Basel III requirements are implemented over a longer period of time (35 quarters), the impact on growth would be minimal (0.03 % per annum below its baseline level during this period) and there would be recovery in growth towards baseline after this period. This is considered affordable as the long-term benefits of stability far outweigh the costs of instability. Keeping this in consideration, the implementation period of Basel III is kept sufficiently long (6 years).

2.2 Impact on Innovation

The crisis has emphatically displayed the ill effects of unbridled innovation, which led to suboptimal and even disastrous results. In the pre-crisis period, financial innovation reached its peak and, in the process, financial markets got delinked from the real sector and assumed a life of their own. For ensuring sustainable development, it is imperative that finance is firmly linked, and be subservient, to the real sector and financial innovation remains responsible. Incorporating lessons learnt from the crisis, the new regulatory framework envisages reducing the complexity and opaqueness of financial instruments and fostering innovation that is socially optimal.

2.3 Simplifying the Regulations

The debate over the efficacy of complex regulations is actively engaging policy makers. The roots of complexity lie in Basel II rules. While much of Basel II was not in operation prior to the crisis, its internal model-based market risk framework was a carryover from the Amendment to the Basel I framework in 1996. This framework was found seriously deficient as most of the impact of the crisis was in the trading books of banks, where the actual losses were several multiples of the regulatory capital requirements. This clearly points to the inadequacy of the models. In fact, there is a more fundamental issue involved here. These risk models can never have the predictive powers of models used in physics, as the financial risk models do not operate in a framework of immutable laws of nature. In fact, they have to contend with human psychology and behaviour, which cannot be modelled, but it is this behaviour that assigns 'value' to financial instruments. Therefore, a question arises against so much model generated complexity.

While simplicity of regulations is welcome, it ought to be recognised that a complex financial system cannot be regulated in a simplistic manner: such an approach would be arbitraged away by banks and would result in riskier portfolios. Further, no single metric would be sufficient as it would likely be gamed. My conjecture is that if the evidence shows that the simple leverage ratio was a more effective predictor of stress in banks, it could, perhaps, be because it was not a closely watched metric. The moment regulations are built around one metric, there would be incentives to game it (Sinha 2013). The regulatory framework, therefore, will have to be a combination of risk based and non-risk based backstops. A combination of various measures differing in their complexity would cover up inadequacies of single measures of risk and, thus, collectively provide a safer framework. To improve simplicity and comparability of regulations, the BCBS Working Paper (BCBS 2013) has proposed measures, such as (i) using additional metrics viz., leverage ratios, risk measures derived from equity volatility, revenue-based leverage ratios; (ii) utilising added floors and benchmarks to address model risks; (iii) reconsidering linkage between internal and regulatory models; (iv) limiting national discretion and improving supervisory consistency and (v) explicitly recognising simplicity as an additional objective along with comparability.

2.4 *Relevance for Emerging and Developing Economies*

The relevance of the Basel III framework to emerging and developing economies (EDEs) is often questioned as the financial system in EDEs did not have the features of the financial system of the advanced economies and they were not the originators of the crisis. However, considering that we live in a globalised and integrated world, no jurisdiction would be completely insulated from the impact of crisis in other jurisdictions. It becomes, therefore, imperative for EDEs to build resilience by adopting the Basel III framework. In fact, there are several jurisdictions: more notably, Australia, Canada, China, India, Japan, Singapore, Switzerland etc., who did not contribute to the crisis but have committed to implement the Basel III reforms realising the obvious benefits. A higher capital and liquidity regime will provide better defence to EDEs both from the perspective of their domestic operations as well as from the spillover contagion from cross-border flows.

3 Unfinished Agenda and Work in Progress

1. The redesigning of regulations distilling the lessons taught by the crisis has been an enormous task for policy makers. While a significant amount of work is already done, work relating to some critical areas is still in progress, such as the framework for forward looking provisioning, management of liquidity risk, cross-border resolution mechanism and oversight and surveillance of the shadow banking system.

2. Some parts of the new regulations, despite having a recently designed framework, need more clarity. For example, there are currently no readily available and widely accepted metrics of systemic risk to help calibrate instruments or gauge policy performance, even *ex post*, with much precision (Caruana 2012). The transmission mechanism of macroprudential policies needs to be better understood and modelled. Similarly, interaction between liquidity coverage ratio (LCR) and monetary policy is an area which is still being examined. The likely asymmetrical effect of macroprudential policies during the upturn and downturn phases of the economy and fine tuning of communication by central banks or designated macroprudential regulators on macroprudential issues and policies are other areas that require focused attention. The possible role of monetary policy in leaning against credit cycles is being researched and debated and it may be a while before a clear direction emerges.

3.1 Summing up

The debate as to whether the regulatory reform is a case of overkill is a continuing one. The broad consensus, however, is that the direction of the reforms is the right one. While there could be differences regarding the 'right' magnitude and the pace and the sequencing of reforms, there can be no ambivalence regarding the necessity of financial sector reforms, which strike a balance between the objectives of supporting growth, fostering innovation and achieving stability.

References

BCBS-Basel Committee on Banking Supervision (2013) The Regulatory Framework: Balancing risk sensitivity, simplicity and comparability. Discussion paper. http://www.bis.org/publ/bcbs258.pdf

Byres W (2012) Regulatory Reforms—Incentives matter. Remarks to the Bank of Portugal Conference on Global Risk Management: Governance and Control, Lisbon, 24 October 2012. http://www.bis.org/speeches/sp121024.pdf

Caruana J (2012) Dealing with financial systemic risk: the contribution of macroprudential policies. Panel remarks at Central Bank of Turkey/G20 Conference on 'Financial Systemic Risk' Istanbul, 27–28 September 2012. http://www.bis.org/speeches/sp121002.pdf

Haldane AG, Madouros V (2012) The Dog and the Frisbee. Given at the Federal Reserve Bank of Kansas City's 366th economic policy symposium "The changing policy landscape", Jackson Hole, Wyoming, 31 August 2012. http://www.bankofengland.co.uk/publications/Documents/speeches/2012/speech596.pdf

Ingves S (2012) Basel III is simpler and stronger. Op-ed published in the Wall Street Journal, 15 October 2012. http://www.bis.org/review/r121017b.pdf

Sinha A (2013) Approach to regulation and supervision in the post crisis world. Address at the programme 'Supervisory Effectiveness in the Post Crisis World' organised by Centre for Advanced Financial Research and Learning (CAFRAL) at Mumbai on February 4, 2013. http://www.bis.org/review/r130312e.pdf

Part IV
A New Framework for Reforming the International Monetary System

Reforming the International Monetary System: an Institutional Perspective

Jyoti Rahman, Ewa Orzechowska-Fischer and Redom Syed

1 Introduction

The international monetary system (IMS) consists of the rules, institutions, political environment and collaborative frameworks that facilitate cross-border exchange of goods and services and flow of capital. The current IMS originated in the aftermath of the Second World War, with the memory of the Great Depression fresh in policy-makers' minds. However, the IMS has evolved greatly since, and would be barely recognisable to the original designers.

The collapse of the Bretton Woods system in the early 1970s and the subsequent widespread adoption of flexible exchange rate regimes are obvious key changes, as are the steady liberalisation of capital accounts around the world. The role played by the G7 advanced economies as an informal 'steering committee' for the system in the past few decades is yet another major change. Perhaps most importantly, over the decades, the system has grown to become a truly global one.

The current IMS has survived for over 40 years, underpinning substantial increases in global trade and cross-border capital flows, contributing to the growth of the global economy and the re-emergence of dynamic emerging markets. As

The authors are from the International Finance and Development Division of the Australian Treasury. The views expressed in the paper are their own, and not necessarily shared by the Australian Treasury. An earlier version of the paper was presented by Matt Crooke, Minister-Counsellor (Economic) at the Australian High Commission in India at the conference titled: *Global Economic Cooperation: Views from G20 countries* organised by ICRIER in New Delhi, October 7–9, 2012. The paper benefitted from the work of Aidan Storer, Nathan Pringle, Thomas Williamson, Kristina Nemet, Adam Hawkins and Vince Barbatano, and comments of Matthew Flavel, Barry Sterland, Michael Callaghan and Sue Vroombout.

J. Rahman (✉) · E. Orzechowska-Fischer · R. Syed
International Finance and Development Division, Department of Treasury, Canberra, Australia
e-mail: Jyoti.Rahman@treasury.gov.au

M. Callaghan et al. (eds.), *Global Cooperation Among G20 Countries*,
DOI 10.1007/978-81-322-1659-9_15, © Springer India 2014

a result, interdependence among the world's economies has grown dramatically, making the existence of a sound system ever more important.

At the same time, the IMS has exhibited symptoms of instability such as frequent exchange rate misalignments, persistent current account imbalances and volatile capital flows (Moghadam 2011). These symptoms, along with internal imbalances and policy mistakes in systemically important economies, culminated in the 2008–2009 global financial crisis (GFC). In the wake of the crisis the IMS was subject to strong criticism—for example, former British Prime Minister Gordon Brown advocated to world leaders the need for a new monetary system (Boughton 2009).

To be effective, the IMS must deliver both sufficient nominal stability in exchange rates and domestic prices and timely adjustments to shocks and structural change. Monetary systems in the past have failed to manage this trade-off. However, as we go on to show, those systems also lacked the international policy frameworks to respond to crises when they did occur. This paper argues that the current system has proven itself resilient in handling the direst of economic conditions.

We propose an alternative perspective on the performance of the IMS following the 2008–2009 crisis, focussing the debate back towards meaningful and achievable action to help guard against future crises. We do not seek to make grandiose statements claiming the need for an alternate framework. Instead we argue that the strength of the international policy frameworks during the GFC, through the actions of the Group of 20 (G20) and the International Monetary Fund (IMF), show that the system is flexible and resilient. In this, we compare the performance of the current system to previous systems before it, which crumpled under the weight of similar turbulent economic conditions.

Of course there are significant economic challenges ahead that will test the operation of the IMS. The multi-speed world recovery will require a careful balancing act by international institutions between providing effective, tailored policy advice and the need to be even-handed. Furthermore, the economic difficulties of the advanced world may lead to greater willingness to protect their domestic industries from import surges at the expense of the developing world.

In the absence of a unified adjustment mechanism, the IMS needs strong, well-functioning international institutions. For this reason, this paper focusses on the role, performance and future of international institutions in the IMS.

Accordingly, we stress the need to improve the legitimacy of international institutions like the IMF as a key area of reform. This involves delivering a quota formula that reflects the rising influence of emerging economies.

We begin in Sect. 2 by profiling the increasingly interconnected nature of the world economy, and recount the events of 2008 and 2009, when the GFC was in its most virulent phase. Section 3 details the renewed role of the G20 and highlights the strength of the IMF's response to the global crisis. Section 4 sheds light on the importance of improving the legitimacy of the IMF and provides some thoughts on how to implement difficult international reforms.

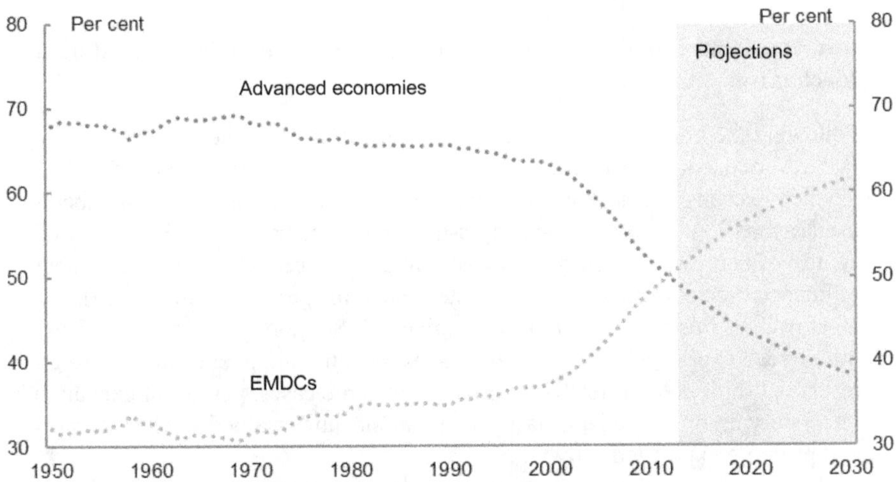

Fig. 1 Share of global GDP (PPP). (Source: Au-Yeung et al. 2013)

2 The Interconnected Global Economy and the Global Financial Crisis

In the decades since the founding of the current IMS, the global economy has grown in size and its composition has significantly changed. As shown in Fig. 1, the world economy is in the midst of a dramatic shift towards emerging market and developing countries (EMDCs). As late as 1950, EMDCs—then home to nearly two-thirds of humanity—produced only about a third of global output. Today, they are poised to overtake the advanced economies in production. If current trends continue, the EMDCs with nearly 85 % of the world population may produce nearly two-thirds of global output by 2050 (UN Population Division 2011; Au-Yeung et al. 2013).

As the global economy has grown, it has also become more complex and interconnected. The shift in global economic activity towards the EMDCs has been accompanied by their increased integration with the IMS. Global gross flows of capital have increased dramatically, from an average of less than 5 % of global GDP during the 1980s and the 1990s to a peak of about 20 % by 2007 (IMF 2012a). This increase has been accompanied by a substantial rise in the volatility of capital flows, visible in their sharp drop in the aftermath of the GFC followed by their moderate recovery.

This rapid rise in capital movements, together with an increase in global liquidity observed over recent decades, facilitated positive spillovers as increased flows of goods, services and capital assisted in lifting millions out of poverty. However, the increasing interconnectedness of the global economy also resulted in cross-country financial linkages becoming increasingly complex. In the absence of effective adjustment mechanisms, this interconnectedness led to a build-up of global imbalances (Box 1). Together with significant failings in financial regulation and

Box 1: Global imbalances and the Lack of a Symmetrical Adjustment Mechanism

Following the breakdown of the Bretton Woods system in the early 1970s, the IMS reverted to a more decentralised, market-based model. Major countries floated their exchange rates, made their currencies convertible, and gradually liberalised capital flows. The move to market-determined exchange rates has increased control of domestic monetary policy and inflation, accelerated the development of financial sectors and ultimately boosted economic growth (Carney 2009).

However, this trend has not been universal. Some major economies frustrated real exchange rate adjustments by accumulating enormous foreign reserves (Table 1) and sterilizing inflows. In some cases, persistent exchange rate intervention served primarily to maintain undervalued exchange rates and promote export led growth.

The flip side of these imbalances was large current account deficit in the United States and other advanced economies (Lim and Pontines 2012). In combination with high savings rates in East Asia, these policies generated low long-term interest rates which, in turn, fed the search for yield and excessive leverage. While concerns over global imbalances were frequently expressed in the run-up to the crisis, the IMS did not promote actions to address the problem and vulnerabilities grew until breaking point.

Flexible exchange rates prevent and limit imbalance problems by providing a symmetrical adjustment mechanism. Monetary systems in the past have failed to manage this trade-off between nominal stability and timely adjustment processes. However, as we go on to show, those systems also lacked international policy coordination in responding to crises when they did occur. The current system, in contrast, has proven itself resilient in handling the direst of economic conditions.

major internal imbalances in systemically important economies, the global imbalances were one of the underlying causes of the GFC.

Of course, the GFC is a stark example of negative spillovers that may arise in an interconnected world economy. While the prospect of a rapid intensification of financial market stress had earlier been identified as a clear downside risk to the global outlook, the speed and extent of the deterioration in global financial and economic conditions exceeded any in living memory.

What started as a problem in the United States housing market in 2007 was eventually transmitted through the international financial system (IFS) to the global economy. After Lehman Brothers collapsed in September 2008, the global financial system experienced severe disruptions. The real economy was hit hard by an unprecedented synchronised fall in world trade and production. By the end of 2008, the financial crisis had hit the world's docks and factory floors. Millions of jobs were lost around the world.

Table 1 International reserves of selected countries (Source: National Statistical Agencies, World Bank, IMF, Economist Intelligence Unit)

	Reserves (US$ billions)	Reserves/GDP		Reserves/monthly imports		Reserves/M2 (%)	
		2000	2008	2000	2008	2000	2008
China	2273	13.8	45	8.1	19	10.1	28
Russia	434	10.8	26.6	5.5	13.9	50.2	74.8
India	278	7.6	22.7	6.6	8.3	14	31.3
South Korea	264	18	21.7	6.0	4.6	29.4	36.8
Brazil	231	5.1	12	5.5	10.6	11.6	23.6
Thailand	135	26.6	42.6	5.5	6.5	25.1	41.7
Malaysia	96	30.6	47	3.6	6.0	25	36.4
Canada	56	4.5	3.1	1.4	1	6.2	2.7

With rapid declines in credit flows, equity values and consumer confidence, strong financial and real economy linkages saw the tremors which rocked financial markets transform into an unprecedented synchronised global contraction of production, trade and capital flows. The result was a global GDP contraction of around 0.60 % in 2009 (Fig. 2). While every country was affected, the impacts were especially stark amongst advanced economies.

Even as policymakers sought to contain the crisis, the financial systems of the crisis-affected countries exacerbated the situation through various channels, including by exposing existing vulnerabilities in the European sovereign debt markets. As bad as the conditions were in late 2008 and early 2009, another Great Depression—and accompanying geopolitical dislocations and human sufferings—did not eventuate. Section 3 will highlight the role and importance of the G20 and the IMF in ensuring that this level of disaster was averted.

3 The Response from International Institutions

The extraordinarily dire economic conditions in the global economy detailed in Sect. 2 forced the current IMS to face its greatest test. Global policymakers, through the G20 and IMF, had to pull together to provide a multilateral policy response or potentially risk the disintegration of the IMS.

3.1 Group of 20

G20 economies account for approximately 80 % of the gross world product, 80 % of world trade (including EU intra-trade) and two-thirds of the world population. At its core, the G20 is designed to address macroeconomic problems pertaining to global demand and price stability. In a broader sense, the G20 stands as the guardian of

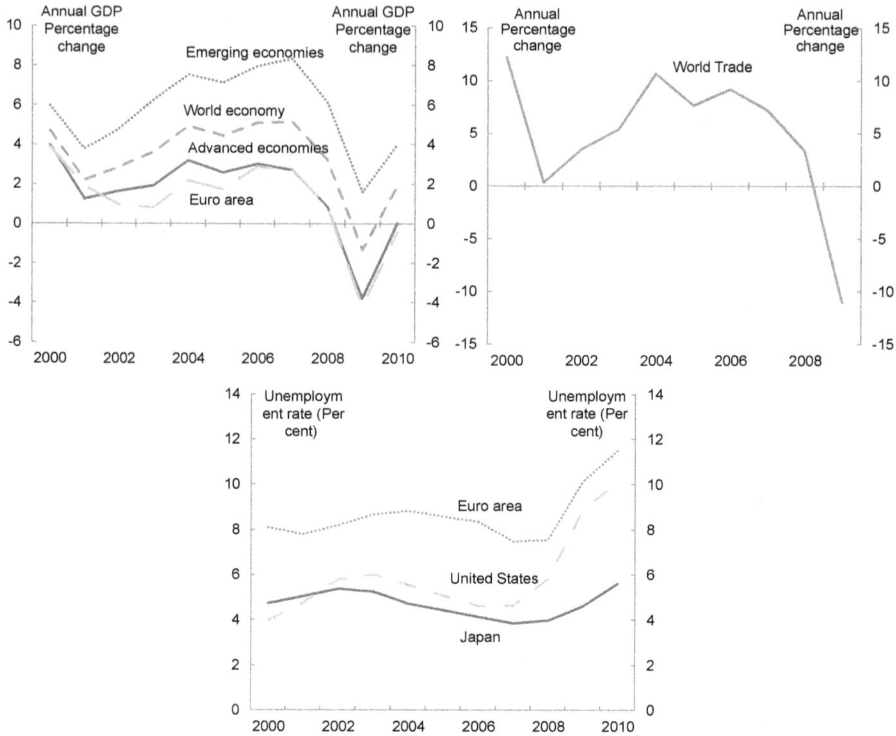

Fig. 2 Economic indicators during 2000s. (Source: IMF 2013a, b; World Economic Outlook Data)

a global common interest, as a way for states to head off the sources of instability, extremism and conflict that proved to be so debilitating in the 1930s.

Against the backdrop of the worst global recession in living memory and continued financial instability, the first G20 Leaders' Summit took place in Washington in November 2008.[1] Seven G20 Leaders' Summits have taken place since, elevating G20 to a leaders-driven forum. In Washington, G20 leaders pledged not to erect trade barriers in response to deteriorating global conditions (Box 2). This was an important policy step and an early sign of strong international political collaboration.

Leaders of the G20 economies reconvened in London in April 2009. Arguably, it was at this summit where the leaders' response to the adverse conditions framed the G20 as the premier forum for international economic cooperation and decision making. At the Summit, the G20 leaders pledged to do 'whatever was necessary' to restore confidence, growth and jobs, repair the damaged financial system and

[1] The G20 was formally established in September 1999 when finance ministers and central bank governors of seven major industrial countries (Canada, France, Germany, Italy, Japan, the United Kingdom and the United States) met in Washington DC in the aftermath of the Asian financial crisis of 1997–1998. Finance ministers and central bank governors started to hold annual meetings after the inaugural meeting on December 15–16, 1999, in Berlin.

Box 2: The Great Depression and Protectionism

To truly appreciate the importance of G20 action during the global financial crisis, it must be viewed in the context of the 1920's Great Depression. In 1929, the decline in the US economy hit most other countries, exposing pre-existing internal weaknesses and resulting in a collapse of economic conditions. By the late 1920s, a steady decline in the world economy had set in, not reaching the bottom until 1933 (Romer 2003) (Table 2).

Governments around the world erected tariff and non-tariff barriers to trade in an effort to direct spending to merchandise produced domestically rather than abroad. However, with other governments responding in kind, the distribution of demand across countries remained relatively unchanged. The main effect was to destroy trade which, despite the economic recovery in most countries after 1933, failed to reach its 1929 peak, as measured by volume, even by the end of the decade. The benefits of comparative advantage were lost. Recrimination over beggar-thy-neighbour trade policies made it more difficult to agree on other measures to halt the slump or assist the recovery.

Despite the magnitude of the economic calamity, economies proved incapable of cooperating to turn things around, refusing to provide mutual aid and engaging in crude protectionism. As economic historian Charles Kindleberger described, '*when every country turned to protect its national private interest, the world public interest went down the drain and with it the private interests of all.*' (Berkeley, Kindleberger 1973).

Table 2 Change in economic indicators 1929–1932. (Source: Eichengreen and Irwin 2009)

	United States	Great Britain	France	Germany
Industrial production	−46%	−23%	−24%	−41%
Wholesale prices	−32%	−33%	−34%	−29%
Foreign trade	−70%	−60%	−54%	−61%
Unemployment	607%	129%	214%	232%

reform international financial institutions to help overcome the crisis and prevent future ones. Specifically, the leaders pledged an additional US$ 1.1 trillion program of support to restore credit, growth and jobs in the world economy.[2] This pledge was described as an unprecedented effort by major countries to stimulate

[2] This pledge consisted of: a trebling of the resources available to the IMF to US$ 750 billion; a new special drawing right allocation of US$ 250 billion; at least US$ 100 billion of additional lending by the multilateral development banks; US$ 250 billion of support for trade finance; and the use of the additional resources from agreed IMF gold sales for concessional finance for the poorest countries.

their economies *together* with expansionary fiscal and monetary policies (Bradford and Wonhyuk 2011).

At the height of the crisis there was a collective sense of danger. Through the most virulent phase of the global crisis, the decisive and coordinated actions of G20 members boosted consumer and business confidence and supported the first signs of economic recovery.

3.2 International Monetary Fund

From its inception in 1944, the IMF's primary purpose has been to ensure the stability of the IMS, which is essential for promoting sustainable economic growth, increasing living standards and reducing poverty. In addition to crisis resolution through financial support to countries undergoing necessary balance of payments adjustments, the way the IMF achieves the stability of the system is through preventative tools, namely the IMF's surveillance activities.

During the mid-2000s, the IMF had been going through somewhat of an existential crisis, with a reduced role in the global economy and a damaged reputation following the Asian Financial Crisis in 1997. Many commentators suggested that the IMF was going through a crisis of legitimacy (Seabrooke 2006), with strong underrepresentation of emerging economies and record lows in IMF lending (Fig. 4).

The IMF's early forecast of the severity of the global recession (IMF 2012b) helped mobilise concerted official action to address quickly and forcefully these extraordinary economic and financial events by providing fiscal stimulus to sustain growth, as well as capital injections and guarantees to ease the credit crunch (Xafa 2010).

Following the emergency summit of G20 leaders in Washington in November 2008, support packages for banks were put together in the United States, Europe, and elsewhere to prevent the disorderly failure of systemically important institutions and to restore confidence in the financial system. Furthermore, the IMF increased and deployed its lending firepower to add confidence to the global economy, created a crisis firewall by mobilising resources on a global scale, introduced structural governance reforms that added layers of legitimacy to the IMF's activities and sharpened its analysis of risks, spillovers and interconnectedness in the global economy.

Increase in IMF resources

At the 2009 London Summit, in response to the rapid fall in global liquidity at the onset of the global crisis, G20 Leaders managed to increase global safety nets through increasing IMF resources via temporarily expanding the IMF's New Arrangements to Borrow (NAB) from US$ 34 billion to US$ 370 billion. Further, in October 2010, IMF members agreed to permanently increase the IMF's resources

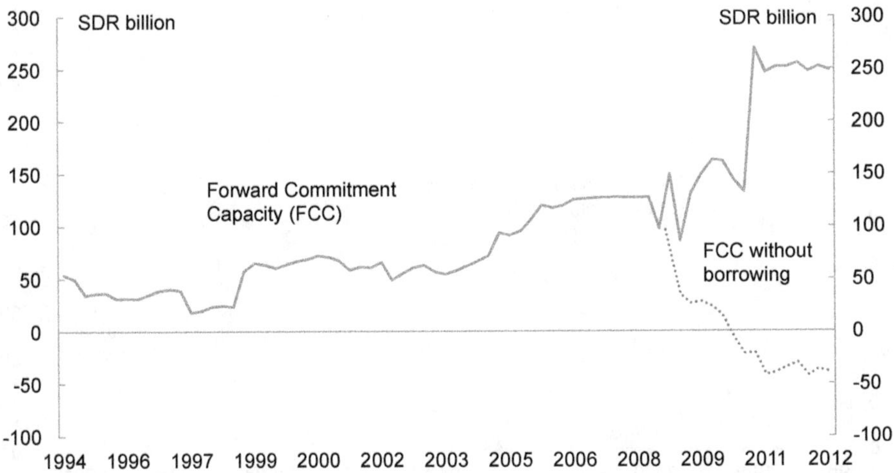

Fig. 3 IMF forward lending capacity with and without borrowing. (Source: IMF Finance Department; Note: Forward commitment capacity refers to the amount of the IMF resources available for new lending at a given point of time)

by doubling its quotas.[3] More recently, at the 2012 Los Cabos Summit, G20 Leaders further supplemented the IMF NAB and quota resources with bilateral loans worth more than US$ 456 billion. As Fig. 3 illustrates, the boost in funding coming from borrowed resources (NAB and bilateral loans), substantially increased the amount of resources available for IMF lending.

This large increase in IMF resources not only bolstered the IMF's lending capacity to support its rapid ramping up in lending activities, but also acted as a powerful symbol that the global community is committed to ensure the stability of the IMS.

At the time of writing, the IMF has provided over US$ 300 billion in loans to its member countries since the onset of the financial crisis in 2007 (IMF 2013a, b). A large part of this lending went to members in dire need of funds. As the European sovereign debt crisis required the most urgent funding assistance, euro area countries accounted for the bulk of IMF lending (Fig. 4).

Furthermore, the IMF also created a flexible credit line (FCL) and a precautionary liquidity line (PLL) for countries with strong economic fundamentals, aimed at bolstering market confidence and moderating balance of payments pressures for members availing themselves of, or expected by markets to, qualify for these programs. As Fig. 5 shows, since the onset of the crisis, between 2009 and 2013, a significant amount of resources (on average over 26 % of total IMF quotas) has been committed to these precautionary lending programs.

[3] The IMF has two main sources of funding to support its lending: quota resources (which are similar to equity contributions from members) and borrowings (which involve a contingent line of credit from member countries, generally under the New Arrangements to Borrow (NAB), more recently bilateral loans). The doubling of IMF quotas, agreed upon in 2010 reforms will come into effect alongside a significant rollback of the NAB.

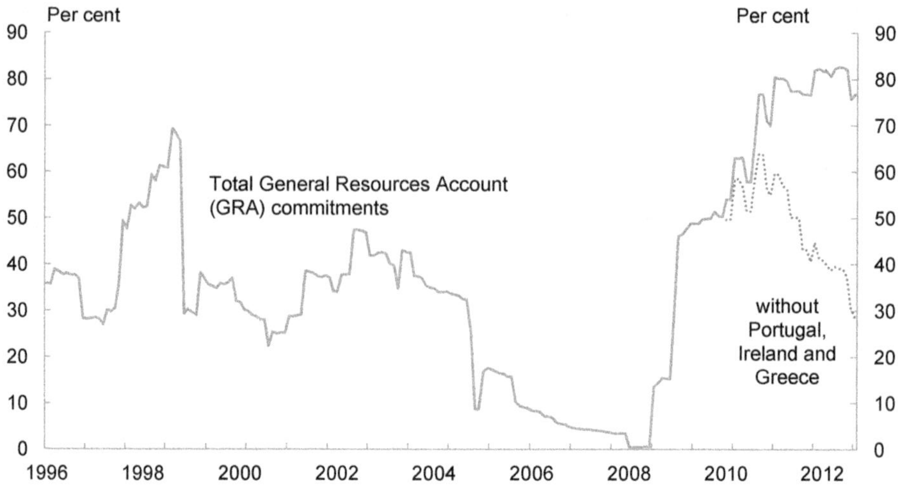

Fig. 4 IMF lending to euro area. (Source: Authors' calculations based on IMF financial data—IMF lending arrangements)

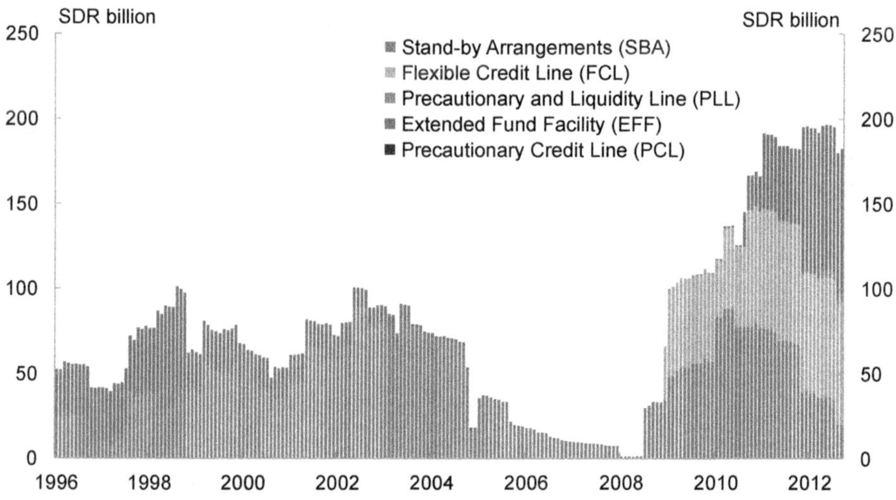

Fig. 5 IMF precautionary lending. (Source: Authors' calculations based on IMF financial data—IMF lending arrangements)

To date, Mexico, Poland and Columbia, have made use of the FCL, while Macedonia and Morocco have made use of the PLL. There has been evidence to suggest that the introduction of these arrangements was associated with sovereign bond spreads falling and exchange rate volatility subsiding in program countries. Also, with a visible corresponding decline in the conditional probability of economic distress in these countries, the FCL and PLL appear to have given markets the necessary assurances, thereby underpinning confidence (IMF 2011c).

IMF Governance

In addition to tackling immediate problems in the global economy, the crisis brought renewed momentum for the IMF to undertake structural governance reforms to improve its legitimacy, and thereby, its effectiveness. These reforms mean that the IMF governance structure has become more reflective of the changing economic and political landscape of the global economy.

Along with a permanent increase in IMF resources through the doubling of quotas with a corresponding rollback of the NAB, the IMF Executive Board approved a far-reaching package of governance reforms in December 2010 that committed the IMF membership to:

- A shift of over 6 % of quotas from over to underrepresented members as well as a shift of similar magnitude to dynamic EMDCs;
- Completing the comprehensive quota formula review and the 15th general review of quotas by January 2013 and January 2014, respectively;
- Protecting the voting power of the poorest IMF members; and
- Compositional changes in the IMF Executive Board allowing for more flexibility and a greater representation by EMDCs.

While these reforms are an important step to strengthen the central role of the IMF in stabilising the global economy, more needs to be done to build on these reforms.[4] In Sect. 4 we will explore thorough, permanent reforms to the arcane IMF quota formula to build in a recognition of the pace of growth of EMDCs.

Strengthening the IMF's analytical capacity

A central cause of the GFC was the build-up of systemic risk due to regulatory and supervisory failures that was not adequately captured by the IMF's surveillance framework. This failure highlighted significant weaknesses inherent in the IMF's surveillance methods (IMF 2011a). In 2009, an examination of the surveillance framework by the Independent Evaluation Office (IEO) found that the prevailing surveillance framework was heavily tilted towards exchange rate policies as the primary contributor to external imbalances failed to sufficiently integrate bilateral and multilateral surveillance and suffered from a serious 'legitimacy deficit' with many members.[5] In addition, IMF surveillance was seen as too fragmented, with

---

[4] Following the Board of Governors' approval, the next step required for the governance reforms to be effective is for member countries to accept the proposed quota increases and the amendment to the articles of agreement. At the time of writing 140 members having 75.69 % of the total voting power (less than the 85 % of the IMF's total voting power required for the amendment to enter into force) had accepted the amendment on the 2010 reform of the IMF Executive Board. Ratification of the reforms is now entirely dependent on United States acceptance, which holds 16.7 % of the remaining voting power.

[5] The IMF reviews the effectiveness of its economic analysis and policy advice—known as surveillance—every 3 years. The next of these 'Triennial Surveillance Reviews' will be completed by

risk assessments lacking depth and having insufficient focus on interconnectedness and transmissions of shocks (IEO 2009).

Following the IEO's examination, the IMF conducted a surveillance review in 2011 which led to major improvements in the surveillance framework. Initiatives flowing out of this review include a heightened focus on spillovers, deeper analysis of risks in the financial system, more detailed assessments of members' external positions and more prompt responses to concerns raised by member countries. Furthermore, the improvements from the 2011 review are beginning to translate into the policy advice the IMF provides its members with the IMF adjusting their policy advice on key issues like capital controls and macroprudential policy.[6]

These initial steps mean the IMF's framework for monitoring the global economy will be better able to identify risks as they emerge and should serve as useful preventive mechanisms to similar crises in the future.

Taken together, international policymakers delivered when it mattered, preventing further job losses and economic disaster. The survival of the IMS, guided by the strong and decisive response by its guardians, through the worst economic conditions since the 1930s suggests the IMS is resilient. Nonetheless, the system requires some maintenance to prepare the IMS for emerging challenges in a post-crisis environment. This is detailed in Sect. 4.

4 Further Reforms to the IMS

The global economy has avoided the worst, but it is by no means out of the woods, with a multi-speed global recovery emerging (IMF 2013a, b). Post GFC, activity has strengthened in many EMDCs, which continue to post relatively high growth rates. In contrast, advanced economies are likely to have slower growth, crippled by high public deficits and the need to undergo structural change (particularly in Europe).

This evolving dynamic is likely to create incentives for the advanced world to clamp down on industrial policies like subsidies, currency manipulation and local content requirements that Asian economies have deployed to good effect in previous decades to foster structural transformations. With or without the support of the WTO, Europe and the United States will exhibit greater willingness to shield their domestic industries from import surges (Rodrik 2013). If used, it is likely that such policies will have an impact on export-led development growth models deployed by developing economies.

---

the IMF's Executive Board in 2014.

[6] In December 2012, the IMF published 'The Liberalization and Management of Capital Flows—An Institutional View'. It marks a shift in the IMF's approach, formally recognising that capital flow management measures, which include capital controls, can be appropriate under some circumstances. In 2013, the IMF published a series of papers stating their view on the usefulness of macroprudential policy in ensuring financial stability, and their effective use in Asia.

While the world relied on the guidance and actions of international policymakers during the crisis, international institutions have work to do, to solidify their improved reputations. The structural shifts in the global economy require international institutions to adjust with it. In managing the risks associated with the evolving world economy, international policymakers must be seen as fair, legitimate and even-handed.

This evolving dynamic underpins the importance of further governance reforms at the IMF, which vastly underrepresent EMDCs in favour of European countries. Such reforms will require long-term structural changes and are difficult to achieve, as evidenced by the current difficulties in passing the 2010 reforms. Nonetheless, a lack of reform will come at the expense of global financial stability and long-term growth. Strong political will is necessary, with the G20 and IMF having a large role to play in delivering these reforms.

4.1 *IMF Governance Reforms*

While the IMF has recognised that '*the 2010 reforms represent a major realignment in the ranking of quota shares that better reflect global economic realities,*' the reforms fail to go far enough (IMF 2012c).[7] Data released in July 2013 show that even if the 2010 reforms were in place, EMDCs would be underrepresented by around 7.50% points in terms of their quota shares relative to their share of the world economy calculated at purchasing power parity (PPP).[8] Advanced countries are overrepresented by a corresponding amount. Therefore, further reforms are needed to make the IMF governance structure truly reflective of the changing global economic realities.

IMF Quota Formula

The next stage of IMF governance reform must start with a thorough, permanent reform of the arcane IMF quota formula (Box 3). The quota formula is the most important element in determining the quota shares a country is given.[9] The underrepresentation of EMDCs is largely explained by the current quota formula which is discriminating against EMDCs, in favour of European members as a group, thereby affecting the legitimacy of the IMF.[10] Therefore, it is crucial that the next set of re-

[7] Each member country of the IMF is assigned a quota, based broadly on its calculated quota shares (CQS). A member country's quota determines its subscription, is the most significant determinant of voting power, and has a bearing on its access to IMF financing.

[8] Based on authors' calculation of IMF Data.

[9] The IMF uses a quota formula to guide the distribution of quotas amongst the membership. However, ad-hoc adjustments may also be made to a member's quota.

[10] If the allocated quota shares of EMDCs matched their calculated quota shares they would still be underrepresented by around six and a half percentage points when compared to their share of

Box 3: Quota Formula

The current quota formula is: CQS=(0.5*GDP+0.3*O+0.15*V+0.05*R)k
Where:

GDP is the GDP measured as a blend of 60 % at market exchange rates and 40 % at PPP rates.

O is openness

V is variability

R is reserves

K is the compression factor of 0.95.

forms delivers a quota formula which better captures the position of EMDCs in the world economy and results in a substantial shift in the IMF quota shares towards those EMDCs who are experiencing strong economic growth.

There are two other relevant principles that should guide reform of the quota formula. First, that the reformed quota formula should be simple and transparent. Second, the formula should also allow for a mechanism for protection of the voice and representation of the IMF's poorest members.

Currently, just half of calculated quota shares (CQS) are determined by relative economic weights, as measured by GDP. This is the most robust component of the formula, and is the best way of taking account of the relative economic and political influence of IMF members. In addition, GDP reflects the importance of a member to the world economy, the ability to contribute to the IMF and the amount of resources that would be required if the need arose for an IMF program.

The remaining components of the formula, to a degree, duplicate and expand on the role of GDP in the formula. The openness variable aims to measure the interconnectedness of a member's economy with the rest of the world. This is justified on the basis that a country's stake in promoting global financial stability relies on the exposure of the domestic economy to the failure of international cooperation. However, it is doubtful that, beyond a certain level of openness, it has a significant bearing on the importance placed by member countries in participation and outcomes of international cooperation on economic issues.

Variability aims to measure the volatility of international flows into and out of a member's economy. The reasoning behind inclusion in the formula is that representation at the IMF should also reflect the potential need of members to call on its resources. However, in practice, this measure has been a poor predictor for a member's need for IMF resources.

As it implies, reserves measures the foreign currency reserves held by a member. As contributions to the IMF are usually made in foreign currency it reflects the capacity of members to contribute as well as the resilience of an economy to external shocks. However, given the relative ease with which most currencies are traded today, the lower need for reserves for floating exchange rate regimes compared

---

the world economy calculated at PPP rates.

to pegged regimes, and the risk that this encourages excess reserve accumulation, there is an open question over the ongoing role of reserves in the formula.

Finally, compression reduces the shares of the largest members to protect the shares of the smallest members. While arbitrary, it is consistent with the principle of protecting the voice and representation of the IMF's poorest members.

Given the shortcomings with the remaining aspects of the formula, it can be concluded that the most fruitful way forward for reforming the quota formula to ensure that it fairly reflects the economic growth of EMDCs is to reduce or modify them and reorient the formula towards GDP.

However, reform will be difficult. Reforming the formula is a zero-sum game. One country can only gain in (CQS) if there is an equal loss by one or a combination of other countries. Yet, if properly reformed, the formula could ensure that EMDCs, in time, receive quota shares that are representative of their position in the world economy. On the other hand, failing to reform the quota formula will undermine the legitimacy of the IMF, undermining its effectiveness. For example, IMF legitimacy concerns have played a role in the rise of alternative sources of finance for the global financial safety net (Box 4).

4.2 *Implementation of Reforms*

Given the interconnectedness of the global economy and the experience of the GFC, which has seen significant spillovers spread across regions, effective multilateral cooperation and coordination will grow in importance. Enhanced cooperation amongst the member countries of the IMF, as well as between the IMF and other global and regional institutions, will be an important part of the IMS going forward.

Aside from the urgent need to address issues with IMF legitimacy, the IMS's evolution should be gradual and should respond to changes in the global economy.

More broadly, Australian policymakers seek to bring a sense of realism about the reform process of the IMS. Based on our domestic experience of reforms over recent decades, we believe that reform should be an ongoing process that is built around engagement and is delivered in a responsible way. As outlined above, we consider that the IMS has proved to be sufficiently flexible and resilient in response to the global crisis. Reforms to the system should therefore be pragmatic and implementable. We believe that traction and trajectory are important, and reform should build on existing strengths. The most important elements for reform will be political will, ongoing collaboration and fair representation.

5 Conclusion

The toughest economic conditions since the Great Depression triggered intense debate about the IMS, with policymakers, academics and even politicians advocating the need for urgent, wide scale reforms.

Box 4: Case Study: The Rise of Regional Financial Arrangements (RFAs)

In recent years, RFAs have dramatically increased their lending resources and prominence in the global safety net, adding another layer that can operate in conjunction with the IMF and other lending arrangements. In Europe and Asia, the rise of RFAs has been so pronounced it has significantly changed the balance in the global safety net, with the IMF no longer dominating the role of lender of last resort.

The rise of RFAs is driven by a range of factors which vary from region to region. In Europe, the creation of large new regional arrangements was driven by recognition that existing lending resources were insufficient to address a large-scale European crisis. In addition, there was sentiment among some EMDCs that Europe should be able to solve its problems internally, given it is a bloc of large industrialised countries. In Asia, the desire to enhance regional capabilities to respond to crises stems from dissatisfaction with the IMF's response to the Asian financial crisis in 1997/1998, including the conditions it imposed on some countries.

In addition, perceived underrepresentation among EMDCs at the IMF compounds perceptions that it is a Western/European-dominated institution, and increases appetite to develop alternative arrangements that are perceived to better serve regional interests and which give a stronger voice to EMDCs.

The rise of RFAs in the global financial architecture brings potential benefits but also carries some risks and costs that need to be carefully managed to ensure they play a productive role in the global safety net and do not undermine the effectiveness of the IMF. On paper, more lending resources in the global safety net and regional expertise could contribute to more effective crisis management, surveillance and technical assistance. However, RFA lending resources may be less reliable than those of the IMF, and a need for cooperation to resolve crises raises complexities and uncertainty. While RFA financing can provide more resources and help spread exposure to risk, it can also undermine IMF conditionality, and regional interests may compromise the effectiveness of joint programs. Responding to crises at a regional level risks disjointed and uneven responses across geographical areas that may be counter-productive, particularly in the absence of coordination or if the effectiveness of the IMF to play a central role is impaired.

In this context, effective reform of quotas and EMDC representation at the Fund is critical, to not only address perceptions about the relevance and legitimacy of the IMF, but also to ensure that the broader global safety net is able to respond to future crises effectively.

This paper details the purposeful, coordinated and decisive actions of the G20 and IMF that protected the global economy when it needed it most. Together, the G20 and IMF deployed immediate crisis prevention mechanisms by: agreeing not to erect trade barriers to protect their own domestic economies at the expense of the global economy; pledging an additional US$ 1.1 trillion programme to support credit, growth and jobs; and increasing the global financial safety net to provide confidence to global markets. Furthermore, measures were put in place to reduce the risk of future crises, with the IMF adjusting their governance arrangements and sharpening its analysis of risks and spillovers.

These actions prove that while the IMS needs maintenance, it is resilient, flexible and able to react to the most extraordinary economic circumstances. We argue that the effective actions from the guardians of the global economy prove that wide scale reform is not necessary.

However, the global economy cannot remain stagnant. The structural shifts in the global economy require international institutions to adjust with it. In managing the risks associated with the evolving world economy, international policymakers must be seen as fair, legitimate and even-handed. One important measure to tackle this emerging challenge is to address serious biases in the IMF's quota formula. Over time, the IMS's evolution should be gradual, built on existing strengths of the system and responsive to developments in the dynamic global economy.

References

Au-Yeung W, Kouparitsas M, Luu N, Sharma D (2013) Long-term international GDP projections, Treasury Working Paper Series. Treasury.

Boughton M (2009) A New Bretton Woods, Finance and Development, IMF

Bradford C, Wonhyuk L (2011) Toward the consolidation of the G20: from Crisis Committee to Global Steering Committee, Brookings Institute

Carney M (2009) The evolution of the international monetary system. Foreign Policy Association

Eichengreen B, Irwin D (2009) The slide to protectionism in the great depression: who succumbed and why? National Bureau of Economic Research.

Independent Evaluation Office (2009) IMF performance in the run-up to the financial and economic crisis, IMF Surveillance in 2004–2007

International Monetary Fund (2011a) Triennial surveillance review

International Monetary Fund (2011c) Review of flexible credit line and precautionary credit line

International Monetary Fund (2012a) The liberalization and management of capital flows—an institutional view

International Monetary Fund (2012b) One year after the 2011 Triennial Surveillance Review

International Monetary Fund (2012c) IMF Quota and Governance Publications

International Monetary Fund (2013a) Managing Directors' Global Policy Agenda

International Monetary Fund (2013b) IMF's response to the Global Economic Crisis—factsheet

Kindleberger C (1973) An explanation of the 1929 depression. In The world in depression, pp 1929–1939. University of California Press, Berkeley

Lim VCS, Pontines V (2012) Global imbalances: a primer. Staff Paper The South East Asian Central Banks Research and Training Centre

Moghadam R (2011) Strengthening the International Monetary System: taking stock and looking ahead, IMF

Rodrik D (2013) The Past, Present and Future of Economic Growth, Working Paper

Romer C (2003) The Great Depression, Berkeley, Forthcoming Paper for Encyclopædia Britannica

Seabrooke L (2006) Resolving the International Monetary Fund's Legitimacy Crises, Working Paper, International Center for Business and Politics, Copenhagen Business School

UN Population Division (2011) World Population Prospects: the 2010 Revision

Xafa M (2010) The role of the IMF in the Global Financial Crisis. Cato J 30(3/Fall):475–489

Strengthening the International Monetary System

Emil Stavrev

The term "International Monetary System" (IMS) refers to the rules and institutions that organize and regulate international payments and foreign exchange systems. Specifically, these include the currency/monetary regimes of countries, the rules for exchange rate intervention, and the institutions that back those rules. Historically, there have been various systems, including several forms of the gold standard and the floating currency system. The Bretton Woods arrangements of a fixed but adjustable foreign exchange system overseen by the International Monetary Fund (IMF) were introduced after World War II. The abandonment of the gold standard in 1971 paved the way to a less regulated system comprising floating exchange and fixed but adjustable rates. A key notion in this setup is that of reserve asset: so long as a country fixes or manages its exchange rate, it needs a liquid international asset of stable value. Since the demise of gold as monetary anchor, the US dollar has been the world's principal reserve asset.

The current IMS has survived for over 40 years, underpinning strong global growth and increasing integration, but has exhibited many symptoms of instability. The past 40 years have seen very rapid growth in global per capita gross domestic product (GDP), as well as in trade and gross capital flows. Links among economies have also become much more complex, both in trade, as supply chains became global, and in finance, as interconnectedness increased drastically. As a result, systemic players that can amplify shocks across the world economy have emerged and symptoms of instability have occurred, e.g., frequent crises, persistent current account imbalances, volatile capital flows and currencies, and unprecedentedly large reserve accumulation. These symptoms have been revealed in full scale by the 2008 crisis and brought renewed international momentum to the idea of reforming the IMS.

E. Stavrev (✉)
Multilateral Surveillance Division, Research Department,
International Monetary Fund, Washington, DC, USA
e-mail: EStavrev@imf.org

M. Callaghan et al. (eds.), *Global Cooperation Among G20 Countries*,
DOI 10.1007/978-81-322-1659-9_16, © Springer India 2014

This note summarizes the key problems facing the IMS and discusses potential reform avenues.[1] The key problems are inadequate global adjustment mechanisms to prevent inconsistent or imprudent policies among systemic countries; lack of a comprehensive oversight framework for growing cross-border capital flows; inadequate systemic liquidity provision mechanisms; and structural challenges in the supply of safe assets. Accordingly, to help prevent crisis and contain costs, if they occur, the IMS reform should focus on strengthening policy cooperation; monitoring and management of capital flows; global financial safety net; and structural improvement of the system through financial deepening and reserve asset diversification.

1 Issues with IMS

The IMS has shown several symptoms of instability, which were clearly exposed by the Great Recession (e.g., see the 2011 Palais Royal Initiative Report). Crises have been a recurring theme throughout the post-Bretton Woods period, with some of these crises taking on a systemic dimension, particularly in recent years. While they have been predominantly among emerging markets, several advanced economies have also suffered, especially during systemic crisis events such as the most recent one.

Going beyond the symptoms, there are four root causes of instability in the current system. Specifically (i) inadequate global adjustment mechanisms to prevent or resolve inconsistent policies among systemic countries; (ii) lack of a global oversight framework for growing cross-border capital flows and linkages; (iii) inadequate systemic liquidity provision mechanisms to ensure continued access to much needed international liquidity; and (iv) structural challenges in the supply of safe assets, reflecting in part the transition underway whereby emerging market economies are becoming systemic and accounting for a fast growing share of global output.

1.1 Inadequate Global Adjustment Mechanisms

Adjustment channels lack mechanisms for burden sharing (across countries) of the changes that are needed to resolve global imbalances. At a country level, current account imbalances must either be resolved through a change in domestic savings/investment balance, which require a change in real effective exchange rates, or must be financed through official/private capital flows. Capital flow imbalances must be addressed through a combination of adjustment in the current account, reserves,

[1] For exhaustive discussion of the root causes and reform agenda, see IMF Board paper: *Strengthening the International Monetary System: Taking Stock and Looking Ahead*, International Monetary Fund, March 2011 (www.imf.org/external/np/pp/eng/2011/032311.pdf). *For broader information on the IMS*, see www.imsreform.org.

and official lending/borrowing. As the country-level adjustments must add up at a global level, how the adjustment in each country is done directly impacts others. Thus, an important component of an IMS should be agreement on the relative burden to be borne by different parties to achieve the needed adjustment, including the role of different adjustment channels (e.g., domestic versus external variables). In the absence of such an understanding, the adjustment is usually one sided, with the deficit countries forced by markets to adjust.

The current system is prone to inconsistencies and externalities. Under the current system, each country can choose its exchange rate and capital account regimes, having domestic policies aimed for domestic stability. This considerably raises the risk of inconsistent regime or policy choices, both across and within countries. For example, if all systemic countries aim ex ante for export-led growth by compressing domestic demand, ex post the outcome is lower global growth, or if a country with a floating exchange rate decides to lower its current account deficit without lowering its domestic demand, it has to revert to higher exports and thus, loosen its monetary policy, which, with open capital accounts, will have spillover effects to the rest of the system.

1.2 No Global Oversight Framework for Cross-Border Capital

Increased volume of cross-border capital flows and related capital account policies have created complex interdependences. The key driver of cross-border capital flows is expectations of rates of return, which, in general, depend on interest rate differentials adjusted for country risk. Therefore, capital flows play an important role in the external adjustment mechanism for countries with open capital accounts and are a stabilizing rather than destabilizing force. However, the domestic focus of macroeconomic, financial, and capital account policies of both source and recipient countries has tended to amplify waves of inflows, undercutting the stability of the IMS.

Despite these complex interdependencies, there is no universal framework that addresses cross-border capital flows. Existing frameworks are mainly regional and bilateral, and do not approach capital account issues from the perspective of global stability. The effectiveness of existing regulation is uneven. This gap leads to risk externalities from large cross-border financial institutions, regulatory arbitrage (facilitated by discrepancies between domestic regulations), excessive risk taking, and contagion. All of these contribute to cross-border flows having a destabilizing influence on the IMS.

1.3 No Systemic Liquidity Provision Mechanism

Inadequate size of collective safety net provides incentives for markets to bet against a country under liquidity pressure. In the current system, the size of the collective financial safety net (IMF resources and regional arrangements) has remained broadly constant as a share of global GDP, but has declined sizably relative to the volume of global capital flows, which determine the size of the external shocks to which countries with open capital accounts might be exposed. This drawback is an incentive for markets to bet against a country at the first sign of liquidity pressure.

There is no mechanism to provide systemic liquidity at the global level. As the recent crisis made clear, stabilizing market conditions in a systemic liquidity crisis requires the availability of potentially substantial resources. Rather, access to global liquidity has occurred through the ad hoc actions of key central banks.

1.4 Challenges

Several challenges need to be addressed to strengthen the IMS. Specifically:

- Shift to a multicurrency system that places less of a burden on a single country[2]. Due to its widespread acceptance and success as a store of value, the US dollar remains preeminent as a unit of account and medium of exchange for international trade and financial transactions and anchor for monetary regimes. However, concentration of many functions of the IMS in the currency of one nation leaves the IMS exposed to risks stemming from idiosyncratic shocks or policy decisions in that country.
- Accommodate the changing core of the IMS, in particular the growing economic role of emerging economies. As a result of the large growth differential between rapidly growing emerging economies and advanced economies, the former now account for half of global output, up from just over a quarter in the 1970s. As key emerging economies develop further, there are likely to be large shifts in global savings and investment behavior.
- Generate the necessary supply of safe assets. Observers have argued that global imbalances have been driven in large part by a structural gap between the ability to generate highly liquid safe assets and a rising demand for such assets, particularly by fast-growing emerging economies, leading to large official reserve accumulation and high saving.

2 Kew Avenues for IMS Reform

All of the above suggest that reform should proceed along four broad ways to strengthen the IMS: strengthened policy collaboration; global monitoring and management of capital flows; more reliable global financial safety net; and structural

[2] See for further discussion Mateos y Lago et al. (2009).

strengthening of the system through financial deepening and diversification in the supply of reserve assets.

2.1 *Strengthened Policy Collaboration*

During the global economic crisis, countries embarked on a coordinated global stimulus to escape the threat of a worldwide great depression. Two key efforts are underway to sustain this multilateral cooperation. First, a mutual assessment process (MAP) has been established by the Group of Twenty (G20). At the Pittsburgh summit, Leaders agreed to adopt policies needed to achieve strong, sustainable, and balanced growth. To meet this goal, they launched a mutual assessment of national and regional policy frameworks, plans, and projections. Second, IMF surveillance has been strengthened. As a follow up to the 2011 Triennial Surveillance Review, the IMF Board approved in July 2012 a new Integrated Surveillance Decision, which aims to better integrate bilateral and multilateral surveillance. It launched a pilot External Sector Report that aims to assess external positions of major countries in a consistent manner.

2.2 *Monitoring and Management of Global Capital Flows*

The IMF is developing a framework to help contain instability from large global capital flows. A first element focusing on dealing with large inflows was considered by the Executive Board (see IMF 2011). Further work will focus on the multilateral aspects of macroprudential policies and capital flow management measures, capital account liberalization, and dealing with capital outflows. There is also a need to strengthen global collaboration among financial supervisors, a goal that could be facilitated by the Fund, in cooperation with others such as the Financial Stability Board.

2.3 *Creation of a Global Financial Safety Net*

There has been a significant change of the IMF's lending facilities. Realization of the magnitude of the global shock in the aftermath of the financial crisis led to a major revamp of the IMF's lending tools (including introduction of a Flexible Credit Line and a Precautionary Credit Line). Support for a tripling in resources of the IMF at the G20 Leaders' Summit in London in April 2009 also contributed to restoring global market confidence, while agreement on a doubling of the Fund's quota resources further strengthened its ability to act as a global safety net. As a key part of efforts to overcome the global financial crisis, the G20 agreed in April 2009 to increase borrowed resources available to the IMF (complementing its quota resources) by up to $ 500 billion which tripled the total precrisis lending resources.

3 Concluding Remarks

This short note has identified several shortcomings in the architecture and functioning of the current IMS. While none of the shortcomings discussed in the note is going to cause big problems, together they add up to significant disturbances that could derail global growth and, potentially, lead to major crises.

The paper also suggests several complementary reform paths. However, the reform proposals would require significant advances in the degree of multilateral collaboration. In addition, there are few, if any, "low-hanging fruits" left in reforming the IMS, and some proposals will require a relatively long time frame to be implemented. Going forward, it is important to agree on a set of initiatives that will improve stability of the system. In this regard, serious consideration should be given to the proposed avenues to provide alternatives to self-insurance and to the potential for other currencies to acquire a greater role in the global reserve system.

References

Mateos y Lago et al. (2009). The Debate on International Monetary System, IMF Staff Position Note 09/26. International Monetary Fund, Washington

IMF (2011) IMF Board paper: Recent Experience in Managing Capital Inflows—Cross-Cutting Themes and Possible Policy Framework. International Monetary Fund, February 2011 (www.imf.org/external/np/pp/eng/2011/021411a.pdf)

Systemic Sudden Stop(s), Credit Lines, and Funding Liquidity

Gurbachan Singh

1 Introduction

Though the analysis in this article is quite general and applies to sudden stop of capital inflows into both developed economies and emerging economies, the exposition here will be, unless otherwise specified, confined to the sudden stop of capital inflows into emerging economies. Furthermore, the term 'sudden stop' will be used to include not only a stop of inflows but also, more broadly, sudden outflows of capital.

Sudden stops can create a serious liquidity crunch. The difficulties can be systemic in the sense that many or even all emerging economies face a possible sudden stop. There is a need for safeguards against sudden stop. There can be several safeguards. This article considers credit lines (CLs) only. The motivation is that these are important, less costly than foreign exchange reserves, relatively new, and less well understood. There can be difficulties for public authorities to raise funds internationally *ex post* once a sudden stop has occurred even if fundamentals are not weak to begin with.[1] In this context, an *ex ante* CL gives an option to borrow in the event of a sudden stop.

In the context of the East Asian crisis in 1997–1998, there were problems of weak fundamentals and also problems of liquidity due to a sudden stop. The literature is still somewhat divided over the role of fundaments and liquidity in causing

A preliminary version of this article was presented in the session on "Reforming the International Monetary System: the Need for a New Framework" at the Conference on 'Global Economic Cooperation: Views from G20 Countries' organized by ICRIER, October 7–9, 2012, New Delhi.

[1] There are similarities between the problem of sudden stop in international economics and the problem of panic run in economics of banking. See Diamond and Dybvig (1983) and Chang and Velasco (2001).

G. Singh (✉)
Independent Researcher and Visiting Faculty, Economics and Planning Unit,
Indian Statistical Institute (ISI), Delhi Center, New Delhi, India
e-mail: gurbachan.arti@gmail.com

M. Callaghan et al. (eds.), *Global Cooperation Among G20 Countries*,
DOI 10.1007/978-81-322-1659-9_17, © Springer India 2014

and aggravating the crisis. One important view in the literature is that the scale of the crisis was primarily due to a panic and liquidity crunch (Radelet and Sachs 1998). This 'liquidity' view of the East Asian crisis is a motivation for this article to focus on the liquidity problems due to a sudden stop.

CLs as a safeguard against sudden stops are, in practice, offered by an international public body such as the International Monetary Fund (IMF) to a public body such as a central bank in an emerging economy. A market for such CLs hardly exists. Singh (2013) deals with the question of why the market fails in providing CLs to deal with sudden stops in 'eligible' economies. This article does not consider a market for CLs. It is taken for granted here that there is a market failure and that there is a need for public authorities to provide such CLs. An important issue in this context is as follows. If many emerging economies buy CLs and if they all need to exercise these simultaneously in the event of a systemic crisis in their economies, then the liquidity requirement is large. How can this requirement be met?

We will explain how, contrary to a somewhat widespread belief, funding liquidity is not a serious problem if appropriate CLs are used to mitigate a sudden stop. This is not to say that there is no problem of any kind at all. As we will see, there can be difficulties of information, enforcement, and so on. In other words, there can be difficulties of implementation even if liquidity is not a constraint. In this context, we will consider CLs that central banks in developed countries extend to central banks in emerging economies. These can be provided in two ways. First, there can be direct CLs. Second, there can be CLs through a mediator or an exchange. The role of a mediator or an exchange can be, as we will see, performed by the IMF. This is a more recent idea and quite different from the perceived role of the IMF in the context of a sudden stop. At present, the IMF is thought of more as a provider of liquidity which is neither possible in the context of a systemic crisis nor required, as we will see.

CLs in this article are for the purpose of macro-financial stability. Though such CLs are recent, the basic idea of CL is all too familiar. Commercial banks routinely extend CLs to firms. The liquidity requirement in such cases is manageable. However, the liquidity requirement in case of CLs used to deal with sudden stop can be, as mentioned already, huge. It is possibly for this reason that there is pessimism with regard to the practical usefulness of CLs in the context of sudden stop. It is, however, interesting that the CLs in the context of sudden stop are actually different from the more familiar CLs such as CLs from banks to firms. They are, in fact, actually similar to some seemingly very different facilities such as the lender of last resort (LLR) facility, which is actually an implicit CL (more on this later). We know that the amount of funding to be provided by the central bank is not a constraint in the latter case. The reason is that the central bank can always issue more money. Similarly, there need not be any serious issue of liquidity in case of swap CLs between central banks, which can be used in the context of a sudden stop. However, there is often a tendency to compare CLs under consideration more with explicit CLs from banks to firms than with the implicit CL in the form of the LLR facility. This has led to some confusion. It is important to clarify this. This motivates a perspective, which this article will provide. This includes a comparison of a variety of

CLs. This perspective will pave the way for understanding the basic message in this article that the main issue in the context of CLs used to mitigate sudden stop is not liquidity, but implementation.

We will broadly classify CLs into two types. Let us label these Type I CLs and Type II CLs. Type I CLs need to be backed by some reserves or liquid assets (hereafter, reserves). In contrast, Type II CLs do not need to be backed by reserves. The reason why some CLs need to be backed by reserves and others do not need such backing will become clear as we proceed.

2 Type I CLs (That Need To Be Backed by Some Reserves)

Within the category of Type I CLs, we will briefly consider six different kinds of CLs in this section.

1 CLs from Banks to Firms As mentioned earlier, banks routinely extend CLs to 'eligible' firms which use these to seize some new and 'perishable' investment opportunity, or to meet some cost overrun of an existing project. The size of the market for these routine CLs is large. '…over three-quarters of bank lending is done using commitment [effectively CL] contracts…' (Loukoianova et al. 2007, p. 3).

2 Home Equity Lines of Credit This CL facility gives a household the option to borrow against the collateral of (the paid-up portion of) its home. This CL is used typically if there is a liquidity shock due to a drop in income or due to a sudden rise in consumption needs.

3 Regional CL Arrangements These CLs include regional arrangements such as the Chiang Mai Initiative in East Asia. Drawing above a certain level can require an IMF program. Hence, there is, in a sense, an overlap between this arrangement and the relevant IMF facilities (see below for more on this). There is also the Latin American Reserve Fund in Latin America, and bilateral arrangements such as a small CL from Japan to India. The purpose of these CLs is to reduce the scale of a possible currency crisis. However, the effective corpus of funds has been a constraint in regional and bilateral CL arrangements.

4 Flexible Credit Lines and Precautionary and Liquidity Lines The IMF offers two kinds of CLs—flexible credit lines (FCLs) and precautionary and liquidity lines (PLLs). The former are for relatively strong countries which may possibly face a liquidity shock (International Monetary Fund 2012a). PLLs are for relatively less strong but nonetheless eligible countries (International Monetary Fund 2012b). FCLs and PLLs were introduced in 2009 and 2011, respectively. FCLs have been bought by three countries—Columbia, Mexico, and Poland. These countries first bought the facility in 2009 and have subsequently renewed the arrangements. They have not exercised the option to borrow so far. The IMF approved US$ 6.2 billion PLL for Morocco on August 3, 2012.

Table 1 Type I credit lines that need to be backed by some reserves

	Is CL explicit or implicit?	Is CL national or international (typically)?	Purpose (typically)?	Is CL direct?
1. CLs from banks to firms	Explicit	National	Investment	Yes
2. Home equity lines of credit	Explicit	National	Consumption	Yes
3. Regional CL arrangements	Explicit	International	Macro-financial stability (external)—a few countries	(Ambiguous)
4. IMF's FCLs and PLLs	Explicit	International	Macro-financial stability (external)—a few countries	Yes
5. IMF's SBAs	Implicit	International	Macro-financial stability (external)—a few countries	Yes
6. Credit cards	Implicit	National	Consumption	Yes

So far, we have dealt with explicit CLs in this section. We will now consider two implicit CLs.

5 Stand-by Arrangement by the IMF Stand-by arrangement (SBA) is an old facility extended by the IMF to member countries. It resembles to some extent a CL facility because, as the name suggests, the IMF stands ready to provide funds though conditions apply.

6 Credit Cards Credit cards can be, unlike debit cards, used as an option to pay in an emergency even if there is inadequate money with the card holder at the time of payment. Therefore, credit cards have an implicit CL-like facility. The use of credit cards has grown over time. It may grow further in future (particularly in emerging and developing economies).

The main features of CLs in this section are shown in Table 1. Except for the last column, the contents in the table are self-explanatory. The last column shows whether the CL is provided directly by the seller to the buyer, or it is provided through a mediator. This aspect will become clearer in the next section. In this section, the CLs are provided directly though there is an ambiguity in one case viz., the *Chiang Mai Initiative*. Several countries are part of the *Initiative* and each country contributes funds to a corpus. If any country needs funds, it can exercise its CL and borrow. It is not clear if the other countries provide funds directly to the country in difficulty, or the funds are provided through some mediator or exchange. However, this is not an important issue in this section. We have included this aspect for comparison with Type II CLs in the next section where mediation plays a crucial role.

What is common between all the CLs in this section is that the seller of CLs needs to hold some reserves to back up the same. This aspect will change for CLs in the next section.

To see how liquidity is provided by the seller of Type I CLs, consider two stylized balance sheets—balance sheet 1 and balance sheet 2. These are very simple. However, these will help understand and contrast the CLs in this section with those in the next section. The two balance sheets in this section are self-explanatory. These are for the seller of CLs (we have not included balance sheets for the buyers of CLs). The important point to note is that the seller of CL holds reserves to back up the same. Several CLs are extended by the seller. Only some of these are exercised by the buyers. Though there is uncertainty on which individual CLs will be exercised, there can be far less uncertainty about the proportion of CLs that will be exercised. This is due to *the law of large numbers* and the assumption that liquidity needs are somewhat independent. It is true that there can be a systemic crisis in which case liquidity needs are correlated. However, this is a case of macro-financial instability, and we will deal with this separately in the next section. Here we will simplify the analysis and assume that there is no aggregate uncertainty at all.

For simplicity, consider two discrete points of time—date 0 and date 1. It is assumed that at date 0, all CL contracts are signed, and the seller receives a fee from the buyer. It is assumed that CLs need to be and can be exercised at date 1 only. However, not all CLs are exercised. Only some are. The other CL contracts simply expire. Balance sheet 1 shows assets and liabilities of the seller after the CL is signed at date 0. Balance sheet 2 shows assets and liabilities of the seller after the CLs are exercised at date 1. Balance sheet 1 shows that the seller holds reserves. Balance sheet 2 shows that the seller of CLs has (new) loans instead of reserves on its balance sheet. The balance sheets shown are stylized and general and can be used to understanding the essence of the six different kinds of Type I CLs in this section though the specific form can differ from one case to another.

The law of large numbers helps to minimize the amount of reserves or liquid assets. However, this is not the only way to economize reserves. Sellers can also rely on synergies with other services[2] and on temporary loans if there are minor fluctuations in the proportion of CLs exercised (not included in the analysis depicted in the balance sheets). However, all these factors only reduce the amount of reserves required. They do not bring the reserves need to zero. The size of reserves is significant in case of CLs considered in this section.

Balance sheet 1: Assets and liabilities of seller of CL (of type 1) at date 0

Assets	Liabilities
Loans/investments	Funds raised in various forms
Reserves or liquid assets (R)	

Balance sheet 2: Assets and liabilities of seller of CL (of type 1) at date1

Assets	Liabilities
Loans/investments	Funds raised in various forms
Loans under CL contracts (=R)	

[2] Credit lines given by banks to firms have synergies with demand deposits. So banks can economize on reserves (Kashyap et al. 2002).

Let us reconsider FCLs and PLLs provided by the IMF. The demand for such CLs has been low so far. Only four countries have bought these CLs. Hence, the IMF would have hardly any problem if any or all of these CLs were to be exercised. It is unlikely that there will be a problem for the IMF in future either if some more countries were to apply for CLs. However, the possible expansion in future can go only up to a point. At some point, the supply can be constrained if the demand were to increase substantially (e.g., if most or all eligible emerging economies were to apply for CLs and there are correlated risks). The substantial increase in demand may seem an unlikely event in the foreseeable future given that at present the demand is really low for CLs. However, there is a need to prepare for the future when central banks in emerging economies may gradually reduce the role of (more costly) foreign exchange reserves and increase the role of CLs in international liquidity management. Then there can be considerable demand for CLs.

Historically cash has given way to CLs. Consider some examples. First, firms have increasingly shifted from cash or reserves to CLs from banks. Second, home equity lines of credit have grown enormously. This can be one of the several reasons why the savings rate has dropped in developed economies. This has in turn reduced the role of liquid assets with households. Third, individuals have increasingly moved from currency and demand deposits to credit cards as a precautionary instrument of liquidity management. Fourth, commercial banks have in the long-run context moved away from cash holding to relying on the LLR for meeting an extreme liquidity situation due to bank runs (see the first item in the next section). There is a lesson from all these examples. By analogy, it is possible that the CLs to deal with sudden stop will grow considerably over time. This may seem unlikely at this juncture, but history of explicit and implicit CLs in general suggests otherwise though there is no denying that there is uncertainty.

There is an interesting issue on the supply side of FCLs and PLLs. If the demand were to increase substantially, it is not clear if the IMF is in a position to extend these to too many eligible countries. This is because there can be very large funding requirements in the event of a systemic crisis in emerging economies. On the other hand, there are limited funds available with the IMF (notwithstanding the fact that resources of the IMF have gone up in recent years). Therefore, there is a limitation of the CLs provided by the IMF in the long-run context even though there is hardly a problem on the supply side at present.

At the root of the liquidity problem is the nature of uncertainty with regard to the scale on which a sudden stop can occur. If there is little aggregate uncertainty, then the IMF can indeed deal with the demand for liquidity even if CLs are sold to very many emerging economies. However, if there is aggregate uncertainty, i.e., if there is a systemic crisis, then most or all emerging economies can need funds somewhat simultaneously. Then the IMF can be constrained financially. Ex ante, it can be reluctant to sell CLs on a very large scale. We will see in the next section what can be done in this case.

3 Type II CLs (That Need Not Be Backed by Reserves)

Within the category of Type II CLs, we will study three different kinds of CLs. Before we consider the relevant CLs that are useful in the context of a sudden stop, we will first review the (domestic) LLR facility.

1 The Lender of Last Resort Though the LLR facility is all too familiar, it is often not realized that this is very much like a CL facility. The central bank acts as the LLR in the event of a liquidity crisis for banks. It is as if commercial banks have bought (implicit) CL from the central bank and the latter has sold the same. There can be an implicit fee in some form (e.g., the central bank pays a low interest on reserves of banks held with it; it is as if the central bank deducts a fee for the LLR facility and for other benefits). The CLs may be exercised by commercial banks in events like a systemic (domestic) bank run. This is a case of aggregate uncertainty. In this case, the reserves of banks and the funds from the interbank market can be grossly inadequate to deal with the situation. In such a situation, the central bank acts as the LLR.

It is elementary but critical that the central bank does not need to hold any reserves in order to be able to act as the LLR. It can simply issue new base money. This is in contrast to the CLs in the previous section. In those cases, the providers of CLs need to hold some reserves.

It may be argued that if a central bank issues new money, this can be inflationary. However, this is usually not the case under the conditions of liquidity crunch in the aggregate. If new central bank money is increased and the money multiplier drops substantially (due to increase in reserve–deposit ratio or currency–deposit ratio), then the total money (as distinct from central bank money) can remain somewhat unchanged. Hence, there need not be inflation due to increase in central bank money, which is used as part of the LLR facility. The economic intuition is simple. Additional base money can lead to inflation if the demand for the same has not increased. However, where additional supply is in response to increased demand (as it is when the LLR facility is used), then there need not be inflation. In fact, the opposite can happen. If there is increased demand for central bank money and this additional demand is not met, then there can be deflation (as was the case in the 1930s in the USA).

2 Swap CLs Between Central Banks The Federal Reserve System (FED) signed up for swap CLs with the central banks in Brazil, Mexico, Korea, and Singapore in April 2009 for US$ 30 billion each (Fernandez-Arias and Levy-Yeyati 2012). The FED previously authorized temporary reciprocal currency arrangements with ten other central banks in Australia, Canada, Denmark, UK, Europe, Japan, New Zealand, Norway, Sweden, and Switzerland (Aizenman and Pasricha 2010).

To understand the analytics of swap CLs, consider a swap CL between two countries—country D and country E. Let us say country D is the representative developed economy and country E is the representative emerging economy. A swap CL is (1) a CL from country D to country E and (2) a CL from country E to country D.

Balance sheet 3: Assets and liabilities of seller of CL (of type 2) at date 0

Assets	Liabilities
Loans/investments	Equity (small)
Reserves or liquid assets (which can be relatively small)	Central bank money (B)

Balance sheet 4: Assets and liabilities of seller of CL (of type 2) at date 1

Assets	Liabilities
Loans/investments	Equity (small)
Reserves or liquid assets (which can be relatively small)	Central bank money (B)
Loans under CL contracts ($=\Delta B$)	New central bank money issued (ΔB)

It is interesting and significant that the central banks which sign up for swap CLs need not hold reserves. To see this, consider an example. Let country D be the USA and country E be South Korea. Suppose that there is a sudden and large outflow of capital from South Korea. Then the Bank of Korea can exercise its CL with the FED and borrow and use US dollars to avoid the currency crisis. The FED on its part can issue new money and lend the same to Bank of Korea. Therefore, the FED need not hold reserves for this purpose.[3]

Next, consider the opposite case where there is large and sudden outflow from country D to country E. Though this is hypothetical at this juncture, it is useful to deal with this case as well. Observe that this is a case of large demand for currency of country E. In this case, country D can exercise its CL and borrow from country E. The central bank in the latter economy can issue its money and lend the same to the central bank in country D. This can be used to avoid a currency crisis in country D. It is interesting that the central bank in country E need not hold reserves for this purpose. The intuition is straightforward. It needs to issue its own money which it can always do. It is significant that this argument holds even though country E is an emerging economy. This is contrary to the usual belief in one way or another that only the central bank in a developed economy can sell a CL.

It is true that a sudden and large outflow from a representative developed economy to a representative emerging economy is unlikely. However, it is important to consider three aspects in this context. First, some emerging economies (e.g., China) are growing rapidly and a sudden and large outflow of capital from developed economies to emerging economies cannot be ruled out altogether in future. Second, the very fact that the agreements between the USA and some emerging economies soon after the financial crisis set in the USA were for swap CLs rather than for one-way CLs from the FED to central banks in emerging economies suggests that there were possible apprehensions about outflow from not only emerging economies to developed countries but also developed countries to emerging economies. Third, con-

[3] For a formal treatment and related issues, see Singh (2013).

sider a bit of history. At present and for a long time the USA has been a developed economy. However, this was not always the case. There must have been a transition period during which the USA was then, what we now call, an emerging economy and a country like the UK was a developed economy by the standards of the time. Under those conditions, there would have been a rationale for a two-way CL. The rationale for the (then emerging) USA to buy a CL from the (then more developed) UK seems obvious. However, there would also be a rationale for UK to buy a CL from the USA even though the former was a developed economy and the USA was then an emerging economy. By analogy, it is conceivable that the FED of the USA (a developed country now) will buy a CL from central banks of other countries that are at present emerging economies.

There is an all too familiar idea in the literature that the US dollar is a reserve currency, that the USA is privileged in this respect, and that the USA does not need to hold reserves. It is argued, in contrast, that other economies in general and emerging/developing economies in particular are very different and that they need to hold reserves to deal with eventualities like sudden stop. All this is historically true at least since the end of World War II, if not earlier. However, theoretically there exist other possibilities as we have already seen above. Theoretically, there can be a sudden and large outflow of capital from a developed country like the USA. In such a (very rare) case, the emerging economy which is the recipient economy is the privileged one.

It may be argued that if a central bank issues new money, this can have implications for the exchange rate. While this is indeed often true, this is not important in the context of the problem under consideration. Additional base money can lead to depreciation of currency if the demand for the same has not increased. However, where additional supply is in response to increased demand (as it is when CLs are exercised), then there need not be depreciation. In fact, the opposite can happen. If there is increased demand for central bank money and this additional demand is not met, then there can be appreciation of the currency (more familiar as depreciation of the currency in the country that faces sudden stop). The basic economic argument why additional central bank money due to exercise of swap CLs need not lead to depreciation is similar to the argument why additional central bank need not lead to inflation in the context of the LLR facility (see the first item in this section).

To clarify how the seller of CL provides liquidity, consider two balance sheets—balance sheet 3 and balance sheet 4. These are stylized and general and can be used to understand swap CLs between central banks. These are self-explanatory. The balance sheets are, for simplicity, shown as if there is one-way CL, and these are shown for the seller of CL (and not for the buyer of CL). The important point to note is that the seller of CL gives a loan by issuing new money. Therefore, the total of assets is higher in balance sheet 4 as compared to that in balance sheet 3. This is in contrast to the balance sheets studied in the previous section. There the total of assets remains the same before and after the CLs are exercised. See balance sheet 1 and balance sheet 2. It follows from balance sheet identity of assets and liabilities that the liabilities too are higher in balance sheet 4 as compared to those in balance sheet 3. Furthermore, total liabilities are the same in balance sheet 1 and balance sheet 2.

As mentioned already, swap CL contracts have been seen already in practice. However, these have been restricted to a small number of countries. This is surprising particularly in the light of the proposition that *liquidity is hardly a constraint in expanding the usage of swap CLs between central banks.* One reason can be simply that such CLs are still new. Therefore, it will take time till these are used more widely. Another reason can be that there is a weakness in direct CLs. In this context, we will next study mediated CLs.

3 Swap CLs Between Central Banks Through the IMF In the previous scheme of direct swap CLs between two central banks, these two banks involved need to deal with each other. If this argument is extended to the case of many countries, then all central banks need to deal with each other to have bilateral swap CLs. There is considerable information and transaction cost involved. Each central bank needs to assess the creditworthiness of each and every other central bank. Furthermore, each central bank needs to be able to enforce repayment of a possible loan that is given under a CL contract. While enforcement of contracts is not a problematic issue within an economy at least in a country with reasonably well-developed institutions and legal framework, this can be difficult in the global economy. The reason is simple. There is effectively hardly any international court whereby contracts can be enforced. This can make loans under CL contracts difficult in the global economy.[4]

All this motivates indirect or mediated swap CLs between central banks—an arrangement in which the IMF acts as the mediator. The CLs can work as follows. Each central bank can extend or sell a CL to the IMF only. In addition, each central bank can buy a CL from the IMF only. Therefore, it is proposed that the central banks deal with only the IMF in the context of sudden stop. No central bank deals with another central bank with regard to CLs under consideration. This kind of an indirect CL arrangement has two advantages over the direct CLs. *First*, the IMF can look after eligibility, surveillance, and implementation. At the international level, the IMF is in a better position to do all this as compared to any central bank. It has much of the information required due to the functions it performs in any case. The central bank of a country is rather handicapped in this matter. *Second*, each central bank needs to have a swap CL with the IMF only (and not with each and every other central bank). This reduces costs substantially as these are not duplicated.

It may help to give an analogy. In standard finance, there are, broadly speaking, two types of contracts. First, there are over-the-counter (OTC) contracts between sellers and buyers. Second, there are cases in which a seller deals with an exchange (and not with the buyer directly). Similarly, the buyer deals with the exchange (and

[4] The problem of enforcement of recovery of loans under CL contracts is particularly acute. It is true that this is a general problem in international economics given that there is effectively hardly any legal way by which capital market transactions can be settled. However, there are some second best solutions. In foreign direct investment (FDI), there is direct control over assets by foreign investors. In equity or bond markets, there is an obvious exit route as there is liquidity and the investor is often free to sell and move funds out of the country (Diamond and Rajan 2001). These kinds of solutions are missing in case of loans under CL contracts.

not with the seller directly). In the second arrangement, there is much less *counterparty risk*, and costs can be less than in the first kind. We may now return to CLs. These can be direct between the sellers and buyers, or these can be through a central body such as the IMF. Carrying the analogy from standard finance, we may view the IMF as an 'exchange'. The IMF takes some risk. It needs to repay its loans even if it is unable to recover partially or fully some of its loans extended under CL contracts.

Fernandez-Arias and Levy-Yeyati (2012), Obstfeld (2009), and Singh (2012, 2013) have proposed variants of such arrangements in the literature.

It is important to make a distinction between (a) the funds that the IMF has raised in the past and again more recently from its member countries and (b) the funds that the IMF raises by exercising the CLs proposed in this article. In case (a), the funds are in the nature of more or less permanent contributions that member countries make to the IMF. These are one-time and one-way contributions.[5] In case (b), the funds are in the nature of temporary loans that different countries give to the IMF in different periods of time. Subsequently, the IMF repays the loans due to these countries. Therefore, these are transitory funds. There is clearly a substantive difference between the two kinds of funds—(a) and (b).

We have earlier seen how direct CL between developed economy D and emerging economy E works. Let us now see how mediated CL between country D and country E works. Suppose investors would like to shift their investments from economy E to economy D. Then the central bank of the former economy can exercise its CL with the IMF. The latter can, in turn, exercise its CL with the central bank of economy D, which can issue money and lend the same to the IMF. The latter can now lend the funds to the central bank of country E. The latter can use the loan to avert a currency crisis. Thereafter, the central bank of country E can gradually accumulate foreign currency and repay the loan to the IMF which in turn repays its loan to country D. *The basic idea is to transform a sudden outflow into a gradual outflow.*

How are the mediated CLs discussed in this section different from the FCLs and PLLs discussed in the previous section? First, in the latter case, the IMF is only a seller of CL and not a buyer. In contrast, in the case of proposed mediated CLs, the IMF is both a seller and a buyer of CLs. Second, in the case of FCLs and PLLs, there is a change in the composition of assets of the IMF after some country exercises CL and borrows from the IMF. Liquid assets with the latter fall and its loans increase. Therefore, the total of assets with the IMF remains the same. Furthermore, there is no change on the liabilities side of the balance sheet of the IMF. In contrast, in the case of mediated CLs, there is an increase in the total of assets accompanied by an increase in the total of liabilities after the IMF borrows funds and lends the same.

It is often argued that the IMF has limited funds and that it cannot issue its own money. Accordingly, it is unable to provide liquidity in the event of a systemic currency crisis. This argument is indeed valid if we are considering FCLs and PLLs

[5] It is possible that some member countries pay up their more or less permanent contributions gradually, while others make an immediate payment but that is a matter of detail. The pending payments from member countries are in the form of receivables. These are substantively different from the funds that the IMF borrows temporarily under CLs exercised.

Table 2 Type II credit lines that do not need to be backed by reserves

	Is CL explicit or implicit?	Is CL national or international?	Purpose?	Is CL direct or mediated?
1. Lender of last resort	Implicit	National	Macro-financial stability (internal)	Direct
2. Swap CLs in practice	Explicit	International	Macro-financial stability (external)—many countries	Direct
3. Swap CLs in the recent literature	Explicit	International	Macro-financial stability (external)—many countries	Mediated by the IMF

as we did in the previous section. However, once we consider mediated CLs as we have in this section, then the funding constraint is no longer an important issue. We have seen that the IMF does not need to provide liquidity from its own funds if mediated CLs are used. It merely borrows and relends funds. Therefore, the fact that the IMF has limited resources is not quite relevant in this context. Hence, it is possible to deal with a systemic outflow of capital from emerging economies to developed economies.

Though mediated swap CLs can be superior to direct swap CLs, these indirect CLs are not yet seen in practice. One reason can be that since the IMF faces a credit risk, it is reluctant to participate in the manner suggested here. However, this argument should not be carried beyond a point. First, in the proposed scheme the IMF extends CLs to eligible economies only. Therefore, the credit risk cannot be high. Second, it can extend CLs to many eligible economies. Therefore, it can diversify and reduce risk. Third, the IMF can be viewed as a permanent body. Therefore, it can consider a long-term horizon. It can extend CLs at present and in the future. Therefore, we may say that it can diversify over time so credit risk cannot be high. Therefore, it cannot be a good enough reason as to why the use of mediated CLs is limited. Another reason why mediated CLs have not become popular can be that CLs for international macro-financial stability are themselves new. They have taken the form of direct CLs as of now. It may be just a matter of time before mediated CLs take shape.

A CL is typically sold for a price. Here we are considering two CLs—one from country D to the IMF and the other from the IMF to country E. As the credit risk, to the extent that it exists, is effectively borne by the IMF, we can consider the price charged by the IMF for the CL it sells to be more than the price it pays to country D for the CL it buys.

Main features of CLs in this section are shown in Table 2. The main contrast with CLs in Table 1 is that there is scope for dealing with *systemic* risks with CLs in Table 2 (and not with CLs shown in Table 1).

4 Summary, Conclusion, and Policy Implications

CLs are pervasive though they are not always explicit. However, the use of CLs in mitigating sudden stop of capital inflows has been limited so far. One reason can be that there is lack of clear understanding of issues involved. This article has provided a broad perspective and clarified the issues involved. In particular, we have explained the meaning of the elusive concept liquidity in the context of CLs.

One contribution of this article is a distinction between two types of CLs: those that need to be backed by reserves or liquid assets and those that do not need such backing. A variety of CLs such as those from banks to firms, home equity lines of credit, Chiang-Mai Initiative, IMF's FCL and PLL facilities, IMF's SBA arrangement, and credit cards are all cases of explicit or implicit CLs that need to be backed by reserves. In these cases, loans under CL contracts are financed by depletion of liquid assets (the total of assets remains the same for the seller of CLs before and after the CLs are exercised). On the other hand, the present day LLR facility within an economy and the swap CLs between central banks are two cases of explicit or implicit CLs that do not need to be backed by reserves. In these cases, the loans given under CL arrangements are financed by issue of new money (the total of assets increases and is accompanied by an increase in total liabilities on the balance sheet of the seller or provider of CLs).

The distinction between the two types of CLs paves the way to understanding that providing liquidity on a large scale to deal with systemic sudden stop is not a major problem. The intuition is simple. The supplier of CL can issue additional money. Though liquidity is not a problem in providing CLs, there can be other difficulties and these can be serious.

There can be reluctance on the part of one country to extend a CL to another country that may face a sudden stop. An important reason for this can be that there are information problems and enforcement problems in the global economy. This can be particularly acute for possible loans under CL contracts.

Policy implications of analysis in this article are as follows. There is need to think of the IMF as a mediator or as an exchange between central banks that use swap CLs for mitigating a sudden stop. The IMF has a comparative advantage in information and enforcement as compared to central banks in the international economy. This role of the IMF as a mediator is different from the current role of the IMF as a provider of liquidity. The IMF can be constrained in providing liquidity in a systemic crisis given that it cannot issue its own money and given that it has limited resources notwithstanding the additional funds raised recently.

A CL is not a panacea in mitigating sudden stop—more so when there is some uncertainty regarding the nature of the instrument itself as it is new. However, CLs are an important step forward at least for eligible countries.

This article has focused on CLs as safeguards against sudden stop. However, there are other safeguards like foreign exchange reserves, capital controls, denomination of foreign debt in local currency, and so on. Further research can see which safeguard or combination of safeguards is suitable in a particular situation of sudden stop.

Acknowledgments I thank Chetan Ghate and Rajat Kathuria for the invitation to make a contribution to this volume. I appreciate the role of ISI and that of my family in making this work possible. I appreciate the comments on an earlier version by Partha Sen and Arti Singh. Last but not the least I am grateful to a referee for useful comments which have helped in writing this revised, longer, and clearer version.

References

Aizenman J, Pasricha GK (2010) Selective swap arrangements and the global financial crisis: analysis and interpretation. Int Rev Econ Finance 19:353–365

Chang R, Velasco A (2001) A model of financial crises in emerging markets. Q J Econ 116:489–517

Diamond DW, Dybvig PH (1983) Bank runs, deposit insurance and liquidity. J Polit Econ 91(3):401–419

Diamond DW, Rajan RG (2001) Banks, short-term debt and financial crises: theory, policy implications and applications. Carnegie-Rochester Conference Series on Public Policy 54(1):37–71

Fernandez-Arias E, Levy-Yeyati E (2012) Global financial safety nets: where do we go from here? Int Finance 15(1):37–68

International Monetary Fund (2012a) Flexible credit line—operational guidance note prepared by the strategy, policy and review department, May 31

International Monetary Fund (2012b) Precautionary and liquidity line—operational guidance note prepared by the strategy, policy and review department, May 31

Kashyap A, Rajan R, Stein J (2002) Banks as liquidity providers: an explanation of the coexistence of lending and deposit taking. J Finance 57(1):33–73

Loukoianova E, Neftci SN, Sharma S (2007) Pricing and hedging of contingent credit lines. J Deriv Spring 14(3):61–80

Obstfeld M (2009) Lenders of last resort in a globalized world, IMES Discussion Paper Series 2009-E-18, August

Radelet S, Sachs JD (1998) The east Asian financial crisis: diagnosis, remedies, prospects. Brookings Pap Econ Act 1998(1):1–90

Singh G (2012) Banking crises, liquidity, and credit lines—a macroeconomic perspective. Routledge, Abingdon

Singh G (2013) Credit lines to mitigate sudden stop: why the market does not exist. https://sites.google.com/site/gurbachansingh61/papers (An early version presented at 7th Annual Conference on Growth and Development, December 15–17, 2011, Indian Statistical Institute, Delhi Centre)

Part V
Capital Control Policy and Emerging Market Economies (EMEs)

Policy Trade-offs in an Open Economy and the Role of G20 in Global Macroeconomic Policy Coordination

Rajeswari Sengupta and Abhijit Sen Gupta

1 Introduction

Emerging economies have been subject to increasingly volatile capital flows in recent years. Sharp swings in volatility, witnessed in recent years, have created a number of challenges for macroeconomic management in these countries, and have reignited the debate on the extent to which emerging economies should subject themselves to the vagaries of capital flows. Moreover, it has been widely agreed that the sharp volatility in capital flows in recent years had little to do with developments in emerging economies. The events up to the collapse of the Lehman Brothers resulted in 'flight to safety' of international capital from emerging economies driven by sharp decline in the risk appetite of global investors. The subsequent pickup in capital flows to emerging economies was a result of widening interest rate differentials due to extremely low interest rates prevailing in the industrialized countries. The worsening debt crisis in Europe and a downgrade of US sovereign rating in the second half of 2011 caused investor sentiment to deteriorate once again and net capital flows to plunge across most emerging economies.

The rise in volatility of capital flows has made macroeconomic management more complex. Unbridled capital flows can exacerbate some of the existing finan-

The views expressed in this paper are those of the author/s and do not necessarily reflect the views and policies of the Asian Development Bank (ADB) or its Board of Governors or the governments they represent.

R. Sengupta (✉)
Visiting Fellow,
Indira Gandhi Institute for Development Research (IGIDR),
Gen. A.K.Vaidya Marg, Goregaon (E),
Mumbai 400 065, India
e-mail:rajeswari.sen@gmail.com

A. Sen Gupta
India Resident Mission, Asian Development Bank,
New Delhi 110021, India

M. Callaghan et al. (eds.), *Global Cooperation Among G20 Countries*,
DOI 10.1007/978-81-322-1659-9_18, © Springer India 2014

cial fragilities and thereby lead to a costly crisis. Furthermore, massive unintended capital inflows can foster rapid real exchange rate appreciation, which can hurt exports of emerging economies. Alternatively, if the central bank intervenes to prevent the exchange rate from appreciating, it is likely to lead to an increase in money supply, fueling inflationary pressures. Many emerging economies have used fiscal, monetary, and exchange rate policies, intervention in the foreign exchange market, domestic prudential regulations, and finally capital controls to counter the impact of volatile flows. The latter has included tax on inflows, additional capital requirements for foreign exchange credit exposure, minimum holding period, and withholding tax to manage capital flow volatility.

India, like other emerging economies, has been subject to these capricious capital flows in recent years. During the pre-global financial crisis (GFC) period, foreign capital poured into India driven by sustained differential in growth potential of the advanced economies and India, easy liquidity, and declining home bias in the developed countries. However, this trend reversed with the outbreak of the subprime crisis resulting in a rapid outflow of capital. The quantitative easing in advanced countries and faster recovery in emerging economies caused capital flows to change direction again in 2010 and early 2011. The deepening of the euro-zone sovereign debt crisis in the second half of 2011 and deteriorating domestic fundamentals resulted in capital reversing direction yet again.

We focus on some of the challenges that have emanated from India's increased integration with global capital markets. India has adopted a gradual and calibrated approach while liberalizing the capital account. This has helped India to negotiate the macroeconomic trilemma—maintaining a stable exchange rate, keeping capital account open, and retaining monetary policy autonomy. In particular, instead of corner solutions, India has opted for an intermediate regime balancing the policy objectives as per the demands of the macroeconomic situation. Capital account management measures also impact the foreign exchange market. We calculate the exchange market pressure (EMP) index in India, and track its evolution over the last couple of decades. We also evaluate the extent to which the EMP index (EMPI) has been influenced by major macroeconomic factors. We find that a deteriorating trade balance and decline in portfolio equity inflows are associated with a higher EMP, while positive changes in stock market returns lower the EMP.

2 Capital Account Management in India

Capital account liberalization in India has been viewed as a continuous process rather than a one-off event. During the post-Independence period until the early 1980s, India had a relatively closed capital account with external financing mainly taking the form of assistance through multilateral and bilateral sources on concessional terms. This approach was associated with an import substitution strategy and relied on tariffs and quotas to limit the need for foreign exchange. During the

1980s, capital flows were liberalized as traditional sources of financing had to be supplemented with additional foreign capital to finance rising current account deficit driven by high oil prices, selective liberalization of imports, and a sharp depreciation of the rupee.

The subsequent phase of liberalization was under the overall reform process that was initiated in 1991. On the external front, the reforms included dismantling of trade restrictions, move toward current account convertibility, a market-determined exchange rate, and gradual opening up of the capital account. However, with the Latin American debt crisis of the early 1980s and the Asian financial crisis of 1997 in mind, India prioritized certain flows and agents in the liberalization process. In particular, non-debt flows were preferred to debt flows. Currently, barring a few sectors, foreign direct investment (FDI) is universally allowed with some of the sensitive sectors being subject to caps. Portfolio flows have also witnessed significant liberalization, though there still exist separate investment caps on sub-accounts of foreign institutional investors (FIIs), individual FII, and aggregate FII investments in a company. In contrast, debt flows are subject to numerous restrictions including eligibility conditions for borrowers and lenders, minimum maturity period, ceilings on interest rate spread, and end-use restrictions.

Table 1 highlights some of the existing guidelines influencing the flow of foreign capital in India. It is evident that there has been a hierarchy in the liberalization of capital flows with equity flows being given preference over debt flows. Within equity flows, FDI has been preferred to portfolio investments, while among debt flows, long-term flows have been preferred over short-term flows. This hierarchy has modified the composition of external liabilities. From comprising 95 % of external liabilities in 1990, the share of debt liabilities has dropped to 33.2 % in 2007. Over the same period, the share of portfolio liabilities has increased from 1 % to nearly 50 %, while that of FDI has increased from 4 to 17.2 %. As shown in Fig. 1, this change in composition of liabilities in India has been in line with international experience.

Another key objective of active management of capital flows in India is to stem rapid appreciation of the exchange rate. Rajan and Subramanian (2005), Johnson et al. (2007), and Prasad et al. (2007) show that excessive capital inflows could result in rapid exchange rate appreciation, which can hurt exports. Bulk of the exports of developing countries like India tends to be concentrated in labor-intensive, low and intermediate technology products with thin profit margins. Hence, sharp exchange rate volatility can have severe employment, output, and distributional consequences. The need for capital flow management measures is also driven by the existing state of financial development. Prasad and Rajan (2008) contend that in an underdeveloped financial system, foreign capital is likely to be channeled toward easily collateralized, non-tradable investments like real estate, leading to asset price booms, with subsequent busts severely disrupting the economy. Moreover, Aghion et al. (2009) argue that higher exchange rate volatility can stunt growth in countries with thin financial markets. Despite significant progress in the last two decades, India's level of financial development continues to lag behind the advanced

Table 1 Regulatory framework for capital account management. (Source: IMF 2012 and various RBI and Securities and Exchange Board of India (SEBI) notifications)

	Inflows	Outflows
Foreign direct investment	FDI is allowed under the automatic route and government approval route. In several sectors, investment up to 100 % is allowed, while a few other sectors have sector-specific caps and guidelines. There are about ten sectors in which FDI is prohibited	Indian companies and registered partnerships may invest up to 400 % of their net worth without approval. The ceiling is not applicable where the investment is made out of balances held in Exchange Earners' Foreign Currency account or out of funds raised through American Depositary Receipts (ADRs)/Global Depositary Receipts (GDRs). Lower limits and extra conditions apply to unregistered partnership and proprietorship firms
Portfolio equity investment	Registered FIIs such as pension funds, mutual funds, investment trusts, etc. and QFIs are allowed to invest in equity. The ceiling for overall investment for FIIs and QFIs are 24 % and 10 % of the paid-up capital of the company. The ceiling for FII investment can be raised up to the sectoral cap, subject to the approval of the board and the general body passing a special resolution to that effect. The limit is 20 % of the paid-up capital in the case of public sector banks. NRIs and persons of Indian origin (PIOs) can invest in equity up to 10 % of the paid-up capital of the Indian company, which can be raised to 24 % subject to the approval of the general body. Holders of overseas citizenship of India certificates have the same rights to invest in India as NRIs (except to invest in agricultural land). QFIs can invest in those mutual fund (MF) schemes that hold at least 25 % of their assets in infrastructure sector under the $ 3 billion sub-limit for investment in MFs related to infrastructure	The overall limit on residents' investments in companies listed abroad is $ 200,000 a year. Resident corporations may invest up to 50 % of their net worth in shares of listed companies abroad. Indian Mutual Funds are permitted to invest within an overall cap of $ 7 billion
Portfolio bond investments	Registered FIIs may invest in debt securities issued by Indian corporates with an overall limit of $ 20 billion, with an additional limit of $ 25 billion in infrastructure bonds and a $ 20 billion limit on government securities. The investor base for G-Secs has been widened to include Sovereign Wealth Funds (SWFs), multilateral agencies, insurance, and pension funds. Infrastructure bonds have mandatory holding period. Different limits apply to NRIs	Only resident individuals may invest in debt securities abroad subject to a yearly limit of $ 200,000

Table 1 (continued)

	Inflows	Outflows
Investments in money market	Only NRIs may invest in money market mutual funds	Residents may purchase these instruments abroad without RBI approval
Derivatives	These transactions are generally subject to limits and approval. Hedging of nonresidents' investments in India is allowed	Commercial banks may purchase such instruments for their asset and liability management. Resident companies may use derivatives to hedge commodity price and foreign exchange debt exposures
Loans	External Commercial Borrowings (ECBs) are allowed through automatic and approval routes. ECBs through automatic route are subject to a cap of $ 20 million for a minimum 3-year average maturity and $ 750 million for a minimum 5-year average maturity. ECBs through approval route can be higher than $ 750 million. External loans are subject to an all-in-cost ceiling and end-use restrictions	Lending abroad is generally subject to approval, except for certain trade credits and lending to foreign subsidiaries

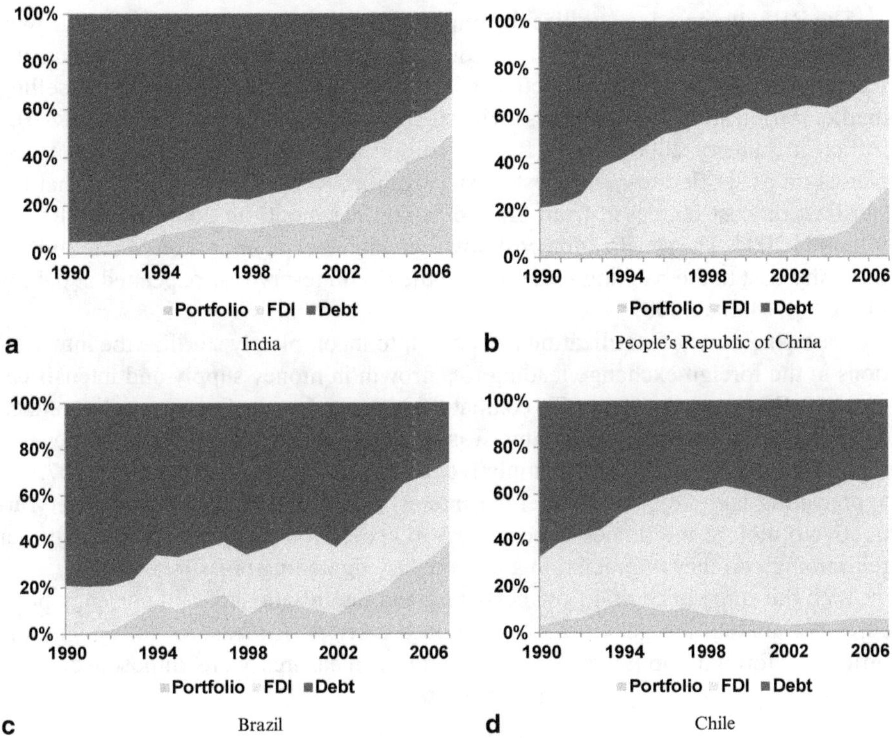

Fig. 1 Composition of liabilities (Source: Lane and Milessi-Ferreti 2007)

economies. The 2012 Financial Development Report of the World Economic Forum ranked India 40 out of the 62 countries covered, with India ranking poorly on institutional and business environment, financial stability, and access as well as banking services.

The calibrated liberalization of the capital account was also driven by fiscal deficit and inflation rates in India being consistently higher than international levels. Both Reserve Bank of India (RBI 2006) and Planning Commission (2009) have argued that the adverse effect of a rising fiscal deficit and high inflation rates would be transmitted much faster in a liberalized capital account regime. These include pro-cyclical fiscal policy, increased volatility of bond yields, rise in monetary base in the absence of sterilizing instruments, and difficulties in securing funds to finance the fiscal deficit.

India started experiencing steadily rising levels of foreign capital since the early 2000s, which surged after 2005 due to excess global liquidity and a strong domestic economy. As a share of gross domestic product (GDP), net capital flows more than doubled from 4 % in 2005–2006 to over 9.5 % in 2007–2008. The initial response to the surge in capital flows was to accumulate reserves with RBI purchasing $ 26.8 billion foreign exchange in 2006–2007 and another $ 78.2 billion in 2007–2008. Such scale of interventions severely strained the monetary base as the reserve money growth accelerated to 30 % in 2007, completely driven by accumulation of foreign assets by RBI. Broad money growth peaked at 25 %, well over the central bank's target of around 15 %.

The RBI attempted to sterilize the impact of intervention and contain the growth in monetary base by reducing its holding of domestic assets and increasing the reserve requirements. The reduction of domestic assets took the form of selling market stabilization bonds (MSBs). The stock of these bonds increased from Rs. 0.4 trillion in January 2006 to over Rs. 1.7 trillion in October 2007. The interest expenses on MSBs led to rising cost of sterilization. Kohli (2011) estimates that the sterilization cost increased from Rs. 7.6 billion per month in 2006 to over Rs. 31 billion in 2007. The sterilization cost, involving interest payments on MSBs and opportunity cost to the banking sector due to the rise in reserve ratio, peaked at 0.42 % of GDP in March 2008.

The rising costs of sterilization forced RBI to incompletely sterilize the interventions in the foreign exchange leading to a growth in money supply and intensification of inflationary pressures. To combat these pressures, outflows were liberalized and the pace of monetary tightening was accelerated with the repo and the reverse repo rates being raised by a cumulative 125 basis points in 2006 and 2007. An appreciating currency and a widening interest rate differential provided a very attractive option to the domestic borrowers to access foreign funds, thereby further reinforcing currency appreciation and monetary tightening pressures.

With the surge in capital flow persisting and the inflationary and currency pressures not abating the government introduced a series of measures to regulate the inflow of foreign capital. A majority of these measures were imposed on debt

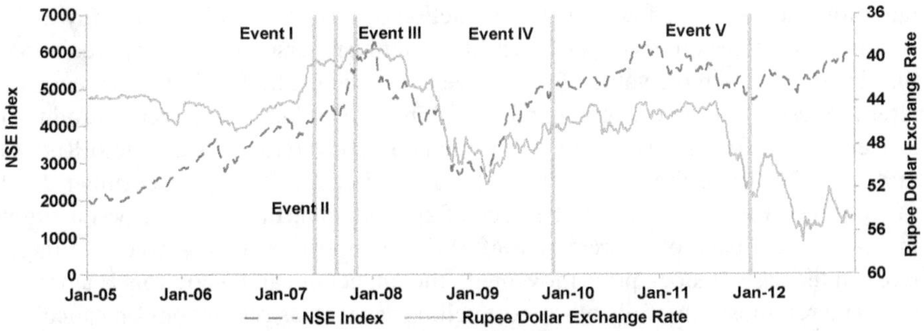

Fig. 2 Impact of capital controls on the currency and stock prices. Note: Event I is the reduction in all-in-cost ceilings for ECBs. Event II refers to measures introduced to restrict conversion of ECBs into Rupees. Event III refers to SEBI's tightening of rules for purchase of shares and bonds in Indian companies through the PN route. Event IV is re-imposition of all in cost ceilings for ECBs that were discontinued during the GFC and discontinuation of the buyback of Foreign Currency Convertible Bonds. Event V refers to restrictions on canceling and rebooking of forward contracts. (Source: Authors' calculations)

Table 2 Impact of capital controls on currency and stock prices. (Source: Authors' calculations)

		Average daily currency appreciation (%)		Average daily stock price increase (%)	
	Date of introduction	Before	After	Before	After
Event I	May 22, 2007	0.198	−0.003	0.395	0.113
Event II	August 7, 2007	0.029	0.027	0.092	0.271
Event III	October 17, 2007	0.125	−0.026	0.670	0.181
Event IV	December 10, 2009	0.023	0.026	0.196	−0.159
Event V	December 15, 2011	−0.259	0.253	−0.385	0.378

flows such as capping of corporates' access to foreign currency funds, restrictions on conversion of foreign currency loans into Rupees, and reduction in ceilings on interest rate for foreign borrowings. Moreover, the use of participatory notes (PNs), an offshore derivative product, allowing overseas investors to participate in the Indian stock market was banned, while interest rates on nonresident deposits were also lowered.

To evaluate the efficacy of some of the measures aimed at managing capital inflow, we look at the currency and stock price movements before and after the introduction of these measures. To be deemed effective, these measures must reverse or at least slow down the rate of change observed prior to their introduction. Figure 2 and Table 2 highlight the impact of some of the capital flow measures on stock prices and the exchange rate. We focus on the average daily change in the exchange rate and stock prices over a 30-day period before and after introduction of the measures. The evidence on the efficacy of capital controls on arresting exchange rate movement is mixed at best. The reduction of all-in-cost ceilings in May 2007 and the restrictions on PNs in October 2007 led to a reversal of Rupee appreciation. Similarly, the fall in the value of the Rupee in the second half of 2011 was reversed after the restriction on canceling and rebooking forward contracts were introduced in December 2011. However, the restrictions on conversion of ECBs into Rupees in August 2007 and the reimposition of the all-in-cost ceilings in December 2009 failed to reverse or slow down the pace of appreciation. In fact, there was a slight increase in the pace of appreciation after the reimposition of all-in-cost ceilings. Even in the case of stock price movement, the impact of capital controls is ambiguous. The reimposition of the all-in-cost ceilings as well as restrictions on canceling and rebooking forward contracts successfully reversed the trend in stock prices. However, the rising trend in stock prices continued after the introduction of various capital controls in 2007, though there was a moderation of the pace of increase after the reduction in ECB ceiling in May 2007 and restrictions on PNs in October 2007. The latter restriction had a particularly strong impact, as the PNs were an important source of FII investment in equities. In contrast, the restriction on conversion of ECBs into Rupees introduced in August 2007 was associated with a sharp acceleration in stock prices.

Our simple analysis indicates that the introduction of capital control measures did not always lead to a reversal or even a slowdown in the rate of exchange rate appreciation or the stock prices. However, this is not to conclude that these measures were ineffective, due to the absence of counterfactuals. Moreover, to rigorously estimate the efficacy of capital controls, one would have to also look at the impact of these measures on the volume and composition of flows (Patnaik and Shah 2011) and the extent to which they allowed policymakers' maneuverability in monetary and exchange rate management. We focus on this point in the next section.

3 Negotiating the Trilemma

India's increased integration with the global capital markets during the last two decades has increased the complexity of macroeconomic management in India. In particular, India had to negotiate the well-known macroeconomic trilemma. The standard formulation of the trilemma argues that it is impossible to attain monetary policy independence, exchange rate stability (ERS), and capital market integration simultaneously. Only two of the three objectives can be obtained at a particular point in time. India, like other emerging economies, seeks to achieve each of the three objectives with varying degrees. While capital flows aid growth by providing external capital to sustain an excess of investment over domestic savings, a competitive exchange rate helps to maintain a sustainable current account balance and an independent monetary policy stabilizes the economy in the face of domestic and exogenous shocks. However, given the impossibility of attaining the three goals simultaneously, India had to balance the conflicting objectives. Moreover, the sharp increase in the volatility of capital flows during recent years has created a tension between monetary management and exchange rate management. As discussed in Sect. 2, excessive capital inflows have been found to result in rapid real exchange rate appreciation, which in turn hurts exports of emerging economies. Even a short-term appreciation can have lingering implications like permanent loss of export market share and reductions in manufacturing capacity. Alternatively, if the central bank intervenes to prevent the exchange rate from appreciating, it is likely to lead to an increase in money supply, fueling inflationary pressures.

In this section, we analyze India's management of the macroeconomic trilemma, the extent to which India has been bound by the trilemma, and whether the trilemma has remained underutilized. Following Aizenman et al. (2010a, b) we quantify the various policy objectives under the trilemma. We use quarterly data and cover the period 1996–1997Q1 to 2011–2012Q3. Our coverage is dictated by the availability of the data at a quarterly frequency, especially data on GDP.

3.1 *Monetary Independence*

Following Aizenman et al. (2010a, b), the monetary independence (MI) is measured as the inverse of the quarterly correlation of the interest rates between India and the USA. The USA is taken as the base country following Aizenman et al. (2010a, b) and Obstfeld et al. (2010) who argue that Indian monetary policy through this period has been most closely linked to the USA. The quarterly indices are calculated using weekly 3-month Treasury Bill yields for India and the USA. The data are taken from Global Financial Database. The index of MI is given by

$$\mathrm{MI} = \frac{corr(i_i, i_j) - (-1)}{1 - (-1)}, \tag{1}$$

where i_i *and* i_j are the 3-month Treasury Bill rates for India and the USA, respectively. This index can theoretically take a value between 0 and 1 with a higher value indicating a greater degree of monetary independence. We find that for India the index ranges between 0.11 and 0.85. Hence, we rescale this index to lie between 0 and 1.

3.2 *Exchange Rate Stability*

We make use of the methodology introduced by Frankel and Wei (1994) to create an index of ERS. The degree of influence that major global currencies have on Indian Rupee can be estimated using the following estimation model:

$$\Delta \log \varepsilon^{CHF}_{INR,t} = \alpha_0 + \beta_{US} \Delta \log \varepsilon^{CHF}_{USD,t} + \beta_{EUR} \Delta \log \varepsilon^{CHF}_{EUR,t} + \beta_{JAP} \Delta \log \varepsilon^{CHF}_{JPY,t} + \mu_t, \tag{2}$$

where $\varepsilon_{i,t}^{CHF}$ is the exchange rate of currency i against the numèraire currency, which in this case is the Swiss franc and the currency i can be the US Dollar, Japanese Yen, and the Euro. For the period prior to the introduction of the Euro, we consider the German Deutsche Mark. Under this estimation, $\hat{\beta}_i$– which is the estimated coefficient on the rate at which currency i depreciates against the numèraire currency indicates the weight of currency i in the basket. In the case where the currency under observation is pegged to a particular currency or a basket of currency, we will have $\hat{\beta}_i = 1$ or $\sum_{i=1}^{I} \hat{\beta}_i = 1$ for the i currencies that are a part of the basket. Moreover, pegging to an individual or a basket of currencies implies a higher goodness of fit. In our estimation, we use daily data, with the data being sourced from the RBI and Global Financial Database. We apply the estimation over a quarter and take the goodness of fit, or the adjusted R^2 as the measure of ERS. A higher R^2 indicates greater pegging to an individual or a basket of currencies. Again, we normalize the index so that it lies between 0 and 1.

3.3 Capital Account Openness (KO)

The index of capital account openness is based on a *de facto* measure instead of a *de jure* one as it is the volume of flows that creates a conflict between MI and ERS as opposed to controls governing the movement of capital. A country with high *de jure* openness can have low capital flows and hence may be able to simultaneously stabilize exchange rate and retain monetary autonomy. Alternatively, a country with low *de jure* openness can witness large flows due to lax capital controls and face a tradeoff between ensuring MI and ERS. The index of capital account openness is based on net capital flows. The index is constructed as the ratio of absolute value of net capital flows to GDP.

$$\text{KO} = \left| \frac{\text{Net Flows}}{\text{GDP}} \right|. \tag{3}$$

The focus on net capital flows is based on the fact that it is the capital account balance that is crucial for the trilemma. If capital inflows in a country were to be matched by an equal amount of outflows, the policymaker can retain MI with a stable exchange rate. Finally, to make this index comparable with others, we normalize it to lie between 0 and 1.

In Fig. 3, we highlight the evolution of the three indices over the period 1996–1997Q1 to 2011–2012Q3. While ERS index exhibited a downward trend since the early 2000s, the KO index witnessed an upswing till the onset of the GFC. The GFC led to a sharp drop in the KO index, as flows to emerging economies, including India, dried up globally. Since 2010–2011, the KO index has shown signs of revival, although the various components of the capital account have displayed considerable volatility. Finally, the MI index witnessed significant volatility, although there is a perceptible upward trend since early 2000s.

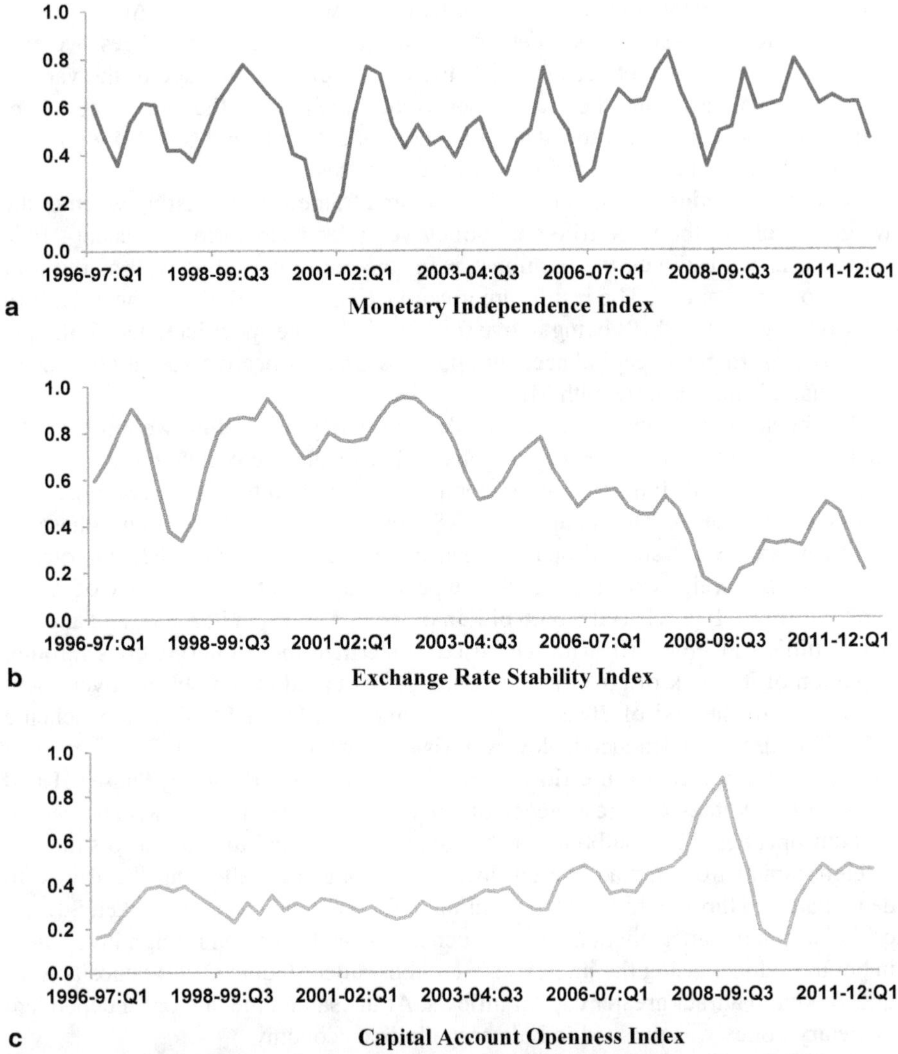

Fig. 3 Evolution of the trilemma indices. **a** Monetary independence index. **b** Exchange rate stability index. **c** Capital account openness index. (Source: Authors' calculations)

The entire period from 1996–1997Q1 to 2011–2012Q3 was one of significant changes in economic conditions, and required balancing of the trilemma objectives. To effectively evaluate the shift in policy stance over the period under consideration, we divide the entire sample into four equal subperiods; Phase I: 1996–1997Q1 to 1999–2000Q4, Phase II: 2000–2001Q1 to 2003–2004Q4, Phase III: 2004–2005Q1 to 2007–2008Q4, and Phase IV: 2008–2009Q1 to 2011–2012Q3.

As pointed out in Aizenman et al. (2010a, b), policymakers can garner greater flexibility vis-à-vis monetary and exchange rate management in the short run by accumulating or depleting reserves. Consequently we also focus on ΔRes, the absolute change in reserves (as a percentage of GDP).[1] Like other indices, we also normalize ΔRes to lie between 0 and 1. Figure 4 shows the average of the various policy dimensions during the four phases. Across the phases, the rise in capital account openness has been associated with a drop in ERS. The index of MI witnessed a drop in Phase II but recovered in subsequent phases.

Next, we examine the validity of the trilemma framework by testing whether the weighted sum of the three trilemma policy variables adds up to a constant—here set to be 2. We estimate the relationship for the entire period as well as the four phases outlined above. The results are given in Table 3. We find that the overall fit is extremely high with R^2 being above 0.93 across all the specifications. While the estimates for ERS and capital account openness are significant across all the specifications, it is not the case with MI.

To obtain the contribution of each trilemma policy orientation we multiply the coefficients with the average for each phase. The results are outlined in Fig. 5. The high goodness of fit implies that the contributions add up to being very close to 2 across all the phases. The increase in ERS from Phase I to Phase II and Phase III was associated with a sharp drop in MI. During Phases II and III, the RBI intervened heavily in the foreign exchange market to prevent appreciation in the face of strong capital inflows. It purchased $ 55.6 billion of foreign assets in Phase II, and another $ 134 billion in Phase III. The RBI tried to sterilize these interventions through depletion of its stock of government bonds. As it started to run out of government bonds toward the end of 2003, a new instrument—Market Stabilization Scheme (MSS) bonds were introduced. However, rising costs of sterilization forced the RBI to only partially sterilize the flows, resulting in loss of MI during Phases II and III. Phase IV witnessed a resurgence of MI with a decline in both ERS and capital account openness. The outbreak of the subprime crisis led to a flight to safety of foreign capital from India. The outflow was managed by allowing the Rupee to depreciate and through limited intervention in the foreign exchange market. Several capital account management measures such as raising the cap on foreign investment in bonds and increasing the interest rate on nonresident Indian (NRI) deposits were undertaken to attract greater capital inflows. At the same time, a more independent monetary policy was pursued to bolster the Indian economy.[2]

Capital flows have remained volatile during most of Phase IV driven by uncertainty over the advanced economies' recovery prospects, large swings in risk aversion, loose monetary policy in the advanced economies, and changing domestic fundamentals. In Phase IV, RBI intervened in a limited manner and allowed the exchange rate to move with greater freedom. While the Rupee appreciated by nearly

---

[1] We use data on actual intervention by the RBI to exclude valuation changes. The data are from Handbook of Statistics on the Indian Economy.

[2] The RBI took a series of measures to counter the drop in liquidity in the aftermath of collapse of Lehman Brothers. These included lowering of key policy rates, cash reserve ratio (CRR) and statutory liquidity ratio (SLR), unwinding of MSS bonds, and lowering of prudential norms related to provisioning.

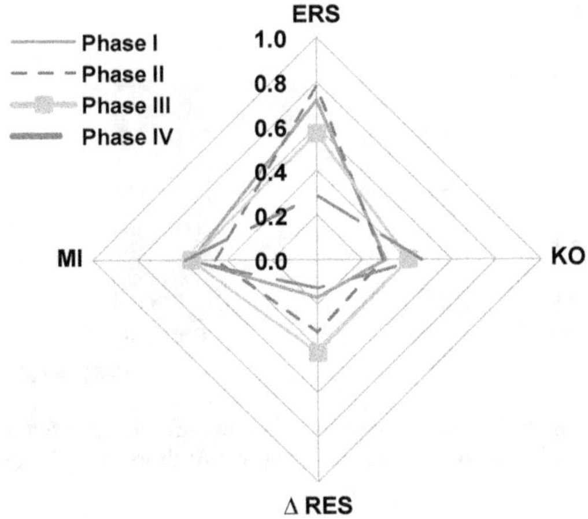

Fig. 4 Configuration of the trilemma objectives and international reserves. *ERS* exchange rate stability, *MI* monetary independence, *KO* capital account openness. (Source: Authors' calculations)

Table 3 Testing the validity of the trilemma framework. (Source: Authors' calculations)

	1996–1997Q1 to 2011–2012Q3	1996–1997Q1 to 1999–2000Q4	2000–2001Q1–2003–2004Q4	2004–2005Q1 to 2007–2008Q4	2008–2009Q1 to 2011–2012Q3
	Whole sample	Phase I	Phase II	Phase III	Phase IV
Monetary independence	0.656***	0.684**	0.125	0.158	1.244**
	(3.448)	(1.986)	(0.516)	(0.861)	(2.711)
Exchange rate stability	1.388***	1.093**	1.511***	1.908***	1.774*
	(9.444)	(2.268)	(5.001)	(7.813)	(1.813)
Capital account liberalization	2.012***	2.419**	2.473***	1.997***	1.357**
	(8.392)	(2.918)	(3.078)	(5.861)	(2.696)
Observations	63	16	16	16	15
R-squared	0.954	0.949	0.980	0.989	0.934

Robust standard errors in parentheses
*, **, and *** indicate significance at 10 %, 5 %, and 1 %, respectively

17 % between March 2009 and April 2010, it weakened by 19 % between August 2011 and December 2011. The drop in capital inflows and greater exchange rate flexibility allowed the RBI to pursue a more independent monetary policy. After the initial softening of monetary policy to stimulate growth, the RBI started tightening monetary policy from March 2010 in response to high inflation. This was in contrast with the advanced economies, which were following a soft monetary policy to stimulate growth.

Overall, we find that instead of opting for corner solutions, India has adopted an intermediate regime while negotiating the trilemma. This has been buttressed by

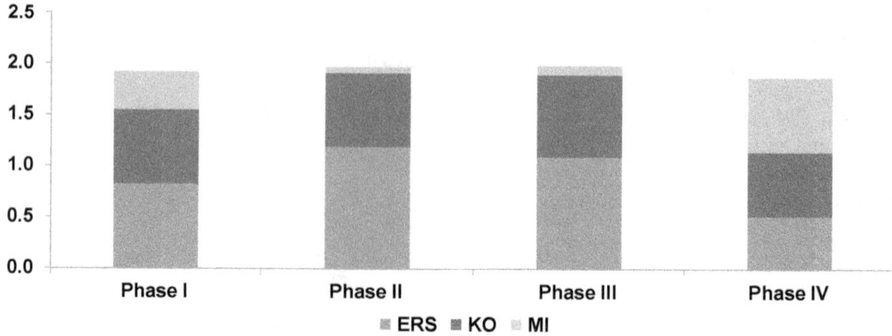

Fig. 5 Contribution to the trilemma. *ERS* exchange rate stability, *MI* monetary independence, *KO* capital account openness. (Source: Authors' calculations)

selective capital flow management measures.[3] In doing so, India has resorted to a multiple instrument approach. The overall policy architecture thus encompasses active management of capital flows, especially volatile and debt flows, moderately flexible exchange rate regime with the RBI intervening at times to prevent excessive volatility, sterilization through various instruments like MSS bonds and changes in CRR, and finally, building up of a stockpile of reserves.

4 Impact on Exchange Market Pressure Index

4.1 Measurements and Evolution of EMPIs

The RBI's management of capital account could be driven by a desire to moderate certain types of capital inflows or to manage ERS. It may be reasonable to conjecture that the goal was the latter in the context of financial trilemma. Accordingly, we measure the EMP in India, discuss its evolution over time, and analyze a few crucial macroeconomic factors that may have affected the EMP over the last couple of decades. EMP is a combination of exchange rate depreciation and international reserves loss—a concept pioneered by Girton and Roper (1977), and applied frequently in the analysis of Emerging Market Economies (EMEs) (Frankel 2009). A positive (negative) EMP indicates a net excess demand (supply) for foreign currency, accompanied by a combination of reserve loss (gain) and currency depreciation (appreciation).

In order to measure EMP in India, we follow Aizenman et al. (2012) who investigate the factors explaining EMP in emerging economies during the 2000s. The first measure of EMP is the unweighted sum of percentage nominal depreciation and percentage loss of reserves:

[3] Our results are broadly consistent with other studies focusing on India's trilemma management such as Hutchison et al. (2011), Aizenman and Sengupta (2013), Sen Gupta and Manjhi (2012), among others.

$$EMP_{i,t} = \frac{\Delta e_{i.t}}{e_{i,t-1}} - \frac{\Delta IR_{i.t}}{IR_{i,t-1}}, \tag{4}$$

where $e_{i.t}$ stands for nominal Rupee exchange rate per US dollar and $IR_{i.t}$ denotes international reserve holdings (excluding gold) by India during quarter *t*. $\Delta e_{i,t}$ and $\Delta IR_{i,t}$ denote changes in nominal exchange rate and international reserve holdings, respectively, between quarters *t* and *t-1*.

Our second measure, EMP (IR/M-base), is defined as the unweighted sum of percentage exchange rate depreciation and reserve loss, with reserve loss deflated by the monetary base:

$$EMP_{i,t}^{IR/M-Base} = \frac{\Delta e_{i.t}}{e_{i,t-1}} - \frac{\Delta IR_{i.t}}{M_{i,t-1}/e_{i,t-1}}, \tag{5}$$

where $M_{i,\ t-1}$ stands for M2 in local currency units of India in quarter *t-1*, and the monetary base is converted to US dollars. According to the monetary model-based EMP measure popularized by Girton and Roper (1977), specification (2) provides a real measure of international reserve loss, normalized by the monetary base.

The third and final measure, EMP (standardized), is the weighted sum of de-meaned percentage nominal exchange rate depreciation and percentage loss of international reserves where the weights are inverses of the historical standard deviation of each series:

$$EMP_{i,t}^{\text{Standardized}} = \frac{1}{\sigma_{i,\Delta e}}\left(\frac{\Delta e_{i.t}}{e_{i,t-1}} - \mu_{i,\Delta e}\right) - \frac{1}{\sigma_{i,\Delta RES}}\left(\frac{\Delta IR_{i,t}}{IR_{i,t-1}} - \mu_{i,\Delta RES}\right), \tag{6}$$

where $\mu_{i,\Delta e}$ and $\mu_{i,\Delta RES}$ denote the historical means of percent nominal exchange rate depreciation and percent changes in international reserve holdings. Similarly, $\sigma_{i,\Delta e}$ and $\sigma_{i,\Delta RES}$ represent historical standard deviations of both these series for India.

Figure 6 shows the time-series evolution of the three EMP indices with the unweighted EMP on the left axis and EMP (IR/M-base) and EMP (standardized) on the right axis.

As can be seen from the figure, all three EMPIs display a fair amount of fluctuations during the early 1990s, representing the period of heightened macroeconomic volatility during and in the aftermath of the 1991 balance of payments (BOP) crisis in India. The unweighted measure of EMP (left axis) indicates that between 1990Q1 and 1990Q4 India went from an average 5 % combined nominal appreciation and gains in international reserve holdings to a 50 % combined nominal depreciation and international reserve loss. The fluctuations in all three EMP series continue throughout the 1990s shooting up during the 1997–1998 Asian financial crisis.

From 1999Q1 to 2008Q1, all three EMP indices are on average negative implying net excess supply of foreign currency, alleviated by a combination of reserve gain and appreciation. According to the unweighted EMP, during this period Indian

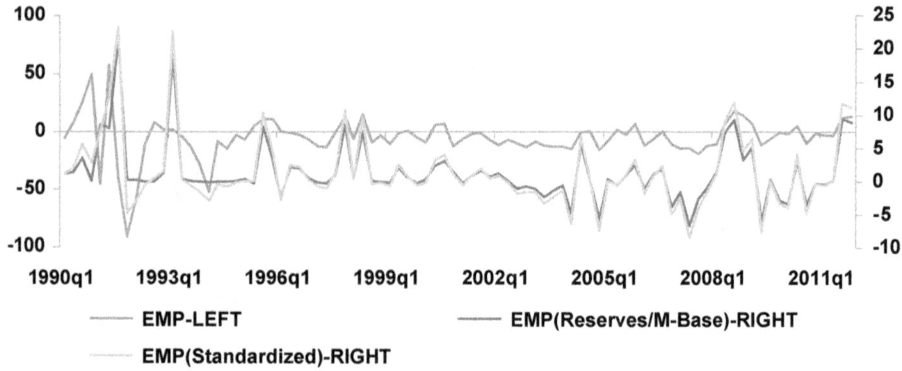

Fig. 6 Evolution of the EMP indices: 1990Q1-2011Q4. (Source: Authors' calculations)

economy experienced on average a 7% combined nominal currency appreciation and gains in international reserve holdings. This also coincides with the period of Great Moderation in the global economy during which all EMEs in general experienced nominal appreciation and massive accumulation of reserves.

The downward/negative trend in the EMPs through the early and mid-2000s gets interrupted by a sharp upward movement between 2008Q2 and 2009Q1—the period of global turbulence centering around the collapse of Lehman Brothers in the US. Between 2008Q1 and 2008Q4, India went from an average 10% combined nominal appreciation and gains in reserve holdings to a 14% combined nominal depreciation and reserve loss. This is comparable to the EMP of other EMEs who during the same period went from an average 10% combined nominal appreciation and gains in international reserve holdings to a 20% combined nominal depreciation and international reserve loss (Aizenman et al. 2012).

Like other EMEs, the EMP in India (by all three measures) came down by 2009Q2 and switched back to net nominal currency appreciation combined with hoarding international reserves. This trend continued in India till the end of 2010. Since then however the EMP has been on the rise again given the massive currency depreciation that India has been experiencing in the wake of the Euro-zone sovereign debt crisis.

4.2 Estimation of EMP Determinants

In this sub-section, we use a multivariate time-series regression framework in order to estimate the link between EMP and a few selected explanatory variables. The objective is to quantify the statistical as well as economic significance of these factors in accounting for EMP patterns over the sample period. Following Aizenman et al. (2012) in our first specification, we include trade balance to GDP ratio, share

Table 4 Factors affecting EMP in India (1990Q1–2011Q4). (Source: Authors' calculations)

Variables	EMP	EMP (reserves/M-base)	EMP (standardized)
Trade balance (% GDP)	−1.420***	−0.096	−0.095
	(0.578)	(0.263)	(0.074)
Net FDI inflows (% GDP)	−1.073	−0.137	−0.083
	(0.944)	(0.448)	(0.124)
Net portfolio equity inflows	−1.667**	−0.661*	−0.206**
(% GDP)	(0.758)	(0.366)	(0.098)
WPI inflation	−1.667	0.198	0.071
	(0.429)	(0.218)	(0.058)
Observations	60	60	60
R-squared	0.1892	0.0858	0.1306

Robust standard errors in parentheses
*, **, and *** indicate correlations significant at 10 %, 5 %, and 1 %, respectively

of net FDI inflows and net portfolio equity inflows in GDP separately and we also control for year on year wholesale price index (WPI) inflation.[4] Estimation results are reported in Table 4. The three columns pertain to the three different EMP measures as detailed in the previous section. The last two measures are used as dependent variables in the time-series regressions as robustness check for our baseline results on column 1.

As can be seen from column 1 of Table 4, a deteriorating trade balance is associated with a higher EMP, a result that makes intuitive sense. When EMP is standardized or deflated by monetary base, the estimated coefficient of trade balance continues to have the predicted sign, but it is no longer statistically significant. An increase in net portfolio equity inflows lowers the EMP. This effect is both statistically and economically significant. For instance, a 10 percentage points rise (decline) in portfolio equity inflows (outflows) is associated with a 16.7 percentage points lower EMP when measured using the unweighted index. The association between EMP and equity flows is also robust to the normalization of reserves by monetary base as well as standardization of the EMP index. Neither inflation nor the share of net FDI inflows in GDP seems to have any significant impact on the EMP over the sample period.[5]

We had also incorporated percentage change in stock market returns (BSE index) as well as the ratio of short-term external debt to GDP in the EMP estimations. Stock market returns happened to be highly correlated with WPI inflation and trade balance. When added without these two explanatory variables in the regression, stock market returns were found to be significantly associated with EMP measured using all three indices. In other words, positive changes in stock returns lower the EMP and vice versa. Quarterly data on short-term external debt are available only

[4] We are constrained by the number of observations and hence have not added too many controls in the EMP estimations for lack of sufficient degrees of freedom.

[5] We also conducted the estimation using Newey–West standard errors and results came out to be the same.

from 2006Q1 onward from the Quarterly External Debt Statistics (QEDS) database maintained jointly by the BIS–IMF–World Bank. When added to the estimation, external debt was found to be negatively associated with EMP—a lower short-term external debt ratio increases the EMP, but the effect was found to be statistically significant only for the unweighted EMPI. These results are not reported here for brevity but are available upon request. Our results thus primarily highlight the importance of portfolio equity flows and also stock market returns to some extent, in accounting for EMP in India from 1990Q1 to 2011Q4.

5 Coordination in Capital Controls: Role of G20

In recent times, there has been a widespread debate among economists and policymakers regarding the efficacy of capital controls in managing volatile cross-border capital flows. While capital controls and similar macro-prudential measures are useful in ensuring macroeconomic and financial stability in countries especially during times of sudden stops and surges, there are considerable risks involved as recently highlighted by the GFC of 2008. A coordinated approach across countries in implementing capital controls is likely to be more effective than unilateral actions, given that any prudential measure adopted to tackle capital flow volatility is bound to have cross-border spillover effects, often times putting the burden of adjustment on other countries.

As argued by Ostry et al. (2012), one of the reasons why countries may wish to impose capital controls on inflows is to maintain an undervalued currency thereby sustaining a current account surplus. By restricting capital inflows, the debtor country may seek to manipulate the inter-temporal terms of trade in its favor. Such a unilateral policy action by one country is likely to have a beggar-thy-neighbor impact by forcing a situation of current account deficit on the importing country. Alternatively, if countries use capital controls in order to mitigate the risks associated with volatile foreign borrowing, it is likely to magnify the macro-financial stability risks for other countries by diverting the unwanted, volatile flows to countries that are less able to absorb the same. Within such a multilateral context, coordination across countries may be useful in producing a globally efficient outcome, especially when imposition of capital controls is associated with welfare costs.

Thus, any decision by a country to impose capital controls may need to take into account the associated multilateral repercussions. In addition, here the G20 can play an effective role by ensuring that the severity of boom–bust cycles in capital flows is mitigated through cooperation and coordination among its member countries thereby fostering global financial stability. In this context, it may be worthwhile to mention that India, a major emerging economy, adopted a series of financial liberalization measures since 1991 and these have mostly been unidirectional since then. Barring a couple of exceptional instances, India has not used capital controls unilaterally to manage volatile capital flows.

6 Conclusion

The recent increase in volatility of global capital flows has reignited the debate about appropriate capital flow management measures. Volatile capital flows tend to complicate macroeconomic management by aggravating real exchange rate misalignment, excesses in credit market, asset price booms and busts, and exacerbating overall financial fragility. Furthermore, they complicate the policy trade-offs related to current account deficit, exchange rate, inflation, availability of external capital to finance investment, and reserve holdings. These policy dilemmas reiterate the need to actively manage capital flows. This can be achieved through a gamut of policy measures of which capital controls are a part. Relying exclusively on the latter would be erroneous—capital controls can be effective, but are not always foolproof, and are vulnerable to leakages through financial engineering.

India's experience highlights the adoption of a calibrated approach toward capital account liberalization to minimize risks associated with financial fragilities and macroeconomic distortions. Furthermore, in dealing with capital flows India has resorted to a multiple instrument approach encompassing capital flow management measures, increasingly flexible exchange rate regime with the RBI intervening from time to time, sterilization of these interventions through multiple instruments like MSS bonds and CRR, and building up of a stockpile of reserves.

India has navigated the well-known macroeconomic trilemma by embracing an intermediate approach and balancing the policy objectives as per the demands of the macroeconomic situation. In recent years, a shift toward greater monetary policy autonomy to tackle growing domestic inflationary pressure has been balanced with greater flexibility of the exchange rate.

In order to assess the impact of capital account management on the foreign exchange market, we also focus on the EMPI and analyze its various macroeconomic determinants. We find that EMP has exhibited a great deal of fluctuation in India during the period 1990–2010 due to global and domestic events and has primarily been affected by changes in the trade balance, portfolio equity inflows, and stock market fluctuations.

References

Aghion P, Bacchetta P, Rancière R, Rogoff K (2009) Exchange rate volatility and productivity growth: the role of financial development. J Monet Econ 56(4):494–513

Aizenman J, Sengupta R (2013) The financial trilemma in China and a comparative analysis with India. Pac Econ Rev 18(2):123–146

Aizenman J, Chinn M, Ito H (2010a) The financial crisis, rethinking of the global financial architecture, and the trilemma. Asian Development Bank Institute Working Paper #213 (April)

Aizenman J, Chinn M, Ito H (2010b) The emerging global financial architecture: tracing and evaluating the new patterns of the trilemma's configurations. J Int Money Finance 29(4):615–641

Aizenman J, Lee J, Sushko V (2012) From the great moderation to the global crisis: exchange market pressure in the 2000s. Open Econ Rev 23(4):597–621

Frankel J (2009) New estimation of China's exchange rate regime. Pac Econ Rev 14(3):346–360
Frankel JA, Wei SJ (1994) Yen bloc or dollar bloc? Exchange rate policies of the east Asian economies. In: Ito T, Krueger AO (eds) Macroeconomic linkages: savings, exchange rates, and capital flows, University of Chicago Press, pp 295–333
Girton L, Roper D (1977) A monetary model of exchange market pressure applied to the postwar Canadian experience. Am Econ Rev 67(4):537–548
Hutchison M, Sengupta R, Singh N (2011) India's trilemma: financial liberalization, exchange rates and monetary policy. World Econ 35(1):3–18
IMF (2012) Liberalizing capital flows and managing outflows. International Monetary Fund, Washington D.C. http://www.imf.org/external/np/pp/eng/2012/031312.pdf. Accessed April 7, 2013
Johnson S, Ostry JD, Subramanian A (2007) The prospects for sustained growth in Africa: benchmarking the constraints. IMF Working Paper 07/52
Kohli R (2011) India's experience in navigating the trilemma: do capital controls help? ICRIER Working Paper 257, June
Lane, P., and Milessi-Ferreti, G.M. (2007), "The External Wealth of Nations Mark II: Revised and Extended Estimates of Foreign Assets and Liabilities: 1970-2004", *Journal of International Economics*, Vol. 73(2):223–250
Obstfeld M, Shambaugh JC, Taylor AM (2010) Financial stability, the trilemma, and international reserves. Am Econ J: Macroecon 2(2):57–94
Ostry, J., Ghosh, A., Korinek, A. (2012) Multlateral Aspects of Managing the Capital Account, Staff Discussion Notes No. 12/ 10, International Monetary Fund, Washington DC
Patnaik I, Shah A (2011) Did the Indian capital controls work as a tool of macroeconomic policy? NIPFP Working Paper # 87
Planning Commission (2009) A hundred small steps: committee on financial sector reforms. SAGE Publications India
Prasad ES, Rajan RG (2008) A pragmatic approach to capital account liberalization. IZA Discussion Paper No. 3475
Prasad ES, Rajan R, Subramanian A (2007) Foreign capital and economic growth. Brookings Papers on Economic Activity 1:153–230
Rajan RG, Subramanian A (2005) What undermines aids impact on growth? IMF Working Paper 05/126
RBI (2006) Report of the committee on fuller capital account convertibility. Reserve Bank of India
Sen Gupta A, Manjhi G (2012) Negotiating the trilemma: the Indian experience. Glob Econ J 12(1):1–20

Managing the Risks Associated with Volatile Capital Flows

Atish R. Ghosh

1 Introduction

The past couple of years have seen a remarkable rekindling of interest in capital controls among academics and policymakers alike. Against the backdrop of the post-war trend of liberalization—first by advanced economies, and then increasingly by emerging market and developing countries—by the eve of the 2008 global financial crisis, the use of capital controls was confined to largely anachronistic legacy cases (India and China) or crisis cases (Malaysia, 1998). Yet today numerous emerging market economies (EMEs)—and even some advanced economies—have imposed, or are contemplating adopting, measures that are either capital controls (i.e., residency-based measures intended to affect cross-border capital flows) or macro-prudential measures that are likely to have at least some incidental impact on cross-border flows.

Three factors account for this renewed interest. First, and most simply, is the sheer volatility of capital flows. Although cross-border flows have always exhibited some volatility, their behavior since the 2008 global financial crisis has been truly remarkable.[1] The onset of the crisis was naturally associated with a sharp reversal of capital flows to emerging markets from their 2007 peak, but by late 2009 and early 2010, some EMEs were contending with massive inflows that both complicated macroeconomic management and raised financial stability risks. By the second half of 2011, amid the US sovereign debt downgrade and the worsen-

Chief, Systemic Issues and Assistant Director, Research Department, International Monetary Fund. This note is based on a presentation made at the ICRIER Conference, New Delhi, 2012. The views expressed herein are those of the author, and do not reflect the views of the IMF, its management, or Executive Board. I am grateful to Jonathan D. Ostry, Mahvash S. Qureshi, other IMF colleagues, and ICRIER conference participants for many helpful comments and suggestions.

[1] On capital inflow surges, see Ghosh et al. (2012a).

A. R. Ghosh (✉)
Research Department, International Monetary Fund, Washington, DC, USA
e-mail: aghosh@imf.org

M. Callaghan et al. (eds.), *Global Cooperation Among G20 Countries*,
DOI 10.1007/978-81-322-1659-9_19, © Springer India 2014

ing global economic outlook, capital flows receded rapidly, eliminating much of the cumulated currency gains of EMEs, only to be partially reversed in the course of 2012. Second, there is growing recognition of the intellectual inconsistency in attitudes toward macro-prudential measures, which are generally viewed as desirable and perhaps even essential for avoiding financial crises, and capital controls, which are often viewed with suspicion as being props for poor macroeconomic policies. The inconsistency arises because, in practice, many prudential measures may be largely indistinguishable from capital controls in their economic effect. Third, the global financial crisis was a rude reminder that not all unfettered borrowing-and-lending decisions are optimal (and the international political economy of this is that EMEs, having been lectured for decades on the merits of "orthodox" policies, are in no mood to be lectured further, given that they have not been responsible for the greatest economic and financial crisis since the Great Depression).

Anticipating this renewed interest, my colleagues in the IMF's Research Department and I started working on these issues in late 2009, preparing three substantial analytical pieces examining the use of capital controls in the face of inflow surges; the nexus between capital controls and macro-prudential measures; and multilateral aspects of managing the capital account.[2] The purpose of this note is to provide a brief summary of this analytical work, which, in turn, has been an important input into the formulation of the IMF's Institutional View on Managing the Capital Account.[3]

2 Three Principles

While the body of analytical work underpinning the Institutional View is quite extensive, the key insights can be summarized in three guiding "principles":

- Neither capital controls nor other policies should be used to avoid warranted external adjustment—nor should capital controls substitute for available macroeconomic tools.
- Both residency-based capital controls and non-residency-based prudential measures may be necessary to safeguard financial stability, depending upon circumstances.
- Policies should take account of multilateral considerations.

What do these mean in practice? Let us take each in turn.

2.1 Warranted External Adjustment

While there are numerous analytical and technical challenges, it is at least conceptually possible to identify each country's multilaterally appropriate current account balance. This "equilibrium" current account balance reflects factors that, on the one

[2] Ostry et al. (2010, 2011, 2012a).

[3] See IMF (2012a).

hand, affect saving (such as demographics and provision of social insurance), and, on the other, affect investment (such as productivity and the "world" interest rate/investor risk aversion). Macroeconomic policies in this calculation should be set at their appropriate values given their primary targets (e.g., monetary policy geared toward closing any output gap and achieving the inflation target[4]; fiscal policy geared to maintaining internal balance and debt sustainability). Since the current account is a net concept, all variables should be measured relative to those of the country's trading partners. This yields the multilaterally consistent "optimal" current account and associated real exchange rate when the country's output gap is closed.[5]

In general, movements (e.g., because of capital inflows) toward these equilibrium values are "warranted," and policy—whether exchange rate, macroeconomic, or capital controls/prudential measures—should not seek to resist them. Thus, in the face of inflows, countries with undervalued (or at least not overvalued) flexible exchange rates should allow them to appreciate, while countries with undervalued fixed exchange rates should either revalue (if the inflow is viewed as persistent) or at least not sterilize their foreign exchange (FX) intervention.

When capital flows are moving the current account and the exchange rate away from equilibrium, a policy response may be required. (Arguably, when a sudden surge of capital is raising financial-stability risks, some policy response may be warranted regardless of whether the exchange rate is moving toward its multilaterally consistent equilibrium value.[6]) Such movements are likely to be temporary (if they were permanent, they would likely be responding to fundamental factors in the economy, which in turn are incorporated in the equilibrium current account).

The policy response will depend, in the first instance, on the nature of the concerns raised by the inflows. These may be macroeconomic (exchange rate appreciation hurting competitiveness and requiring costly reallocations of resources when the inflows reverse; overheating of the economy; and general asset price booms) or financial stability (excessive unhedged FX exposure on domestic balance sheets; fragile external financing structures; and asset price bubbles in specific markets). Of course, inflows may raise both sets of concerns simultaneously, but for analytical purposes, it is useful to separate them. Although emerging market and developing countries are especially susceptible to these risks (for instance, because less-developed financial markets mean that firms can less easily obtain financing to tide them over when the currency is temporarily strong), the global financial crisis has served as a reminder that no country, however advanced its economy, is completely immune.

---

[4] By "divine coincidence," meeting the inflation target should be consistent with closing the output gap.

[5] This is the logic underlying the IMF's External Balance Assessment (see IMF 2012b).

[6] In the case where inflows are raising financial-stability risks, the essential argument for policy intervention is that the private sector does not fully internalize the externalities, e.g., crisis risks associated with more risky forms of borrowing (see Korinek 2011). Another form of externality is learning-by-doing in the traded goods sector. As discussed in Ghosh and Kim (2008), while the optimal intervention is a production subsidy, a viable alternative strategy to address the externality would be to maintain an undervalued exchange rate through sterilized intervention cum capital controls; see Ostry et al. (2012a) for a discussion of whether such learning-by-doing externalities justify the use of capital controls.

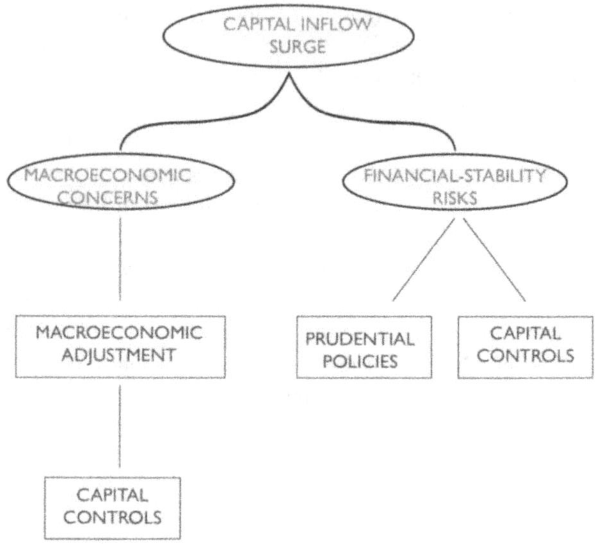

Fig. 1 Policy responses to capital inflow surges. (Source: Ostry et al. (2010))

When the concerns are mainly macroeconomic, it is natural that macroeconomic policies be deployed (Fig. 1).[7] As already noted, if the exchange rate is not already overvalued, the first response is to allow the currency to appreciate. Beyond that, macroeconomic policies should be deployed to the extent that doing so does not prejudice their primary targets. For example, in the face of the inflows, the central bank can use the opportunity to accumulate reserves for country insurance purposes (sterilizing the impact of the accumulation on the money supply, as necessary). However, if reserves are already ample, it may not make sense to accumulate more, given that there are sterilization costs.[8] Likewise, lowering the policy interest rate may help reduce the incentive for capital inflows (at least fixed-income securities), but since the economy is likely to be overheating during a period of inflows anyway, the scope for doing so without prejudicing the inflation target is likely to be limited. By contrast, the very cyclical overheating of the economy argues for fiscal tightening, which would also help reduce capital inflows.

To the extent that such deployment of the available macroeconomic policy tools still leaves a macro problem of excessive inflows, restrictions on capital inflows might be imposed or strengthened. Such controls would typically be widespread (since the form of the inflow is largely immaterial for its impact on the exchange rate), be price-based, and temporary (since the inflow problem is temporary).

[7] The flowchart is not intended to imply temporal precedence of measures (for instance, fiscal policy adjustments may take time, and the country may wish to impose capital controls even before the fiscal adjustment is implemented), nor is intended to imply that capital controls are a "last resort." However, in the face of macroeconomic challenges there is logical precedence of using macroeconomic tools, one reason being that such adjustments (e.g., lowering policy interest rates) reduce the incentive for capital inflows.

[8] For recent IMF policy advice on holding of reserves for precautionary purposes, see IMF (2011b); on emerging market countries' motivations for accumulating reserves, see Ghosh et al. (2012b).

Whether such controls are likely to be effective is an open question. Outright illegal evasion aside, there is generally some scope for circumventing controls, including by relabeling flows (for example, making loans of 366-day maturity to avoid taxes on short-term capital flows) or by using the derivatives markets. Empirical evidence on whether capital controls can affect aggregate inflow surges (and hence the exchange rate) is mixed, with cross-sectional studies usually finding more favorable evidence than time-series studies.[9] This may reflect econometric endogeneity problems whereby countries impose or tighten controls precisely when they are facing inflow surges, yielding a spurious positive correlation between inflows and capital controls that masks the underlying negative correlation (which may be difficult to detect because it is hard to construct the counterfactual). The cross-sectional variation in the use of capital controls is likely to be much less endogenous to inflow surges. Moreover, studies that find controls to be ineffective presumably mean that controls *as implemented* have had little detectable effect on aggregate flows. There is little doubt that sufficiently Draconian controls would be effective—the only question is whether their costs would exceed their benefits.

2.2 Capital Controls vs. Prudential Measures

When capital inflows are raising financial-stability concerns, it is natural that prudential tools be deployed. However, the distinction between prudential measures and capital controls is not clear-cut, and which one should be deployed will depend on the nature of the inflows and the attendant risks. First, it is worth clarifying terms. Prudential measures are applied to the regulated financial sector (typically banks) and, at least as the term will be used here, do not discriminate on the basis of the residency of the parties to the capital transaction, but may discriminate according to the currency of the transaction. Capital controls, which may apply to the financial sector or to the broader economy (or to both), do discriminate on the basis of residency.[10]

From these very definitions, it is clear that if the flows are not being intermediated by the domestic banking system (for instance, domestic agents are borrowing directly from abroad or from foreign bank branches), then prudential measures will be useless: the only option will be capital controls. If the flows are being intermediated through the domestic banking system, then both prudential measures (which apply to banks) and capital controls (which can apply to banks or to ultimate borrowers—households and corporates—directly) are at least feasible instruments. Which should be used then depends on the nature of the risk that is of concern. If

[9] See Cardarelli et al. (2007), Ostry et al. (2010), and Ghosh et al. (2012a).

[10] The IMF Institutional View classifies measures into capital flow management (CFM) and macro-prudential measures (MPMs). CFMs are any measure that, by constructive design, are intended to reduce cross-border capital flows. This would include residency-based measures (what are traditionally termed capital controls), but may also include currency or other non-residency-based measures where, by design of the measure—but regardless of the primary purpose of the measure—there is likely to be substantial effect on cross-border flows; see IMF (2012a).

the main concern is the fragility of the external financing structure (too much reliance on wholesale funding; short-term debt instruments; and portfolio flows), then specific capital controls that discourage the most risky types of flows are called for. Conversely, if the main concern is FX exposure on domestic balance sheets, then prudential measures on banks (limits on open FX positions and higher capital requirements for domestic lending in FX) would be appropriate. Finally, if the concern is mainly an asset price boom that could fuel a bubble, then a nondiscriminatory prudential measure (such as a maximum loan-to-value (LTV) limit) would be appropriate (Ostry et al. 2012b).

Several other considerations in the choice between capital controls and prudential measures are worth mentioning. First, it is sometimes asserted that capital controls impose microeconomic costs on the economy, including loss of access to capital by small and medium enterprises (SMEs)—Forbes (2007). While this may certainly be true, it is also true of prudential measures. Indeed, given that SMEs typically rely on bank financing, and—unlike major corporations—cannot borrow directly from abroad, prudential measures are likely to hit them disproportionately more severely than capital controls. Second, prudential measures applied to the banking system may make the flows migrate to the less-regulated part of the financial system, such as finance companies, that is not subject to prudential regulation (hence, the distinction made above between flows that are intermediated by the banking system and those that are not, may be endogenous to the imposition of prudential measures). Third, there may be legal or treaty obligations that preclude the imposition of capital controls (though, in some cases, these limitations apply also to prudential measures that, while not being strictly residency based, are likely to have a significant impact on cross-border flows). All other things equal, measures that do not discriminate on the basis of the residency or nationality of the parties to the transaction are preferable to those that do.[11] In practice, the institutional set up may determine whether capital controls or prudential measures are more likely to be imposed—whether, for instance, it is the Ministry of Finance imposing a tax or the central bank imposing an unremunerated reserve requirement (URR) or the macro-prudential regulator tightening prudential regulations.

Evidence on the effectiveness of capital controls in shifting the composition of flows is rather stronger than evidence that controls affect the overall volume of flows. In fact, the empirical evidence lines up quite neatly with theoretical priors: thus, countries with capital controls tend to have less fragile external financing structures (more FDI and less portfolio debt); countries with FX-related prudential measures have less foreign currency-denominated domestic lending; and countries

[11] This follows from basic principles of fairness, which dictate that measures/penalties should be applied according to behavior rather than identity. Thus, if cross-border lending by nonresidents is more risky because they typically lend in foreign currency, then a restriction on FX-lending (rather than nonresident lending) would be preferable because some nonresidents may be willing to lend in local currency (and some residents may be lending in FX). Restrictions for financial-stability purposes based on residency make sense when the risks are inherent to the residency/nonresidency of the parties to the transaction (for instance, if nonresident investors are more skittish because they lack political representation in the country) or when nondiscriminatory measures would be ineffective.

with nondiscriminatory prudential measures have fewer credit booms. Interestingly, FX-related prudential measures are also associated with lower debt financing (though the effect is not as large as that of capital controls), and capital controls are also associated with less foreign currency-denominated lending (though the effect is not as large as that of FX-related prudential measures). Finally, in looking at resilience during crises, including the global financial crisis, emerging market economies that had capital controls in place prior to the crisis (and hence avoided excessively risky external financing structures) fared better than those that did not have such controls (Ostry et al. 2011, 2012b).

To the extent that capital controls are used for financial-stability purposes, the argument that they should be temporary is less pertinent than when controls are being used for macro reasons. As discussed above, when capital flows are expected to be "permanent" or persistent, then they form part of the equilibrium current account to which the economy should be allowed to adjust. However, regardless of whether the flows are temporary or persistent, they may raise financial-stability risks—and thus policy responses to these risks may need to be part of the permanent financial architecture (though the "tax rate" could be allowed to vary according to the risk at any particular moment). In contrast to controls imposed for macro reasons, moreover, those imposed to address financial-stability risks may need to be quantity-based (like most other macro-prudential tools such as capital requirements) and specific to the flows that pose risks rather than being broad-based.

2.3 Multilateral Aspects

The discussion thus far has centered on the policy responses of an individual country. Yet these responses may have multilateral consequences.[12] For example, imposition of capital controls against inflows by one recipient country could deflect capital to others, exacerbating their macroeconomic and financial-stability challenges. In addition, from the perspective of a country that is receiving an inflow surge, it makes little difference whether the capital flows are the result of deflection from another recipient or the result of policies in the source countries. In other words, both recipient and source countries may need to take account of the multilateral aspects of their policies in regard to capital flows.

A first, if somewhat obvious point is that if capital controls are ineffective (that is, investors find ways of bypassing them), then there cannot be any multilateral ramifications of imposing controls. Supposing then that controls are effective in reducing inflows to the country posing them, do they result in deflection to other recipient countries or do they simply keep the capital in the source country? Evidence on deflection is very weak, with just a couple of studies that tend to find that either there is no effect, or there is no average effect but that capital is deflected toward other countries that markets deem as less likely to impose controls themselves (IMF 2011a; Forbes et al. 2012).

[12] See Ghosh (1991); Ostry et al. (2012a).

Assuming such deflection does occur, is this an argument for the "first" country not to impose controls? Not necessarily. If capital controls are not costly, then all countries experiencing unwanted surges should take appropriate policy measures, including imposing controls (as discussed above). However, even if controls are costly (impose administrative, compliance, or economic costs), it is still optimal that countries that do not welcome the deflected capital should impose controls. In this case, however, the global optimum is achieved when countries imposing controls internalize the possible deflection and response of other countries. In practice, this means impose "lower" controls than would be chosen unilaterally since the deflection is a zero-sum game that is needlessly costly to the countries imposing the controls.

What about countries that are the source of the flows? If the costs of controls are convex (i.e., the distortions associated with controls are increasing at an increasing rate), then economic efficiency requires splitting the burden of controlling excessive flows between source and recipient countries. This is difficult to do when there are generalized outflows (say in response to monetary loosening), because some recipient countries may welcome the higher flows, while others feel that they are excessive. However, in particular instances where, for example, banks in a source country are lending excessively in a recipient country, it may be easier for the regulators in the source country to help curtail the flows than to rely solely on the inflow controls in the recipient country. Why would the source country be willing to cooperate? There are a couple of reasons. First, if the recipient country suffers a financial crisis, it may be the source country's banks that incur losses, which ultimately might rebound on taxpayers in the source country. Second, the terms of trade (i.e., the interest rate) move in favor of the source country when there are restrictions on outflows. Finally, such cooperation may be an important contribution to global financial stability.[13]

3 Conclusions

The global financial crisis was a rude reminder that not all borrowing and lending decisions—within and across borders—are rational or welfare improving. While cross-border capital flows bring substantial benefits—provision of finance, risk sharing, and sometimes transfer of knowledge and technology—they may also be too much of a good thing.[14] Large surges of capital can bring both macroeconomic and financial-stability challenges, especially—though by no means exclusively—in developing and emerging market economies. At times, these surges call for policy responses—including exchange rate and intervention policies, macroeconomic policies, prudential measures, and capital controls. The three principles or rules-of-

[13] See also "Modernizing the Legal Framework for Surveillance—An Integrated Surveillance Decision" available at: http://www.imf.org/external/np/exr/facts/isd.htm.

[14] Recognizing this, the G20 issued its *Coherent Conclusions for the Management of Capital Flows Drawing on Country Experiences* (October 15, 2011); the discussion here is consistent with—but helps flesh out—the *Coherent Conclusions*.

thumb outlined here are intended to help policymakers reap the benefits of cross-border capital flows while also protecting their economies against the damaging effects of sudden surges.

Not surprisingly, interest in capital controls in both academic and official circles tends to wax and wane with the flows themselves. Yet it is precisely because there will be subsequent—and possibly disruptive—outflows that careful management of capital inflows is so essential. One thing is clear: as Group of 20 (G20) countries become ever more integrated and interconnected, dealing with volatile capital flows will remain on the G20 agenda for many years to come.

References

Cardarelli R, Elekdag S, Kose MA (2007) Managing large capital inflows. World Economic Outlook, October 2007, Chapter 3. International Monetary Fund, Washington DC

Forbes K (2007) One cost of the Chilean capital controls: increased financial constraints for smaller traded firms. J Int Econ 71(2):294–323

Forbes K, Fratzscher M, Kostka T, Staub R (2012) Bubble thy neighbor. NBER WP 18052

Ghosh AR (1991) Strategic aspects of public finance in a world of high capital mobility. J Int Econ 30:229–247

Ghosh AR, Kim J (2008) Export subsidies, undervalued exchange rates, and consumption taxes—some equivalence results of relevance to Bretton Woods II. Mimeo. International Monetary Fund, Washington

Ghosh AR, Kim J, Qureshi MS, Zalduendo J (2012a) "Surges," IMF Working Paper WP/12/22. International Monetary Fund, Washington DC

Ghosh AR, Ostry JD, Tsangarides C (2012b) Shifting motives: explaining the buildup in official reserves in Emerging Market Economies since the 1980s. IMF Working Paper 12/34. International Monetary Fund, Washington DC

International Monetary Fund (2011a) The multilateral aspects of policies affecting capital flows. International Monetary Fund, Washington DC. http://www.imf.org/external/np/pp/eng/2011/101311.pdf

International Monetary Fund (2011b) Assessing reserve adequacy. International Monetary Fund, Washington DC. http://www.imf.org/external/np/pp/eng/2011/021411b.pdf

International Monetary Fund (2012a) The liberalization and management of capital flows—an institutional view. International Monetary Fund, Washington DC. http://www.imf.org/external/pp/longres.aspx?id=4720

International Monetary Fund (2012b) External balance assessment (EBA): technical background of the pilot methodology. International Monetary Fund, Washington DC. http://www.imf.org/external/np/res/eba/pdf/080312.pdf

Korinek A (2011) The new economics of capital controls imposed for prudential reasons. IMF Working Paper 11/298. International Monetary Fund, Washington DC

Ostry JD, Ghosh AR, Habermeier K, Chamon M, Qureshi MS, Reinhardt DBS (2010) Capital inflows: the role of controls. IMF Staff Position Note 10/04. International Monetary Fund, Washington, DC

Ostry JD, Ghosh AR, Habermeier K, Chamon M, Qureshi MS, Laeven L, Kokenyne A (2011) Managing capital inflows: what tools to use? IMF Staff Discussion Note 11/06. International Monetary Fund, Washington, DC

Ostry, JD, Ghosh AR, Korinek A (2012a) Multilateral aspects of managing the capital account. IMF Staff Discussion Note, 12/10. International Monetary Fund, Washington, DC

Ostry JD, Ghosh AR, Chamon M, Qureshi MS (2012b) Tools for managing financial-stability risks from capital inflows. J Int Econ 88(2):407–421

On an Asian Monetary Union: What does the Evidence Tell us?

David Kim

1 Introduction

This chapter reviews the conditions required for a successful monetary integration in the context of the optimal currency area literature and assesses the future prospects with particular reference to recent research on the prospects of a monetary union in East Asia. The chapter also provides the policy implications for G20, judging from the experience of the Eurozone as well as empirical evidence on one of the preconditions for a monetary union in East Asia, the extent of business cycle synchronisation and output adjustments to shocks.

The economic turmoil in the Eurozone has renewed, among others, the question of what pre-conditions need to be satisfied before forming a successful monetary (or currency) union among a group of countries. In particular, it serves as an important lesson for other regions in the G20 contemplating a monetary union. Regions such as East Asia, Mercosur and Trans-Tasman are possible candidates for a monetary union.[1] Together with the Eurozone countries, countries in these regions contemplating a monetary integration constitute about 70 % of the entire G20 memberships.

With the growing significance of the Asian region in the world economy, East Asia is often considered to be a region that may potentially benefit further from deepening monetary integration. Following the Asian financial crisis, East Asian countries have stepped up the discussion of regional financial and monetary coordination in order to enhance the stability of exchange rates as well as increased intra-regional trades. More recently, the Chiang Mai Initiative Multilateralisation (CMIM) Agreement involving the ASEAN5 plus Japan, China and Republic of Ko-

[1] Most of the fastest growing emerging economies are constituents of these regions, in particular, East Asia and Latin America. The Trans-Tasman region mainly comprises Australia and New Zealand, in which the possibility of a common currency has been an occasional subject of discussion. See, for example, Kim and Sheen (2007) for an empirical assessment of this region.

D. Kim (✉)
School of Economics, University of Sydney, Sydney, Australia
e-mail: kim.david@sydney.edu.au

M. Callaghan et al. (eds.), *Global Cooperation Among G20 Countries*,
DOI 10.1007/978-81-322-1659-9_20, © Springer India 2014

rea is seen as a practical step in the direction of the increased financial and monetary integration in the region. The stability of exchange rates and avoiding any future financial crisis are at the heart of such attempt at an increased regional coordination, while the countries witnessed the instability of yen–dollar exchange rates and the rising Yuan as a currency of increasing international significance. However, the onset of the Eurozone crisis put a temporary halt, at least, to the discussion of the region as a possible optimal currency area (OCA). Despite a large volume of research on the OCA, it is not easy to determine whether a region is even close to being an OCA justifying the formation of a monetary union, and how the membership of the union has to be determined.

There are a number of difficulties facing East Asia, mainly the ASEAN5 plus Japan, China and Korea, among other candidates for a monetary union.[2] The region is far more heterogeneous than both the European Union and Mercosur in terms of per capita income, geographical proximity, industrial composition as well as political and legal institutions. The varying stages of economic development are particularly well reflected in their key industries spanning the entire spectrum of high-end manufacturing, mass manufacturing, financial and services industry and primary industry. However, the significant growth in intra-industry trade and foreign direct investment, while having caught up with the developed world in recent decades, facilitated escalating discussions of the need for closer regional economic integration. Furthermore, China's recent emergence as a major economic and political power adds a further dimension to the already complex interrelationships in the region.

2 Literature and Evidence

The OCA literature initiated by Mundell (1961) suggests a number of criteria for a successful monetary integration. A key criterion is the synchronisation of business cycle co-movement, also referred to as the symmetry of shocks, because the cost of losing an independent monetary policy would be small enabling common policy responses, if countries are subject to shocks of similar nature and size. Various empirical studies have been conducted to examine the extent of (dis)similarities of the business cycle co-movement across East Asia, so as to provide an assessment of the status of synchronisation of cycles and adjustments to the shocks in the region. Other important criteria include the degree of trade and financial integration because countries with a high degree of trade and financial integration are likely to benefit more from a currency union. Lee et al. (2004) assessed the prospects of an East Asian currency union by focussing on the trade and financial integration. Bayoumi et al. (2000) analysed whether the Association of Southeast Asian Nations (ASEAN) region, a subset of East Asia, satisfies these criteria. There are also studies that examined the potential welfare gains from a currency union. Kim et al.

[2] Throughout this chapter, other countries in East Asia were not included in the study due to their relative economic insignificance.

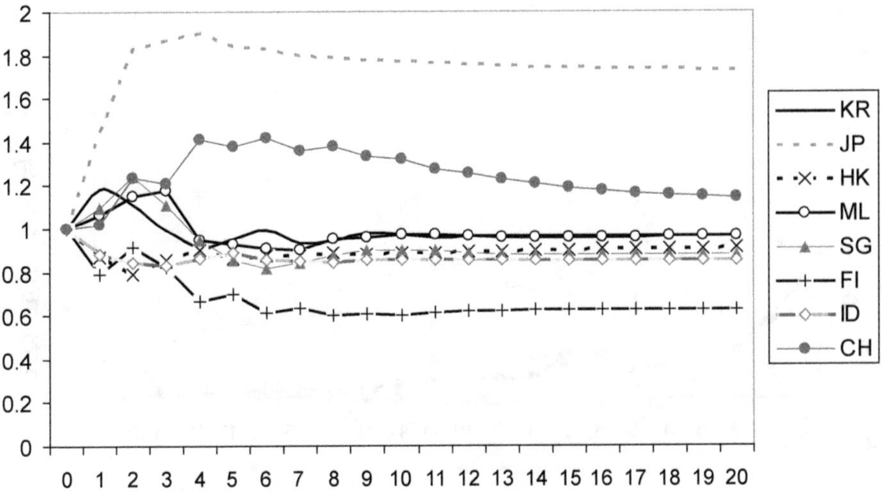

Fig. 1 Responses of output to supply shocks across East Asia. *KR* Korea, *JP* Japan, *HK* Hong Kong China, *ML* Malaysia, *SG* Singapore, *FI* Philippines, *ID* Indonesia, *CH* China. (Source: Kim 2007)

(2006) provide estimates of risk-sharing and potential welfare gains for East Asia. To date, there has been no clear evidence supporting a currency union in the region.

However, regarding the criterion of symmetry of shocks and adjustments, the findings appear to be least consistent and inconclusive. In what follows, two recent studies on East Asian business cycles are discussed to outline the evidence concerning the symmetry of shocks and adjustments. In the first, Kim (2007) analysed the nature of output shocks hitting each country in the region and also discussed how much of the historical output fluctuations are driven by demand or productivity (or supply) shocks. Understanding the nature of shocks (i.e. whether the shocks are due to demand or supply, or of permanent or transitory nature) and how countries respond to them would be important as a first check on the criterion of the symmetry of shocks. Figures 1 and 2 display how the countries in the region respond to supply and demand shocks, respectively. Figure 1 shows that the output responses to supply shocks vary widely in terms of the size. Japan and China show strong positive responses to a unit supply shock, while the effects are much less pronounced for the other countries. However, for short-term macro-policy responses, it is important to investigate whether demand shocks are symmetric. Figure 2 shows that there are substantial variations in the size of responses, although all responses are positive, with the exception of Indonesia. However, except for Hong Kong, all countries show relatively rapid output adjustments to the demand shocks after about a year.

Empirical studies also analysed whether shocks are global, regional or country specific. The cost of joining a currency union will be less burdensome when potential member countries are mostly affected by common shocks, both global and regional, rather than idiosyncratic or country-specific shocks. Another recent study

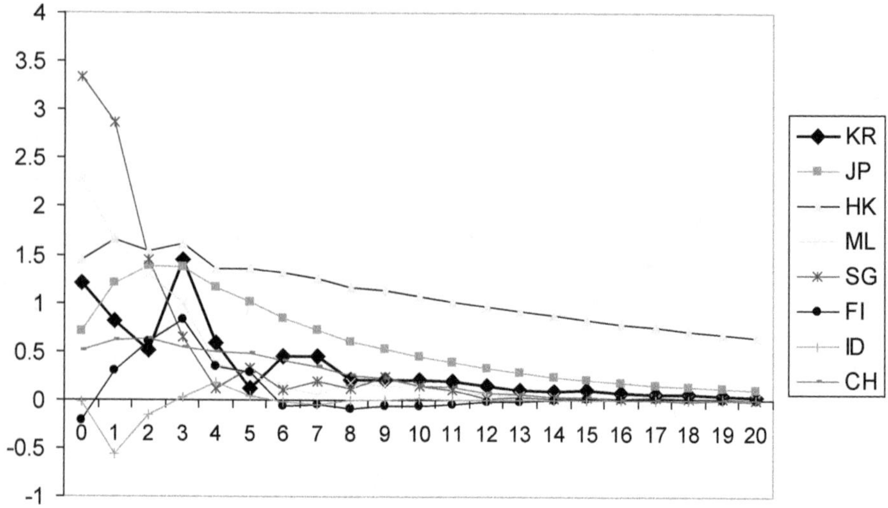

Fig. 2 Responses of output to demand shocks across East Asia. *KR* Korea, *JP* Japan, *HK* Hong Kong China, *ML* Malaysia, *SG* Singapore, *FI* Philippines, *ID* Indonesia, *CH* China. (Source: Kim 2007)

by Huh et al. (2012) provides further evidence on the degree of business cycle synchronisation in East Asia: ASEAN5 (Indonesia, Malaysia, Singapore, Thailand and the Philippines), Japan, Korea and Greater China (China, Taiwan and Hong Kong). Using the methodology proposed by Stock and Watson (2005), they identify and estimate three types of shocks; global, regional and country-specific idiosyncratic shocks from a set of real, nominal and external variables. Figures 3 and 4 show the responses of output to global and regional demand shocks, respectively. For global shocks, the signs and patterns are similar across all the countries, while there is substantial variation in the size of the responses. Indonesia shows the least responsive output while Hong Kong and Singapore show outputs that are highly responsive to the global shocks. The output responses to regional shocks appear to be more congruent, showing less wide variations across the countries. For regional shocks, the difference measured in percent deviation of output responses between the most and least responsive countries is around 4 %. For global shocks, the difference is more than 6 %. However, once the most and least responsive countries are excluded, the difference across eight countries is reduced to about 3 % in the face of global shocks and to 2 % in the face of regional shocks. This indicates that East Asia displays more uniform responses implying the potential benefit of common macroeconomic policy responses if the regional shocks constitute a significant fraction of all disturbances. Huh et al. also report the decomposition of output in each country to world, region and country-specific shocks. Their estimates indicate that regional demand shocks are the most important driver accounting for about 50 % of output variance in the very short run (less than two quarters) but are replaced by the world demand shocks as the most important driver of output fluctuations in the short-to-

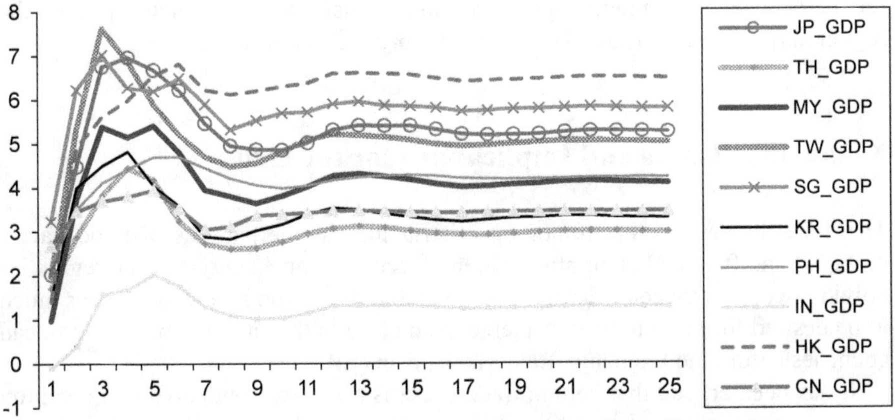

Fig. 3 Output responses to global demand shocks. *KR* Korea, *JP* Japan, *HK* Hong Kong China, *MY* Malaysia, *SG* Singapore, *PH* Philippines, *IN* Indonesia, *TH* Thailand, *TW* Taiwan, and *CH* China. (Source: Huh et al. 2012)

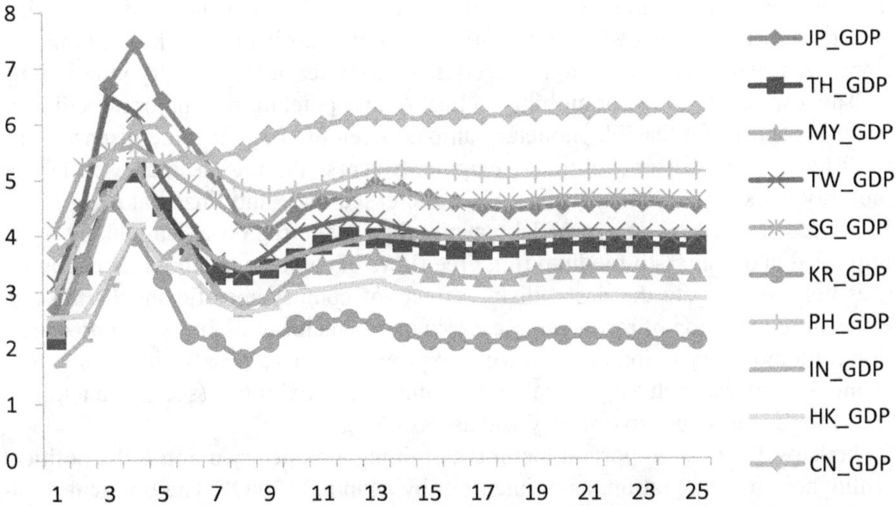

Fig. 4 Output responses to regional demand shocks. *KR* Korea, *JP* Japan, *HK* Hong Kong China, *MY* Malaysia, *SG* Singapore, *PH* Philippines, *IN* Indonesia, *TH* Thailand, *TW* Taiwan, and *CH* China. (Source: Huh et al. 2012)

medium run over the horizon of eight quarters. When domestic output fluctuates a lot in response to country-specific or idiosyncratic factors, forming a monetary union requiring coordinated policy responses would not be feasible. Across the ten countries studied, country-specific shocks do not account for more than 5 % of output fluctuations over the horizon of eight quarters. The evidence outlined above seems to suggest that regarding the criterion of business cycle synchronisation the region may be almost as good as Europe before the Maastricht Treaty.

3 Further Issues and Implications for the G20

There are, however, other important criteria such as the patterns of trade, factor mobility, and financial integration. On these criteria, some subsets of the region involving two or three countries may fare well but the region as a whole leaves much to be desired for them to be considered even close to the situation of the European countries before the Exchange Rate Mechanism (ERM).

It has been argued that certain trade patterns are more conducive to a common currency arrangement than others. In particular, a highly fixed form of exchange arrangements would benefit a group of countries characterised by a high level of intra-industry trades. In East Asia, intra-industry trades have grown significantly over the last couple of decades, largely through foreign direct investments in China and Southeast Asia. Improving financial integration to a significant degree is also seen as an important precondition for a monetary union. Although financial integration would be further enhanced *ex post*, a high level of coordination in the banking and financial system would need to be precipitated for a feasible monetary integration.

The low degree of factor mobility in East Asia is potentially a major impediment to the prospect of a feasible monetary union. Given the large income disparity due to different stages of economic developments across the region, increased labour mobility is likely as a consequence of the increased trade and financial integration. In particular, the low degree of labour mobility in the region is least likely to be improved in the short-to-medium run. Free flows of capital and labour across countries help to mitigate the destabilising effects of country-specific shocks through efficient reallocation of resources. Research on the factor of mobility as a precondition for a monetary union is still a work in progress. There are also important non-economic criteria such as political and institutional proximities (see Barro and Lee 2011) for a comprehensive survey and assessment).

Perhaps, the most important factor determining a monetary union is the political willingness for integration, as pointed out by Mundell (2003). The political motivation behind a common economic community in East Asia is much less than that which emerged in the post-war Europe. Another significant challenge is the lack of an obvious anchor currency in the region, as a common currency arrangement requires a country whose currency provides the role of an anchor to other currencies in the transition process. While there is no single currency that could be an anchor currency, a weighted basket of currencies comprised of the dollar, yen and Euro may be able to provide an anchor, to create a notional Asian currency unit.

While the preceding discussion was centred around the East Asian region, the evidence on the region and the lessons of the Eurozone have important implications for the G20 as a whole. Since a significant fraction of the G20 member countries are either already in a monetary union or are candidate countries for a future union, the economic cooperation of the G20 cannot be considered separately from how a region or a subset of the G20 chooses its monetary and exchange rate arrangement. This is particularly important as emergence of a new monetary union within the G20 may reshape the current framework for policy discussion in the G20. In the foreseeable future, any new monetary union in the G20 is very unlikely and the resolution of the current turmoil in the Eurozone would have a major bearing on any progress in the discussion of a future monetary union.

References

Barro R, Lee J-W (2011) East Asian Currency Union. In: Barro R, Lee J-W (eds) Costs and benefits of economic integration in Asia. Oxford University Press

Bayoumi T, Eichengreen B, Mauro P (2000) On Regional Monetary Arrangements for ASEAN. J Japanese Int Economies 14:121–148

Huh H-S, Kim D, Kim W-J (2012) A FAVAR analysis of the Asian Business Cycle. Paper presented to the APEA Conference, Singapore, June

Kim D (2007) An East Asian currency union? the empirical nature of macroeconomic shocks in East Asia. J Asian Econ 18:847–866

Kim D, Sheen J (2007) Consumption risk-sharing within Australia and with New Zealand. Econ Rec 83:46–59

Kim S, Kim H, Wang Y (2006) Financial integration and consumption risk-sharing in East Asia. Japan World Economy 18:143–157

Lee J-W, Park Y, Shin K (2004) A currency union in East Asia. In: Asian Development Bank (ed) Monetary and financial integration in East Asia, vol 2. Palgrave Macmillan

Mundell R (1961) A theory of optimum currency areas. Am Econ Rev 51:657–665

Mundell R (2003) Prospects for an Asian currency area. J Asian Econ 14:1–10

Stock J, Watson M (2005) Implications of dynamic factor models for VAR analysis. NBER Working Paper No. 11467

Part VI
Austerity and Growth

The Macroeconomic Policy Response to the International Financial and Economic Crisis and the G20

Alok Sheel

1 Overview

During the *Great Depression* of the 1930s, an event to which the recent crisis is often compared[1], the animosities of the interwar period prevented a coordinated policy response to what was essentially a global problem. Indeed, it is often argued that this failure resulted, inter alia, in the cascading competitive protectionism triggered by the Smoot–Hawley tariffs that may well have magnified a deep recession into the Great Depression. In sharp contradistinction, the G20 orchestrated a much acclaimed globally coordinated policy response to the *Great Recession*, in the process effectively putting in place a new institution to manage globalization.

The first G20 Summit was held in November 2008 in Washington DC under the shadow of the greatest financial crisis in the post-war era. While central banks had already taken steps to inject liquidity into a faltering global financial system, G20 Leaders now supplemented these efforts through an unprecedented concerted global policy response to prevent the global economy from falling over a cliff. At the second G20 Summit in London in April 2009, as the crisis worsened, Leaders pledged to do whatever was necessary to restore confidence, growth and jobs through concerted fiscal expansion and monetary easing. They also pledged to keep international trade and investment open, and reached an agreement to provide over a trillion dollars of additional resources through international financial institutions to counteract the spillovers on emerging markets and developing economies (EMDEs) of a crisis emanating, rather unusually, from advanced economies. These coordinated actions are widely credited for forestalling a second Great Depression, with the G20 declaring victory at their third Summit at Pittsburgh in September 2009 ("It worked").

[1] While the fall in aggregate national income was not as rapid and been as sharp in major countries as during the Great Depression—except in the Eurozone periphery—in several other respects parallels are quite striking.

A. Sheel (✉)
Economic Advisory Council to Prime Minister of India, New Delhi, India
e-mail:ioksheel@gmail.com

M. Callaghan et al. (eds.), *Global Cooperation Among G20 Countries*,
DOI 10.1007/978-81-322-1659-9_21, © Springer India 2014

The focus of the Pittsburgh Summit was on strengthening the recovery and making it durable. With this end in view, the G20 launched its signature '*Framework for Strong, Sustainable and Balanced Growth*', while declaring the G20 to be the premier international forum for economic cooperation, ostensibly replacing the G7. The G20 also turned its attention to addressing other long-standing structural problems in the global economy such as setting an ambitious agenda for regulatory reform of the financial sector; phasing out and rationalizing inefficient fossil fuel subsidies; raising resources for effectively dealing with climate change; combating cross-border tax evasion and havens; bridging the development gap and making the governance of the Bretton Woods and other institutions of global economic governance more representative of tectonic shifts in the structure of the global economy.

Meanwhile, the market reaction to mounting public deficits and debt in some Eurozone countries led G20 Leaders to make commitments for fiscal consolidation at the fourth G20 Leaders' Summit at Toronto, Canada, in June 2010. By the time of the sixth G20 Summit in November 2011 at Cannes, France, it was clear that the global recovery was again in trouble. The Summit deliberations were largely dominated by the Eurozone crisis and on how to restore growth and jobs. The G20 and indeed economists and policymakers, generally, were now on the horns of a dilemma that pitted the need for austerity demanded by markets, against the need for growth and jobs demanded by electorates. This dilemma, most vividly captured in the ambiguous construct 'growth-friendly fiscal consolidation', remains as paramount as ever, having once again dominated the seventh G20 Summit at Los Cabos on June 18–19 under the Mexican Presidency, and also likely to dominate the eighth Summit to be held in St. Petersburg, Russia, on September 5–6, 2013.

With the prospects of global economic recovery uncertain, and the IMF repeatedly downgrading its forecasts for global economic growth[2], the initial accolades received by the G20 for having forestalled a second Great Depression have been dented by increasing scepticism regarding both its effectiveness and credibility as the premier forum for international economic cooperation. The two questions uppermost in the minds of those who have observed the G20 policy response to the crisis are, firstly, how appropriate was this response, and secondly, whether the G20 is indeed an effective forum for international economic cooperation.

2 The State of Play of Macroeconomic Policy on the Eve of the Global Financial Crisis

Any critical review of the G20 policy response to the global financial crisis needs to take stock of the broad consensus on macroeconomic management prevailing as the crisis set in, as this consensus shaped the policy response. This macroeconomic stabilization consists of monetary and fiscal policies conducted by central banks and

[2] See Table 1.

treasuries. Central banks generally use a combination of interest rates and monetary aggregates to stimulate or depress demand, depending on the stage of the business cycle. To ensure financial stability, central banks provide liquidity as 'lender of last resort' through their discount windows to prevent financial panic. Treasuries use taxpayer resources—fiscal policy—to bail out critical segments of the financial system that appear to be collapsing, and to substitute for the decline in private demand.

Extant policies for short-term macroeconomic and financial stability were in turn shaped by what was done, but more importantly what critics later pointed out should have been done, and was not done, during the Great Depression of the 1930s. There were, of course, some critical policy constraints, as 'fiat currency' policy tools were unavailable under the gold standard.

2.1 Milton Friedman and the Great Depression

Milton Friedman famously argued that the catastrophic economic collapse of the Great Depression could have been averted had the Federal Reserve lowered, rather than increased, interest rates in the face of deflation. Deflationary tendencies in turn arise from the rapid deleveraging following financial panic that leads to a sharp fall in the money multiplier. During the Great Depression the Federal Reserve felt compelled to raise rates to protect the value of the dollar as speculators demanded gold for currency. The Federal Reserve also failed to provide liquidity necessary for financial stability, which exacerbated deflationary tendencies, bankruptcies and bank failures. The banking system was eventually stabilized by setting up the Federal Deposit Insurance Corporation (FDIC), and abandoning the gold standard for some time. The first measure reassured depositors that their money was safe. The second measure enabled the Federal Reserve to pump liquidity into the financial system.

Temporary abandonment of the gold standard also facilitated expansionary new—Keynesian—fiscal policies (President Franklin Roosevelt's 'New Deal') that according to several economists led to a smart recovery in the mid-1930s.[3] It is widely believed that premature fiscal tightening on account of worsening public deficits and debt pulled the USA back into a second dip recession in 1937. Ultimately it was the fiscal stimulus of the 'War Economy' that finally pulled the USA out of the Great Depression.

2.2 The Post-War Period and the Dominance of Keynesian Economics

Keynesian economics enjoyed a bull run in the post-Second World War period. Even Milton Friedman, who effectively sounded the death knell of fiscal policy as

[3] The relative role of monetary and fiscal policy during the Great Depression is a matter of continuing debate. Rangarajan and Sheel (2013, p. 47).

a macroeconomic tool, could say that "we are all Keynesian now." Theoretically, Keynesian demand management policies should not be inflationary, since fiscal expansion merely substitutes for the contraction in private demand to restore the economy to trend growth and full employment. When domestic demand destruction is combined with external demand shock, there may even be no alternative to fiscal expansion to restore growth. Fiscal policy works over the long run however only if used in a contra-cyclical manner, by targeting the structural rather than the nominal fiscal deficit.

This means, firstly, estimating growth potential, a hazardous exercise in the best of times, and often a shifting target as well, and secondly, creating fiscal space when output is above potential by running fiscal surpluses for use when it is below potential. Fiscal policy is however a political minefield, easy to navigate while expanding, but difficult to exit even during boom times. In practice, therefore, governments, fortified by the Philips curve that postulated a trade-off between inflation and growth, kept pushing the envelope to increase growth. Central banks, no longer constrained by the gold standard, were now in a position to accommodate the expansion by monetizing any level of fiscal deficit. Fiscal policy therefore had an inherent inflationary bias.

While some amount of financial repression may have been necessary to reduce the huge burden of the World War II debt in advanced economies, the War Debt hangover was no longer a destabilizing issue at the time of the oil price hikes in the 1970s following the oil price hike, by that time. Fiscal policies however expanded, rather than adjusted, in the face of what was a big and permanent demand shock—a steep rise in oil prices. This led to hyperinflation even as growth remained below trend ('stagflation'), with the widely acclaimed Phillip's curve breaking down.

2.3 The Ascendancy of Monetary Policy

Milton Friedman sounded what appeared at the time to be the death knell of Keynesian economics by placing monetary policy at the heart of macroeconomic stabilization policies. He identified inflation as basically a monetary phenomenon. It was however Paul Volcker's dogged and aggressive monetary tightening that finally tamed the dragon of hyperinflation, although it is still disputed whether the costs in terms of growth foregone was too high a price. Be it as it may, inflation rates were brought down sharply and have been well anchored ever since in advanced economies. Over time, even though the strict 'monetarism' of Milton Friedman was not strictly adhered to, monetary policy tools were streamlined and became more rule bound. The US Fed has by and large followed the Taylor rule, adjusting short-term interest rates to attain targeted inflation and growth rates. Other central banks also followed variants of the Taylor rule, with single or multiple targets. The entire credit for low and stable consumer price inflation cannot of course be given entirely to inflation targeting, the Taylor rule or the US Fed. 'Benign' deflationary forces deriving from productivity gains wrought by globalization, especially following the integration of large developing countries like China (for manufactures) and India (for services) into the global economy, were also at work.

While discretionary fiscal policy fell into disrepute, fiscal policy continued to play a role in macroeconomic stabilization through 'automatic stabilizers', such as unemployment benefits that automatically kicked in as economic activity fell below trend. These additional expenditures, along with the revenue decline associated with lower growth, were however expected to make fiscal deficits contra-cyclical, keeping the structural balance stable.

Till the outbreak of the recent global financial crisis, Japan stood out as the outlier in the developed world as a country that persisted with fiscal policy as a major tool for macroeconomic stabilization. Since this stabilization has still not occurred, its public debt to national income ratio has risen to unheard-of levels. In retrospect, the Japanese experience in several respects anticipated what was to happen in much of the developed world in the wake of the Great Recession. The Euro Union Maastricht Treaty imposed a ceiling of 3 % on fiscal deficits on its member states, which approximated to their expected real growth rates. As a result, debt–GDP ratios in advanced countries tended to decline over time, until such time adverse demographics started affecting their balance sheets. At any rate these ratios remained significantly below those in EMDEs where fiscal discipline remained by and large lax until a big spurt in trend growth sharply increased the size of the denominator.

2.4 *The Emergence of Unconventional Monetary Policies*

There are apparent limits to the use of conventional rule-based monetary policy since interest rates cannot dip below zero. These limits are breached as inflation rates drop and the output gap grows, and there is little demand for credit even when the central bank discount rates are at the lower zero bound. This is the liquidity trap, into which Japan fell in the 1990s, and arguably the USA and much of the developed world in the wake of the recent global financial crisis.

In such circumstances central banks may be constrained to resort to unconventional monetary policy, expanding money supply not only through the short-term discount window, but also through purchase of long-term government (quantitative) and/or private (credit easing) assets. This can neutralize the sharp decline in the multiplier due to rapid deleveraging during a severe financial crisis. Such liquidity injections are also expected to stimulate growth by raising both investment (by keeping the cost of credit cheap) and consumption (through the wealth effect of appreciating asset prices).

The current chairman of the US Federal Reserve is closely associated with another variant of unconventional monetary policy, sometimes referred to as a money financed as opposed to a bond-financed tax cut, giving him the epithet 'Helicopter Ben', as this is tantamount to dropping money by helicopter. This is outright money creation, with no associated government debt. The first real-life experiment with quantitative easing (QE) was done in Japan in the 1990s. However, QE could neither prevent deflation nor stimulate growth in Japan. Ben Bernanke argued that this was because Japanese QE was far too timid to be effective[4]. A 'helicopter drop' has however never been attempted so far (Sheel 2013a).

3 The Monetary Policy Response to the Global Financial Crisis

The turmoil in US financial markets was in evidence as early as 2007, with rising defaults in the subprime housing market in the USA as interest rates rose consequent on monetary tightening by the US Federal Reserve, and a long, unprecedented bull run in US housing prices ended. The market for complex structured products that fuelled the housing boom was particularly affected, leading to a crisis of confidence in interbank markets that pushed up TED (T bills Euro Dollar) and OIS (overnight indexed swap) spreads to unusually high levels in August 2007. However, the global economy still grew at a robust 5.2 % in 2007, and inflationary expectations were on the upward side. Corporate bond markets were quite unaffected. There was therefore some uncertainty regarding the extent to which perturbances in exotic financial products would spill over into the real economy.

In retrospect such speculation appears strange, because the financial system had become much interconnected. The financial system also intermediates real sector economic activity. The response time is no doubt asymmetrical, with financial markets adjusting immediately, even as the real economy adjusts with a lag, like an inverted J curve. Be it as it may, the US Federal Reserve was the first off the block to tackle what was clearly seen as an emerging financial panic. Monetary tightening had peaked on June 29, 2006, with the benchmark Fed Funds Rate set at 5.75 %. From September 2007, almost as soon as the first tremors in the financial system were felt, the US Federal Reserve embarked on a rapid easing of monetary policy. At a time other central banks, such as the European Central Bank (ECB) and the Bank of England, were still concerned about inflationary pressures and rising interest rates; the direction of US monetary policy indicated that the US Federal Reserve was presciently looking beyond current inflation rates and worrying about deflationary pressures down the road. By January 2008, the benchmark Federal Funds Rate (FFR) was down to 3 %, and by April to just 2 %. Within 3 months of the collapse of Lehman Brothers US monetary policy was zero bound, well ahead of other central banks that followed suit (Figs. 1, 2, 3 and 4).

Alongside lowering its benchmark policy rate, the US Federal Reserve also started injecting liquidity into the financial system through its short-term discount window by selling off assets, even as its balance sheet (total assets) remained flat. At this point it was the ECB that expanded its balance sheet to inject liquidity into

[4] The Bank of Japan has however recently embarked on a much more aggressive round of quantitative easing, comparable to what the US Federal Reserve is doing, in an attempt to defeat deflation and raise growth.

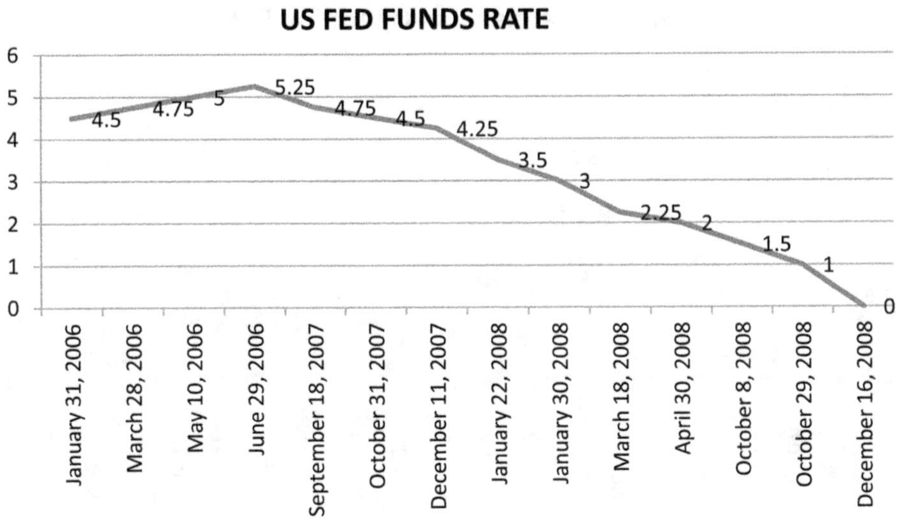

Fig. 1 US Federal Reserve benchmark interest rates. (*US Federal Reserve.* http://www.federalreserve.gov/monetarypolicy/openmarket.htm)

the financial system when the Paris-based bank *BNP Paribas* ran into a liquidity problem in August 2007 with three of its funds heavily exposed to US mortgage-based securities.

The expansion of the ECB's balance sheet was relatively modest compared to what the Bank of England and the US Federal Reserve embarked upon in the wake of the collapse of Lehman Brothers and the associated credit freeze. The US Federal Reserve and the Bank of England were the most aggressive, with their balance sheet expanding in a spectacular fashion through lending to banks and purchase of long-term treasury bonds and mortgage securities. The size of central bank balance sheets continued to grow through various rounds of QE. The composition (mix of short-term liquidity facilities, treasury bonds, mortgage and other assets) and maturity profile (such as through Federal Reserve's '*operation twist*') also changed over time as they calibrated their strategies to new challenges. The ECB however started catching up with the US Federal Reserve and the Bank of England from the second half of 2011 as it stepped up to the plate to backstop sovereign debt through its long-term refinancing operations (LTRO) as the Eurozone crisis unfolded. The balance sheets of all three central banks continue to remain at historic highs. From early 2013 the Bank of Japan started charting a similar path of aggressive QE to try and beat deflation. [5]

The Federal Reserve's balance sheet has quadrupled from $ 869 billion on August 8, 2007, to almost $ 3.5 trillion currently (Fig. 5). In its current phase QE 3 it

[5] A comparative picture of the expansion of the balance sheets of the four major central banks, including their composition and source of financing, can be gleaned from IMF's GFSR (2013b, p. 97).

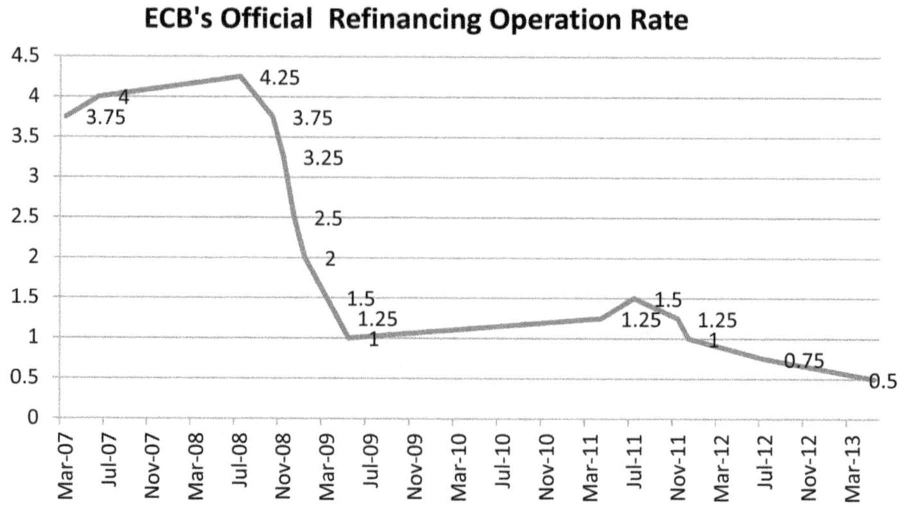

Fig. 2 European Central Bank benchmark interest rates. (*Eurostat.* http://appsso.eurostat.ec.europa.eu/nui/show.do)

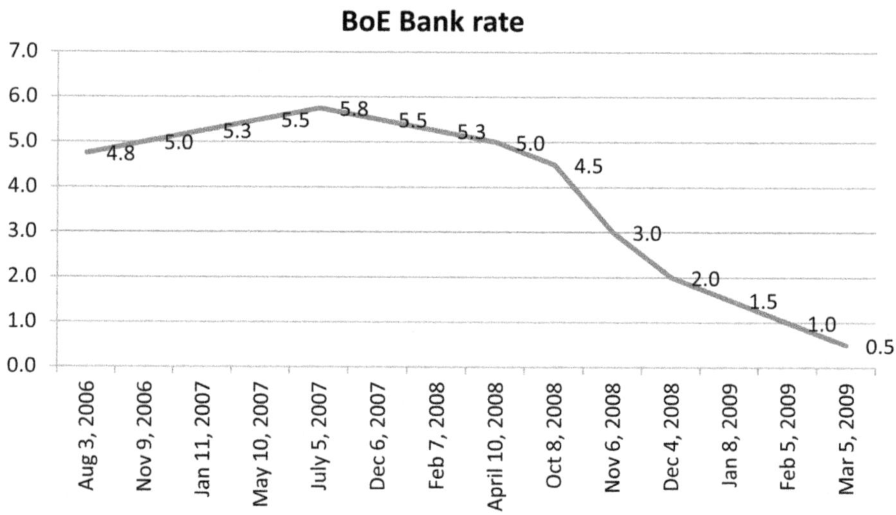

Fig. 3 Bank of England benchmark interest rates. (*Bank of England.* http://www.bankofengland.co.uk/monetarypolicy/Pages/decisions.aspx)

is expanding its balance sheet by $ 85 billion every month, and has announced its intention to continue doing so for an indefinite period as long as conditions, chiefly the unemployment situation, so warrant. The Bank of Japan is currently expanding its balance sheet by about $ 75 billion a month.

Conventional and unconventional monetary easing on such a scale was perhaps the reason why deflation was averted in the face of rapid private sector deleverag-

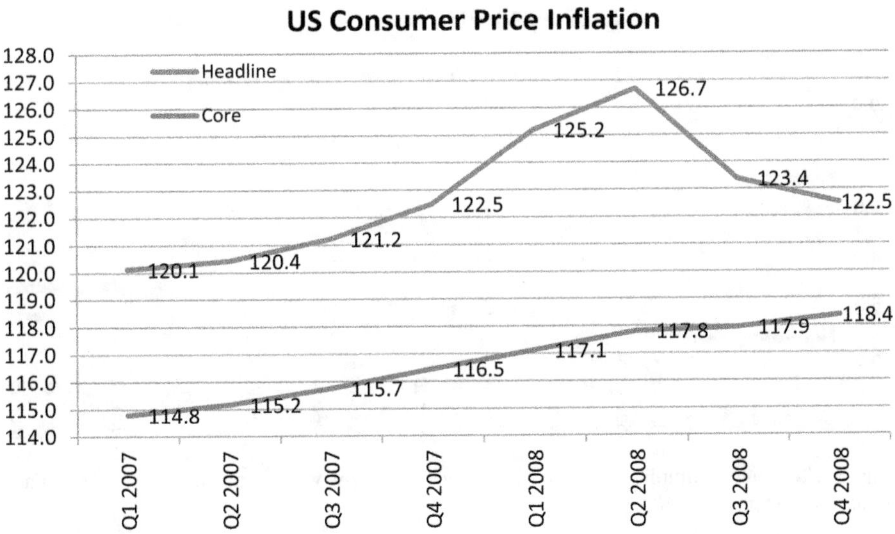

Fig. 4 US consumer price inflation. (*Bureau of Labor Statistics, US Department of Labor.* http://www.bls.gov/cpi/)

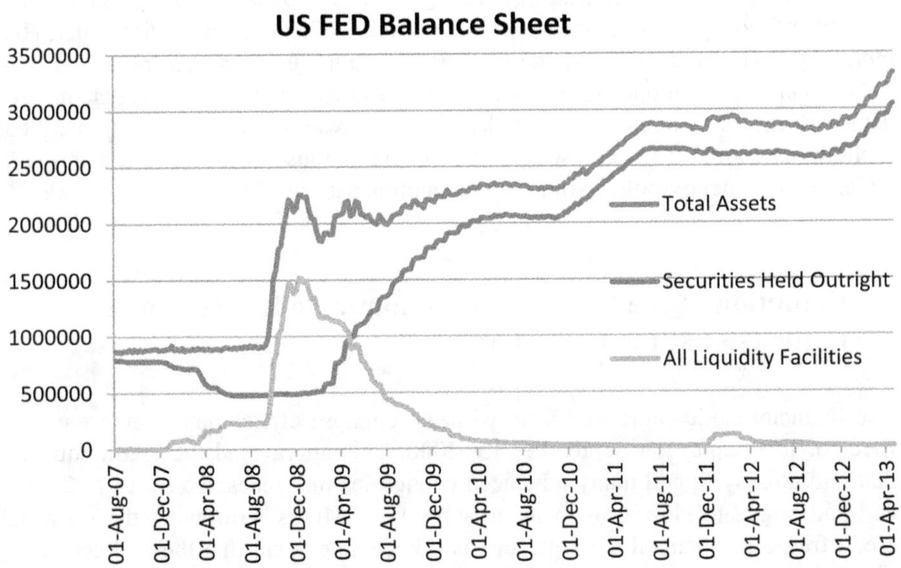

Fig. 5 US Federal Reserve balance sheet. (*US Federal Reserve.* http://www.federalreserve.gov/monetarypolicy/bst_recenttrends.htm)

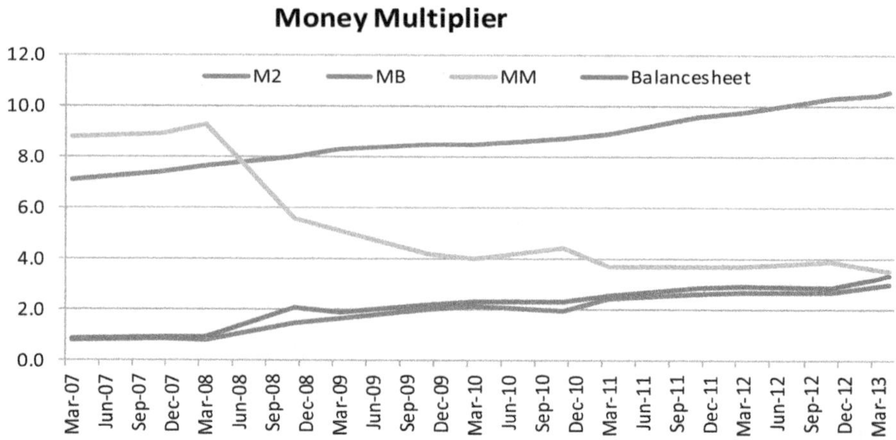

Fig. 6 US money multiplier. (*US Federal Reserve*. http://www.federalreserve.gov/econresdata/statisticsdata.htm)

ing. The massive liquidity injection, however, did not have a commensurate impact on credit expansion through the banking system (M2), as the money multiplier (MM)—the velocity of money in circulation—plunged on account of a large increase in reserve assets. Instead of lending, depositary banks started parking huge amounts of money with central banks, far in excess of mandated requirements. The monetary base is currently expanding more through the increase in reserve assets rather than through monetization. These reserve assets continue to increase in tandem with the size of central bank balance sheets, resulting in what is often called a "liquidity trap"—a breakdown of the monetary transmission channels through which easy monetary policy stimulates economic activity (Fig. 6).

4 Evolution of the G20 Macroeconomic Policy Response to the Global Financial Crisis

The financial panic came to a head with the collapse of Lehman Brothers which filed for bankruptcy on September 15, 2008. This aggravated the credit squeeze that had already tipped many advanced economies into recession by early 2008[6], and had begun to slow growth in fast-growing EMDEs. Following the growing credit freeze in financial markets, and as it became evident that the real economy was being adversely impacted, both Europe and EMDEs were inclined to blame

[6] The Business Cycle Dating Committee, of the National Bureau of Economic Research, has determined that economic activity in the US peaked in December 2007, and "that the subsequent decline in economic activity was large enough to qualify as a recession." *Determination of December 2007 Peak in Economic Activity, National Bureau of Economic Research*, http://www.nber.org/cycles/dec2008.html.

lax financial regulation in the USA for bringing down a robustly growing global economy. President Sarkozy of France contemplated hosting an international summit where it was expected that the USA would be put on the mat. Any such initiative was pre-empted by President Bush's announcement to hold a meeting of the G20 for the first time at Summit (Leader) level in Washington DC, thereby reasserting US global leadership.

The G20 was a forum of finance ministers and central bank governors of systemically important economies, representing almost 80 % of global GDP, set up in the wake of the Asian financial crisis a decade earlier. Since such a role was the traditional preserve of the G7, the move was widely welcomed by EMDEs who were full members of the G20, who had along resented sitting on the margins of G7 Summits as part of the L'Aquila or Heligendamm process.

4.1 The Washington Summit

The first G20 Summit was preceded by a meeting of G20 Finance Ministers and Central Bank Governors in Sao Paulo, Brazil, on November 8–9, 2008. The crisis had deteriorated to the point of warranting a coordinated policy response by systemically important economies, but the severity of its impact on the real economy was still unclear.[7] Nevertheless, it was at this meeting that the broad contours of the G20 assessment of the problem and the policy response emerged. This was more fully articulated in the Leaders' Declaration[8] in Washington DC a week later, and carried forward into subsequent communiqués.

At Sao Paulo, Brazil, G20 Finance Ministers identified the root causes of the crisis as global macroeconomic imbalances on the one hand, and a gradual weakening of regulation of the financial sector on the other. The suggested policy response was a fiscal stimulus to supplement action being taken by central banks, consistent with country-specific fiscal situations. Two aspects of the early policy response are especially worthy of note. First, the reference to "non-inflationary growth" is an indication that the G20 did not consider deflation as a serious danger at this stage, although the reference to an appropriate monetary response to dangers arising from "financial deleveraging" would indicate that it was not entirely oblivious of the threat. Second, while there was a close consensus on supporting the financial sector, differences between the USA and Europe on the role of fiscal policy in stimulating economic activity were already apparent, with the latter drawing attention to its automatic stabilizers that made discretionary stimulus less critical.[9]

[7] In its *World Economic Outlook* of October 2008, the IMF was still forecasting global growth at 3 %, and that of advanced economies at 0.5 %, in 2009. This was subsequently revised downwards to 0.5 and −2 % in its January 2009 *Update* , and further to −1.3 and −3.8 % in its *World Economic Outlook* of April 2009, around the time of the London (second) G20 Summit.

[8] *Declaration of the Summit on Financial Markets and the World Economy, Washington DC, November 15, 2008.* http://www.g20.utoronto.ca/2008/2008declaration1115.html.

[9] Para 9: " We noted that fiscal policies have served as an important instrument to address the current financial crisis, including through government support to the financial sector and have

Several other essential ingredients of the overall G20 policy response to be fleshed out in future meetings were all in evidence in Sao Paulo and Washington DC: keeping international trade open, including quick conclusion of the Doha round; insulating innocent developing country bystanders from the financial crisis through additional capital provisions for the World Bank and the IMF and reforming global economic governance by giving developing countries greater voice and representation in the Bretton Woods Institutions and the Financial Stability Forum.

4.2 The London Summit

Nuanced differences between the USA and Europe on the policy response were again in evidence in the run-up to the second G20 Summit in London. When G20 Finance Ministers met in Horsham, UK, on March 13–14, 2009, while there was a broad consensus on tightening financial regulation and coordinated use of fiscal and monetary policies to combat the economic crisis, the USA advocated aggressive use of fiscal policy, relatively lighter regulation, and a more far-ranging reform of the governance structure of the Bretton Woods Institutions. The Europeans rooted for tighter financial regulation, more prudent use of fiscal policy with an eye to medium-term sustainability, and a more defensive posture to safeguard their pre-eminent position in the governance structure of the Bretton Woods Institutions in the face of their economic decline.

In view of the rapidly worsening economic outlook, and with monetary policy falling into a liquidity trap, the differences on fiscal policy were however, more muted, with stability concerns now pushed to the long term.[10] It appeared that the global economy was on the verge of another Great Depression. The IMF's April 2009 *World Economic Outlook* that appeared just before the London Summit on

---

performed an important stabilization role and in mitigating further negative effects on markets and on economic activity. Some countries are also considering additional fiscal measures to stimulate the economy and we agreed that countries must use all their policy flexibility consistent with their circumstances, to support sustainable growth, while we recognize the importance of fiscal sustainability for macroeconomic stability and growth…." *Communiqué. G20 Meeting of Ministers and Governors, Sao Paulo, Brazil, 8–9, November, 2008.* http://www.g20.utoronto.ca/2008/2008communique1109.pdf The International Monetary Fund was also of the view that "In Europe, with its relatively large automatic stabilizers, the additional fiscal impulse can probably be somewhat less than in the United States," Blanchard (2008, p. 12).

[10] These differences were more clearly in evidence in the closed-door deliberations, than in the official Communiqués, from where these can be deduced by reading 'between the lines'. Thus in the Horsham Communiqué, while paragraph 6 makes a strong statement on strengthening financial regulation, bullet # 3 clarifies that "it is vital that capital requirements remain unchanged until recovery is assured." Paragraph 5 states that while "fiscal expansion is providing vital support for growth and jobs….we will ensure the restoration of growth and long-run fiscal sustainability." Likewise paragraph 8 tried to limit the gains of the larger EMEs by protecting the share of the poorest developing economies. *G20 Finance Ministers' and Central Bank Governors' Communiqué, March 14, 2009.* http://www.g20.utoronto.ca/2009/2009communique0314.pdf.

April 2, 2009, projected global growth in 2009 at −1.3 %, with advanced economies shrinking by −3.8 %, and EMDEs expanding at a very modest 1.6 %. G20 Leaders now resolved to do "whatever it takes" to use the full strength of monetary and fiscal policies to pull the global economy back from an economic cliff. They put together a trillion-dollar package to cushion the impact on EMDEs through the IMF and the World Bank, in addition to committing G20 countries to taking "…unprecedented and concerted fiscal expansion, which will save or create millions of jobs which would otherwise have been destroyed, and that will, by the end of next year, amount to $ 5 trillion, raise output by 4 per cent…. Our central banks have also taken exceptional action. Interest rates have been cut aggressively in most countries, and our central banks have pledged to maintain expansionary policies for as long as needed and to use the full range of monetary policy instruments, including unconventional instruments, consistent with price stability…. Our actions to restore growth cannot be effective until we restore domestic lending and international capital flows. We have provided significant and comprehensive support to our banking systems to provide liquidity, recapitalize financial institutions, and address decisively the problem of impaired assets. We are committed to take all necessary actions to restore the normal flow of credit through the financial system and ensure the soundness of systemically important institutions…. Taken together, these actions will constitute the largest fiscal and monetary stimulus and the most comprehensive support programme for the financial sector in modern times."[11]

4.3 The Pittsburgh Summit

IMF's forecast for 2010 in its WEO of April 2009 was that while the global economy would grow at 1.9 %, advanced economies would not grow at all. From its July 2009 WEO *Update*, however, the IMF started revising its forecasts for the global economy sharply upwards. By the time of the third G20 Summit in Pittsburgh, USA, towards the end of September 2009, G20 Leaders congratulated themselves that their unprecedented globally coordinated policy response to what was now a financial and economic crisis had succeeded. [12] In its October 2009 World Economic Outlook, the IMF now projected global growth in 2010 at 3.1 %, with advanced economies growing at 1.3 % and EMDEs at 5.1 % (Table 1).

While G20 Leaders stated that "A sense of normalcy should not lead to complacency" (*para 8*), at the Pittsburgh Summit the focus of the G20 clearly shifted from short-term macroeconomic stabilization policies to addressing medium- to long-term structural challenges to strengthen growth and sustain the recovery.[13] It

[11] *London Summit—Leaders' Statement, 2 April 2009,* http://www.g20.utoronto.ca/2009/2009communique0402.pdf.

[12] *Para 5* of the Pittsburgh Declaration consisted of just two words: "It worked." IMF's (20010) was appropriately entitled "*A Policy-Driven, Multispeed Recovery*."

[13] *Para 10*: "We pledge today to sustain our strong policy response until a durable recovery is secured. We will act to ensure that when growth returns, jobs do too. We will avoid any premature

Table 1 IMF growth projections

WEO	2008			2009			2010			2011			2012			2013		
	Wd	Ad	Em	Wd	Ad	Em	Wd	Ad	Em	Wd	Ad	Em	Wd	Ad	Em	Wd	Ad	Em
Apr-08	3.7	1.3	6.7	3.8	1.3	6.6	4.8	2.7	7.1	4.9	3.1	7.0	4.9	3.0	7.0	4.9	2.9	7.0
July Update	4.1	1.7	6.9	3.9	1.4	6.7												
Oct-08	3.9	1.5	6.9	3.0	0.5	6.1	4.2	2.0	6.7	4.8	2.9	6.9	4.8	2.8	6.9	4.7	2.5	6.9
January Update	3.4	1.0	6.3	0.5	−2.0	3.3	3.0	1.1	5.0									
Apr-09	3.2	0.9	6.1	−1.3	−3.8	1.6	1.9	0.0	4.0	4.3	2.6	6.1	4.9	3.0	6.8	4.9	3 .0	6.8
July Update	3.1	0.8	6.0	−1.4	−3.8	1.5	2.5	0.6	4.7									
Oct-09	3.0	0.6	6.0	−1.1	−3.4	1.7	3.1	1.3	5.1	4.2	2.5	6.1	4.4	2.6	6.4	4.6	2.5	6.6
January Update	3.0	0.5	6.1	−0.8	−3.2	2.1	3.9	2.1	6.0	4.3	2.4	6.3						
Apr-10	3.0	0.5	6.1	−0.6	−3.2	2.4	4.2	2.3	6.3	4.3	2.4	6.5	4.5	2.4	6.6	4.5	2.4	6.6
July Update	3.0	0.5	6.1	−0.6	−3.2	2.5	4.6	2.6	6.8	4.3	2.4	6.4						
Oct-10	2.8	0.2	6.0	−0.6	−3.2	2.5	4.8	2.7	7.1	4.2	2.2	6.4	4.5	2.6	6.5	4.6	2.6	6.6
January Update				−0.6	−3.4	2.6	5.0	3.0	7.1	4.4	2.5	6.5	4.5	2.5	6.5			
Apr-11	2.9	0.2	6.1	−0.5	−3.4	2.7	5.0	3.0	7.3	4.4	2.4	6.5	4.5	2.6	6.5	4.5	2.5	6.5
July Update				−0.5	−3.4	2.8	5.1	3.0	7.4	4.3	2.2	6.6	4.5	2.6	6.4			
Oct-11	2.8	0.1	6.0	−0.7	−3.7	2.8	5.1	3.1	7.3	4.0	1.6	6.4	4.0	1.9	6.1	4.5	2.4	6.5
January Update							5.2	3.2	7.3	3.8	1.6	6.2	3.3	1.2	5.4	3.9	1.9	5.9
Apr-12	2.8	0.0	6.0	−0.6	−3.6	2.8	5.3	3.2	7.5	3.9	1.6	6.2	3.5	1.4	5.7	4.1	2.0	6.0
July Update							5.3	3.2	7.5	3.9	1.6	6.2	3.5	1.4	5.6	3.9	1.9	5.9
Oct-12	2.8	0.1	6.1	−0.6	−3.5	2.7	5.1	3.0	7.4	3.8	1.6	6.2	3.3	1.3	5.3	3.6	1.5	5.6
January Update										3.9	1.6	6.3	3.2	1.3	5.1	3.5	1.4	5.5

was widely believed at that point that, the recovery notwithstanding, a return to pre-crises levels of global growth on a sustainable basis was unlikely without a major rebalancing of the global economy, since US saving rates were rising in response to the severe mauling of household balance sheets on account of the financial crisis. The drop in US consumption expenditure would need to be countervailed by higher domestic demand in China and elsewhere. Such rebalancing was also expected to reduce the risks to the global financial system.

The institutional mechanism to achieve this—*The Framework for Strong Sustainable and Balanced Growth* based on a 'mutual assessment process'—was launched at Pittsburgh, and was soon to be described as the 'heart and soul' of the G20. The *Framework* was seen by G20 Leaders as a compact that committed their Finance Ministers to consult and work together on a continual basis to assess how their policies fitted together, to evaluate whether they were collectively consistent with strong, sustainable and balanced growth, and to act as necessary to meet the common objectives of G20 countries. The compact was that G20 members would agree on shared policy objectives, which would be updated from time to time as conditions evolved; they would set out medium-term policy frameworks and work together to assess the collective implications of national policy frameworks for the level and pattern of global growth and to identify potential risks to financial stability. G20 Finance Ministers would subsequently present the results of their mutual assessment to Leaders at each Summit, who would in turn agree on actions to meet these common objectives.

To an extent the *G20 Framework* could be seen as another attempt to augment IMF's bilateral macroeconomic '*Article IV*' surveillance system with multilateral macroeconomic surveillance which was more suitable to an age of enhanced globalization and policy spillovers IMF (2007). Two features of the G20 Framework exercise are particularly relevant: it is firstly, a mutually consultative process, rather than driven by the IMF[14], and secondly, any commitments/targets are country driven rather than imposed externally. While this makes the exercise uniquely democratic and inclusive, it is also less likely to result in rules-based outcomes.

4.4 The Toronto Summit

By the time the fourth G20 Summit was held in Toronto, Canada, on June 26–27, 2010, the global recovery was unexpectedly robust, considering that the general view at the time, based on the work done by Rogoff and Reinhart, (Rogoff and

withdrawal of stimulus. At the same time, we will prepare our exit strategies and, when the time is right, withdraw our extraordinary policy support in a cooperative and coordinated way, maintaining our commitment to fiscal responsibility." *Para 11:* "Even as the work of recovery continues, we pledge to adopt the policies needed to lay the foundation for strong, sustained and balanced growth in the 21st century." *G20 Leaders Statement: The Pittsburgh Summit, September 24–25, 2009, Pittsburgh.* http://www.g20.utoronto.ca/2009/2009communique0925.html.

[14] IMF's official role in the *G20 Framework* exercise is to act as 'technical advisor'.

Reinhart 2009a) was that a recovery from a financial crisis is slow and protracted. Following the contraction (−0.6 %) in 2009, the WEO of April 2010 projected global growth in 2010 at 4.2 %, with advanced economies growing at 2.3 % (not far below the average of 2.8 % between 1992 and 2001), and Emerging and Developing Economies growing at 6.3 %, far higher than the average of 3.8 % between 1992 and 2001.

The global recovery, however, was accompanied by a storm brewing in the Eurozone, with the focus of financial instability now shifting from the USA and UK. Whereas financial instability in the first phase of the financial crisis centred on the banking system, with treasury bonds providing a safe haven, the second stage of the crisis was marked by sovereign debt risks in the Euro area when markets discovered the flaw that was always known to economists: that sovereign debt in these countries did not have a central bank backstop on the one hand, and their tax base was too small to bail out their pan European banks on the other (Table 2).

A protracted and tepid recovery severely mauled budgetary revenues, while the need for stimulus and supporting the financial sector kept expenditures high. As a result, there was a dramatic rise in budget deficits, the lagged effect of which was a steep rise in debt–GDP ratios unheard of in peace time in advanced economies. This once again opened fissures within the G20 on fiscal policy, with European countries arguing for front-loaded fiscal exit in the face of market revolt, and the USA and UK (right up to the dramatic shift in stance with the defeat of the Labour Party in the May 2010 elections) for fiscal exit calibrated to the recovery. The final outcome, reflected in the Toronto Leaders' Declaration[15], was to make the fiscal consolidation mix 'growth friendly', albeit 'date' rather than 'rate (of recovery)' contingent, with advanced G20 economies agreeing measures to halve deficits by 2013 and to stabilize or reduce government debt-to-GDP ratios by 2016. The unstated assumption was that the heavy lifting was now left to monetary policy which was, however, still in a liquidity trap on account of continued deleveraging and dysfunctional transmission channels. The G20 has been living with this dilemma ever since.

At Pittsburgh the G20 had turned its attention to medium- to long-term macroeconomic policies to raise and sustain global growth through its *Framework for Strong, Sustainable and Balanced Growth,* to be conducted through a consultative *Mutual Assessment Process*. The first MAP exercise was undertaken by the Framework Working Group which was co-chaired by Canada and India, with technical advice from the IMF, and its results presented to G20 Leaders at Toronto. The overall assessment was that when the G20 country frameworks were combined into a global framework the outcomes appeared unrealistic, as all countries expected to export their way out of low growth. Leaders were therefore of the view that "we can do much better," with advanced deficit countries committing to take actions to boost national savings and enhance export competitiveness, and surplus countries committing to reforms to reduce their reliance on external demand and focus more on domestic sources of growth and keep exchange rates flexible. Therefore both

---

[15] *The G20 Toronto Summit Declaration, Toronto, June 27, 2010*. http://www.g20.utoronto.ca/2010/to-communique.html.

Table 2 General government fiscal balance and gross debt

% of GDP	2007		2008		2009		2010		2011		*2012*[a]		*2013*[a]	
	Bal	Debt	Bal	Debt	Bal	Debt	Bal	Debt	Bal	Debt	Bal	Debt	Bal	Debt
Advanced	−2.7		−3.5	81.3	−9.0	94.9	−7.8	101.5	−6.6	105.5	−5.9	110.2	−4.7	109.3
France	−2.8	64.2	−3.3	68.2	−7.6	79.2	−7.1	82.3	−5.2	86.0	−4.6	90.3	−3.7	92.7
Germany	0.2	65.4	−0.1	66.8	−3.1	74.5	−4.1	82.5	−0.8	80.5	0.2	82.0	−0.3	80.4
Greece	−6.8	107.3	−9.9	112.5	−15.6	129.3	−10.7	147.9	−9.4	170.6	−6.4	158.5	−4.6	179.5
Iceland	5.4	29.1	−0.5	70.4	−8.6	88.0	−6.4	90.6	−5.0	102.3	−3.0	99.1	−1.3	91.9
Ireland	0.1	25.0	−7.4	44.5	−13.9	64.9	−30.9	92.2	−13.4	106.5	−7.7	117.1	−7.5	122.0
Italy	−1.6	103.3	−2.7	106.1	−5.4	116.4	−4.3	119.3	−3.7	120.8	−3.0	127.0	−2.6	130.6
Japan	−2.1	183.0	−4.1	191.8	−10.4	210.2	−9.3	216.0	−9.9	230.3	−10.2	237.9	−9.8	245.4
Portugal	−3.2	68.3	−3.7	71.6	−10.2	83.1	−9.8	93.2	−4.4	108.0	−4.9	123.0	−5.5	122.3
Spain	1.9	36.3	−4.5	40.2	−11.2	53.9	−9.7	61.3	−9.4	69.1	−10.3	84.1	−6.6	91.8
UK	−2.9	43.7	−5.1	52.2	−11.4	68.1	−10.1	79.4	−7.9	85.4	−8.3	90.3	−7.0	93.6
USA	−2.7	66.5	−6.7	75.5	−13.3	89.1	−11.1	98.2	−10.0	102.5	−8.5	106.5	−6.5	108.1
BRICS	*0.3*	*39.3*	*−1.2*	*37.9*	*−5.6*	*40.4*	*−4.3*	*42.8*	*−2.9*	*41.6*	*−3.5*	*42.3*	*−3.3*	*41.6*
Brazil	−2.7	65.2	−1.4	63.5	−3.1	66.9	−2.7	65.2	−2.5	64.9	−2.8	68.5	−1.2	67.2
Russia	6.8	8.5	4.9	7.9	−6.3	11.0	−3.4	11.0	1.5	11.7	0.4	10.9	−0.3	10.4
India	−4.8	75.0	−8.6	73.3	−10.1	75.0	−8.7	68.5	−8.4	66.4	−8.3	66.8	−8.3	66.4
China	0.9	19.6	−0.7	17.0	−3.1	17.7	−1.5	33.5	−1.3	25.5	−2.2	22.8	−2.1	21.3
South Africa	1.4	28.3	−0.4	27.8	−5.5	31.3	−5.1	35.8	−4.0	39.6	−4.8	42.3	−4.8	42.7

IMF, Fiscal Monitor April 2013 Bal: General Government Nominal Balance

[a] Projections

internal and external rebalancing were envisaged. G20 Leaders recognized "that these measures will need to be implemented at the national level and will need to be tailored to individual country circumstances. To facilitate this process, we have agreed that the second stage of our country-led and consultative mutual assessment will be conducted at the country and European level and that we will each identify additional measures, as necessary, that we will take toward achieving strong, sustainable, and balanced growth."[16]

4.5 The Seoul Summit

By the time of the fifth G20 Summit in Seoul a few months later on November 11–12, 2010, the global recovery was in full swing. Global growth was forecast by the IMF in its WEO of October 2010 to expand by 4.8% in 2010. Although economic activity appeared to be slowing from the second half of 2010, global growth in 2011 was nevertheless projected to be at a relatively healthy 4.2% in 2011. The recovery was 'two-speed', with developing countries recovering more strongly. The focus at the Seoul Summit, therefore, remained on medium- to long-term issues, namely the 'Framework' exercise and 'Development', a new G20 stream injected by the Summit Chair, Korea.

The second-stage MAP Framework exercise was expected to be at the country level on the basis of forward-looking projections given by each G20 country. This quickly brought into the open dormant fissures within the G20 apparent, reflected in the careful choice and balancing of words in G20 Communiqués. These fissures were exacerbated by IMF's technical assessment to the G20 that after putting together G20 country submissions it appeared that countries were again overoptimistic in projecting growth through reliance on external demand. While fiscal rebalancing seemed to be on track, external rebalancing was not happening, and there was little clarity on structural reforms.

The USA and some other advanced countries were of the view that China's exchange rate continued to be substantially undervalued. China was not ready to accept this, accusing the USA of causing global imbalances through large current account and fiscal deficits, and also causing currency (dollar) devaluation through large QE. There were also concerns that monetary easing on a large scale, combined with financialization of commodity markets, were distorting commodity prices.[17] Other emerging markets, led by Brazil, also complained about volatile capital flows appreciating their currencies consequent on continuing loose monetary policies in

[16] Ibid.

[17] The G20 Study Group set up to study the issue however did not come up with conclusive evidence of this, pointing instead to the steep rise in physical demand for commodities in recent times, especially in emerging markets. These conclusions were keenly debated in G20 meetings, especially since there was continued pressure on commodity prices despite a collapse in global demand. *Report of the G20 Study Group on Commodities under the chairmanship of Mr. Hiroshi Nakaso*, November 2011 http://www.cmegroup.com/education/files/G20Nakaso-November202011.pdf.

advanced economies.[18] Germany was very touchy about any attempt to discuss intra-zone imbalances in the G20, and any mention of staggering fiscal consolidation in the short term in the Eurozone. By now the UK had also started leaning towards fiscal austerity following the victory of the Conservatives in May 2010, leaving only the USA and Japan as the major advanced G20 countries who fully agreed with the IMF's advice to backload fiscal consolidation in view of worsening economic conditions. Global consensus on policy actions to deal with the new headwinds now became increasingly difficult.

In the event, the G20 continued to reiterate constructive ambiguities such as committing to 'growth friendly fiscal consolidation' and 'exchange rate flexibility and avoiding competitive devaluations'. An alternative proposal, attributed to the USA, for an indicative quantitative cap of 4 % of GDP on current account imbalances was turned down largely on account of strong resistance by China, Brazil, Germany, Australia and Japan. There was however an agreement that "persistently large imbalances, assessed against indicative guidelines to be agreed, would warrant an assessment of their nature and the root causes of impediments to adjustment as part of the Mutual Assessment Process." [19]

4.6 The Cannes Summit

Following the 'dead cat bounce' of 2010, the global recovery started fading away in 2011 and 2012, with Europe falling into a second dip recession, US growth weakening and the strong recovery in emerging markets and developing economies stalling. The smouldering crisis in the Eurozone erupted once more, this time in Greece, just prior to the (sixth) Cannes Summit on November 3–4, 2011. However, another grand global rescue comparable to the 'trillion dollar' London Summit was quickly ruled out since, unlike London, policymakers went into the Summit with empty

[18] These developing country concerns were carried forward into subsequent Summits leading to a debate within the G20 on external spillovers of monetary policies in reserve currency issuing countries which basically respond to domestic business cycles. At the next Summit at Cannes, G20 Leaders agreed to *G20 Coherent Conclusions for the Management of Capital Flows Drawing on Country Experiences* (http://www.g20.utoronto.ca/2011/2011-finance-capital-flows-111015-en.pdf) that were earlier endorsed by G20 Finance Ministers and Central Bank Governors on October 15, 2011. While there were several constructive ambiguities in this agreement, reflecting sharp differences between G20 countries on the issue, this nevertheless endorsed the view that as a last resort countries could put in place 'capital flow management' measures to insulate them from the volatility in cross-border capital flows inherent in the shifting monetary policy stance in reserve issuing currencies. The real significance of this agreement was that it pressured the IMF into abandoning its long-held view that the final objective of all countries should be to move towards full convertibility on the capital account. While re-iterating the benefit of capital flows, the IMF now concluded that there was "no presumption that full liberalization is an appropriate goal for all countries at all times" IMF (2012c) .

[19] *The G20 Seoul Summit Leaders' Declaration, Seoul, November 12, 2010*. http://www.g20.utoronto.ca/2010/g20seoul.html.

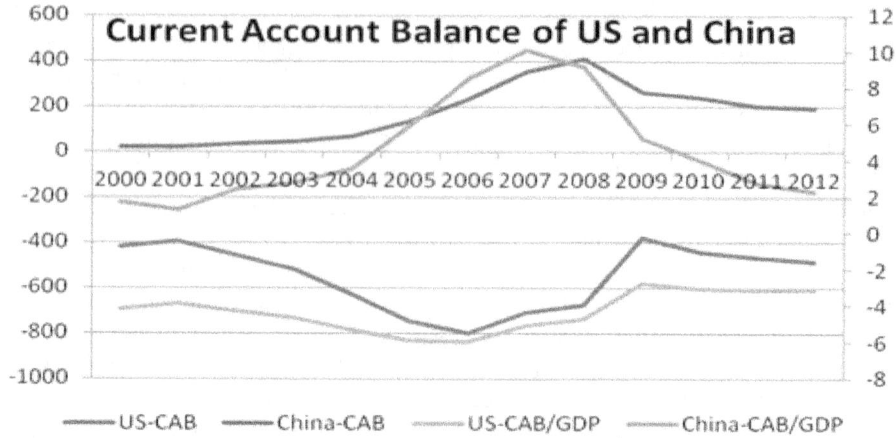

Fig. 7 USA and China current account balance. (IMF 2012b)

pockets and depleted policy instruments. There was nevertheless a resolve to garner more resources for the IMF for short-term macroeconomic support, although no number could be put on the table.

The gravity of the situation compelled G20 Leaders to turn their attention once again to short-term macroeconomic management to stabilize the global economy, with the growth–austerity dilemma now taking centre stage. These concerns were reflected in the way the Framework exercise panned out, with specified countries committing to specific short-term policy actions, in addition to long-term objectives such as demand rebalancing that retreated into the background.[20] Long-term objectives also lost focus on account of some appreciation of the Chinese currency, the sharp reduction in China's current account surplus (Fig. 7) even as those of oil-exporting countries rose, China's own resolve in its 12th Five Year Plan to increase domestic consumption so as to reduce external vulnerabilities to its growth and a new narrative on trade developed by the World Trade Organization (WTO) that highlighted the growing importance of processing trade that had the effect of sharply reducing China's bilateral trade surpluses with the USA.[21] While it can plausibly be argued that pressure within the G20 forum also influenced Chinese policy, other

[20] In its *World Economic Outlook* of September 2011 the IMF observed that "While imbalances decreased during the crisis, this was due more to a large decrease in output in advanced relative to emerging market economies than to structural adjustment in these economies. Looking forward, the forecast is for an increase rather than a decrease in imbalances." Its tune had changed, however, by the time of its next *World Economic Outlook* in April 2012, where it stated that "latest developments suggest that global current account imbalances are no longer expected to widen again, following their sharp reduction during the Great Recession.", and by July 2012, in its *Staff Report* for the Article IV Consultations with China it assessed the Chinese currency as only "moderately undervalued." IMF (2012d). .

[21] WTO (2011). If the same exchange rate that led to rising trade surpluses with the US—and could therefore considered undervalued—also led to rising trade deficits with East Asia, what, then, was the equilibrium exchange rate?

imbalances, such as those of oil-exporting countries, are taking its place. At best this could be seen as an illustration of discretionary, rather than rules-based policy coordination.

At Seoul G20 Leaders had resolved to develop indicators for identifying large imbalances that require corrective action. Following this, more stringent surveillance criteria were developed at Cannes for seven G20 countries found to be systemically important as their individual share of aggregate G20 GDP exceeded 5 % at either market exchange rates or purchasing power parity. These included the USA, Japan, Germany and China (both criteria), UK and France (MER criteria) and India (PPP criteria).

The irony, however, was that just as the focus of the Framework was shifting to systemically important economies, the world was confronted with a crisis emanating from a relatively small economy, namely Greece. While the subprime housing crisis showed how a problem in a small market in a large economy could be systemically magnified by financial markets, the Eurozone crisis now showed that large imbalances even in a small economy in a large currency union can be similarly systemically magnified through the same transmission channel. The new surveillance criteria developed by the Framework Working Group therefore appeared flawed from inception, and in any case did not go very far. At Cannes[22], following the adoption of the indicative guidelines, G20 Leaders commissioned an 'Accountability Framework', which has in effect meant country-led presentations and justifications of their own policies, of which other countries and the IMF were wary of being too critical.

By this time the Eurozone imbroglio had clearly supplanted global imbalances from the G20 centre stage. The Eurozone had moved to address the problem by first setting up the EFSF, subsequently rolled into the ESM to provide fiscal support to troubled governments and banks, and in March 2011 Eurozone governments agreed to reform their Stability and Growth Pact through a 'six pack' reform to penalize countries that failed to comply with fiscal rules, as a prelude to a more comprehensive new Treaty on Stability, Coordination and Governance one year later.

The market response to the outcome at Cannes was not kind. The Eurozone problem had not only not been addressed to its satisfaction, but also there was no acknowledgement that structural flaws—monetary union without a fiscal and banking union, and the absence of a mechanism to deal with intra-EMU imbalances—needed to be fixed quickly. There was also no clear strategy of how the Eurozone could get back to a path of sustainable growth from a situation where countries were being forced into austerity at a time of collapsing growth. The message that appeared to go out was that Europe did not take too kindly to the G20 meddling into what it saw to be intra-Eurozone issues.

The takeaway from G20's handling of the austerity–growth dilemma seemed to be that while medium-term fiscal consolidation plans were necessary, countries should continue to stimulate in the current circumstances till such point as they

---

[22] *Cannes Summit Final Declaration—Building Our Common Future: Renewed Collective Action for the Benefit of All Cannes, November 4, 2011*. http://www.g20.utoronto.ca/2011/2011-cannes-declaration-111104-en.html.

were penalized by markets, at which point fiscal consolidation should commence irrespective of the output gap or state of recovery. All this could hardly have been reassuring to markets. A number of Eurozone sovereign bonds went into free fall following the Summit as the contagion spread, denting the image of the G20 as the premier multilateral forum for international policy cooperation and crisis management. It was the ECB's LTRO announced in December 2011 that temporarily helped stabilize peripheral sovereign bond yields.

4.7 The Los Cabos Summit

The seventh G20 Summit was held at Los Cabos, Mexico (June 18–19, 2012), close on the heels of the Cannes Summit, with the two imminent threats confronting the global economy, to all intents and purposes, the same as what was confronted by Leaders at their last Summit in Cannes. If anything, these old challenges had become even more daunting.

First, the Cannes Summit agenda was hijacked by the gathering storm in the Eurozone, specifically the Greek question. The Summit failed to address the problem squarely. As a result, the contagion spread beyond Portugal, Ireland and Greece (PIG, all of whom had lost sovereign market access before Cannes) to the bigger Eurozone economies of Spain and Italy, and even threatened France. Their sovereign bond spreads started spinning out of control within weeks of the Summit. It was the ECB that temporarily rescued Eurozone sovereign bonds. Once 'Big Bertha' felt silent, however, sovereign bond markets went into revolt again, with the spreads of Spain breaching the dreaded 6% barrier and Italian yields in hot pursuit. Leaders now confronted a much worse situation in the Eurozone than at Los Cabos, with governments quietly planning for the exit of Greece, or even a catastrophic break-up of the monetary union. Whereas sovereign bond yields rose after the Cannes Summit, they were now rising prior to the Summit. The Eurozone once again threatened to hijack the G20 agenda at Los Cabos.

G20 Leaders agreed to augment IMF's firewall again by another $ 450 billion at Los Cabos. Since the bigger EMDEs were already self-insured through their large foreign currency reserves, this further augmentation seemed to be directed towards the Eurozone crisis. This, however, had no impact on Eurozone sovereign bond yields, since the amount raised was too small relative to the size of the problem. It was once again the announcement by the ECB in September 2012 of its intention to buy sovereign bonds, without any limits on size or time, through its new Outright Monetary Transactions (OMT) that battered high bond yields into submission.

The second threat facing Leaders at Cannes was the faltering global recovery and the persistence of high levels of unemployment, particularly youth unemployment. The Cannes Action Plan was subtitled "Growth and Jobs" because unemployment had become a political hot potato, with the concerns over growth, global imbalances and exchange rates stemming primarily from this. If the sleight of hand in the employment data was discounted to take stock of discouraged workers who had abandoned their job search, the employment scenario had only worsened in most parts of

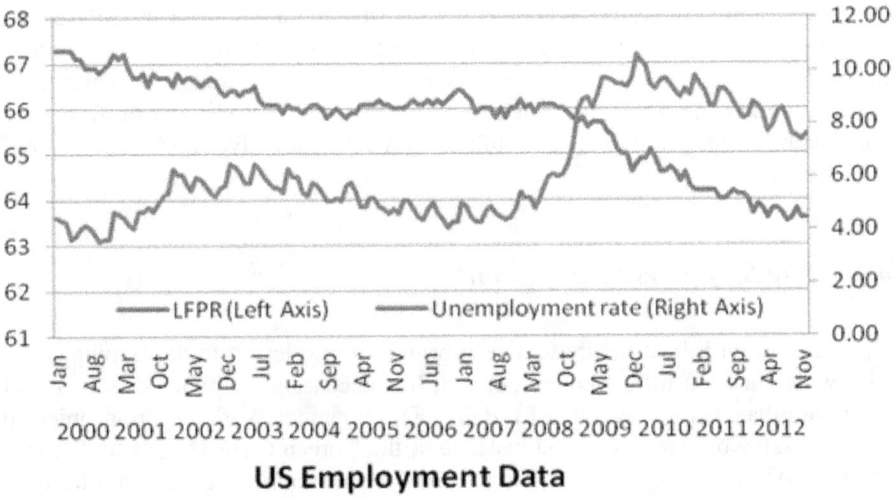

Fig. 8 US unemployment and Labor Force Participation Rate. (*Bureau of Labor Statistics, US Department of Labor*. http://www.bls.gov/data/)

the developed world since Cannes. While a long-term decline in the US Labor Force Participation Rate (LFPR) was discernible even before the onset of the global financial crisis (Fig. 8), it had stabilized during the boom since 2003. A true recovery is consistent only with a reversion, or at least near reversion, to pre-crisis unemployment *and* labour participation rates. Growth and jobs were, therefore, once again at the top of the Los Cabos agenda, especially with near-term economic data from the USA, the UK, the Eurozone and even major emerging markets like China, Brazil and India pointing towards another synchronized downturn.

The dilemma facing Leaders at Cannes of having to choose between austerity (market-induced fiscal consolidation) and growth (fiscal expansion to help bridge the output gap) was now compounded by the realization of a new paradox. While the flight to quality—sovereign bonds—seems to have created an illusion of fiscal space in a number of advanced countries that enabled them to continue to stimulate, or stagger their consolidation, the same process shrank the fiscal space in peripheral Eurozone countries. Capital flowed out of the latter, elevating sovereign borrowing costs. Since there was no central bank backstop, the recovery was left hostage to markets. Electorates had by now joined issue with markets, voting against austerity by unseating governments wherever elections were held. Leaders were therefore expected to devise a coordinated workable strategy to revive flagging global growth with markets and electorates revolting in different directions.

With economists divided on what was to be done, it is not surprising that there was no rabbit to pull out of the hat. On the trade-off between austerity and growth, neither the Leaders' Declaration nor the Los Cabos Action Plan went one whit beyond Cannes: continue to stimulate if you have the fiscal space, and start consolidating if you do not. In the event, the Cannes and Los Cabos Action Plans were essentially similar in design and objectives, albeit with three significant differences. First, there was a greater willingness in Mexico on the part of European countries to let the G20 discuss and render policy advice on intra-Eurozone imbalances[23]; second, the bar for what constituted fiscal space was lowered[24] and third, serious consideration was given to the possibility of infrastructure investment as a driver of the global recovery.

4.8 *The St. Petersburg Summit*

Up to this point infrastructure was seen primarily as relevant to developing countries which had big infrastructure deficits. It was consequently included as one of the nine pillars on the agenda of the G20 Development Working Group injected into the G20 work streams at the instance of the Korean Chair at the fifth Summit at Seoul. At the next Summit in Cannes, the French Chair had accorded priority to infrastructure financing, but this was still seen from a purely developing-country perspective, with the High-Level Panel on Infrastructure assigning the central role to an action plan developed by multilateral development banks (MDBs). The macroeconomic policy (Framework) and Development streams proceeded on separate tracks, as infrastructure investment was not envisaged as a possible driver of the global recovery. At Los Cabos, G20 Leaders seriously considered, perhaps for the first time, a role for infrastructure investment in reviving growth and creating jobs in developed countries and subsumed the subject within the Framework Working Group dealing with macroeconomic issues.

The synergies between the 'Macroeconomic' and 'Infrastructure' streams were explored further at the next (eighth) Summit held in St. Petersburg, Russia, on September 5-6, 2013, where a work plan was adopted to improve the overall investment climate to boost economic growth, job creation and development. Country specific strategies are expected to be worked out by the time of the next (Brisbane) Summit.

[23] The G20 had for long talked about global rebalancing, but the Los Cabos Action Plan was the first G20 document that acknowledged the need for internal rebalancing in the Eurozone. Also, while no specific commitments were given, pointers to the banking union, the severance of the negative "feedback loop between sovereigns and banks" and measures to support growth agreed at the EU Summit 10 days later were all there in the Los Cabos Leaders' Declaration and Action Plan. It is true that nothing definitive was stated about fiscal union or the conversion of the European Central Bank into a regular central bank that can insulate sovereign bonds from market revolt. But there was no consensus amongst European leaders themselves on these issues. G20 commitments, it must be remembered, are country led. *G20 Leaders Declaration, Los Cabos, Mexico, June 19, 2012*. http://www.g20.utoronto.ca/2012/2012-0619-loscabos.html.

[24] While the Los Cabos Leaders' Declaration exhorted countries with fiscal space to continue with stimulus in general terms, the country-specific linkage between fiscal space and stimulus that featured prominently in the Cannes Action Plan was dropped in the Los Cabos Action Plan. This severance allowed the USA, which was not included in the group of countries with fiscal space at Cannes, and now faced a "fiscal cliff" deriving from the double whammy of automatic federal expenditure cuts and expiry of tax cuts, to commit to continuing stimulus at Los Cabos.

The G20[25], however, is perhaps still too sanguine about private investment taking the lead in infrastructure investment in view of weak animal spirits, continuing deleveraging, and the leading role played historically by governments in financing and supporting infrastructural investments on account of long gestation periods, low returns and attendant risks. Public investment, including public works on a large scale, was part of President Franklin Roosevelt's 'New Deal' and therefore a feature of the fiscal policy response during the Great Depression. During the Global Financial Crisis, however, this tool was not widely used, with the possible exception of China, where it seems to have worked quite dramatically. This is perhaps because public investment creates jobs directly, and gives a sense of permanent income increase that neutralizes Ricardian equivalence by giving households the confidence to spend the additional income.[26] Public investment in infrastructure can also crowd in private investment.[27]

Pressured by the need to enhance their tax base to reduce mounting fiscal imbalances G 8 countries launched a new initiative at their Summit in Lough Erne held on June 17, 2013, which was subsequently endorsed by G20 leaders at St Petersburg G20 Leaders launched a new initiative to protect their tax bases from 'Base Erosion and Profit Shifting' (BEPS) in an age of rapid globalization. The full implications of this initiative are still unclear. TNCs have long been migrating Industrial production, and increasingly services as they become more tradable, to EMEs, lured by low wages, productivity shifts and attractive tax rates. While much of the final consumption deriving from these activities continues to remain in OECD countries, this shift in economic activity has raised growth in EMEs, and along with economic activity and growth has come higher tax revenues. The initiative is likely to prove more contentious as it proceeds. Be it as it may, the timing of this initiative is at cross purposes with the G20's initiative to boost private investment in a broken global economy low on investment confidence. When growth and animal spirits are low, and governments want private investment to take over the load from public expenditure for a sustainable recovery, an international initiative to tighten or aggressively target tax avoidance, especially when corporate tax receipts have not dipped out of proportion to the fall in growth, can only make the recovery more difficult. Of the two 're-balancings' identified by the G20 itself for a sustainable recovery, global demand rebalancing is clearly in evidence, but a question mark still hangs over the second rebalancing, namely from public to private.

Macroeconomic stabilization, growth and jobs, which dominated the first two G20 Summits at Washington and London Summits, came back to occupy centre stage

---

[25] 25 G20 Leaders' Declaration, St. Petersburg, September 6, 2013. http://www.g20utoronto.ca/summits/2013stpetersburg.html

[26] Brad DeLong and Lawrence Summers recently argued that when economic activity is depressed, and monetary policy is zero bound, fiscal multipliers should be larger than usual. DeLong and Summers (2012). The IMF came to a similar conclusion in its findings that fiscal multipliers were higher in the early phase of the crisis, although they tended to decline over time. Blanchard and Leigh (2013).

[27] A fuller discussion on the issues relating to infrastructure and the recovery can be seen in C. Rangarajan and Alok Sheel, Growth or Austerity, op. cit. pp. 77–81.

in the last two Summits at Cannes and Los Cabos in the wake of the Euro Zone crisis and fears of a double dip. These concerns remained paramount despite some improvement in the near term data, and despite this being the first Summit where growth was seen strengthening in the US and Japan, and recovery in the UK and the Eurozone, but further weakening in EMEs. Growth concerns in EMEs were magnified in the run up to the St Petersburg Summit by market expectations of imminent rollback of the abundant global liquidity arising out of non-conventional monetary policies in advanced economies, pressuring the financing of the current account deficits of EMEs and their currencies. They were caught in a catch-22 type situation—standing to gain through the trading channel on account of the US recovery, but standing to lose through the financial channel on account of the US Federal reserve's response to the recovery.

Since the initial reaction of EMEs to QE was on the whole negative because it appreciated their currencies, they found it difficult to take a stronger position against this roll back at St Petersburg. While monetary policy all over the world responds to the domestic business cycle, the case of the US Fed is singular in that its policies also shape cross-border capital flows by virtue of the dollar being the effective global reserve currency. This constrains the monetary stance of other countries in ways that may be inappropriate for their own business cycles. In 2007-08, when the Fed turned on the liquidity tap EMEs, who recovered relatively quickly from the crisis, hesitated to tighten monetary policy for fear of attracting more capital inflows. India's currency appreciated despite a widening current account deficit. Now, when growth is weakening, EMEs hesitate to loosen monetary because, whatever the Fed's real intention, the resultant monetary tightening is drawing capital out of EMEs. Reserve build up in EMEs is as much a defensive response to US monetary policy as the pursuit of export led growth by some EMEs. It is for this reason that EMEs had earlier argued for greater policy flexibility in dealing with cross border capital flows in the run up to the Cannes G20 Summit.

5 Concluding Remarks

5.1 Assessing the G20 Macroeconomic Policy Response

The global financial and economic crisis of 2007–2008 elicited a strong, globally coordinated policy response orchestrated by G20 central banks and Leaders which was without precedent. This policy response was tempered by lessons learnt from the Great Depression, and the use of macroeconomic policy tools following the shift from the gold standard to the free-float Bretton Woods system, in particular the interplay between monetary and fiscal policies. Consequently, central banks and governments by and large eschewed the cardinal sins, such as contractionary monetary and fiscal policies, and the kind of extreme protectionism embodied in the infamous Smoot—Hawley tariffs of the 1930s, that culminated in the Great Depression.

The near-term impact of these extraordinary policy measures was a spectacular recovery in global economic growth in 2010. However, this recovery was fleeting. The G20 perhaps declared victory too soon at Pittsburgh, since advanced economies were still on monetary and fiscal life support. Private investment and consumer confidence—animal spirits—that alone can drive a sustainable recovery had not returned, and unemployment levels remained at near crisis highs if the discouraged workers who had stopped looking for employment are included. Recent studies, including those of the IMF itself, underscored that slow and protracted recoveries from past financial crises, especially those associated with housing busts, should have also sounded a note of caution IMF (2009b); Claessens (2008); Reinhart and Rogoff (2009b).

By 2011 the global economy was again on a downward trend. The global economy and financial system were still in shambles in advanced economies[28], and a big question mark hung over the resilience of EMDEs that were widely considered to be the new nodes of stability in the global economy. A new and dangerous fault line has opened up in the Eurozone that has slipped into a double-dip recession. This has raised questions regarding the appropriateness of the policy response, in particular whether the protracted use of essentially discretionary short-term policy instruments has more negative medium- to long-term consequences than short-term gains, and what should be the appropriate policy stance going forward.

In particular, concerns over public debt, and inflation down the road, have divided economists and policymakers into two major camps[29]. Those who are of the view that there can be no fiscal consolidation in the absence of strong growth favour continuing with macroeconomic stimulus.[30] Despite the dramatic increase in public sector deficits and debt, and large liquidity injections by central banks, sovereign borrowing costs by and large remain low and inflationary expectations continue to

---

[28] Barring periodic quarterly recoveries that have proved to be false dawns each time, as they indeed did during the long Great Depression of the 1930s. The recent rebound in US housing prices, which is widely expected to drive the recovery of consumer demand in the USA, should be read with the sobering data that shows that the housing mortgage market is now entirely dependent on state support through Fannie Mae and Freddie Mac that are now guaranteeing about 90% of all residential mortgages, and even these are being ultimately bought by the US Federal Reserve. Tett (2013).

[29] It is moot whether it was the sharp divide in policy, or bond market revolt, that originally pushed peripheral European countries towards austerity. Altman (2013). Be it as it may, the USA (fiscal stimulus) and Germany (austerity) in particular have clashed lately on the issue in international forums such as the IMF, G20 and G7. UK's about-turn from stimulus to austerity was also a conscious policy decision rather than induced by bond markets.

[30] The Nobel Laureate Paul Krugman has from the very beginning been a consistent votary of this point of view, arguing that fiscal stimulus in the US was ineffective because it was too small. Krugman has written prolifically on the subject over the years. The main arguments are summarized in a recent piece, viz. Krugman (2013). Lawrence Summers, former US Treasury Secretary is of a similar view. Summers (2013). Martin Wolf, chief economics commentator of the *Financial Times* is another high profile protagonist of the stimulus and growth camp. Wolf (2013a). It would appear that the IMF itself holds this view. Cottarelli and Jaramillo (2012); Eyraud and Weber (2013); IMF (2013c).

be well anchored. Innovations in monetary policy, such as QE, seem to have opened up unlimited monetary space even beyond zero-bound interest rates, and virtually unlimited fiscal space through rock-bottom sovereign borrowing costs. The general risk aversion in financial markets—'flight to safety'—has also increased the demand for sovereign bonds of major advanced countries. Extraordinarily high levels of public sector deficits and debt normally considered unsustainable in normal times now cohabit with rock-bottom interest rates.

The second camp is of the view that the current downturn is not entirely cyclical. There has been permanent loss of demand on account of household wealth destruction, deleveraging and rising savings. A strong, sustainable recovery from the Great Depression in the post-war period was greatly facilitated by the demographic profile of, and the large investment needs in, the worst affected economies. The worst affected economies of the Great Recession, however, had been slowing and ageing even prior to the Great Recession, and labour income that drives final consumption demand was stagnant. Their fiscal balance sheets were being strained by rising welfare expenditure. These trends were exacerbated by the recession. There are therefore lingering market concerns that the downturn in growth may not be just a short-term problem, and markets may need credible assurances that structural problems in the way of a sustainable recovery will be, and are being, fixed for animal spirits to fire again.

This camp points to the relative ineffectiveness of monetary and fiscal policies to stimulate growth, and to the lasting damaging impact of high levels of public debt on market confidence and growth potential. There is also a fear that huge liquidity injections by central banks would eventually be inflationary. An extreme view within this camp favours front loaded adjustment and austerity. The argument is that after a sharp, one-time downward adjustment, growth would revert to normal levels, while the deadly spiral of rising indebtedness would be arrested.[31]

A less extreme view that draws attention to the German experience under Chancellor Gerhard Schroeder more than a decade earlier points to the need for structural reforms alongside fiscal stimulus that should be used to cushion the pain. This approach also underpins the 'three arrows' of 'Abenomics' currently being adopted by Prime Minister Shinzo Abe in Japan. It is pertinent that IMF's macroeconomic stabilization programs in developing countries combine liquidity provision with painful structural reforms that restore and raise growth potential on a sustainable basis.

[31] The Bank of International Settlements, which has underscored that extended stimulus is only delaying the structural reforms that alone can drive a sustainable recovery, also appears to fall into this camp. The BIS view differs significantly from that of the IMF, which is clearly on the side of extended stimulus. Bank for International Settlements (2013). There are clear indications that after its disastrous brush with austerity, the European Union may be heading in this direction. The European Commission has recently decided to permit France, Spain and the Netherlands to breach the 3 % budget deficit cap for a short period provided they undertake far-reaching labour reforms. Spiegel and Daneshkhu (2013). These countries, however, still have market access to finance deficits. The big challenge in the Eurozone is on how to finance stimulus in countries such as Greece and Portugal that have effectively lost market access.

The G20 Framework initially focused aggressively on external structural adjustments, and a fair degree of rebalancing was achieved.[32] However, a similarly sharp focus on internal structural reforms and adjustment that could have restored or even raised growth potential was perhaps missing. While the immediate need was for fiscal expansion that targeted consumption, including ramping up provision for automatic stabilizers where these existed, as these can yield results quickly, spending on investment provides the added benefit of increasing long-run growth prospects, which consumption does not. In a protracted downturn, associated with financial crises, there was a manifest need for a better balance between consumption and investment-oriented fiscal expansion Baldacci et al. (2009).

The growth–austerity debate is about the short term, as nobody disputes the urgency of fiscal consolidation and structural reforms to improve competitiveness over the medium term. There are at least six sets of troubling forward-looking questions over the medium to long term for the G20 to ponder.

The first question is, how long should policymakers persist with the extraordinary macroeconomic stimulus? Although interest rates are zero bound, and fiscal deficits and public debt have risen dramatically, fiat currency appears to give almost bottomless policy space during a severe downturn: despite unprecedented levels of liquidity injection by central banks and large fiscal deficits by central banks, neither inflation nor sovereign borrowing costs have gone up in advanced economies.[33] National income in a number of major advanced economies—with the notable exception of the USA and Germany—is still below the 2007–2008 level. They have also entered a second dip recession, despite large amounts of monetary and fiscal stimulus. Their current average annual growth rates are far below the 1994–2003 (pre-boom) average. This is clearly the worst recovery from recession in the post-war period. Nevertheless, the recovery in the USA, which has had the largest and most sustained monetary and fiscal—before the recent sequestration—stimulus, is so far the most robust amongst advanced countries. The IMF is of the view that when private and external demand are in retreat, and monetary policy in a liquidity trap, fiscal multipliers are higher than usual.[34] It is therefore possible to argue that over the short term, at least, continued stimulus is necessary, and there is adequate policy space to persist with it. The US Federal Reserve has indicated that it would start exiting from its extraordinary monetary policy only when the unemployment rate dips below its target of 6.5 %, or inflation exceeds its target of 2 % U.S Federal Reserve (2013).

[32] While initially it seemed that the unwinding was mostly cyclical, it now appears likely that it has large structural components as well on account of the rise in US savings and China's new focus on domestic demand reflected in its 12th Five Year Plan.

[33] Peripheral Europe is of course the exception. But this is because sovereign debt in the Eurozone does not have the central bank backstop.

[34] In its October 2012 World Economic Outlook the IMF concluded that "consistent with research suggesting that in today's environment of substantial economic slack, monetary policy constrained by the zero lower bound, and synchronized fiscal adjustment across numerous economies, multipliers may be well above 1", *IMF, WEO, October 2012*, Chap. 1, Box 1.1, pp. 41–43.

The second set of questions pertain to the size of fiscal multipliers. If fiscal multipliers are potentially high, why was the Japanese recovery so tepid, and why is the US recovery not more robust currently? Could this be because of the fiscal mix? Governments can stimulate the economy either through tax cuts or by directly increasing expenditure. Tax cuts have the advantage of easier rollback, unlike sticky public expenditure, and also give additional income to households for consumption and expenditure. However, when balance sheets are impaired, additional income might be used to draw down debt rather than consumed or invested. If tax cuts are perceived as temporary because of the huge build-up in public debt, Ricardian equivalence may also come in the way of translating additional income into expenditure. In a recession induced by a financial crisis, therefore, tax cuts may be less effective than direct government expenditure in stimulating the economy.

Since the impact of aggressive short-term stimulus has been relatively limited so far, it could be argued that the fiscal mix needs mid-course correction; that, while the overall (expansionary) fiscal stance has been appropriate, they have mostly overlooked the role of public investment, particularly public works on a large scale undertaken during the Great Depression. The latter could substitute for the lack of private investment, create new jobs and therefore the confidence to spend as the increase in income is seen as permanent, thereby counteracting Ricardian equivalence.

Public infrastructure investment also has the potential to lay the foundations of medium-term growth since it raises growth potential and crowds in private investment, unlike other kinds of government expenditure which may actually crowd this out. Infrastructure investment has both supply-side and demand-side features. Capital expenditure also typically has higher fiscal multipliers. Some recent studies also indicate that there is a strong correlation between investment in fixed capital, growth and job creation Spilimbergo et al. (2009); UNCTAD (2012). The demand for infrastructure in developing countries, which have several shovel-ready projects, is potentially almost without limit. Accelerated financing and implementation of these projects would therefore hasten both global and internal demand rebalancing, while the associated demand for capital goods can create jobs in advanced countries as well.[35]

Since fiscal multipliers have not had the expected impact on output, particularly on employment that is more politically sensitive, there is a danger that policymakers might pin the blame on fiscal slippages abroad through international trade. The G20 has from the very beginning been alert to the dangers arising from protectionism that could amplify recessionary trends, as had happened in the 1930s. It has therefore repeatedly extended agreements on 'trade standstills', tasked the WTO to monitor protectionist measures taken by G20 countries on a continuing basis and put its weight behind initiatives for a speedy conclusion of the Doha Round of international trade negotiations to further open up trade. While it has failed spectacularly

[35] According to one estimate, $ 1 increase in investment in developing countries is likely to cause a $ 0.35 increase in capital goods exports from high-income countries. Lin (2013).

on the Doha front so far[36], it nevertheless succeeded in its efforts to keep traditional forms of protectionism at bay.[37]

This restraint, however, could also, at least in part, be on account of the changing structure of international trade[38] that has left few domestic stakeholders in favour of traditional protectionist measures, such as high tariffs and quantitative restrictions, on account of the growing import intensity of exports and the trade in intermediates. Traditional trade defence measures or tariff increases are yielding to new forms of protectionism, such as discriminatory investment measures, fiscal measures, export subsidies, discriminatory bailouts, wage subsidies, visa and residence permits including reversing offshoring, central bank measures, regulating transactions of sovereign wealth funds and so on, that are not captured in WTO's trade protectionism metrics[39].

The third set of questions concern the impact of the extraordinary monetary stimulus. There is broad consensus that the enormous liquidity injection through non-conventional measures like quantitative and credit easing was necessary to ward off the deflationary spiral during the Great Depression of the 1930s. This is because in a financial crisis, rapid deleveraging in the private sector can lead to a rapid fall in the money multiplier.

However, beyond preventing deflation, and keeping sovereign borrowing costs artificially low, monetary policy has had limited impact in stimulating the economy as traditional transmission channels of monetary policy seem to be broken. The liquidity created has instead been directed back to the central bank by depository banks, spilled over into emerging markets and into commodity and asset price infla-

[36] Practically each G20 Leaders' Communique resolved to take the Doha Round to a speedy but balanced conclusion, even setting timelines for achieving this objective. Leaders were perhaps too optimistic regarding the possibilities of trade liberalization during a steep recession when the natural instinct is to close markets.

[37] WTO, OECD and UNCTAD (2012). While a large number of minor trade restrictive measures have accumulated over time, in the aggregate, they affect only about 3.5 % of world imports and 4.4 % of G20 imports. http://www.oecd.org/daf/inv/8thG20report.pdf As a result, but for a slight dip during the deep recession in 2009 and early 2010, the ratio of global exports to global GDP (measured at market exchange rates), which had risen sharply during the preceding boom, did not decline.

Year	1995–2004	2000	2001	2002	2003	2004	2005	2006
Exports/*GDP*	23.7%	24.7%	24.0%	24.3%	25.1%	27.1%	28.4%	30.2%
Year	2007	2008	2009	2010	2011	2012	2013	
Exports/*GDP*	31.1%	32.4%	27.4%	29.8%	31.7%	31.3%	31.7%	
IMF *WEO*	October 2008 & April 2013							

[38] See footnote 24.

[39] An important caveat to WTO's measurement of protectionism is that several new measures are not included in their inventory, such as fiscal stimulus that differentiates between domestic and foreign or non-resident investors, local production requirements, visas and residence permits, financial support to domestic companies and central bank measures to enhance the functioning of credit markets and the financial system that influence international capital movements in complex ways. *Reports on G20 Trade and Investment Measures*, op. cit. p. 57. See also Evenett (2013).

tion[40] and fuelled fears of currency wars. The current disconnect between consumer and asset prices is reminiscent of the unsustainable housing sector boom in the run-up to the current crisis, with nuanced differences: the current asset inflation is in commodities and capital markets rather than in housing; the consequential 'wealth effect' had little impact on investment and economic growth Feldstein (2013) and the source of liquidity creation this time round is central, rather than shadow, banks. This situation could change, however, when private deleveraging runs its course, which it may well have in the USA.[41]

With the return of private demand and the money multiplier to normal levels, the enormous liquidity created by central banks would need to be rolled back to contain inflation. While entry into extraordinary monetary policies had a stabilizing effect on financial markets, exit from such policies could be destabilizing. Reversing QE and raising rates prematurely could choke the green shoots of recovery; reversing QE and raising rates too slowly risks unhinging inflationary expectations, as the huge amounts parked by depository institutions with central banks could quickly lead to a surge in credit. It would be well to keep in mind that just a statement by the Chairman Ben Bernanke in late May 2013 that the US Federal Reserve may reduce its asset purchases sooner rather than later sent strong tremors in international financial markets, with EMDE currencies and bond prices crashing, clearly indicating how destabilizing withdrawal of financial steroids is likely to be if not deftly managed. As interest rates rise, the price of the huge stock of assets on central bank—and also those of other banks who also moved into the safe haven of sovereign bonds—balance sheets earning near zero interest rates would also fall sharply, exposing them to potentially huge losses. The central banks losses would be passed on to the tax payer, increasing the burden of public debt.

The fourth set of perplexing forward-looking issues concerns the dramatic rise in public debt in advanced economies. This has so far not resulted in market revolt beyond the Eurozone periphery, as sovereign bond yields have fallen in inverse proportion to the increase in deficits and debt. This is not as counter-intuitive as it ap-

[40] Even Ben Bernanke, the driving force behind the creation of this liquidity, has warned that reckless speculation and search for yields in a low interest rate environment could inflate new asset bubbles. Harding et al. (2013). The Dow Jones has risen almost continuously over the past few years, scaling new highs, despite practically everybody being consistently downbeat on the prospects of global growth going forward. Junk bond yields are now where US Treasuries used to be in 2007. There is also a surge of 'low quality' capital flows to emerging markets strongly suggesting that push, rather than pull, factors are the driving force. "In the four years leading up to the Lehman Crisis in 2007 (2004–07), cumulative capital flows into EM totaled some USD3.1 trillion. This amount was substantially higher than the cumulative total of USD800 billion registered during the prior four years, 2000–2003. During the GFC (Global Financial Crisis), capital flows heading to EM collapsed, though they did not turn negative.... In the four years since the GFC (2009–2012), the cumulative capital flows into EM totalled USD3.9 trillion—even larger than the four years leading up to the GFC." Jen and Dreisin (2013).

[41] Private non-financial sector debt as a proportion of the GDP in the USA, which increased sharply during the boom preceding the credit crunch, has been declining since and is now consistent with its long-term growth trajectory. See *Bank for International Settlements, 83rd Annual Report*, op. cit. Graph II.8, p. 23.

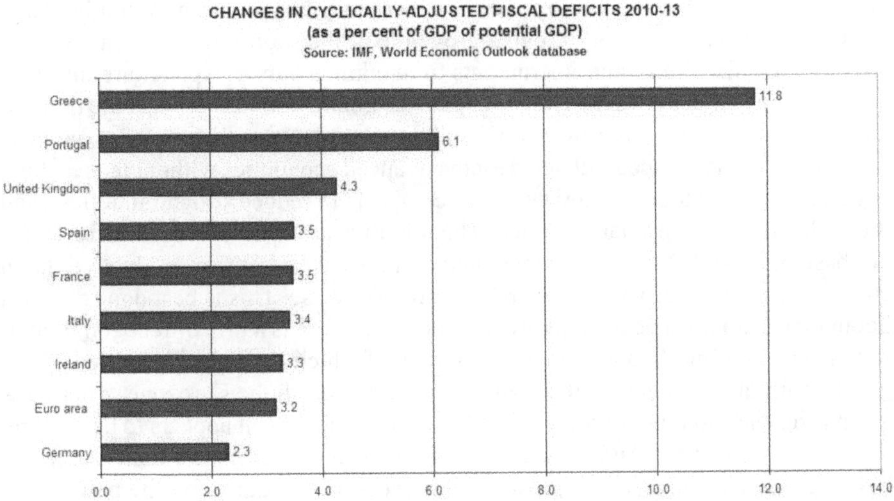

Fig. 9 Fiscal adjustment in Europe. (*Martin Wolf's Exchange* (Wolf 2013b))

pears, as deleveraging and general risk aversion in financial markets have increased the demand for risk-free assets. Large-scale purchase of long-term sovereign bonds by central banks through QE has further reduced pressure on sovereign bond yields.

However, as central banks in advanced economies normalize monetary policy current levels of debt in major advanced economies may become unsustainable, especially if trend growth remains low by historical standards on account of demand destruction and adverse demographics. At that point even if markets do not revolt outright, sovereign borrowing costs could increase significantly. It is even argued that sovereign bonds could also lose their risk-free status as the threat of sovereign default would increase substantially. Sovereigns however do not generally nominally default on domestic currency debt—they do so through inflation, or financial repression. The threat of such de facto default in advanced economies is very real, and may indeed have already begun through negative real interest rates. High levels of debt incurred by advanced countries during World War II were brought down through a combination of high growth and inflation (savings taxed through negative real interest rates). Although the western financial system has become market oriented since, with independent central banks setting monetary policy in a rule-bound manner, the toxic combination of low trend growth and high debt makes it difficult to see advanced economies simply growing their way out of high levels of debt. A return to financial repression looks inescapable.

The issue is no doubt, complex, double-edged and cutting edge, and it encapsulates the great macroeconomic conundrum of the day in advanced economies: slowing growth is associated with rising debt on the one hand; 'expansionary fiscal consolidation' is not possible when both domestic and external demand have collapsed, on the other. Therefore, as long as inflation remains low (i.e., as long as private demand is not being crowded out), there may be no option to running large deficits and increasing debt to revive growth over the short term. One can quibble over the best fiscal mix and instruments to maximize public expenditure multipliers, but John Maynard Keynes' dictum that 'the boom, not the slump, is the time for austerity' holds good. It is however difficult to see a number of advanced economies grow out of the large accumulated debt in advanced economies without far-reaching structural reforms that renegotiate social compacts to reduce structural deficits and move them towards primary balance. The initiative at St Petersburg to increase the tax base may be difficult ro achieve, and could even be counter-productive, in an environment where private investors are still risk averse. This is best done during a boom than a slump. The most likely out-come therefore is a mix of renegotiation of social compacts and financial repression, both of which have already started.

The fifth question is how the G20 should engage with the Eurozone, where it is clearly too early to talk of policy exit. Sharp fiscal adjustment appears to be pushing it into a prolonged recession. As a result it has become the biggest fault line in the global economy. There was a greater willingness at Los Cabos on the part of Eurozone Leaders to let the G20 deliberate their internal macroeconomic imbalances. However, this is a perplexing addition to the G20's menu of problems, as traditional instruments of macroeconomic stimulus and adjustment, such as the exchange rate and central bank backstop of fiscal policy, are not available to individual countries on the one hand, and there are political sensitivities arising out of the concept of the Nation State on the other. Sharp adjustments forced externally through nominal wage adjustments not only are more painful but also risk the kind of social unrest that characterized Europe in the 1930s. To the extent that the Eurozone anticipates several issues of macroeconomic management in an increasingly globalizing world that lie beyond the Nation State, the G20's success or failure to address the Eurozone question might well foretell its own fate as the institution of global economic governance of the future (Fig. 9).

The sixth and final question relates to the roadmap to guide policymakers in exiting extraordinary stimulus measures. Since there is a strong likelihood that a return to the Great Moderation growth rates may not be possible, policymakers should not be looking at the output gap, or to growth rates, to begin exiting, but to rising treasury yields and inflation. This point has already been reached in several EMDEs, but not in advanced economies. Inflation and rising yields on sovereign bonds are like distressed canaries in a goldmine, signalling the revival of animal spirits and closing of the output gap. At that point monetary policy would need to take over the mantle of macroeconomic stabilization from fiscal policy, finely balancing the need to anchor inflationary expectations by gradually normalizing interest rates and unwinding unconventional monetary measures, with the need to gradually inflate away high public debt through a degree of financial repression.

This balancing act is made even more difficult by the fact that long-term deflationary forces, predating the financial crisis, may have weakened the role of consumer price inflation as a robust marker of business cycles. Consumer price inflation was subdued despite unprecedented levels of growth and liquidity in the run-up to the global financial crisis, even as the overheating spilled over into asset markets. In the light of their experience in the run-up to the global financial crisis, central banks may now be more willing to call asset bubbles before they burst even if consumer price inflation is below their targets Sheel (2013b).

These are all difficult questions to which there are no ready answers, as the past provides little guidance. Perhaps it is because of these complexities of macroeconomic policy formulation in a rapidly integrating global economy that even economists seem to be wringing their hands in despair, Blanchard et al. (2010, 2013) and policymakers are having to turn elsewhere for sage advice, such as *St Augustine* for the short term (Lord make me chaste, but not yet), or *Alice in Wonderland* for the long term (Jam yesterday and jam tomorrow, but never jam today), and even to Aesop's Fables such as *The Ant and the Grasshopper* (to understand the dynamics of global imbalances) and *The Fox who Lost its Tail* (building a consensus on back-breaking debt).

5.2 Assessing the G20 as the Premier Institution of Global Economic Governance

The first two summits at Washington DC and London marked the first stage of policy cooperation, culminating in the trillion-dollar London Summit. G20 Leaders resolved to do whatever was necessary to stall the slide in the global economy through an aggressive, coordinated macroeconomic response to the financial crisis. It is pertinent, however, that no country-specific commitments were asked for, and none were given. The policy response was also fairly undifferentiated across countries. The G20 deliberations fed into domestic policy, with each country doing what it considered appropriate. Though there were no country-specific commitments, this policy coordination was, nevertheless, a spectacular success, even though questions are now being asked whether the recipe itself was fully appropriate. A second Great Depression and deflation have been avoided but growth remains below trend.

At the third G20 Summit at Pittsburgh, it seemed that the coordinated response had pulled the global economy back from the brink of a second Great Depression. The G20 now turned its attention to long-term structural problems impeding a return to strong, sustainable and balanced growth, going forward. The G20 Framework, or Mutual Assessment Process, was conceived at Pittsburgh while preparing to exit from the aggressive and coordinated stimulus.

The second stage of policy cooperation at the fourth Summit at Toronto (2010) was differentiated across countries because of market reactions, a two-speed recovery and the need to rebalance global demand for strong, sustainable and balanced growth. Consequently, unlike the first stage, the G20 arrived at different policy prescriptions for different groups of countries: advanced deficit, advanced surplus, developing surplus, developing deficit and resource-rich economies. Perhaps because it was quite clear to what group each G20 country belonged, once again there were no country-specific commitments, apart from some general fiscal commitments given by advanced economies to reassure financial markets, since the G20 seemed mindful of the potential divisiveness of 'naming and shaming'.

The third stage was at the fifth Summit at Seoul, where there was a realization that there was little forward movement in the desired direction. The possibility of country-specific commitments was seriously considered for the first time. A consensus was, therefore, arrived at to develop indicators on the basis of which country-specific commitments could be worked out and, therefore, made more acceptable.

The fourth stage of policy cooperation was at the last G20 Summit at Cannes, in the form of the Cannes Action Plan, which contains country-specific commitments. However, problems regarding measurement and timelines persist and are still unresolved, especially since these commitments were made at a time when a cloud was hanging over the global recovery, and this cloud appears even darker now. An attempt was, therefore, made to distinguish between short-term and long-term policy commitments. Also, commitments were 'country-led' in the best G20 tradition, and mostly what the countries had committed as part of their own domestic policies in the public domain. The G20 debate is, nevertheless, clearly weighing on the trajectory of domestic policies.

Although the G20 *Framework* exercise has not resulted in an agreed set of enforceable macroeconomic rules, these four stages nevertheless indicate that the G20 has incrementally committed itself to more intrusive policy coordination within a relatively short period of time. As the G20 moves towards its fifth stage of macroeconomic policy coordination of assessing country commitments and holding them accountable, caution is warranted in placing unrealistic expectations on the budding G20 process going forward.

First, it is for the first time that the world's biggest advanced and developing economies are sitting at the same table and talking to each other, rather than talking past each other from separate forums. Although economic interests are beginning to converge, the trust necessary for even effective discretionary policy cooperation will take some time to be on a firm footing. Beyond this, agreement on enforceable rules-based policy coordination would run into issues of sovereignty, as they have in the case of the European Union. The past record of rules-based policy coordination gives little cause for optimism (Bird 2012).

Second, domestic policies respond to changing circumstances. For instance, prospects for the global economy have deteriorated considerably since commitments for fiscal consolidation were given at Toronto. How can commitments and assessments accommodate the need for such dynamic policy shifts? In the deliberations leading up to the Toronto Summit, there were differences of opinion over whether fiscal commitments should be date specific or benchmarked to the pace of recovery. This issue remains as relevant as ever.

Third, a huge divide now appears to have opened up between what electorates and markets expect from governments. Both electorates and markets are in revolt. Electorates are voting against severe austerity in country after country in Europe, unseating governments. While sovereigns should not allow themselves to be held hostage by the markets, they ignore markets at their own peril, as the taxpayer has to foot the bill of market revolt upfront. They have already started footing the bill through negative real deposit rates. A sharp rise in public debt always follows deep crises and recessions, but this time round, markets do not seem too sanguine regarding the prospects for long-term growth necessary to bring down debt ratios going forward in countries where public debt has risen appreciably, and are, therefore, demanding higher returns. As a result, policymakers need to reassure markets how debt dynamics would be managed by persuasively clarifying or creating the engines of future growth.

Fourth, how can the G20 nudge countries' policies in mutually agreed directions and hold sovereigns accountable for commitments given, especially since these are not legally binding, and in the absence of any enforcement mechanism? The sovereignty of internal policies of nation states has been well recognized at least since the Treaty of Westphalia that is almost three-and-a-half centuries old. A distinction needs to be drawn between coordination and commitment. In the early stages the G20's focus was on coordinating policies—developing a consensus on what needed to be done, with each country contributing what it could, depending on individual-country circumstances. The G20 has been much less successful as it moved towards trying to obtain country commitments and holding their feet to the fire. The spirit of cooperation quickly evaporated amidst 'naming and shaming', which some members of the G20 had warned against in the early G20 deliberations.

Alongside these four negatives, however, is the fifth, which is a clear positive for global cooperation going forward. It is increasingly clear that economic integration is moving far ahead of political integration. The success of domestic policy actions in a fast-integrating world with growing market and policy spillovers is increasingly linked to global outcomes. Domestic business cycles are becoming more and more globally aligned. If rebalancing does not take place, growth will decline everywhere, but if rebalancing is uncoordinated, the outcomes could be even worse. Policy cooperation, and beyond that policy harmonization or convergence, is potentially a win–win. This harmonization is of course the work of specialized multilateral fora like the WTO (trade), Basel Committee on Banking Supervision (BCBS) (financial regulation), United Nations Framework Convention on Climate Change (UNFCCC) (climate policies), Global Forum (Tax), etc. However, given the systemic importance of the G20 aggregation, the forum could give the decisive push where required if their Leaders are firm in their resolve, as they were at the high point of the global financial crisis. The resolve has understandably weakened as the recovery takes hold. The benefits and hazards before such cooperation and harmonization are most clearly manifest in the case of the Eurozone and the EU, which is pushing the envelope of the Nation State beyond the limits of Westphalian sovereignty in place since 1648. To a great extent, the challenges ahead facing the G20 are similar. What is needed at this juncture is a new political economy and institutional structure to manage globalization, built on mutual trust and cooperation. Seen in this perspective, the G20 is a brave new experiment pushing the boundaries of globalization to harvest this cooperative dividend, and its Leaders will no doubt learn how to do so as they go along.

References

Altman R (2013) A Response to Martin Wolf, Financial Times, May 13, 2013. (http://blogs.ft.com/the-a-list/2013/05/13/a-response-to-martin-wolf/?#axzz2TE0DXTBd)

Baldacci E, Gupta S, Mulas-Granados C (2009) How effective is Fiscal policy response in systemic banking crises? IMF Working Paper, WP/09/160, July 2009. (http://www.frpii.org/english/Portals/0/Library/Fiscal%20Policy/How%20Effective%20is%20Fiscal%20Policy%20Response%20in%20Systemic%20Banking%20Crises.pdf)

Bank for International Settlements (2013) 83rd Annual Report, 1 April 2012–31 March 2013, Basel, June 23, 2013. (http://www.bis.org/publ/arpdf/ar2013e.pdf)

Bird G (2012) Dealing with global economic imbalances: the political economy of policy coordination. Global Econ Rev 41:4. (Perspectives on East Asian Economies and Industries, December 2012, pp 299–317. http://dx.doi.org/10.1080/1226508x.2012.738781)

Blanchard O, Leigh D (2013) Growth forecast errors and Fiscal multipliers, IMF, WP/13/1, January 2013. (http://www.imf.org/external/pubs/ft/wp/2013/wp1301.pdf)

Blanchard O, Spilimbergo A, Symansky S, Cottarelli C (2008) Fiscal policy for the crisis, IMF Staff Position Note SPN/08/01, December 29, 2008. (p 12)

Blanchard O, Dell'Ariccia G, Mauro P (2010) Rethinking macroeconomic policy, I M F Staff Position Note SPN/10/03, February 12, 2010. (http://www.imf.org/external/pubs/ft/sdn/2010/sdn1303.pdf)

Blanchard O, Dell'Ariccia G, Mauro P (2013) Rethinking macro: getting granular, I M F Staff Position Note SDN/13/03, April 2103. (http://www.imf.org/external/pubs/ft/sdn/2013/sdn1303.pdf)

Cannes (G20) Summit final declaration—building our common future: renewed collective action for the benefit of all Cannes, November 4, 2011

Claessens S, Kose MA, Terrones ME (2008) What happens during recessions, crunches and busts? IMF, WP/08/274. December 2008. (www.aeaweb.org/annual_mtg_papers/2009/retrieve.php?pdfid=208)

Communiqué. G20 Meeting of Ministers and Governors, Sao Paulo, Brazil, 8–9, November, 2008

Cottarelli C, Jaramillo L (2012) Walking hand in hand: fiscal policy and growth in advanced economies, IMF. Working Paper, WP/12/137, May 2012. (http://www.imf.org/external/pubs/ft/wp/2012/wp12137.pdf)

Declaration of the (G20) Summit on financial markets and the world economy, Washington DC, November 15, 2008

Evenett SJ (2013) Protectionism's quiet return: the GTA's Pre-G8 Summit Report, VOX, June 13, 2013. (http://www.voxeu.org/article/protectionism-s-quiet-return-gta-s-pre-g8-summit-report)

Eyraud L, Weber A (2013) The challenge of Debt reduction during fiscal consolidation, IMF. Working Paper, WP/13/67, March 2013. (http://www.imf.org/external/pubs/ft/wp/2013/wp1367.pdf)

Feldstein M (2013) The federal reserve's policy dead end. The Wall Street Journal, May 10, 2013. (http://online.wsj.com/article/SB10001424127887324326504578467592090881604.html)

G20 Coherent Conclusions for the Management of Capital Flows Drawing on Country Experiences, October 15, 2011

G20 Finance Ministers' and Central Bank Governors' Communiqué, March 14, 2009, issued from Horsham, U.K

G20 Leaders Declaration, Los Cabos, Mexico, June 19, 2012

G20 Leaders Statement: The Pittsburgh Summit, September 24–25, 2009, Pittsburgh

Harding R, Mackenzie M, Ross A (2013) Bernanke warns banks on excessive risk, Financial Times, May 10, 2013. (http://www.ft.com/intl/cms/s/0/b4b474d4-b978-11e2-9a9f-00144feabdc0.html#axzz2T2e9ZV00)

IMF (2007) Staff Report on the Multilateral Consultation on Global Imbalances with China, the Euro Area, Japan, Saudi Arabia, and the United States June 29, 2007

IMF (2008) World Economic Outlook, October 2008

IMF (2009a) WEO Update, January 2009
IMF (2009b) World Economic Outlook, April 2009. (p 113, http://www.imf.org/external/pubs/ft/weo/2009/01/pdf/text.pdf)
IMF (2010) WEO Update January 26, 2010
IMF (2011) World Economic Outlook, September 2011
IMF (2012a) World Economic Outlook, April 2012
IMF (2012b) World Economic Outlook, October 2012
IMF (2012c) The Liberalization and Management of Capital Flows—An Institutional View, November 14, 2012. (http://www.imf.org/external/np/pp/eng/2012/111412.pdf)
IMF (2012d) People's Republic of China, 2012 Article IV Consultation, IMF Country Report No. 12/195, 2012. (http://www.imf.org/external/pubs/ft/scr/2012/cr12195.pdf)
IMF (2013a) Fiscal Monitor April 2013
IMF (2013b) Global Financial Stability Report, April 2013
IMF (2013c) Greece: ex post evaluation of exceptional access under the 2010 Stand-By Arrangement, IMF Country Report No. 13/156, June 2013. (http://www.imf.org/external/pubs/ft/scr/2013/cr13156.pdf)
Jen SL, Dreisin A (2013) Assessing the 'Sudden Stop' risks for EM. SLJ Macro Partners, May 10, 2013. (http://research.sljmacro.com/rp//521/process.clsp?EmailId=169330&Token=20228271CE54C7EC69DE041C97831318D)
Krugman P (2013) How the case for austerity has crumbled, The New York Review of Books, June 2013. (http://www.nybooks.com/articles/archives/2013/jun/06/how-case-austerity-has-crumbled/?pagination=false)
Lin JY (2013) How to kick-start a global recovery. The Wall Street Journal, July 1, 2013. (http://online.wsj.com/article/SB10001424127887324183204578567542350561774.html)
London (G20) Summit—Leaders' Statement, 2 April 2009
National Bureau of Economic Research (2010) Determination of December 2007 Peak in Economic Activity, April 13, 2010
OECD (2013) Action Plan on Base Erosion and Profit Sharing. http://www.oecd.org/ctp/BEPSActionPlan.pdf
Rangarajan C, Sheel A (2013) Growth or austerity: the policy dilemma,. Money and Finance, ICRA Bulletin, February 2013. (p 47)
Reinhart CM, Rogoff KS (2009a) This time is different. Eight Centuries of Financial Folly, Princeton University Press, 2009
Reinhart CM, Rogoff KS (2009b) The aftermath of financial crises, NBER Working Paper Series # 14656, January 2009. (http://www.nber.org/papers/w14656.pdf?new_window=1)
Report of the G20 Study Group on Commodities under the chairmanship of Mr. Hiroshi Nakaso, November 2011
Sheel A (2013a) The Central Banker's Brahmastra, Business Standard, New Delhi, April 2, 2013. (http://www.business-standard.com/article/opinion/the-central-banker-s-brahmastra-113040100582_1.html)
Sheel A (2013b) Misunderstood dog has not barked, yet, Financial Times, April 19, 2013. (http://www.ft.com/intl/cms/s/0/48b1b55e-a770-11e2-bfcd-00144feabdc0.html#axzz2XWqCwN8n)
Spiegel P, Daneshkhu S (2013) EU Eases Hard Line on Austerity, Financial Times, May 29, 2013. (http://www.ft.com/intl/cms/s/0/22348284-c7a6-11e2-be27-00144feab7de.html#axzz2UpgvJHU1)
Spilimbergo A, Symansky S, Schindler M (2009) Fiscal Multipliers, I M F Staff Position Note SPN/09/11, May 20, 2009
Summers LH (2013) It is no time for faster cuts to the US budget deficit. Financial Times, June 3, 2013. (http://www.ft.com/intl/cms/s/2/13ce15ac-c878-11e2-8cb7-00144feab7de.html#axzz2V6oICF8C)
Summers LH, DeLong JB (2012) Fiscal policy in a depressed economy, March 20, 2012. (http://www.brookings.edu/~/media/Files/Programs/ES/BPEA/2012_spring_bpea_papers/2012_spring_BPEA_delongsummers.pdf)

Tett G (2013) Markets insight: US Mortgage Market Depends on State Support, Financial Times, April 25, 2013. (http://www.ft.com/intl/cms/s/0/1d311082-adba-11e2–82b8-00144feabdc0.html#axzz2YFiLIkyy)

The G20 Toronto Summit Declaration, Toronto, June 27, 2010

The G20 Seoul Summit Leaders' Declaration, Seoul, November 12, 2010

UNCTAD (2012) Background note: macroeconomic policies to promote growth and job creation. Special high-level meeting of the Economic and Social Council with the Bretton Woods institutions, the World Trade Organization, and the United Nations Conference on Trade and Development. New York, March 12–13, 2012. (http://www.un.org/esa/ffd/ecosoc/springmeetings/2012/Unctad_BGNote.pdf p.3)

U.S Federal Reserve (2013) Transcript of Chairman Bernanke's Press Conference June 19, 2013. (http://www.federalreserve.gov/mediacenter/files/FOMCpresconf20130619.pdf)

Wolf M (2013a) The sad record of fiscal austerity, Financial Times, February 26, 2013. (http://www.ft.com/intl/cms/s/0/73219452-7f49-11e2-89ed-00144feabdc0.html#axzz2XWqCwN8n)

Wolf M (2013b) Austerity in the Eurozone and U.K: kill or cure? Financial Times, May 23, 2013. 6 a.m. (http://blogs.ft.com/martin-wolf-exchange/2013/05/23/austerity-in-the-eurozone-and-the-uk-kill-or-cure/)

WTO (2011) Trade patterns and global value chains in East Asia: From trade in goods to trade in tasks, 2011. (http://www.wto.org/english/res_e/booksp_e/stat_tradepat_globvalchains_e.pdf)

WTO, OECD and UNCTAD (2012) Reports on G20 Trade and Investment Measures (Mid-May to mid-October 2012), October 31, 2012

Austerity, Growth, and Public Policy

Denis Medvedev and Smriti Seth

Since the onset of the 2008–2009 economic crisis, global growth decelerated to 2.8 % from 4.8 % during 2003–2007. In addition to slower growth, fiscal buffers in high-income and developing economies are much weaker than prior to the crisis. The average general government deficit has increased from 2.5 to 6.7 % of gross domestic product (GDP) for high-income and from 0.1 to 1.8 % of GDP for developing economies between 2003–2007 and 2008–2011. General government debt in advanced economies reached an unprecedented level of 105 % of GDP in 2011, compared to an average of 77 % between 2003 and 2007.

There is broad consensus in the literature that high debt can significantly depress growth. Reinhart et al. (2012) showed that a vast majority of high-debt episodes coincide with substantially slower growth regardless of the effects on real interest rates.[1] Furthermore, they find that the average duration of high-debt overhang was 23 years and, once a debt overhang lasted 5 years, it was more likely to last 10 years or more. Thus, the deterioration in fiscal indicators and weak demand conditions in a number of advanced economies have reignited the debate on the role of fiscal policy in supporting economic growth.

Two diverging views on ways to stimulate economic activity without compromising long-term solvency have emerged. One view, following Keynesian tradition, proposes that fiscal stimulus can increase the rate at which the output gap is closed, minimizing the total cost of a recession and bringing down debt ratios. Another

The original version of this note was prepared for the 4th Annual International Conference on issues of concern for G20 countries, organized by ICRIER on 7–9 October 2012 in New Delhi, India. The views expressed here are those of the authors and should not be attributed to the World Bank, its Executive Directors, or the countries they represent.

[1] See also Kumar and Woo (2010), who find a significant negative impact of high initial debt-to-GDP ratio (above 90 %) on subsequent growth in per capita income.

D. Medvedev (✉) · S. Seth
Economic Policy and Poverty Unit, The World Bank,
70 Lodi Estate, New Delhi, India
e-mail: dmedvedev@worldbank.org

M. Callaghan et al. (eds.), *Global Cooperation Among G20 Countries*,
DOI 10.1007/978-81-322-1659-9_22, © Springer India 2014

view, more in line with neoclassical thought, suggests that fiscal stimulus under the current conditions could further weaken macro fundamentals and be detrimental to growth; conversely, austerity could be good for growth through the process of "expansionary consolidation."

Seminal work by Keynes (1936), published during the Great Depression, argued that reigning in demand when output falls below potential could exacerbate economic downturns. The observed response of economic activity to fiscal consolidation depends on the sign and magnitude of the fiscal multiplier, which most authors find to be positive. For example, International Monetary Fund (IMF) (2010), DeLong and Summers (2012), and Batini et al. (2012) argue that immediate fiscal consolidation can worsen the ongoing recession and further raise debt–GDP levels. IMF (2010) identified deficit-reducing policy actions in 15 economies during 1980–2009 and concluded that consolidations equal to 1 % of GDP reduce output and domestic demand by 0.5 % and 1 %, respectively, within 2 years and raise unemployment by 0.3 %.[2]

Recent studies show that the magnitude of the fiscal multiplier may vary depending on the interest rate environment and the phase of the economic cycle. Christiano et al. (2011) find that the government-spending multiplier is much larger when interest rates are at near-zero levels, than when monetary policy follows the Taylor rule. Denes et al. (2012) also note that a cut in public spending, when interest rates face a lower bound, can worsen the budget deficit by shrinking the tax base. In addition, DeLong and Summers (2012) express caution about the presence of hysteresis effects under the current conditions in the USA and suggest that fiscal stimulus can help address these, making the 'stimulative' deficit self-financing. Batini et al. (2012) find that fiscal multipliers are significantly larger during downturns than in upturns and front-loaded consolidations during recessions can aggravate output loss and delay the reduction in debt-GDP ratios. Similarly, Auerbach and Gorodnichenko (2012) find that fiscal multipliers associated with government spending can fluctuate from being near-zero in normal times to about 2.5 during recessions. Eggerston and Krugman (2012) argue that lower output and lower income, together with a poorly functioning financial system, could imply that consumption and investment may depend more on current than on future income, leading to larger multipliers.

On the other hand, some authors argue that fiscal consolidations can stimulate growth by reducing expected future taxation and strengthening the credibility of fiscal policy. Giavazzi and Pagano (1990) first explored the possibility of an 'expansionary consolidation' using evidence from Denmark and Ireland in the 1980s. They found that fiscal consolidation could generate expectations of a permanent increase in private income and thereby stimulate today's private demand and output. More recently, Alesina and Ardagna (2010) identified episodes of fiscal consolidation

[2] The identification methodology used by IMF is similar to the historical approach of Romer and Romer (2010). See Perotti (2012) for a critique of this methodology.

during 1970–2007 as a decline in the cyclically adjusted primary balance (CAPB).[3] Using this data set, they found that spending cuts, in several episodes, were associated with economic expansions. Alesina et al. (2012) repeated the analysis using the Devries et al. (2011) data set (also used by IMF 2010) and showed that these results are robust to alternative ways of identifying episodes of fiscal adjustments. More specifically, Ilzetzki et al. (2010) show that in countries with central government debt above 60 % of GDP, fiscal stimulus can be counterproductive in the long run and, at best, neutral in the short run.

The likelihood that a fiscal consolidation may be expansionary depends crucially on the type of consolidation. According to Alesina and Ardagna (2010), reduction in government spending is much less likely to be reversed (compared to tax adjustments) and, therefore, has a positive wealth effect on individuals via a reduction in future taxation, which in turn stimulates consumption. The authors find that, in expansionary cases, almost 60 % of the adjustment came from spending cuts. Instead, more than 60 % of the budget correction was on the tax side in the case of unsuccessful and contractionary adjustments. Spending cuts are usually considered more credible, reducing risk premia on long-term interest rates and boosting confidence. Therefore, spending cuts can have a positive effect on private investment, while tax increases can hurt investments through the labor market and firm profitability, as shown in Alesina et al. (2002). IMF (2010) also suggests that central banks may view spending-based deficit cuts more favorably, possibly because they interpret them as a signal of stronger commitment to fiscal discipline and are, therefore, more willing to provide monetary stimulus.[4]

Reorientation of spending toward more productive uses can help minimize adverse effects on growth. Early work by Barro (1990) and Baxter and King (1993) showed that a change in the composition of government spending toward more productive expenditures can improve the economy's growth rate over the long term. This effect stems from the positive impacts of government spending on private sector productivity through the supply of infrastructure, research and development (R&D), education, or health services which the private sector does not provide in optimal quantities. Moreover, a consolidation based on cuts to less productive but politically sensitive items, such as transfers may be less contractionary because it signals a credible commitment to long-term deficit reduction. Gemmell (2007) notes that more recent studies for developed countries tend to find significant positive growth impacts from education, health and/or transport, and communications spending, with 'productive spending' in Organisation for Economic Co-operation and Development (OECD) countries—especially when financed through reductions in nonproductive spending or through increases in 'non-distorting' taxes—generally having a positive impact on growth, while 'distortionary taxes' have a generally negative effect.

---

[3] Authors of IMF (2010) argue that using a decline in the CAPB as an indication of fiscal consolidation ignores exogenous improvements in the primary balance and could result in an expansionary bias on its effect on output.

[4] However, Alesina et al. (2012) argue that robust heterogeneous response of output to tax-based and expenditure-based consolidations does not hold for monetary policy.

Complementary policies can enhance the expansionary effects of fiscal consolidation. Policies such as liberalization of goods and labor markets can limit the potential negative effects of consolidations on output and improve the likelihood of expansionary effects. Income policies such as wage agreements can reinforce the effects of fiscal adjustments that slow down the growth of public sector wages. Alesina and Ardagna (2012) and Perotti (2012) find that such wage moderation, generated through supply side reforms, can more than compensate for the small recessionary effects of spending cuts on the demand side. IMF (2010) also highlights the impact of fiscal tightening on net exports, with a considerably larger improvement in exports under spending-based measures but a larger decline in imports during tax-based adjustments. However, since exports cannot increase everywhere, simultaneous consolidations are likely to be more challenging.

Overall, studies show that fiscal consolidation can have a positive impact on growth, but these effects are not guaranteed and are more likely to work when policy commitments are credible, spending cuts focus on unproductive expenditure, and consolidation is accompanied by complementary policies. The mixed nature of the evidence is also reflected in the state of debate on these issues in the G20. During the earlier stages of the global financial crisis (e.g., 2008 and 2009 G20 summits), the consensus was oriented toward expansionary macroeconomic policies (Nelson 2013).[5] However, during later stages, amid growing uncertainty in Europe and the Greek sovereign crisis (e.g., the 2010 summit), most high-income G20 members embraced "growth-friendly" fiscal consolidation following the advice of Reinhart and Rogoff (2010) and others who warned against the perils of debt overhang. The adoption and intensity of austerity policies were, however, not uniform across members. Some of the more vulnerable EU countries, such as Greece, Ireland, Portugal, and Spain, initiated immediate consolidation as part of financial bailout packages by European Central Bank (ECB) and IMF. On the other hand, the USA adopted a more gradual approach through a budget sequestration program, which was adopted in 2011 but went into force in 2013.

References

Alesina A, Ardagna S (2010) Large changes in fiscal policy: taxes versus spending. In: JR Brown (ed) Tax policy and the economy, vol 24. The University of Chicago Press, Cambridge

Alesina A, Favero C, Giavazzi F (2012) The output effect of Fiscal Consolidations. National Bureau of Economic Research, Working Paper 18336, August 2012.

Alesina A, Ardagna S, Perotti R, Schiantarelli F (2002) Fiscal policy, profits and investment. Am Econ Rev 92(3):571–589

Auerbach A, Gorodnichenko Y (2012) Measuring the output responses to Fiscal Policy. Am Econ J: Econ Policy 4:1–27

[5] Latvia was a notable exception. Suffering from capital flight and a balance of payment (BoP) crisis after the onset of the global financial crisis, Latvia responded with fiscal austerity in 2008/2009 and subsequently experienced one of the fastest recoveries in Europe.

Barro RJ. (1990) Government spending in a simple model of endogenous growth. J Polit Econ 98(October):s103–s125
Batini N, Callegari G, Melina G (2012) Successful austerity in the United States, Europe, and Japan. IMF Working Paper WP/12/190
Baxter M, Robert GK (1993) Fiscal policy in general equilibrium. Am Econ Rev 83(3):315–34
Christiano L, Eichenbaum M, Rebelo S (2011) When is the government spending multiplier large? J Polit Econ 119(1):78–121
DeLong JB, Summers L (2012) Fiscal policy in a depressed economy. Brookings Papers on Economic Activity, March.
Denes M, Eggertsson GB, Gilbukh S (2012) Deficits, Public Debt Dynamics, and Tax and Spending Multipliers. Federal Reserve Bank of New York, Staff Report No. 551
Devries P, Guajardo J, Leigh D, Pescatori A (2011) A New Action-Based Dataset of Fiscal Consolidation. IMF Working Paper WP/11/128
Eggertsson GB, Krugman P (2012) Debt, deleveraging, and the liquidity trap. Q J Econ 127(3):1469–1513
Gemmel N (2007) The composition of public expenditure and economic growth: a Report to the World Bank. Manuscript, January 2007
Giavazzi F, Pagano M (1990 May) Can severe Fiscal Contractions be expansionary? Tales of two small European Countries. National Bureau of Economic Research, Working Paper no. 3372
Iltzetzki E, Medoza EG, Vegh CA (2010, October) How big (small?) are Fiscal Multipliers? National Bureau of Economic Research, Working Paper 16479
International Monetary Fund (2010) World Economic Outlook, Chapter 3
Keynes JM (1936) The general theory of employment, interest and money. Macmillan, Cambridge University Press
Kumar M, Woo J (2010) Public Debt and Growth. IMF Working Paper WP/10/174
Nelson RM (2013) The G20 and International Economic Cooperation. Congressional Research Service
Perotti R (2012) The austerity myth: growth without pain? forthcoming In: Alesina A, Giavazzi F (eds) Fiscal policy after the great recession. University of Chicago Press and NBER
Reinhart C, Rogoff K (May 2010) Growth in a time of Debt. Am Econ Rev 100(2):573–578
Reinhart C, Reinhart V, Rogoff K (2012) Public debt overhangs: advanced-economy episodes since 1800. J Econ Perspect 26(3):69–86
Romer CD, Romer DH (2010) The macroeconomic effects of tax changes: estimates based on a new measure of fiscal shocks. Am Econ Rev 100(3):763–801

India and Fiscal Austerity

Shankar Acharya

1 Introduction

Following the global financial crisis of 2007–2009 and the "Great Recession" of that period, there was remarkable consensus across economists and policy-makers in most major nations, especially industrial countries, that governments and central banks had to follow strongly expansionary fiscal and monetary policies to counter the recessionary impact of the financial crisis and prevent the "Great Recession" from degenerating into another Great Depression of the 1930s kind. The G20 summit communiqués of the time, especially those of the London Summit (June 2009) and the Pittsburgh Summit (September 2009), reflected this broad consensus. By the time of the Toronto Summit (June 2010), this consensus had begun to fray. Economic recovery had begun in much of the world by late 2009, prompting calls for gradual exit from exceptionally expansionary policies. The calls for prudence were strengthened by the Greek fiscal crisis, which, over the spring of 2010, snowballed into a wider threat to sovereign debt in southern Europe, to the viability of the euro and the durability of the global economic and financial recovery. Within a remarkably short span of time, the consensus in favour of fiscal stimulus was rent by growing calls for fiscal prudence and austerity. Since then, the policy and intellectual debates over issues of stimulus, timing of "exit," and need for austerity have been centre-stage in industrial nations.

In India, the fiscal policy narrative runs somewhat differently. First, as Fig. 1 shows, over the last 30 years, fiscal austerity has been notable by its absence in India. The combined deficit of central and state governments has typically been in the range of 7–10 % of gross domestic product (GDP), except for 5 years, two in the mid-1990s and three in the mid-2000s. The revenue deficit (government

The views in this chapter are personal

S. Acharya (✉)
Indian Council for Research on International Economic Relation (ICRIER),
New Delhi, India
e-mail: acharya.shankar@gmail.com

M. Callaghan et al. (eds.), *Global Cooperation Among G20 Countries*,
DOI 10.1007/978-81-322-1659-9_23, © Springer India 2014

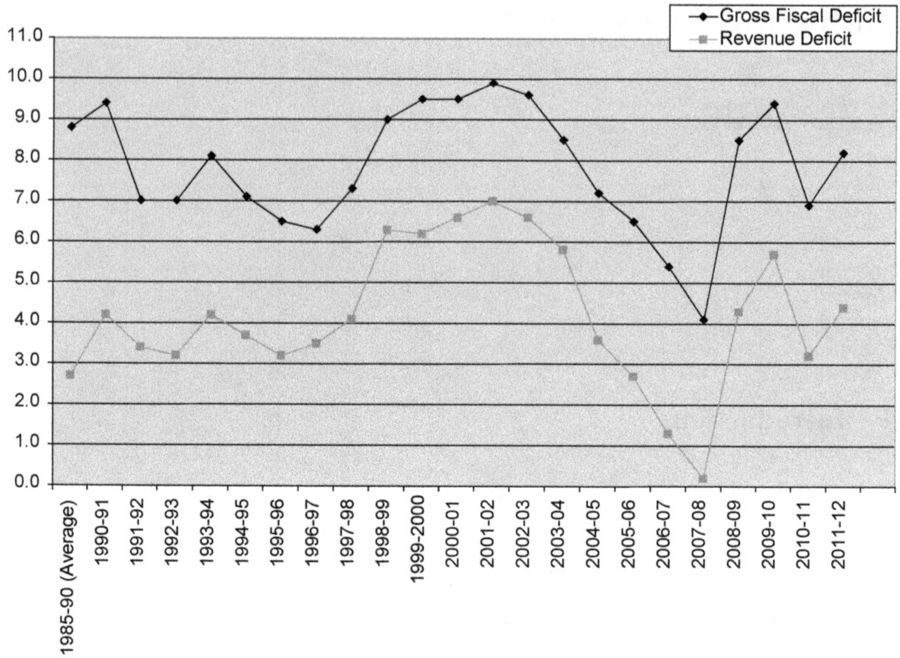

Fig. 1 Combined deficits of Central and State Governments (% of GDP). (Sources: Handbook of statistics of the Indian Economy, RBI 2011–2012 and RBI Annual Report for 2011–2012)

dis-savings, approximately) has often been high. This reflects a number of factors, including a bias towards fiscal populism in the country's democratic, competitive politics and a somewhat narrow tax base. Second, in the last 20 years, the two best periods of economic growth, 1992–1997 and 2003–2008, have been associated with significant fiscal consolidation, if not "austerity" (Fig. 2). Periods of high fiscal deficits have not engendered high growth. Third, the latest period of resurgent fiscal populism, beginning 2008, did help counter the recessionary impact of the global crisis, initially. However, the persistence of large deficits fuelled high inflation, stoked growing external imbalances and contributed to the sharp slowdown in economic growth in the past 2 years. Fourth, because of the nature and content of the spending surge in 2008/2009 and since, the next round of fiscal consolidation is likely to be difficult. These points merit some elaboration.

2 Fiscal Policy and Growth: A Heuristic Account

It is widely accepted that the balance of payments crisis of 1991 had manifold roots, including the series of large fiscal deficits (averaging around 9% of GDP in 1985–1990), an overvalued exchange rate, excessive regulation of industry and trade and growing recourse to external commercial borrowing to fund rising external

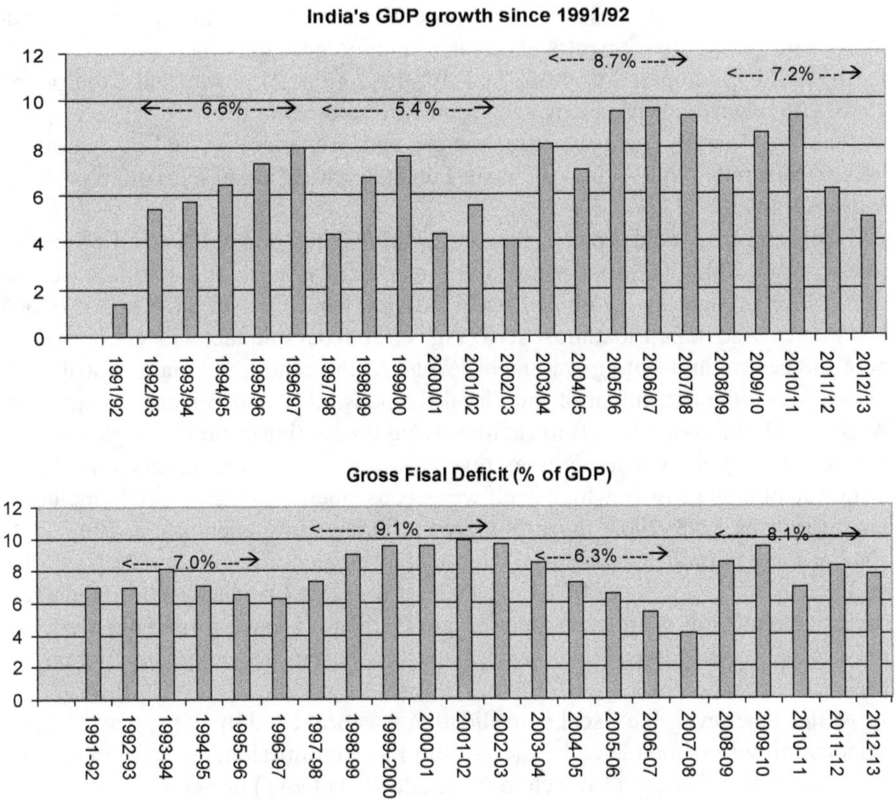

Fig. 2 India's growth and deficits. (Sources: Economic Survey 2012–2013 and handbook of Statistics of the Indian Economy, RBI 2011–2012 and RBI Annual Report for 2011–2012)

deficits[1]. The partial fiscal consolidation that was carried out post-crisis and brought the fiscal deficit down from 9 % of GDP to around 6.5 % by 1996 certainly supported the stabilization and structural reform programme undertaken by the government in response to the crisis. However, it is likely that most of the impetus for a quick and strong growth recovery came from the decontrol of industry, devaluation of the rupee and the opening up to foreign trade and capital flows.

The 5 years of strong growth, 1992–1997, faltered thereafter as India underwent 3 years of unstable coalition governments; the Asian financial crisis of 1997–1998 took some toll and the partially successful fiscal consolidation was abruptly reversed, mainly on account of massive government pay increases at central and state levels, resulting from implementation of the Fifth Pay Commission recommendations. As a result of this and low revenue buoyancy, the combined fiscal deficit shot back up to 9 % of GDP in 1998/1999 and stayed at these high levels for the

[1] See, for example, Acharya (2006), Ahluwalia (2002), Joshi and Little (1996) and Panagariya (2008).

next 4 years. The penalties were paid in terms of high real interest rates, crowding out of private investment and lower economic growth, which averaged 5.4% in 1997–2003, compared to 6.6% in 1992–1997 (Fig. 2). Fortunately, the period 1998–2003 was quite productive for economic reforms at the sectoral level (such as telecom, finance, highway infrastructure and insurance) as well as continuing tax reforms, reductions in import barriers and the advancing of legislation on fiscal responsibility.

Fiscal and revenue deficits peaked in 2001/2002 at 9.9 and 7% of GDP, respectively. From 2002/2003, one witnessed a remarkably successful fiscal consolidation, which brought the combined fiscal deficit down to 4% of GDP in 2007/2008 and the revenue deficit to almost zero (Fig. 1).[2] Favourable factors were at work at both the central and state government levels. At the centre, the main contributory factors were: the enactment of the Fiscal Responsibility and Budget Management Act of 2004, the concerted efforts at improving tax administration through information technology and the surge in tax revenues (especially direct taxes) from the resumption of high growth, which itself was a consequence of many factors including the reforms of 1998–2003, the strong growth in the world economy in 2002–2007 and the surge in India's domestic savings and investment from around 25% of GDP in 2002 to 35% plus by 2007. About half of this extraordinary leap in aggregate savings came from sharp reductions in government dis-saving (revenue deficits), illustrating some of the virtuous cycles at work during this exceptionally buoyant period.

At the state level, the fiscal consolidation was propelled by the spread of fiscal responsibility laws mandated by the Twelfth Pay Commission, the spurt in tax revenues from the widespread switch to value added tax (VAT) principles in state sales taxes, the increased devolutions from the centre's revenue boom and higher nontax receipts on various accounts.

A heartening feature of the remarkable fiscal consolidation of this period was that it was the product of sustained technical, administrative and political efforts invested by two successive governments at the centre and many different state governments. Aside from the direct increase in public savings, the exceptional fiscal consolidation of 2003–2008 supported the excellent macroeconomic outcomes of this period (Table 1), by inducing higher investment through lower nominal and real interest rates and greater availability of investible funds and assisted the prevalence of low external deficits in this period.

Unfortunately, the enormous gains in fiscal consolidation in 2003–2008 were all lost in 2008/2009, a year of extraordinary fiscal profligacy, influenced perhaps by the imminence of the general election of spring 2009. Well before the dramatic collapse of Lehman Brothers in September 2008, spending by India's central government was running far above budget levels on account of government pay increases (resulting from the adoption of Sixth Pay Commission recommendations), fertilizer and food subsidies, the new farm loan waiver scheme and the National Rural

[2] For a detailed account of fiscal and macroeconomic policies and developments during this period, see Acharya (2010).

Table 1 Macroeconomic indicators: the "Best Years, 2003–2008", but weaken thereafter. (Sources: Central Statistical Organization and Reserve Bank of India)

Indicator	Average (2003/4–2007/8)	2007/8	2008/9	2009/10	2010/11	2011/12	2012/13
Economic growth (GDP, percent per year)	8.7	9.3	6.7	8.6	9.3	6.2	5.0
Inflation (GDP deflator, percent per year)	5.6	6.6	8.8	7.5	10.5	8.7	8.2
Current account balance (percent of GDP)	−0.3	−1.3	−2.3	−2.8	−2.7	−4.2	−4.8
Combined fiscal deficit (percent of GDP)	6.3	4.1	8.5	9.5	7.0	8.2	7.5[a]
Gross domestic investment (percent of GDP)	33.8	38.1	34.3	36.6	36.8	35.0	34.0[a]
Gross fixed investment (percent of GDP)	29.6	32.9	32.3	31.6	31.7	30.6	30.0
Gross domestic savings (percent of GDP)	33.4	36.8	32.0	33.8	34.0	30.8	29.2[a]

GDP gross domestic product
[a] Author's projections

Employment Guarantee program (NREG).[3] Some of these, like pay increases, farm loan waiver and NREG, had been under-budgeted. Others, such as fertilizer and oil subsidies, were the result of the international commodity price boom, which hit the Indian economy from early 2008. With the government choosing to hold down controlled prices, explicit and implicit (through oil and fertilizer bonds) subsidies soared. The net result (together with steep, post-Lehman cuts in central excise duties) was that the central government's fiscal deficit for 2008/2009 went from the 2.5 % of GDP budgeted in February 2008 to over 6 % in the actual accounts and to an even higher 8 % of GDP, when the off-budget items like petroleum and fertilizer bonds were included. This massive fiscal overshoot more than wiped out, in a single year, all the hard-won fiscal consolidation achieved in between 2003/2004 and 2007/2008. While storing up fiscal and inflationary problems for the future, it had the salutary effect of countering the deflationary shock from the global financial and economic crisis. Whether this order of fiscal stimulus (or profligacy) was really necessary remains debatable. What is clear is that the composition of the fiscal expansion, in the form mainly of higher government wages, much larger subsidies for fuel, fertilizer and food and the ramping up of entitlement programmes, seriously constrained the scope for subsequent fiscal retraction.

The persistence of the high fiscal deficits beyond 2008/2009, while contributing to India's economic resilience in 2008–2010, also helped fuel the high inflation of the post-crisis years, reduced domestic savings and helped induce the worrisome

[3] See Acharya (2012a, b) for accounts of India's policies and outcomes during after the global crisis.

widening of external deficits (Table 1). By helping to keep interest rates high, the large deficits also contributed to the slowdown in investment and economic growth in the last 2 years, though, quite obviously, other factors were also at work. These included: the prolonged absence of productivity-enhancing economic reforms; the mounting disarray in key infrastructure sectors of power, coal, highways, telecom and mining; several high-profile economic scams, reflecting serious governance weaknesses and resulting in widespread policy and decision deadlocks; and, of course, the weakness of the post-crisis global economy.

Looking ahead, the need for successful fiscal consolidation (including compression of revenue deficits) remains strong, especially given the record high (and unsustainable) levels of the current account deficit in the balance of payments and the associated high vulnerability of the economy to external and internal shocks. In this context, the limited reduction targeted by the 2013/2014 Central Budget in the centre's revenue deficit from 3.9 % of GDP to 3.3 % of GDP is disappointing, especially given the optimistic projections for tax revenues, disinvestment proceeds, telecom spectrum auction earnings and subsidy containment. After all, as a matter of accounting, a reduction in the country's current account deficit has to be matched (enabled) by an equivalent reduction in the domestic investment–savings gap. In the current context of low growth, it would be better to achieve this reduction through increases in domestic savings (including public savings) rather than any further fall in aggregate investment.

Despite the evident need for long-delayed fiscal consolidation, the short-term prospects are clouded by political compulsions emanating from the general elections to be held before May 2014. Against that background, it may be difficult to break out of the current predicament of high fiscal and external deficits, modest economic growth and persistent inflation.

This brief review of India's fiscal policies in the last 25 years also cautions against accepting a uniform policy paradigm for all nations at all times on issues of fiscal policy. Thus, the ongoing industrial nation debate on austerity versus stimulus may have little practical relevance for India's current fiscal priorities.

References

Acharya S (2006) Essays on macroeconomic policy and growth in India. Oxford University Press, New Delhi

Acharya S (2010) Macroeconomic performance and policies, 2000–2008. In: Acharya S, Mohan R (eds) India's economy: performance and challenges. Oxford University Press, New Delhi

Acharya S (2012a) India after the global crisis. Orient Blackswan, New Delhi

Acharya S (2012b) India and the global crisis. In: Bergsten CF, Henning R (eds) Global economics in extraordinary times. Peterson Institute for International Economics, Washington DC

Ahluwalia MS (2002) Economic reforms in India since 1991: has gradualism worked? J Econ Perspect 16(3):67–88

Joshi V, Little IMD (1996) India's economic reforms, 1991–2001. Oxford University Press, New Delhi

Panagariya A (2008) India: The emerging giant. Oxford University Press, New York

ERRATUM

Asian Perspectives for Financial Regulatory Reforms after the Asian Financial Crisis

Jae-Ha Park

M. Callaghan et al. (eds.), *Global Cooperation Among G20 Countries*,
DOI 10.1007/978-81-322-1659_12, pp. 135-141, © Springer India 2014

DOI 10.1007/978-81-322-1659_12

In the original publication of the print and online versions of this book the title is wrong. The title should read:

Asian Perspectives for Financial Regulatory
Reforms after the Global Financial Crisis

The online version of the original chapter can be found at
http://dx.doi.org/10.1007/978-81-322-1659_12

Index

M. Callaghan et al. (eds.), *Global Cooperation Among G20 Countries*,
DOI 10.1007/978-81-322-1659-9, © Springer India 2014

www.ingramcontent.com/pod-product-compliance
Lightning Source LLC
LaVergne TN
LVHW012323171026
850499LV00003B/76

* 9 7 8 8 1 3 2 2 1 6 5 8 2 *